"At last a wrecking crane which will help black people break down some of the barriers which block our access to each other. This book is about four hundred years overdue, but right on time."

—Dr. Na'im Akbar, Ph.D.
Speaker, Author, Educator

"If you share George Fraser's view, as I do, that black people must do better at getting together if we are to truly get ahead, then this book will be mighty useful to you. If you do not share this view, please read this book anyway, because we need you in the network."

—Dr. Johnnetta B. Cole
President, Bennett College

"When it's good, it's very good, and when it's bad, it's gruesome. That's true of life, love, but especially networking, and nobody tells it better than George Fraser. *Success Runs in Our Race* is an account of networking's high points and its ugly underbelly; the good, the gruesome, the helpful, and the humorous. Whether you're a new kid on the block or have been around it a few times, there are important lessons and powerful reminders in this must-read for black folk on the move and those who want to run with us."

—Dr. Julianne Malveaux
Columnist, Author, Speaker

"This valuable book can help people to expand their horizons and their careers."

—John E. Jacob, Jr.
Former President, National Urban League

"*Success Runs in Our Race* is a masterpiece. This is a book all Americans can use to increase their ability to network, get together to get ahead, grow spiritually, and develop the resources leading to greater wealth and relationship success. This book allows us to realize our connectedness to one another and to share, give, and maximize all of our community and business resources."

—ANNE BOE
AUTHOR OF *Is Your "Net" Working?*

"A thoroughgoing how-to on the art and practice of networking—and so much more, George Fraser's *Success Runs in Our Race* probes profound cultural dimensions of black reality. It is the state of the art of this crucial aspect in our cultural offense. It powerfully removes any remaining doubt about whether we are afraid to succeed. It is empowering, entertaining, and sure enough on time."

—DR. RAMONA HOAGE EDELIN, PH.D.
FORMER DIRECTOR, CONGRESSIONAL
BLACK CAUCUS FOUNDATION

"I love Fraser's view that networking transcends individualism, selfishness, and profits and that Afrocentric networking is designed to benefit the 'least of these.' Great book!"

—DR. JAWANZA KUNJUFU
AUTHOR, LECTURER, SPEAKER

"*Success Runs in Our Race* is a road map to individual success that also gives basic skills and tools to help in achieving your goals and dreams. No library will be complete without it."

—WALLY AMOS
"THE COOKIE MAN"

"George Fraser understands that there is opportunity for everyone, and that working together through networking greatly enhances everyone's opportunity."

—ALBERT B. RATNER
CHAIRMAN OF FOREST CITY
ENTERPRISES

"This is a blueprint for thousands of potential entrepreneurs who take what some define as 'stumbling blocks' and turn them into stepping-stones. George Fraser's refreshing book accentuates the positive, empha-

sizes synergy, and incorporates a world view that can truly build a growing chain of success for hardworking, ambitious African Americans."
—HARRIET R. MICHEL
EXECUTIVE DIRECTOR, NATIONAL
MINORITY SUPPLIER DEVELOPMENT
COUNCIL, INC.

"Wow! Great job, wonderful book. I really enjoyed reading it. A monumental job of presenting an inspirational how-to book on building community. It provides insight into the black world in an authentic, compelling way. George Fraser will help millions of blacks and whites."
—ARTHUR J. NAPARSTEK, PH.D.
GRACE LONGWELL COYLE PROFESSOR,
CASE WESTERN RESERVE UNIVERSITY

"George Fraser, through an unrelenting reach for excellence, is a living testimony of success. Now, in his first book, he provides a legacy of motivation and inspiration for each of us and the next generation."
—THE REVEREND DR. OTIS MOSS, JR.
PASTOR, OLIVET INSTITUTIONAL
BAPTIST CHURCH, CLEVELAND, OHIO

"George Fraser has written a very timely and important book which is an indispensable aid to even the best college or professional school education."
—VIRGIL ECTON
RETIRED COO, UNITED NEGRO
COLLEGE FUND

"George Fraser's book is an excellent tool for achieving personal and professional success. . . . His readers will be inspired."
—EDWARD B. BRANDON
RETIRED CHAIRMAN AND CEO,
NATIONAL CITY CORP.

"Descendants of Africans throughout the Diaspora, and by extension, the entire human family, stand at the crossroads on the eve of a new millennium. In times of human need, learned leadership often surfaces, and

George Fraser has joined a long list of historic visionaries. He has cleared the path, developed the strategy, and stands ready to lead. *Success Runs in Our Race* incorporates the incarnated generalship of Hannibal, the organizational architecture of Marcus Garvey, and the fiery determination of Harriet Tubman.

"George has given us the twenty-first-century primer on black unity as well as the 'blueprint' for the enhancement of African people and the restoration of universal harmony."

—David W. Whitaker, Ph.D., J.D.
President and Founder, Phoenix
Village Academy

"There has never been a more important time for networking in the black community. Opportunities abound, and it is critical that blacks become well versed in the techniques of networking. *Success Runs in Our Race* provides not only the vision, but the specifics that will empower the black community to stengthen its own commitment to excellence."

—The Honorable Michael R. White,
Mayor of Cleveland, Ohio, Retired

"*Success Runs in Our Race* is a reservoir of important information. It is full of great ideas, strategies, and tactics for effective networking. As multiculturalism grips America, everyone seeking to build new and productive relationships needs to read this book now; it could change your perspective and perhaps your life!"

—Steve Lewis,
Past Chairman,
National Black MBA Association

"This is a worthy book, and it ought to be embraced by all black people interested in achieving success as a by-product of mutual empowerment."

—Armstrong Williams
President, Graham/Williams Group

"George Fraser's book sounds the alarm for black people to use networking as the primary focus for strengthening the black community. It is a powerful vision, beautifully written . . . a must for every library."

—Jerry Roebuck
Chairman and Founder,
Black Expo U.S.A.

"Thank you for the wake-up call. This explosive new literary tool was an ambitious undertaking. It will dominate discussions in many black circles for years to come. Fraser forces us to take another look at the importance of effective networking—it works!"

—CAROLYN SHELTON
FORMER EDITOR, *The Houston Sun*

"In *Success Runs in Our Race*, George Fraser lifts networking to the level of sophistication it deserves. One of the real values of this book is that it urges black people to aggressively utilize the assets already available to us."

—BOB LAW
FORMER HOST OF *NIGHT TALK*,
AMERICAN URBAN RADIO NETWORK

SUCCESS
RUNS IN
OUR RACE

Also by George C. Fraser

Race for Success: The Ten Best Opportunities for Blacks in America

SuccessGuide Worldwide: The Networking Guide to Black Resources

REVISED AND UPDATED EDITION

SUCCESS RUNS IN OUR RACE

The Complete Guide to Effective Networking in the Black Community

GEORGE C. FRASER

Amistad

An Imprint of HarperCollins*Publishers*

HarperCollins books may be purchased for educational, business, or sales promotional use. For information, please write: Special Markets Department, HarperCollins Publishers Inc., 10 East 53rd Street, New York, NY 10022.

First published in 1994 by William Morrow and Company, Inc.
First published in paperback by Avon Books in 1996.
Revised and updated edition published by Amistad in 2004.

Designed by Renato Stanisic

Printed on acid-free paper

Library of Congress Cataloging-in-Publication Data
Fraser, George C.
    Success runs in our race: the complete guide to effective networking in the
    Black community / George C. Fraser.—Rev. and updated ed.
        p.   cm.
    Includes bibliographical references and index.
    ISBN 0-06-059417-9 (acid-free paper)
    1. African Americans—Social networks. 2. African American
businesspeople—Social networks. 3. African Americans—Economic
conditions. 4. Success in business—United States. I. Title.
E185.86.F725 2004
650.1'3'08996073—dc22   2003045146

04 05 06 07 08 BVG/RRD 10 9 8 7 6 5 4 3 2 1

*To those whom I have helped and/or who
have helped me . . . my network*

Todd Abbey
Diane Abbott
James Abbott
Eric Abercrumbie
Jean Abernathy
Pat Ackerman
Robert Acquaye
Phyllis Acres
Charles Adams
David Adams
Janus Adams
M. E. Adams
Rod Adams
Ron Adams
Roosevelt Adams
Tanzie Adams
Valencia Adams
Michele Adams-Proctor
John Addison
Wilford Adkins, Jr.
Selom Adogah
Gerald Adolph
Herbert Adrine
Ron Adrine
Russell Adrine
Ahneva Ahneva
Na'im Akbar
Bruce Akers
Lisa Alaimo

Steve Alcorn
Kurt Aldag
Alicia Alexander
James Alexander
Carlean Alford
Omar Ali-Bey
Carolyn Allen
Clyde Allen
Hector Allen
Judith Allen
Robert Allen
Stefanie Allen
Lavonia Allison
Tanya Allmond
Paul Altig
Goldie Alvis
John Amos
Wally Amos
Anna Anderson
Carl Anderson
Claud Anderson
Donald Anderson
Ken Anderson
Kernie Anderson
Warren Anderson
Lamont Andrews
Richard Andrews
Ron Andrews
Mary Ann

Debra Anthony
Ed Anthony
Henrietta Antoinin
Ana Aponte-Curtis
Jay Apple
J. B. Appling
Marsialle Arbuckle
Susan Arceneaux
Josh Archer
Christi Archibald
Tom Arco
Carroll Armstrong
J. L. Armstrong
Anna Arnold
Eddie Arnold
John Arnold
John Arrington
Karen Asher-Osbourne
Lavalle Ashley
Robert Ashley
Nana Ashong
Brett Ashton
Ken Askew
Giovanna Athias
Pat Atkin
Connie Atkins

Elizabeth Atkins-Bowman
Susan Au-Allen
Anthony Austin
Clarence Avant
Lenora Avery
Lillian Ayala
Roy Ayers
Sonia Babers
Barry Backmon
Pierre Bagley
Anthony Bailey
J. T. Bailey
Lee Bailey
Marietta Bailey
Tom Bailey
Lawrence Bain
Art Baker
John Baker-Brown
Dee Baldwin
John Baldwin
Myra Baldwin
Carolyn Baldwin-Byrd
Angelique Ball
Charles Ballard
Stacey L. Balsley
Tom Baltimore
Andrew Banks
Anna Banks

Monica Banks
Will Banks
Milt Barbee
Don Barden
Skip Barner
John Barnes
Ken Barnes
Ronald Barnes
Ron Barnett
Joe Louis Barrow
Willie T. Barrow
Alexander Barton
Dawn Baskerville
Phyliss Batson
Tom Baylock
Bernard Beal
Tracy Bean-Oliver
Thomas Beaver
Hal Becker
Ella Becton
Alex Beerlerman
Mike Belkin
Alice Bell
Ed Bell
Terri Bell
Walter Bell
Brandon Bellamy

Werten Bellamy

Siddiq Bello

Erline Belton

Y. Marc Belton

Frances Benko

Lerone
  Bennett, Jr.

Keith Benson

Michael Benz

Bob Bergman

Antonia Bernard

Margaret
  Bernstein

Paul Besson

Isisara Bey

Adam Beyah

Charles Bibb

Deb Bibb

Leon Bibb

Lee Bickley

James Biggar

Bob Billingslea

Jerry Birch

Marvin Bishop

Scully Black

Wilbert Black

JoAnn Blackman

Barry Blackmon

Pat Blackmon

Gene Blackwell

Joseph Blackwell

Nakato Blair

Norman Bliss

William Blue

Rena Blumberg

Edward Blunt

Roma Blunt

Carol Bolden

Tom Boles

Roger Bond

Michael Boney

Gail Boone

Monica Boone

Ron Boone

Dawnyell Bower

Angie Bowie

Regina Bowie

Claudette
  Bowles

Keith Bowles

Wendell Boyce

Jarmell Boyd

Pepper Boyd

Mary Ann Boykin

Pete Boyle

Reg Brack, Jr.

Irene Branch

Richard Branch

Ed Brandon

Charles Bremer

Paul Bresnick

Moses Brewer

Glenda
  Bridgeforth

Camille Bridges

Ken Bridges

Sam Briggery

Roslyn Brock

Ralph Brody

Sheila Bronner

Arthur
  Bronner, III

Dennis Brooks

James Brooks

Jesse Brooks

Laura Brooks

Sylvia Brooks

Ann Brown

Baron Brown

Charles Brown

Damon Brown

Darian Brown

David Brown

Ed Brown

Eric Brown

Ernestine Brown

Frances Brown

Gasby Breely
  Brown

Gloria Brown

Jesse Brown

Les Brown

Lorie Brown

Majid Brown

Malcolm Brown

Matt Brown

Ona Brown

Paulette Brown

Renee Brown

Rochelle Brown

Rodney Brown

Roger Brown

Ron Brown

Tamara Brown

Theresa Brown

Tony Brown

Virgil Brown, Jr.

Virgil Brown, Sr.

Winford Brown

Paul Brownridge

Tommy Bruno

Marian Bryan

Donna Bryant

John Bryant

Paul Bryant

William Bryant

Janice Bryant-
  Howroyd

A. Deane
  Buchanan

Silas Buchanan

Alonzo
  Buchanan, Jr.

Ruth Buczynski

Phyllis Buford

Carol Bugg

Janet Bullard

Steve Bullock

Jill Bunton

Todd Burden

Bill Burges

Caesar Burkes

Charles Burkett

Earli Burks

Eral Burks

Len Burnett, Jr.

Dargan Burns

Khephra Burns

LaWanda Burrell

John Burry, Jr.

Barbara Burton

Fred Burton

Rodney Buscher

Andre
  Bustamante

John H.
  Bustamante

Tuan
  Bustamante

Minnie Butcher

Annette Butler

John Butler

John Sibley
  Butler

Marlene Butler

Michael Butler

Rita Butler

Leisa Byars

Gilda Byers

Liz Byers

William Byers

Juanita Bynum

Erskine Cade

Jolie Caldwell

Deborah
  Calhoun

Danny Cameron

Pam Cammady

BeBe Moore
  Campbell

Gerald Campbell

Jane Campbell

Tony Campbell

Cheryl Canady

Joyce Cannady

Tracey Capers

Rick Capretta

Victoria Cargill

Wendy Carlton

Eric Carmichael

Maria Carothers

Austin Carr

Frank Carson

Bev Carter

James Carter

Jocelyn Carter-
  Miller

Karl Carter

Kevin Carter

Marquietta
  Carter

Robert Carter

Ruth Carter

Juluis Cartwright

Denette Casey

Paula Casey

Ray Cash

Jorge Castillo

E. T. Caviness

Janet Century

Audrene
  Chakmakjian

Mary Anne
  Chambers

Theo Chambers

Joseph Champ

Nathan
  Champman,
  Jr.

Ed Chanantry

James Chandler

Wayne Chandler

Kelly Chapman

Mike Chapman

Veronica
  Chapman

Emma Chappell

Carl Character

Nick Charles

Clark Chasen

David Chavez

Tom Chema

Bill Cherry

Chahn Chess

Farai Chideya

Faye Childs

Dwight
  Chillious

Robert Chinn

John Chisell

Hunter Chisolm

Jim Chones

Rose Christian

Maurice
  Christopher

Susan Claiborne

Dana Clark

Frank Clark

William Clark

Andre Clarke

Constance
  Clarke

Faye Clarke

Frank Clarke

Leslie Clarke

William Clay

Kevin Clayton

Xernona Clayton
Frank Clayton, III
Susie Claytor
Phillip Cleaver
Mike Clement
Jill Clements
Linda Clemmons
Mack Clemmons
Polly Clemo
Bonita Cleveland
Gregory Clifford
James Clingman
Keith Clinkscales
Kenneth Cloud
Ed Coaxum
Delmarie Cobb
Leonard Cobbs
Gail Cochran
Johnnie Cochran, Jr.
Raiford Cockfield
Gwen Cohen
Virgis Colbert
Johnnetta B. Cole
Johnnie Coleman
Lonnie Coleman
Lonzo Coleman
Al Collins
Annis Collins
Keith Collins
Retanya Collins
Robert Collins
Ed Comwell
Lester Coney
Culbreth Cook
Debert Cook
Thelma Cook
Lawrence Cooke
Barry Cooper
Judy Cooper
Margot Copeland
Terrence Copeland

Carole Copeland-Thomas
Sherman Copelin, Jr.
John Costen
Ludie Couch
Pat Council
Shaun Court
Cynthia Cousins
Lee Cox
Maurice Cox
Paul Cox
Roosevelt Cox
Michael Craig
Norm Craig
Charlie Crawford
Cody Crawford
L. Marilyn Crawford
Bruce Crawley
George Crawley
Leroy Crayton
Henry Creel
Marvin Creel
Claude Crenshaw
James Croll
Fred Crosby
Ricky Crosby
Stanley Crouch
Andy Crowe
Melvina Crowell
John Crump
Thomas Cuffie
Sherry Culpepper
Donna Cummings
Tanya Cummings
Bob Cunningham
Fatima Cunningham
Jimmy Cunningham
Karl Cureton
George Curry
Dee Cutter
Michel Daley

Stephen Dalton
Ronald Daly
Anthony Daniels
Diane Daniels
Ron Daniels
Monica Daniely
Vernetta Daniely
Tom Darden
Aaron Dare
Sean Daughtry
Michael Daum
Hezekiah Davidson
Ralph Davilla
Ben Davis
Chad Davis
Cherisse Davis
Crystal Davis
Darwin Davis
Dawn Davis
Dwayne Davis
Edward Davis
Greg Davis
Kelly Davis
Ken Davis
Maceo Davis
Michael Davis
Pat Davis
Phil Davis
Sylvia Davis
Tim Davis
Wayne Davis
Tom Davis, Jr.
Asfilofio De Oliveria Filho
Curtis Dean
Donna DeBerry
James DeBerry
Clarence Dees
Normando DeHalle
Dino DeLoach
Norman DeLoach
Gary Dennis
Sheila Dennis
Reginald Denson
Bill Derrick

Billy Dexter
Harlan Diamond
Ralph Dickerson
Cheryl Dickson
Wendy Dickson
Tanya Diggs
Flora Dillard
Dennis Dillon
Christine Dinez
Nancy Dinger
David Dinkins
Jeffrey Diver
George Dixon
Bob Dockery, Jr.
Howard Dodson
Xavier Dominesis
Virgil Dominic
Bob Donaldson
Kyle Donovan
Linda Dorman
Julius Dorsey
Keith Dorsey
Tommie Dortch
Larry Doss
Janice Douglas
Shawn Dove
Norma Downs
George Ducas
Joe Louis Dudley, Sr.
Mabrey Duff
Mike Duncan
John Dunn
Michael Dunn
Cal Dupree
Donald Durrah
Ed Dwight
Michael Dye
Michael Eric Dyson
Berthel Eagle
Michael Eanes
Julian Earles
Willie Eason
Robert Eaton
Virgil Ecton
Alfred Edmond, Jr.

Jerome Edmonson
Al Edwards
Buck Edwards
Eddie Edwards
Henry Edwards
Karen Edwards
Ron Edwards
Rondle Edwards
William Edwards
Henry R. Edwards, Jr.
Preston Edwards, Sr.
Adele Eisner
E. David Ellington
William Ellis, Jr.
Nolen Ellison
Tereasa Embry
Wayne Embry
Ollie Emerson
Curtis English
Larry Eskridge
Glenn Estelle
Emma Etuk
Doris Evans
Josulyn Evans
Lisa Evans
Monica Evans
Therman Evans
Benny Evans, III
Jon Everett
Mary Everhart
George Faison
Nabii Faison
Mel Fallis
William Fambrough
Robert Farling
David Faroo
Walter Fauntroy
Tom Feelings
Cedric Fellows
J. R. Fenwick
Ken Ferguson
Tom Ferguson
Valerie Ferguson

Gerald Fernandez
Jose Ferrer
Chad Fields
Ed Fields
Pat Fields-Davison
Melvin Finch
Robert Finch
Dale Finley
Fred Finley
Jim Fisher
Lee Fisher
Gloria Fitchpritch
Floyd Flake
Charles Fleming
Greg Fletcher
John Flowers
Kim Folsom
Kia Fomby
Janine Fondon
Joan Fonseca
Emory Foote
Muffet Foote
Bob Foraker
George Forbes
Allen H. Ford
Henry E. Ford
Harold Ford, Jr.
Margaret Ford-Taylor
Randy Forrest
Carol Foster
Gerry Foster
Willa Fox
Sherrie Foxman
Sheila Fraizer
George Frame
Bryan Franklin
Cedric Franklin
Rachelle Franklin
Rebecca Franklin
Rodney Franklin
Adam Fraser
Edward Fraser
Gregory Fraser
Hyacinth Fraser

Jean Fraser
Joseph Fraser
Kyle Fraser
Millicent Fraser
Scotland Fraser
Scott Fraser
Walter Fraser, Jr.
Shirley Frazier
Maxine Fredericks
Don Freeland
Leroy Freelon, Jr.
Claire Freeman
Craig Freeman
Dee Dee Freeman
Henry Freeman
Shine Freeman
Ann Fudge
Sam Fulwood, III
Johnny Furr
Mildred Gaddis
Roderick Gains
Collen Gallagher
Greg Galore
Gloria Gamble
Gwendolyn Garnett-Thomas
Tulio Garonzi
Willie Gary
Gina Gates
Greg Gates
Jacquelyn Gates
Reginald Gates
Luther Gatling
Jim Gelarden
Vic Gelb
Marvin Gentry
Karl George
Lewis Gibbs
Andy Gibson
Jill Gibson-Bell
Russ Gifford
Richard Gilchrist
Erick Gilkesson

Robert Gillespie
Reginald Gilliam, Jr.
Robert Ginn
Louise Gissendaner
Stephanie Gitner
Henry Givens
Norma Givens
Dean Gladden
Celeste Glasgow
Jerry Glazer
Everett Glen
Emanuel Glover
John Glover
Sterling Glover
Paul Goggin
Don Goins
Thomas Goins
Adam Goldstein
Margarete Goodall
Valerie Goodman
Bob Goodwin
Ida Goodwin-Woolfolk
Bruce Gordon
Ed Gordon
Kerry Gordy
Sam Goss
Mirian Graddick-Weir
Donald Graham
Stedman Graham
Mudcat Grant
Melvin Gravely
Don Graves
Earl Graves, Jr.
Earl Graves, Sr.
Paula Graves
Shirley Graves
Darrius Gray
Holloway Gray
William Gray, III
Delilah Grayer
Hermenia Grayson

Dorothy Riley Green
Lee Green
Mark Green
Maryjoyce Green
Robert Green
Amie Greer
Michael Greer
Thomas Greer
John Gresham
Mark Gresham
Rosey Grier
Robert Gries
Curtis Griggs
Donald Griggs
Nadine Guerrier
Mathis Guice
Udayan Gupta
Roberta Gutman
Rick Hackley
Jim Hagen
Ken Hail
John Hairston
Teresa Hairston
Ken Hale
Janice Hale-Benson
Sangue Hales
Don Haley
Brian Hall
Delora Hall
Regina Hall
Steve Hall
Wesley Hall
Aundrella Hamed
Charlotte Hamilton
John Hamilton
Leonard Hamilton
Neal Hamilton
Scott Hamilton
Yvonne Hamilton
Jaron Hamlett, Sr.
Demetrius Hammett

Kevin Hampton
Mami Hampton
Kim Hankerson
John Hankins
John Hanson
Constance Haqq
James Hardiman
Darren Hardy
Lawrence Hardy
Pat Hardy
Solomon Harge
Blanton Harper
Carolyn Harper
Tom Harrington
Anthony Harris
Brock Harris
David Harris
Nancella Harris
Portia Harris
Rey Harris
Robert Harris
Stayce Harris
Wallace Harris
Yusef Harris
Leon Harrison
Tony Harrison
Reginald Hart
Earl Harvey
Richard Harvey
Steve Harvey
Randy Hasty
RoNita Hawes
Shirley Hawk
Delores Hawthorne
Darlene Hayes
Eleanor Hayes
Helen Hayes
Jimmy Hayes
Marschell Head
Rufus Heard
Dorothy Height
Angelo Henderson
John Henderson, III
Lewis Henderson
Ron Henderson

Shirley Henderson
Allie Hendricks
Jim Henley
Ernestine Hennings
Vanessa Henry
Glo Herbert
Soloman Herbert
Marva Herman
James Hewitt
Joseph Hewitt
Ilene Heyward
Jonathan Hicks
Patrick Hicks
Randy Hicks
William Hicks
Michael Hilber
Darrell Hill
David Hill
Deborah Hill
Muzette Hill
Pat Hill
Paul Hill
Valerie Hill
Amy Hilliard
Asa Hilliard
I. V. Hilliard
Larry Hines
Greg Hinton
Melody Hobson
Gerri Hodby
Daryl Hodnett
Latrelle Hogg
Ben Holbert
Larry Holeman
Victor Holiday
Melvin Holliman
Reuben Holloway
Scott Holloway
Howard Holly
Joann Holly
Lee Holmes
Pam Holmes
Stephan Holmes
Bert Holt
Don Holt

Dundee Holt
Rachelle Hood-Phillips
Carole Hoover
Mary Hoover
Horace Hord
Isaac Horton, III
Mike House
Bessie House-Soremekun
J. D. Houston
Samuel Howard
Wes Howard
C. Diane Howell
Hamp Howell
Marilyn French Hubbard
Cheryl Hudson
Mickie Hudson
Thomas Hudson
Charles Huffman
Hosiah Huggins, Jr.
Cathy Hughes
Jim Hughes
Mary Ellen Hughes
Vera P. Hughes
Al Hunt
Jim Hunter
Jim Hurley
Sam Hyman
Andy Ingram
Oliver Issac
Leon Isaac-Kennedy
Al Jackson
Charone Jackson
Derrick Jackson
Elaine Jackson
Frank Jackson
Hayes Jackson
Jesse Jackson
Leonard Jackson
Maynard Jackson
Rita Jackson
Debrina Jackson-Gordy
John Jacob, Jr.

Hanifa Jahi
T. D. Jakes
Leonard James
Myra James
Charles James, III
Sandy Jamison
Mabel Jasper
Mario Jean
Murial Jeffries
Tony Jeffries
Hensley Jemmott
Al Jenkins
George Jenkins
Rodney Jenkins
Sebetha Jenkins
Lorretta Jennings
Larry Jennings, Jr.
Renaldo Jensen
Lynn Jeter
Satish Jethani
William Jiles
Daymond John
Allison Johnson
Andrew Johnson
Byron Johnson
Carolyn Johnson
Charles Johnson
Chris Johnson
Diane H. Johnson
Eric Johnson
Fred Johnson
Genita Johnson
Harry Johnson
Henry Johnson
Hortence Johnson
Janette Johnson
Jeff Johnson
Joe Johnson
John H. Johnson
Khalil Johnson
Laura Johnson
Mickey Johnson
Richard Johnson
Roger Johnson

Ron Van Johnson
Shelby Johnson
Alexandria Johnson-Boone
Joseph Joiner
Felicia Jolivet
Bev Everson Jones
Carolyn Jones
E. Edward Jones, Sr.
Ed Jones
Geneva Jones
James Earl Jones
Jakki Jones-Nance
Jefferson H. Jones, III
Jefferson J. Jones
Kevin Jones
Lafayette Jones
Larry Jones
Lonnie Jones
Marilyn Jones
Martin Jones
Melvin Jones
Paul Jones
Paula Jones
Penny Jones
Reginald Jones
Robert Jones
Sylvia Jones
Zemira Jones
Charles Jordan, Jr.
Vernon Jordan, Jr.
Consuella Jordon
Eugene Jordon
Oscar Joyner
Tom Joyner
A. Keith Kaid
Bichlien Kaldahl
David KanKam
Brett Kaufman
Peter Keay
Floyd Keith
Anthony Kellum

Charles Kelly
Gwen Kelly
Richard Kelso
Anthony Kendall
John Kendall
Rose Kendrick
Claude Kennard
John Kennedy
Arif Khatib
Saad Khayat
Fred Khoury
Vivian Kidd
Dennis Kimbro
Leon Kimloch
Barbara King
Bridget King
Cecil King
Gayle King
Les King
Oona King
Richard King
Bernard Kinsey
Gerald Kisner
Mami Kisner
Ron Kisner
Jennifer Kit
Gayle Klaber
Fred Kleisner
Ronnie Knight
Ronnie "Freebie" Knight
Jackie Knox-Kelly
Amy Krakow
Diane Kugel
Matt Kuhn
Steven LaBroi
Aida LaChaux
Excell LaFayette, Jr.
Dennis Lafferty
Reginald Lake
John Landry
June Landry
Darrel Lane
Randell Lane
Bob Lanier
John Lanier

Robert Lavelle
Bob Law
Mark Lawrence
Charles Lawson
Peter Lawson-Jones
Mark Lay
David Lazik
Charmaine Leary
Kathryn Leary
Asfilofio Lee
Bertram Lee
Clayton Lee, Jr.
Creighton Lee
Debra Lee
JoAnn Lee
Mack Lee
Richard Lee
Rotan Lee
Janice Leek
John Lenear
Tony Lesesne
Liz Leslie
Wanda F. Lester
Anne Levert
Jay Levert
Michael Lewellen
Bracy Lewis
Fannie Lewis
Jerry Lewis
John Lewis
Lionel Lewis
Melissa Lewis
Steven Lewis
Virginia Lewis
Cathy Lewis-Wright
Henry Liang
Mychal Lilly
Josie B. Lindsay
Barbara Lindsey
Fred Linley
Richard Lippman
Alan Lipson
Jane Lockhart
Keith Lockhart

Lance London
Mel London
Sheryl London
Ted Long
Jerry Lopes
Mike Lorenze
Pat Lottier
Pam Loury
Bobby Love
Clarence Love
Helen Love
Mother Love
Tracy Love
Jay Lovinger
Jerry Lowe
Victoria Lowe
Barbara Lowenstein
James Lowery
John Lowery
Sonya Lowery
James Lowry
Kay Lucas
Maxine Lynch
Jay Lynn
Bates Lyons
Guy Mack
John Mack
Miranda Mack
Ramon Maddox
Robert Madison
Dee Magic
Amos Mahsua
Paul Major
James Malone
Ken Malone
Julianne Malveaux
Gary Manuel
Hannah Manuel
Robert Marks
Lonnie Marsh
Vickie Marsh
Betty Marshall
Brian Akil Marshall
Carl Martin
Carol Martin

Franklin Martin
Guy Martin
Joe Martin
Joel Martin
John Martin
Maxine Martin
Dave Martinson
Byron Mason
Marilyn Mason
Michael Mason
Winnie Mason
Jim Mastandrea
Judy Matheson
Kent Matlock
C. J. Matthews
Dee Matthews
Darryl Matthews, Sr.
Westina Matthews-Shatteen
Fred Mattingly
Bernadette Mayfield
Leslie Mays
Norman Mays
Cassandra McCall
Richard McCann
Nolan McCants
E. Lance McCarthy
Phyllis McCarthy
Bernie McClain
Jerry McClain
Gerri McClamie
Nancy McClaran
William McCleave
Carol McClendon
D'Joane McCorkle
Quentin McCorvey
Anna McCoy
Darlene McCoy
Richmond McCoy
Denise McCray
Mel McCray

Ruby McCullough
Donna McCurvin
Cynthia McDaniels
Lolita McDavid
Bobby McDonald
Robert McDonald
Rushion McDonald
Monica McDonell
Gerald McDonough
Barbara McEachern
Ron McFadden
Maria McFarlane
Renee McGee
Sherry McGee
Jeffrey McGuire
Jimmie McGuire
Lloyd McHamm
Emmit McHenry
Dwight McKee
Crystal McKenzie
Wanda McKenzie
Patrice McKinley
Antonio McKinney
Lois McKinney
Don McKneely
Angela McLowan
Stephany McManus
Marvin McMickle
Michael McMillian
Fran McNeal
Glenda McNeal
Eric McNish
Abner McWhorter
Pat Means
Michael Medcalf

Leon Merrick
Idris Merriman
William Merritt
Harriet Michel
Fred Middleton
Harvey Milam
Bennie Miles
Avis Miller
Darrell Miller
John Miller
Larry Miller
Marcellus Miller
Ray Miller
Ronnie Miller
Stanley Miller
Scott Mills
Howard Mims
Tony Minor
Steven Minter
Bert Mitchell
Maya Mitchell
Mello Mitchell
Fred Mitchem
N. Denise Mitchem
Owen Montague
Mark Monteverdi
Lewis Montgomery
Marvin Montgomery
David Moody
John Moody, Jr.
Deanna Moore-Latimore
Kelvyn Moore
Louie Moore
Madeline Moore
Melba Moore
Parasada Moore
Shelton Moore
Jovino Morales, Jr.
Madeleine Morel
Allen Morgan
Andrew Morgan
Beverly Morgan
Clint Morgan
Lori Morgan

Sheila Morgan
Deborah Morris
John Morris
Chuck Morrison
Joyce Morrow
Ariah Morse
Evan Morse
Charles Morton
Avis Mosby, II
Edwina Moss
Otis Moss, Jr.
Kofi Moyo
Akbar Muhammad
Laura Mullens
Joe Munoz
Myles Munroe
Bruce Murphy
Donald Murphy
Melvin Murphy
Jerry Murphy, Jr.
Hilton Murray
Bashirah Muttalib
Kalam Muttalib
Masequa Myers
Glenda Myhand
Ibrahim Naeem
Chris Nance
Donald Nance
Fred Nance
Art Naperstak
Mike Nash
Muhammad Nasserdeen
Jeff Nathenson
Carol Neal
Cathy Nedd
Greg Neely
Carl Nelson
Debra Nelson
Michael Nelson
Mickey Nelson
Norma Nelson
Ed Nesfield
Lisa Neu
Ozzie Newsome
Richard Newsome

Marlon Nicholes
Liz Nolley
Randy Norfus
Beverly Norman
Carl P. Norman
Percy Norwood, Jr.
Kirk Nugent
Irv Nunn
Afi Nur
Cyrus Oaks
John Odom
Dan Okrent
Mary Oldham
Patrick Oliver
Lea O'Neal
Richard Orange
Sam Orum
Anthony Overton
Lisa Overton
Jerry Sue Owens
Dominic Ozanne
James Pace
Janis Pace
Gloria Pace-King
Pamela Page
Charles Panky
Anthony Papa
Al Parham
Patty Park
Amelia Parker
Armetta Parker
Debra Parker
Ed Parker
Jennifer Parker
Jerry Parker
Kathyee Parks
Richard Parnell
Kimberly Parsons
Carol Patterson
Charles Patterson
Don Patterson
Lisa Patterson
Mari Lynn Patterson
Randi Patterson

Carol Patterson-Brooks
Charles Patton
Paul Patton
Hubert Payne
Anthony Peebles
Richard Peery
Richard Pelzer
Jose Pena
David Pendleton
Emma Pendleton
George Pendleton
Kevin Pendleton
Richard Pendleton
Ricky Pendleton
Benita Perkins
Milton Perkins
Dick Perlmuter
Dee Perry
F. E. Perry
Jeff Perry
Marc Perry
Pamela Perry
Richard Perry
Lavonia Perryman
Susan Peters
Cynthia Petrus
Ted Pettus
Regina Petty
Linda Pharr
Jeff Phelps
Allison Phillips
Vivian Pickard
William Pickard
Arnold Pickney
Raymond Pierce
Betty K. Pinckney
Jerry Pinckney
Mark Pinn
Mary Pitt
Marcia Pledger
Richard Pogue
Yvonne Pointer-Triplett
Tina Polite

Flip Pollack
Flo Pollack
Charles Poole
Tom Popes
Norman Potiker
Bill Potts
Alvin Poussaint
Caletha Powell
Inez Powell
Charlie Pratt
Pam Pratt
Delores Pressley
Bernice Prewitt
Art Price
Chuck Price
Earnest Price
Richard Priory
Michele Proctor
Patrick Prout
Joe Prude
Everett Pruitt
Mike Pruitt
Fred Pryor
Don Puchensky
Gary Puckrein
Catherine Pugh
Marino Puhalj
Gene Pulley
Carol Pusateri
Melvin Pye, Jr.
Alfred Quarles
Oliver Quinn
Roberto Quinones
Noraphine Rackley
John Rae
Donna Rae-Smith
Tina Rahman
Franklin Raines
Pemon Rami
Marya Randolph
Marty Raphael
Kelley Raspberry
Talut Rasul
Albert Ratner
Dori Ray
John Raye

Charles Reaves
Richard Reaves
Futrell Redditt
Nedra Redditt
Darrin Redus
Robert Redus
Gregory Reed
Larry Reed
Mike Reed
Raymond Reed
Ted Reed
Noel Reede
Jeffrey Reeves
Marsha Reeves-Jews
Octavius Reid, III
Tim Reid
Robert Reitman
Robert Render, III
Dannette Render-Reynes
Barbara Reynolds
Julian Reynolds
Rodney Reynolds
Sylvia Rhone
John Ribbins
Mark Ribbins
Bricelia Rice
Deanna Rice
Linda Rice-Johnson
Yannick Rice-Lamb
Henry Richards
Larry Richards
Chuck Richardson
Hank Richardson
Kellie Richardson
Gye Riddick
Dorothe Riley-Green
Scott Ringer
Gisele Rivera
Mike Rivers

Susie Rivers
Zie Rivers
Ken Roberts
Martha Roberts
Christ Robertson
Darnell Robertson
Kevin Robertson
Babidiya Robinson
Ben Robinson, III
Denise Robinson
Derrick Robinson
Edwin Robinson
Elaine Robinson
John Robinson
Ken Robinson
Larry Robinson
Myron Robinson
Randall Robinson
Rhonda Robinson
Shanna Robinson
Stacia Robinson
Tom Robinson
Vince Robinson
Pamela Rodgers
Jerry Roebuck
Clarence Rogers
Pam Rogers
Wilson Rogers
John Rogers, Jr.
Richard Romero
Pat Roper-Sanders
Lee Rosenburg
Michele Ross
Rose Ross
Sharon Roth
Wayne Rothman
Stephen Rowan
Philip Rowell
Victor Rubell
Montrie Rucker
Reggie Rucker
Ben Ruffin

Renee Ruffin-Price
Judy Ruggie
Diogenes Ruiz
Barbara Russell
Frank Russell
Herman Russell
Mark Russell
Janet Saboor
Oscar Saffold
Synthia Saint James
Anika Sala
Warren Salmon
Carol Sam
Cynthia Samples
Thomas Samuels
Chuck Sanders
Clarence Sanders
Shauna Sanders
Harry Sandler
TiaMarshae Sanford
Dick Satterfield
Brett Savage
John Schambach
Nick Scheele
Edna Schenkel
Lynn Schiffman
Paul G. Schloemer
Charlie Schnell
Bonnie Schollianos
Glen Shumate
Janet Schupe
Belinda Scott
Darrell Scott
George Christopher Scott
Winifred Scott
Don Scott Scully
Laura Seaburn
Eric Dean Seaton
Jay Seaton
Shirley Seaton
Jan Sebastian
Jean Sebastian

Lee Seidman
Alan Seifullah
Deborah Seller
Laurie Shakur
Larry Shane
Amir Shariff
Al Sharpton
Alan Shatteen
Curtis Shaw
Juanita Shealey
Terrence Shelton
Cyril Shepherd
Charles Sherill
Chris Shick
Dee Dee Shine
Michael Shinn
Leslie Short
Katie Shorter
Lawrence Shorter
Betty Shorts
Glen Shumate
Sandra Sibley
Sondra Sibley
John Sidley
Esther Silver-Parker
Robert Silverman
Carole Simpson
Jane B. Simpson
Larry Simpson
Yvonne Simpson
Ted Sims
Brian Sisak
Saikouba Sisay
Dawn Slade
Ron Slaughter
Toney Sledge
David Slutzkey
Eric Small
Sydney Small
Wayne Smalls
Janice Smallwood-McKenzie
Ken Smikle
Tavis Smiley
Athena Smith

Barbara Smith
Bev Smith
Clarence Smith
Connie Smith
Herb Smith
Hilton Smith
Jane Smith
Michael Smith
Monica Smith
Myles Smith
Rosie Smith
Sylvester Smith
Wes Smith
William Smith
Willie Smith
Sonny Snead
Curtis Snipes
Ray Somich
Ratanjit Sondhe
Mark Spain
Michele Spain
Ricky Spain
Lori Spano
Darlene Spencer
Herb Spencer
Kelly Spencer
Steve Spencer
Peter Spitter
Lenny Springs
Pamala Springs
Renee Squires
Tonya Stancel
Hilbert Stanley
Suzanne Stanley
Bud Stanner
Suzanne Stantley
Cedric Steele
Joe Steele
Warren Steele
George Steinbrenner
Tim Stephens
Brooke Stevens
Keith Stevenson
David Steward
Burma Stewart
Daryl Stewart
Lisa Stewart

Pam Stewart
Louis Stokes
Aubry Stone
Harold Stone
Tom Stone
Robert Storey
William Strickland
Denise Stroder
George Subira
Thelma Sullivan
Lauren Summers
Pierre Sutton
Ed Swailes
Cathy Swartz
Floyd Swoope
Harry Sykes
Dave Synder
Olive Tabor
Booker Tall
Zel Talley
Steve Tanruther
Janice Tarachowski
Meg Tarada
Pauline Tarver
Beth Tassinari
Charles Taylor
Hilary Taylor
James Taylor
Marlene Taylor
Michael Taylor
Mikki Taylor
Susan Taylor
Ricardo Teamor
Buddy Teaster
William Tedford
Ted Teng
Ruby Terry
Rudolph Terry
Dennis Thatcher
Charles Thigpen
Clyde Thomas
Franklin Thomas
Gerald Thomas
Herb Thomas
Norman Thomas

Patricia Thomas
Winston Thomas
Al Thompson
Dallas Thompson
Geraldine Thompson
John Thompson
Tiona Thompson
Yvonne Thompson
Margaret Thoren
Charles Thoroughbred
Denise Thurman
Carol Tidmore
Larry Tidmore
Sam Tidmore
Jerald Tillman
June Tims
Jaime Tineo
Roger Tinsley
Lynn Toliver
Stanley Toliver
Barbara Tomczyk
Nathan Townsend
Onetha Trammer
Jane Tresville
Lee Triggs
Lee Trotter
Lloyd Trotter
Glendora Troy
Stephanie Tubbs-Jones
Edris Tucker
Howard Tucker
Marion Tucker
Sheryl H. Tucker
Earl Turner
Karen Turner
Mary Turner
Patricia D. Turner
Stephanie Turner

Wendall Turner
Lorna Turpeau
Ross Turpeau
Debra Tyler
Ralph Tyler
Lisa Urbanch
Betty Vadenbosch, Jr.
Isabella Varrasso
Phillip Vassell
Lorraine Vega
Andrew Venable
John Villanueva
Jose Villanueva, Jr.
Claire Villarosa
Vic Vionovich
Fred Virgous
George Voinovich, Sr.
Burton Waddy
James Wade
Tola Wahab
Maurice Wainwright
Mylion Waite
Adele Walker
Blair Walker
Carol Walker
Dwayne Walker
Earl Walker
Juliet E. K. Walker
LeQuisha "Sunni" Walker
Seturah Walker
Curtis Wallace
Tom Wallace
George Walters
Aaron Walton
Eugene Ward
Alan Ward-Robinson
Reggie Ware
William Ware, Jr.
Shawn Warner
True Warner
Gerri Warren-Merrick

Angela Washington
Gordon Washington
Jan Washington
Nichole Washington
Sherita Washington
Simone Washington
Steve Washington
Omar Wasow
Maxine Waters
Sean Waters
Charles Watkins
Brian Watson
Charles Watson
Harry Watson
Darlene Watts
Robin Weaver
Darcel Webb-Shumaker
Rob Weber
Tina Weed
Michael Weil
Cornel West
Darryl West, Jr.
Natalie Wester
Pat Weston
Larry Wheeler
Lorna Whisham
Kwaw David Whitaker
Addie White
Albert White
Coleen White
Earl White
Eric White
Eugene White
George White
Jay White
Michael R. White
Monifa White
Ann White-Harris
David Whitehead
Reginald Whitehead

Anthony Whitfield
Cecil Whiting
James Whitley
Elaine Whitlow
Leonard Whitlow
Arnold Whitmore
Tony Whitmore
Deborah Whitt
William Whitten
Denver Wilborn
Michael Wilkens
Richard Wilkens
Larry Wilker, Sr.
Yvonne Wilkes
Alex Williams
Alonda Williams
Armstrong Williams
Ben Williams
Bruce Williams
Daisey Williams
Diane Williams
Dick Williams
Donald "Corky" Williams
E. J. Williams
Earl Williams
Edna Williams
Edwin Williams
Erlene Williams
Faye Williams, Jr.
Gregory Williams
Ivan Williams
Ivy Williams
Jay "The Gospel Kid" Williams
Judy Williams
Keith Williams
Kenneth Williams
Pamela Williams
Reggie Williams
Rita Williams
Steve Williams
Suzanne Williams

Tanya Williams-Bell
Terrie Williams
Vernona Williams
Willie Williams
George Willis
Greg Willis
Ione Willis-Hancock
Matthew Willmore
Cheryle Wills
Eddie Wills
Guy Wills
Gloria Wilson
John Wilson
Josleen Wilson
Ken Wilson
Mary Wilson
Raymond Winbush
Jesse Wineberry
Mike Winlock
Judy Winston
James Winston, Sr.
Michael Winston
Peggy Winston
Sherry Winston
Sherma Wise
Lorna Wisham
Cherise Witherspoon
Bill Witten
Bart Wolstein
Carter Womack
Daisy "Dee" Wood
Rhonda Woodard
Al Woodcock
Wona Wossen
Bill Wright
Clarence Wright
Frances Wright
Janice Wright
Michael Wright
Nadine Wright
Wallace Wright

Leslie Wyche

Lynn Wyman

Leon Wynter

Malika Yamini

George
Yarbourough

Bill Yingling

Ed Young

Michael Young

Nick Young

Ricky Young

Sandra Zabinski

Muhammad
Zahir

Calvin Zanders

Harvey Zay

Sharvishia
Zeigler

Joe Zion

Robert Zion

Peggy Zone-
Fisher

To be
continued . . .

CONTENTS

Foreword by Les Brown   xxv

Acknowledgments   xxix

Introduction   xxxv

PART ONE: SUCCESS RUNS IN OUR RACE

Chapter 1: Twenty Thousand Personal Guides to Success   3

A New Millennium: A New Underground Railroad   4

The Next Phase of the Civil Rights Movement   11

Working Toward Unity   19

The Networking Guru   19

Success Runs in Our Race   32

Portrait of Success: Keith Clinkscales   36

Chapter 2: It Takes a Village to Raise a Child   37

The Enemy Within   41

Seeking Acceptance Versus Equality   48

In Search of Our Family   49

Memorializing Black Excellence   52

The Renewed Urban Village   54

The Rites of Passage   57

Afrocentricity Versus Eurocentricity   62

A Spiritual Connection   65

Portrait of Success: Mellody Hobson   70

Chapter 3: Perceptions, Reality, and Excellence 71
Used but Not Abused 74
Our Violent Image 78
Fixing the Image Problem 79
Cashing In on Our Intellectual Capital 84
Community Versus Individual Success 86
Excellence Redefined 87
Tapping Our Own Roots 89
The Seven Principles of Kwanzaa 91
A New Agenda 91
The Birth of the Urban Village 95
Portrait of Success: Oprah Winfrey 103

**PART TWO: PARTY FOR A PURPOSE: THE POWER
OF NETWORKING**

*Chapter 4: Entrepreneurship and Networking:
Closing the Wealth Gap* 107
Starting More Businesses in the Twenty-first Century 110
Overcoming the Business Start-up Barriers 111
Doing Well While Doing Good 114
Four Key Factors for Entrepreneurial Success 119
Reciprocity: Leveraging Our Purchasing Power 122
Ten Steps to Starting Down Your Entrepreneurial Path 123
Ten Reasons for Doing Business with Minorities 124
Portrait of Success: Teresa Hairston 127

Chapter 5: Getting Together to Get Ahead 128
Sharing the Wealth by Networking 131
The Success Network for You 134
Getting Together to Get Ahead 136
Networking for Access and Success 139
Building Mutually Beneficial Relationships 141
Network Nurturing 144

The Big Four of Networking   146
Portrait of Success: Willie Jolley   153

Chapter 6: Make Networking Work for You   154
Defining Your Networking Goals   157
Setting Goals   159
Your Network Huggers and Shakers   161
Network Nemeses   164
Networking Tools   165
Starting Your Own Networking Event   173
Planning and Networking at Awards Ceremonies   176
Networking in Action   180
Portrait of Success: Marilyn French Hubbard   183

Chapter 7: The Art of Network Conversation   184
People Skills and Networking   186
What Is Your Agenda?   195
Overcoming Fears and Doubts   197
Remembering What's-His-Name   203
The Etiquette of Introductions   204
Rules and Tools of Conversation   205
Portrait of Success: Willie Gary   211

Chapter 8: Networking for a Purpose   212
Networking for a Job   215
Job Hunting for the New College Graduate   224
Keep the Network Plugged In   228
Networking for Customers or Clients   229
Networking for Career Success   232
Networking at Conventions and Conferences   236
Networking for Information   240
Networking for Board Appointments   243
Network Marketing   247
Networking Versus Neck-Working   248
Portrait of Success: Damon Dash   252

PART THREE: CREATING A SUCCESS STEREOTYPE

Chapter 9: Networking as a Way of Life   *255*
The Fraser Guidelines for Effective Networking   257
Networking Dos and Don'ts   277
Ten Tips for Whites Seeking to Network with Blacks   280
Portrait of Success: Cheryl Broussard   *283*

Chapter 10: Networks at Work   *284*
Networking for Economic Empowerment   285
One Hundred Multiplied by Millions   289
Creating Economic Inroads   290
Preaching Economic Redemption   295
Private Enterprise Does Public Good   298
In Conclusion: Networking for the Success of All   306
Portrait of Success: Bruce Gordon   *308*

Appendix A: The FraserNet Workbook   309
Appendix B: The Thirty Best Places to Network   332
Appendix C: The Most Influential Black Speakers in
America: "The Fabulous 50"   336
Appendix D: The Best Black Clubs and Organizations   340
Glossary   349
Suggested Reading   354
Your Comments, Please   356
About the Author   360
Index   363

FOREWORD

It has been over thirty years now since I first met George Fraser and learned of his vision and his dream. Dreams were mostly all that we had back then—not much else but those dreams, and this powerful, compelling desire to live them.

I realize now, as I reflect on those days, that both of us were testing out smaller versions of our dreams back then, preparing ourselves, even though we did not know it. I was broadcasting a message of inspiration and motivation to radio listeners in a midwestern market. And George—well, George was out there trying to do well by doing good in our community, just as he is doing today with his successful businesses and, of course, this inspiring and information-packed book.

When I first met George Fraser, I was a radio disc jockey in Columbus, Ohio, pushing the limits of what my station managers would allow. They had hired me to entertain, but as I became more conscious of the power for positive change in that microphone, I could not resist the opportunity to call out to the community, telling them to stand up and *be somebody*!

George showed up one day at the station with a mutual friend. Of course, he was networking—need you ask? I am telling you, this guy is so plugged in that the folks at BET are talking about going up against Ted Turner, with the George News Network. That's right. Look out, Ted, here comes GNN!

Back on that day when we first met, George was networking as an encyclopedia salesman. Now, I had some experience myself in door-to-door sales. So, when George told me back then that he was an encyclopedia salesman, I was fully prepared to inform him that he was intruding on my air time and to please close the door to my sound booth on his way out.

Of course, that didn't happen. Nobody chases away the King of Networking that easily. And, as I quickly discovered, George was not simply selling encyclopedias. He was selling self-esteem in his community. He was selling pride and information and knowledge. Now, if that sounds like part of a sales pitch, it was, and it still is. It was George's sales pitch then, and it is now. And I bought it. And then, before I knew it, I was selling it, too, on my radio show. George has this effect on people. His dream is contagious, as all good dreams are.

George had come to Columbus to sell the *International Library of Negro Life and History* encyclopedias. He sold me a set. He probably sold me ten sets, because in no time at all, I was selling those encyclopedias, too. At every opportunity, I put in a good word on my radio show for those encyclopedias because I believed in what they represented and I believed in what George was doing. Obviously, I still do.

I think we sold more of those encyclopedias in Columbus than anywhere else in the country. And if we didn't, I would still say we had more fun than any other encyclopedia sales people in the country. That is what happens when you do something that follows your dream, when you do something that is positive for your community, when you live a dream that by its very nature inspires others to dream. How can you help but have fun and enjoy life when you are inspiring others to dream and succeed? There is such power in that.

After George and I had sold a set of the *International Library of*

Negro Life and History encyclopedias to every man, woman, child, and Seeing Eye dog in Columbus, Ohio, he moved on. But naturally, Mr. Networking stayed in touch. Cards, newspaper articles, telephone calls "just to catch up on things." Oh, Lord.

And I was not easy to catch in the years that followed. The radio station owners finally pulled the plug on my microphone when my message became too powerful in the community. That led to my running for state representative and three successful terms in the Ohio legislature before I embarked on my journey to becoming a public speaker. George, in the meantime, went to work for Procter & Gamble, and then the United Way, and then into the Ford dealer-training program.

Each of us carried our dreams along, keeping them alive, strengthening them. George was still in the Ford program when I got one of those "just catching up on you" phone calls. He told me he was putting on a networking forum and wanted me to be his first principal speaker. He explained that he was not so sure that his future lay in the automobile industry. He wanted to get back to living his dream of selling people on their own value and greatness, rather than selling them Taurus cars and F-10 pickup trucks.

Again, George had no trouble selling me. I spoke at that first SuccessNet Forum in Cleveland, and every time he has asked me since, I have gone and spoken, many, many times. It will always be like this for George and me because we share essentially the same dream. And we have seen each other struggle mightily as we stretched to achieve our own versions of it. I lived for months in my office because I couldn't afford to have an apartment, too. George somehow managed to put out *SuccessGuides* that look like a million dollars at times when he didn't have enough change for the parking meter.

We have watched each other struggle, and I think in some ways, we were inspired by each other. We each endeavored to stay on the high road even when we literally had to jump over the toll gates to get on it because we couldn't afford the toll. We were poor, but we didn't act poor or live poorly. Our spirits were rich, and we drew strength from the challenge of seeing our visions through to reality.

George has created and nurtured this vision and has refused to let it go. He has enlisted the help of many people, me included, and that is what it takes—networking and cooperation. George had a dream, and now that dream is his to live, and yours to share. He is going to be part of the solution, and this book will help many, many people.

You have probably read or at least picked up other networking books, but I guarantee you, this is like no other one. *Success Runs in Our Race* is far more than a how-to book by someone with training and knowledge in a particular field. This book is a powerful voice for change, for social action. Other books have exhorted us to take control of our destinies. This one shows us how to do it and why we must do it. This book gives us an agenda.

And there is something else in this book that is different from and so much more powerful than those other books that deal with networking. Most of those books, or at least the ones that I have seen, are rather like textbooks written by professors who have studied the field and come up with their own theories and conclusions. That is not the nature of *Success Runs in Our Race*.

This is a book rooted in life, in our cultural traditions and history. Life's blood flows through these pages because this book was not written by a man who studied the subject; it was written by a man who lived his dream. I urge you to read this book and then live its messages. It may well change your life, and the lives of many others around you. This is an important book for you and for our community.

I must go now—my telephone is ringing. Need you ask who it is? Yes, George, I'll be there. I'll be there.

—LES BROWN

ACKNOWLEDGMENTS

This book in its original and revised version had been brewing in my mind for nearly two decades, and had it not been for my friends, family, and associates . . . my network, I probably would have died with my experiences still inside of me, a mistake all too many of us make. First I must acknowledge the Creator for his divine guidance in providing me the inner strength and vision to write the words that spilled onto blank sheets of paper. A special thanks also goes to my spiritual leader, Rev. Allison Phillips, retired pastor of Mt. Zion Congregational Church, who provided great encouragement as well. These words, ideas, and insights came from everywhere and who knows where, but they were there when I needed them to share with you. It is impossible to write a book about networking and not literally acknowledge everyone in your network. For me that would add another chapter to the book, so instead I dedicated this book to my network. It is they who are responsible for this collection of knowledge; I am the sum of them, and through me you hear their voices.

So many seeds of ideas float around the universe, and eventually the good ones take root. A warm and special thanks goes out to Don Anderson for his insightful suggestions and, most important, to Sherry Winston, who found the first opportunity to plant the seed for this book in the minds of Mel and Sheryl London, without whose thoughtfulness and outreach the book would have not been written.

Few new authors are gifted with agents who fight hard for the right deal for the right idea. Madeleine Morel and Barbara Lowenstein were nothing short of spectacular. Paul Bresnick, my then dedicated senior editor at William Morrow and Company, added encouragement, faith, and savvy to this project, therefore altogether providing me one of the best literary teams in America.

When compiling any list of people who have been instrumental in bringing a project of this size to life, it is usually difficult to single out one person, but in this case it is not difficult. I can't think of anyone who deserves more credit than my friend, researcher, and alter ego, Wes Smith. "Radar," as he is affectionately known, anticipated my every need and helped to shape my ideas, thoughts, themes, and voluminous manuscript into a cohesive whole. His knowledge, sensitivities, and skills contributed greatly to the end product you are about to read.

Then there are those who have contributed lifelong intellectual, financial, and—most important—moral support. It begins with the next generation: my sons Kyle and Scott. Then there is Jean, my caring wife. Other special people who continue to influence me include my brother, Edward Fraser, one of my first role models; sister Emma Pendleton, who keeps my ego in check; best friend Corky Williams, who never stops giving; and finally, my partner, Gregory Williams, who watches my back and gives all that he has all of the time. I am eternally grateful to have such people as a part of my life.

Writing a book requires a few skills I do not possess, one of which is typing. My heartfelt thanks goes out to Millicent Fraser (my sister-in-law) for the long hours she put in typing and retyping my ninety-thousand-word manuscript, and Jarmell Boyd-Sims for her insightful assistance on the tenth-anniversary revised edition of this important book. Getting good advice at the beginning of the process can save you countless hours and steps; Michael and Judy Winston gave me the best advice ("Write about what you know and feel"), and Dennis Kimbro gave me the second-best advice ("Who says so other than you?"). Their advice led me to search my soul for answers, and led me to the Cleveland Public Library, where Angie Bowie, director of the research center, took good care of me. My good friend Tony Brown has always provided me important insights, many of which are reflected in the text of this book. Les Brown, my good friend of thirty years, gave me continued inspiration and his heart in the Foreword. My personal guru and adviser, Dr. David Whitaker, has opened my eyes, broadened my horizons, and illuminated my thinking. My understanding of the importance of Afrocentricity, rites of passage, and the Kwanzaa principles are attributable to him, and to his kindred spirit, Paul Hill. A special thanks goes out to James Earl Jones for the use of his voice and image for my company's fifth-anniversary audio and video presentation on Black Excellence, which helped to inspire this book. Mr. Jones has been a model of excellence and personal achievement for me. While I knew the power and importance of networking, no one made it clearer or more effectively punctuated its importance from a black perspective than Dr. Alvin Poussaint. Dr. Poussaint was one of many people we interviewed for the book. Each person gave of their time generously and helped to round out and broaden my thinking.

I'm especially grateful to the following people for their revealing thoughts: Pat Fields-Davidson, Dr. Floyd Flake, Earl Graves, Jr., Shirley Henderson, Dennis Kimbro, Julianne Malveaux, Caletha Powell, Steve Minter, Dr. Myles Munroe, Pat Roper-Sanders, Pat Tobin, Armstrong Williams, Terrie Williams, Reverend Otis Moss, Jr., and Peggy Winston.

The writing of this book dominated my life for about two years. Running a business is difficult at best when you are operating on all cylinders, let alone when you are preoccupied with a major project. The fact of the matter is that my team really ran the business, starting with my incredible board of directors: Julius

Dorsey, Bob Donaldson, Carl Anderson, and Carole Hoover. There was also a group of dedicated consultants, like the great Margaret Thoren, who stood by me when things were tough and helped to shape my vision. Others include Josh Archer; Maurice Christopher; Edward Fraser; Jim Moore; Marino Puhalj; Dave Faroo; Janet Century; Mack Clemmons; John Schambach of Northern Ohio Live Publishing; George Walters in New York; Rebecca Franklin, William Ware, and Owen Montague in Atlanta; Antonio McKinney, Anthony Daniels, and Lisa Stewart in Chicago; Marilyn French Hubbard, Steve Lewis, and Dorothe Riley-Green in Detroit; William Byers and Nadine Wright in Los Angeles; James Carter, Rey Harris, and Muhammad Zahir in Washington, D.C.; Caletha Powell and John Hankins in New Orleans; and John Wilson in Philadelphia. Frances Wright and Sheila Dennis of WSD, Inc., experts in training and instruction, contributed greatly to the SuccessNet workbook in Appendix A. Their generosity on this and other projects is greatly appreciated.

Latrelle Hogg, then manager of the Xerox Copy Center in Cleveland, had the task of making the many bound copies of the three-hundred-seventy-page "first draft" manuscript. The contribution of her time and the Xerox team spirit made this tedious task easy and pleasurable for me and the forty-five brave souls who agreed to preview and critique the book before printing. I know this may sound like writing a book by committee, but what a committee! I'm indebted to my network of friends who read the first manuscript and gave me valuable comments and contributions: Richard Andrews, Arthur Baker, Margaret Bernstein, Wilbert Black, Edward Blunt, Angela Bowie, William Byers, James Carter, Kevin Carter, Margot Copeland, Paul Cox, Anthony Daniels, Robert Donaldson, Julius Dorsey, John Dunn, Buck and Karen Edwards, Kenneth Ferguson, Rebecca Franklin, Aisha Fraser, Edward Fraser, John Glover, Don Goins, Jonn Hankins, Rey Harris, Gerri Hodby, Latrelle Hogg, Hosiah Huggins, Jr., Alexandria Johnson-Boone, Jefferson H. Jones, Lafayette Jones, Marilyn Jones, Tony Minor, James Moore, Irv Nunn, Emma Pendleton,

George Pendleton, Rev. Allison Phillips, Flo Pollack, Deborah Seller, Ralph Tyler, George Walters, Dr. David Whitaker, Corky Williams, Sherry Winston, and Frances Wright.

Aside from the generous advance provided by William Morrow and Company, additional longer-term financial support was needed to get me to the point where my business and ideas were viable enough so that anyone would pay me or even ask me to write a book. That financial support came by way of my many good friends who shared in my vision. Without this infrastructure of financial support, FraserNet, Inc. and this book would not have become a reality.

Included among those relationships I cherish are: Russell T. Adrine, Ed Anthony, Erline Belton, James Biggar, Robert Donaldson, John Dunn, Ollie Emerson, Allen H. Ford, George Frame, Victor Gelb, Robert Gries, Leon Hogg, Carole Hoover, Dr. Rey Jensen, J. Richard Kelso, Vivian Kidd, Gayle Klaber, John Lewis, Steven Lewis, Josie B. Lindsay, Alan Lipson, Dr. Lonnie Marsh II, Gerald McDonough, John R. Miller, Mello Mitchell, Richard Perlmuter, Richard Pogue, Albert Ratner, Robert Reitman, Paul G. Schloemer, Margaret Thoren, Patricia D. Turner, Dr. Eugene White, David W. Whitehead, Corky Williams, and Frances Wright.

I would like to especially acknowledge Hubert Payne, Bob Donaldson and the Bustamante family—John, Andre, and Tuan—for their support in the incubation of my business. Their outreach enabled me to make enormous strides during the writing of this book and during the most important period of my entrepreneurial development.

Last, I believe it is important to recognize the pioneers of networking in America, those who have written about it, preached its importance, and continue to teach it as a part of their life's work. They include people like Earl Graves, John Naisbitt, Marilyn Ferguson, Susan RoAne, Harvey Mackay, Anne Baber, Lynn Waymon, Anne Boe, Bettie Youngs, Donna and Sandy Vilas, Mel Kaufman, Stacia Robinson, Ivan Misner, Ph.D., and Mary Scott

Welch. Just as important are those modern-day pioneers who have used the power of the media to enhance our image, build our self-esteem, and tell the stories of our networks at work. They include John H. Johnson, Ed Lewis, Clarence Smith, Preston Edwards, the late Robert Maynard, Robert Johnson, Susan Taylor, Kelvin Boston, Keith Clinkscales, and again Earl Graves. We should all be inspired by their individual and collective achievements.

I started this extensive list by saying that it barely scratches the surface of the many people who have influenced me and helped me grow. I would like to end by saying I am ever so grateful for the many that have given so much to enrich my life.

INTRODUCTION

Thank you for stopping here first! I'm told most people skip the introduction to a book, but I think an introduction is needed for *Success Runs in Our Race*, because you may be surprised by what you find on the following pages. By starting here, you will have a road map for your journey into the world of networking.

Because this is the first major book of its kind targeted to black people around the world, I didn't want to write a networking book full of trite tips, facts, and ideas about an important movement only now taking center stage in the black community. There are lots of reasons for our "late blooming," if you will. I felt it was important to explore some of the background, history, and psychological warfare we have come through to make networking a permanent and meaningful part of our lives.

To that end, the first several chapters build the foundation from a historical, biographical, and cultural perspective. The remaining chapters are full of practical and useful networking techniques, strategies, and tactics peppered with true-to-life stories from the famous and not so famous; everyday people with real problems and effective solutions. Some are seasoned networkers and some are beginners; all of them you can relate to, because they share in your culture and in the history, values, and beliefs that culture carries with it. This book was written for you and to you, because sharing what I know is the only way I can grow, learn, and get to heaven.

Let me warn you about the difficulty in grasping real-life networking as I envision it. This is not the "What's in it for me?" brand of networking. It is the brand of networking that calls upon you to give until it hurts, and then give until it feels good. It is the kind of networking that over time delivers to your doorstep your every dream and every hope.

If it sounds like *American Idol*, I assure you it's not. It took me almost half a century to learn the lessons of life I am sharing with you. Many of these lessons are very personal; some you will be able to mirror with your own experiences; others could be classified as small miracles, maybe even unbelievable. But this is a book of facts, not fiction. The most important lesson you will learn from this book is that networking is a mind-set, an attitude, an approach to life and all its twists and curves.

Networking is driven by our experiences and exposures, both good and bad, by our values and beliefs, by our self-esteem and cultural orientation. My networking experiences have grown more meaningful and more productive as I have grown older and wiser and have learned more about myself and my capacity to give, to receive, and to love. When I finally reached the point in my life where I truly understood who I was and why I was here, my "net" began "working." So will yours if you internalize the lessons of this book and read between the lines—because this is the line *you* will be writing, and your story will become our story, and our story will become legacy.

All of this from a simple networking book, you say? I say, *yes*, and it is not so simple. Nothing of substance is as simple as it seems. The overarching themes that have been woven into this book have strong moral fibers. Some of them may already be woven into your life, some may be new, others may just be a fresh approach to a complex problem, but all of them are worthy of consideration.

Networking is rampant among blacks who are hungry for success. Many, however, still are not masters of the process. On my travels across the country, and after my speeches to scores of black organizations every year, I hear tale after tale about blacks who network feverishly but without achieving the desired results, because they are not networking skillfully. And far too often, I see networking done for individuals or narrow purposes. We must network for the good of all of our people, not just for our own prosperity, but because as long as one of us is living in poverty, we all are impacted by those images of poverty.

And so, in this book, you will be presented with new ideas, goals, and an agenda for the further advancement of our successful race, and then you will be provided with some very practical and applicable instructions on how to network for that cultural success. You will also be presented with scores of networking success stories and anecdotes from the lives of black people. Some of them you may already know; others are simply unsung heroes and heroines. They have agreed to share their stories for the same reason that I have written this book. We believe in the Afrocentric principles of cooperation and community. We believe that by working together for the good of all of our people, we all will benefit and, more important, our children and the world they grow in will benefit. Yes, success does run in our race!

I have gone into my soul for some of the lessons and ideas in this book, and I am hopeful that you will identify both with those it pained me to explore, and with those it has given me joy to delve into. There is nothing clichéd about networking in my life. Networking has elevated my life, and I have come to recognize that the only networking that works is networking for the benefit of others. I believe that you will be motivated to adopt that philosophy as you read this book. I think you will find that it is quite contagious.

Part One

SUCCESS RUNS IN OUR RACE

1

Twenty Thousand Personal Guides to Success

God bless the Underground
Great praise to it shall ever resound.
The train, it never left the track.
No one was lost. No one turned back.
— FRANK MORRIS

Atop a bale of hay in the back of a badly dented pickup truck, Juliet E. K. Walker, Ph.D., rides through a rutted hog run in a remote corner of the Midwest. When the lurching truck reaches the edge of a cornfield, the University of Illinois history professor, who has done postdoctoral work at Harvard, jumps out and plunges in between the tight rows.

She walks for fifty yards through the clawing cornstalks until she comes to a wooded patch of ground overgrown with Queen Anne's lace and shaded by hundred-year-old evergreens. Filtered sunlight lands upon the bleached faces of twenty weathered tombstones in the clearing. One of the stones, a simple cracked tablet that has been knocked flat to the ground, marks the final resting place of Walker's personal and professional inspiration: her great-great-grandfather, Free Frank McWorter.

The offspring of a West African slave woman and her Irish-Scot slave master, McWorter was born into servitude in 1777 in South Carolina. As a young slave, he became manager of his master's farm in Kentucky, and earned extra wages by hiring his work out to others. He put those wages toward the establishment of his own business mining and selling saltpeter for the manufacture of gunpowder. With the profits from these ventures and others, Free

Frank eventually purchased not only his own freedom, but that of his wife, Lucy, and fourteen other family members spanning four generations. He later moved his freed family to Illinois, where he used his entrepreneurial skills to buy land and become the first African American to legally establish his own town, New Philadelphia. From this town, populated by both blacks and whites, Free Frank operated a station in the Underground Railroad, covertly shuttling some of the hundred thousand runaway slaves who found freedom from slave masters and bounty hunters to the North and Canada.

In her doctoral dissertation, "Free Frank: A Black Pioneer on the Antebellum Frontier," Walker wrote of her little-known ancestor's dedication to improving not only his own life, but that of all black people.

Free Frank achieved success that was almost unheard-of for blacks of his time, and once he achieved that success, he dedicated himself to reaching back and elevating the lives of others of his race.

A NEW MILLENNIUM: A NEW UNDERGROUND RAILROAD

With this book, I am calling for the revival of that Afrocentric communal spirit among the millions of black Americans who are seeking personal and professional success, as well as for those who have already achieved success and now wish to build upon it and to spread it to others of our race.

Afrocentricity, which will be discussed at length later in this book, promotes the oneness of all things. Cooperation, collectivism, and sharing are the essential elements. Community is considered before the individual. Many of our black organizations have come to embrace Afrocentric principles. It is my belief, and that of many other blacks, that the image of the black community and in too many cases the actions of black people do not reflect the image and actions of our success-oriented ancestors. I'm speaking of great people such as the kings and queens of Africa, and more

modern figures such as Sojourner Truth, Free Frank, Harriet Tubman, Malcolm X, and the Reverend Martin Luther King, Jr.
These are the role models for a successful black community. These
are the people who fought for us all.

Consider this then your personal guidebook for a modern version of the Underground Railroad; an Afrocentric Networking
Movement that hopefully will deliver you to a destination called
"Success" in both your personal and your professional life—a success marked by compassion and striving for the enrichment of all
our people.

In many ways, it is understandable why so many blacks came
to view their struggle in a hostile, racist, and exclusionary environment as an individual struggle. But the time has come to join
together so that those who have succeeded can use their collective
power to raise up those who are still struggling. "Networking
helps people share psychological as well as political and economic
interests, and it provides the sense that someone cares and is willing to help, easing the feeling that a black person is alone and at
the mercy of an institutionalized white system that might be
overtly or covertly against him or her," said Dr. Alvin Poussaint,
Harvard psychologist and expert on black families.

Like the Underground Railroad, networks with an Afrocentric
philosophy are dedicated to improving the lives of blacks and elevating our race as a whole. Afrocentric networks come in many
forms. If you belong to a black fraternity such as Alpha Phi Alpha
or a black sorority such as Delta Sigma Theta or Alpha Kappa Alpha—or any organization devoted to uplifting the lives of its
members—then you belong to an Afrocentric network. Many
black on-line discussion groups, professional organizations,
alumni groups, service clubs, and mentor or role-modeling programs are essentially Afrocentric networks.

Looking quickly in my own electronic organizer, which I affectionately call my "Soul-O-Dex" and which has grown from one
thousand to twenty thousand names since 1992, I find the National Association of Black Social Workers, the National Society

of Black Engineers, the American Association of Blacks in Energy, the National Association of Black Journalists, and hundreds more black networking groups. (See pages 340–48.)

There is no doubt that we know how to form organizations. But do we know how to use them to network for the good of our entire race of people? Or do we use them to further our personal ambitions, and maybe the agenda of our profession or special-interest group, rather than as sources of collective strength and self-determination for the good of all?

An organization of black lawyers is a professional network, but if its only goal is to benefit the lawyers, then it is too narrowly focused and, from my perspective, selfish. If that same organization, however, networks by putting the collective knowledge, energy, and talents of those lawyers to work to provide legal aid to the poor, or to draft legislative reforms to benefit the black community, or to mentor children and college students so that they might have positive role models, then that is Afrocentric networking for the benefit of our race. *That* is the sort of networking that we must advocate within all of our organizations.

If you belong to the congregation of a black church and you attend church social events, then you are part of that network, and it is a benevolent network. But it can also be a powerful force for change and good if, as has happened in various locations across the country, its congregation members pool their economic resources and put them to use to revitalize their neighborhoods or to conduct special educational programs for neighborhood children. That is the kind of Afrocentric networking that uplifts a community.

While many people think of networks as business tools, they have historically been used to implement social change. The Underground Railroad is an amazing example of networking for social change, as was the civil rights movement, in which a network of like-minded people came together, expanded their network, and forced a nation to change. Often, people turn to networking when they become frustrated by traditional power structures and by hierarchical institutions that refuse to listen. Leaders emerge in any group, but in networks, leadership is generally shared more readily and spread across the group rather than organized in the traditional pyramid style. Information becomes the source of power, and information flows to anyone willing to receive it. It is not racist or elitist or exclusive. That is what makes networking so effective: Many voices are heard, many minds are tapped. Ideas flourish in this environment. Power builds.

The rapidly expanding economic power of networking among blacks has not gone unnoticed. Every year, publications like *Black Enterprise, Fortune,* and *Newsweek* document several powerful examples of high-level networking among a group of the nation's most prominent and affluent blacks. Carolyn M. Brown wrote an article in *Black Enterprise* entitled "Come together with colleagues and private groups to build a community of profitable black-owned business." The article spotlighted Athletes Building Better Communities LLC (ABBC). AABC came into being when Mike D. Jones, Jason Fisk, Eddie Robinson, Jr., and Henry Ford of the Tennessee Titans decided to come together to reinvest in their communities by starting businesses. Each invested $100,000 into the Nashville-located AABC. The goal of the LLC is to invest in housing developments, franchises, real estate, and retail outlets located in Nashville's underserved communities. Another one of AABC's goals, according to the *Black Enterprise* article, is to form alliances with community development organizations, banks, faith-based organizations, and educational institutions. Titan defensive end Mike D. Jones stated in the article, "We took the seeds of the notion and developed a viable business plan."

Another example, former basketball great Magic Johnson, has redefined himself as a businessman who focuses his efforts on revitalizing neglected communities and providing quality entertainment and services. As chairman and chief executive officer of Johnson Development Corporation, Johnson partnered with Kenneth Lombard, who serves as president of the corporation. Lombard had been regional director for Grubb & Ellis Real Estate

Company. There he raised over $100 million by developing and executing creative investment programs targeted for pension funds and other institutions. Using his expertise and Magic's desire to focus his efforts on revitalizing neglected communities, the company has successfully negotiated partnership ventures with Sony/Loews Cineplex Entertainment, Starbucks, T.G.I. Friday's, Fatburger, and CALPERS. The development projects and related operations create jobs and employ local minority contractors and service vendors. All Johnson Development partnership entities perform in the top 10 percent of their respective businesses.

Other black "power networking" has also proven successful. There's the collaboration between J Bruce Llewellyn, CEO of Philadelphia Coca-Cola Bottling Company (the only African American among Coke's 394 U.S. bottlers), and a group of investors that included basketball star Julius "Dr. J" Erving, which bought a controlling interest in Philly Coke and has since built an enterprise that produces nearly 40 million cases of Coke products each year and earned $400 million in annual sales in 2001. Presently, the company is the third largest black-owned firm in the United States. Roy Johnson, former editor-in-chief of *Savoy*, a lifestyle magazine for anyone interested in how blacks affect the areas of business, politics, and art, forged collaboration with Keith Clinkscales, chairman and CEO of Vanguarde Media. Don Coleman, president of Global Hue (formerly Don Coleman Agency), made a strategic business alliance and joined the New American Strategies Group. Global Hue, Coleman's full marketing services company, merged with several minority agencies that represent $270 million in billings. The rapidly expanding economic power of networking among blacks has not gone unnoticed.

Blacks are asserting themselves in positions of power in education, finance and banking, small business development, technology, publishing, real estate development, and entertainment and music.

I will give you more detailed examples of Afrocentric networks that work for our mutual benefit rather than individual gain in later chapters, particularly Chapter 10, "Networks at Work." One of my premises is that blacks still have not used networking as a social reform tool, at least not as wholeheartedly or as effectively as other cultural groups. I find this perplexing, because the basic philosophy of networking—cooperative effort for the common good—is very much a part of our African tribal heritage.

In most African tribes, there was no such thing as private property; everything was considered community property held for the benefit of the group. Even in more recent history, certain segments of black society in other countries have worked together for the good of all much more enthusiastically than black people in America. The late Robert Maynard, editor and president of the *Tribune* in Oakland, California, often spoke of how his father's small trucking company benefited from a network of men who, like his father, were natives of Barbados who immigrated to the United States. This "Barbadian network" had a communal spirit that somehow had not been allowed to flourish throughout the black community, Maynard frequently noted. But that can be changed, particularly in these ripe times in which thousands and thousands of successful blacks are in a position to join together for the good of their race.

The "twenty thousand personal guides to success" referred to in this chapter title come from the pages of *SuccessGuide Worldwide; The Networking Guide to Black Resources,* a resource guide published by my company, FraserNet, Inc. The *SuccessGuide Worldwide* provides resources and contacts from around the world, including Australia, Bahamas, Brazil, Cameroon, Canada, East Africa, Ghana, Jamaica, Japan, Puerto Rico, Senegal, South Africa, Switzerland, The Netherlands, United Kingdom, U.S. Virgin Islands, United States, West Africa, West Indies, and Zambia. They are modern examples, just as Free Frank is a historic example, of why I believe that success runs in our race. There are millions of blacks who are still impoverished, yes. But millions have been successful not only as individuals who have survived slavery, segregation, and American apartheid but as an enduring race of people who developed highly complex and sophisticated civilizations in Africa long before the white man evolved on the European continent. In other words, more than we have ever really acknowledged, success is a tradition in our race. We have it as our history, and we have it now.

As the only immigrants to come to this country in shackles and chains, we have come a great way. The questions that remain are: How can those of us who have succeeded use our success to empower those still locked in the struggle of poverty? How can we better educate and elevate our young? How can we build upon our successes to create a new legacy, one of service to our own people and to the larger world?

Large segments of our black community, commonly referred to as "the underclass," have become isolated from success. My goal is to help bring those abandoned people back up from "under" by reaching out to them with our Afrocentric network of talent, energy, and financial resources. I am not alone in my goal, by any means. "The middle class wants a structured way to share talent and advantage with those less fortunate who are of their families and group, and to reverse the brain-drain that depletes our still-segregated cities," according to Dr. Ramona Hoage Edelin, former executive director of the Congressional Black Caucus Foundation. Dr. Edelin suggests a "successful cultural offensive" to reunite the black community, one that "would unite us and coordinate and focus our leadership; create markets, businesses, and jobs; reestablish mastery in learning; and materially change the lives of our poor, near-poor, and middle classes so that our group substantially enhances the productivity and competitiveness of this nation."

I agree with Dr. Edelin and all the other black scholars, political leaders, and businessmen who have been calling for such a movement. In this book, I will offer you ideas, themes, and an agenda for that movement, and the tools to bring it about.

THE NEXT PHASE OF THE CIVIL RIGHTS MOVEMENT

Media images that still portray blacks only as exceptional athletes or entertainers fail to understand where we have been and where we are going, not only as individuals, but as a community of people. Civil rights legislation and social programs helped millions of individual blacks enter the white-dominated business world, and through hard work and intelligence, most are succeeding beyond the dreams of previous generations.

In this book, I will focus on the successes of blacks, but not because I do not see and fully understand the problems that still ravage black America. I was born into the underclass. I know those problems, and I know what they are doing to my racial family. But I do not believe in dwelling on the problems. I believe, instead, in offering solutions. As my daddy used to tell me: "What you do speaks so loudly I can't hear what you say." Rather than moan about the miseries that plague black society, rather than look for the ones to blame, I prefer to look at our successes and achievements and offer ways to build upon them in order to pull more blacks out of the underclass, out of the gangs and the ghettos and into productive and rewarding lives. We all know the problems too well. We have discussed it ad nauseam. Let us now devote ourselves to taking action and to looking to our strengths.

The unemployment and poverty rate for blacks are both at the lowest levels on record. In 2000, the average unemployment rate was 7.7 percent, down from 14.2 percent in 1992. The poverty rate in 1999 was 23.9, down from 33.1 percent in 1993. Presently, there are now fifteen million blacks employed in this country, nearly half of them in professional and technical positions in the business world. There are 823,500 black-owned businesses in this country. The top one is World Wide Technology Inc., the largest black-owned business in the nation, with $802 million in revenues. Among the more established of the top black-owned businesses is sixty-year-old Johnson Publishing of Chicago, a publishing, broadcasting, and cosmetics empire founded by John H. Johnson, which has annual sales of about $412.4 million. Some of the newer black-owned franchises exist in the "hip-hop" arena. One facet, hip-hop music, is ranked second behind country music, according to *Black Enterprise*. Hip-hop produced over $2 billion in U.S. sales in 2000. Other industries spawning from hip-hop include clothing designers like FUBU and Karl Kani and national and local publications. In fact, according to *Black Enterprise*, *The Source* is one of the top-selling magazines in the nation that cater to the hip-hop audience. Russell Simmons, CEO of Rush Communications of NYC, Inc., was a *BE* Company of the Year, with $192 million in sales. Once dismissed as a fad, hip-hop is now a lifestyle, language, and, most notably, a $5 billion industry. Black power has definitely gone green. " 'Sup, y'all?"

One of my favorite Afrocentric-based new businesses is the MATAH network. The MATAH program, launched in 1997 by the late Ken Bridges and Al Wellington, endeavors to teach blacks the importance of redirecting their almost $600 billion plus spending power into the black community and black businesses. The MATAH concept was born from Wharton School graduates following the 1995 Million Man March. In one of his last interviews, Ken Bridges said, "MATAH seeks relationships with excellent manufacturers," citing Dudley Products, which will produce hair care products for MATAH. Unfortunately, Ken became the tenth victim of the Washington, D.C.–area snipers in October 2002. He had a wife, six children, and a dream that is certain to continue well into the future.

If you read newspapers or check out the skin tone of the bad guys in most television dramas and screenplays, you rarely see glimpses of this hardworking, intelligent, and successful class of blacks. Oddly, though, with the rise of the hip-hop generation, Madison Avenue is very much aware of it these days. In case you've missed it, we are the hottest market in the country. Ten years ago, when an advertisement for the then-new *E-Style* catalogue was run in *Ebony*, requests for it ran at double the normal rate: one hundred thousand compared with the usual fifty thousand for other catalogues. Surely it was not all those dope dealers and street thugs dropping their weapons to fill out subscription forms. Spiegel did not launch the new catalogue because of some benevolent urge to outfit blacks. Its corporate chiefs simply read the marketing figures and determined that there are millions of successful blacks out there with expendable income. According to *Target Market News*, a Chicago-based research firm that tracks black spending patterns, blacks spent $43.2 billion on automobile purchases in 2001. If you've seen the latest television commercials, you'll notice that marketing divisions across the automobile industry have finally "awakened" to cater to the black community in media, specifically to young urban black professionals. Evidently, there has been a shift in the retail industry, which ten years ago focused on the expendable clothing dollars of black and white females.

Back in 1992, black-owned auto dealerships had their best year ever at a time when most white-owned dealerships were laying workers off—and probably black workers, at that. But according to a 2002 *Black Enterprise* magazine study, despite the challenges facing black auto dealers, the top 100 increased their total number of employees from 11,296 in 1999 to 12,257 in 2000, up 8.5 percent, and expanded their total sales from $7.3 billion in 1999 to $8.7 billion in 2001, a jump of 20.4 percent. Ten years ago, the ominous addendum to reports that black-owned enterprises fared well during the recession was the report that black workers were the only group to experience a net loss of jobs during the 1990–91 recession. Back then, *The Wall Street Journal* studied government labor figures and found what most blacks could have told them: that some large corporations shed black workers disproportionately. Blacks were the only cultural group to have a net loss in jobs during that recession. Asians gained jobs. Hispanics gained jobs. And whites gained jobs. We had a net loss. In fact, we lost nearly one third of the 180,210 blue-collar jobs that disappeared during that recessionary period. This clearly pointed out a great need for blacks to own their own businesses to ensure job security.

I mention these statistics to illustrate the undeniable and

growing success of blacks in business. And for those who still deny that blacks are successful, I refer you to a widely published 2001 Census report showing that there are more than 823,000 U.S. businesses owned by blacks. In addition, black-owned businesses employed 718,300 people and generated $71.2 billion in revenues in 1997, according to the Commerce Department's Census Bureau. The report went on to say that businesses owned by blacks made up 4 percent of the 20.8 million nonfarm businesses in the nation and 0.4 percent of the $18.6 trillion in receipts for all businesses. Black-owned firms, excluding C corporations, increased 26 percent from 1992 to 1997, compared with a 7 percent increase in this category for all U.S. firms. Receipts of black-owned firms rose 33 percent, from $32 billion in 1992 to $43 billion in 1997, compared with a 40 percent increase for all U.S. firms over the same period.

Further, *Black Enterprise* magazine reported in its June 2001 issue that the timing of the nation's largest black-owned businesses was impeccable. Even as the economy slowed, total revenues for firms on the BE Industrial/Service 100s topped the $10 billion mark for the first time, moving up from $8.7 billion in 1999 to $10.9 billion in 2000. The 25.1 percent increase in revenues was powered by 80 percent of firms on the list showing an increase in revenues and the emergence of three companies debuting on the list with revenues of $200 million or better. In fact, twenty-two of these enterprises grossed more than $150 million; there were sixteen such firms in 1999. Our entrepreneurs are no longer limited to a few niche markets. Our business expertise ranges from manufacturing to high-tech, and we are well represented in the global market. More and more black professionals have left high-ranking jobs in corporate America and stepped out on their own to run more and more businesses, using their savvy and skills in entrepreneurial endeavors aimed at their own communities. Over the last decade, we have rapidly learned to play this game, and we are playing it well. We have elevated it to a higher plane.

But despite leaps and bounds, the strong growth in revenues

from black businesses has been offset by a slight decline in employment among the nation's largest black-owned businesses. In 2000, 65,898 workers were employed by the BE Industrial/Service 100s, a 2.5 percent decrease over 1999. Detroit-based Hawkins Food Group employed 5,833 workers, the greatest number of personnel among the BE Industrial/Service 100s list of employment leaders.

One of the primary themes of this book is that those of us who have "gotten ours" in the game need to reach back and assist those who are still striving. We need to build upon social gains by building economic strength for all blacks, particularly by encouraging and assisting our own people to become entrepreneurs and establish their own businesses.

In *Tao of Leadership*, John Heider writes, "Power comes through cooperation, independence through service and a greater self through selflessness." Such development of economic power, financial independence, and personal growth through networking by blacks is the key theme of this book, and of my own business.

There is no charge paid by those black professionals and entrepreneurs who are listed in our *SuccessGuide*. Each person pays only in networking time. Each signs a consent form agreeing to be listed at no charge in our *SuccessGuide Worldwide* and also to welcome inquiries from anyone who uses the guide to contact them. In effect, they sign a pact to network. There are more than fifteen thousand individuals listed in *SuccessGuide Worldwide*. Each of these individuals is a source of inspiration, each is a success story. Just flipping randomly through the guide I come upon:

- Werten Bellamy, Jr., is a partner in the law firm of Lewis & Murray and is responsible for managing the corporation's law department.
- Carolyn Baldwin Byrd is chairman and chief executive officer of GlobalTech Financial, LLC, a financial services company headquartered in Atlanta.
- Kyle Donovan is the publisher and CEO of *NV Magazine*

(*New Vision in Business*). He is the youngest publisher of a
national magazine.
• Reginald R. Denson is recognized as one of the pioneers
in urban radio marketing. He is the director of Urban Radio
Sales for ABC Radio Networks.
• Marc Belton was born in West Hempstead, New York. He
is president of the Big G cereal division at General Mills and
is responsible for marketing the company's cereals and new
cereal ventures.
• George R. Carruthers, Ph.D. is senior astrophysicist and
head of the Ultraviolet Measurements Group, Space Science
Division of the Naval Research Laboratory. His scientific
investigations include the first detection of interstellar
molecular hydrogen.
• Margot James Copeland is executive vice president-
director of civic affairs and corporate diversity for KeyCorp,
one of the nation's largest multiline financial services
companies. Copeland serves as chair of the Key Foundation
and manages the company's $20 million social investment
and workforce diversity initiatives.
• Stayce D. Harris is a first officer on the Boeing 747-400
aircraft for United Airlines. While on active duty in the
United States Air Force, Harris was rated as a C-141 aircraft
commander, logging over twenty-five hundred hours.
• Patricia Russell-McCloud is president of Russell-McCloud
& Associates. *Black Enterprise* magazine named her one of the
top five business motivators in America.
• Bert N. Mitchell is the founder, chairman, and CEO of
Mitchell & Titus, LLP, the nation's largest African
American–controlled CPA firm.
• William Pickard, Ph.D., has been a successful businessman
in the metropolitan Detroit area for more than twenty years
and is currently the chairman and chief executive officer of
the GlobalAutomotiveAlliance. GlobalAutomotiveAlliance is
made of five entities: Regal Plastics company,

Commonwealth Regal Industries, Vitec, ARD Logistics, and Grupo Antolin-Wayne.
• Ingrid Saunders-Jones is senior vice president of the Coca-Cola Company and chairperson of the Coca-Cola Foundation. She is also senior vice president of corporate external affairs and directs the vision and involvement of the Coca-Cola Company in community, philanthropic, and civic affairs.
• Maceo K. Sloan is chairman, president, and chief executive officer of Sloan Financial Group, America's largest African American diversified financial and communications firm.
• Hilton O. Smith is corporate vice president and director of community affairs at Turner Construction Company. He is responsible for forty business units and six subsidiaries internationally.
• Janine Fondon and husband Tom (Fondon) publish one of the most well-read email newsletters as president and CEO of UnityFirst.com and African American/Diversity Newswire. *Unity First Online* is a direct email service that carries regional and national multicultural news to over 250,000 mailboxes of African Americans and other diverse populations.
• U.S. Representative Harold E. Ford, Jr., is one of the youngest members of Congress and serves on the House Education and Workforce Committee. He authored the Make College Affordable Act to help working families meet the rising costs of higher education.
• Melody Hobson is president of Ariel Capital Management, Inc., a Chicago-based investment management firm with over $5 billion in assets under management.
• Glenda G. McNeal is vice president and general manager of New Industries Development in Global Establishment Services at American Express Company.
• Gwendolyn Garnett-Thomas is a senior vice president at Bank of America, with twenty-two years in the technology

and operations industry. She presently serves as a consumer real estate loan fulfillment executive and manages one thousand employees across the Florida, Georgia, Tennessee, and Central regions of the United States in consumer banking and retail mortgage.

These individuals are just a sampling of the many Black success stories listed in *SuccessGuide Worldwide*, and I consider them to be the foundation of an Afrocentric Networking Movement. You should consider them part of your network, too.

If you page through *SuccessGuide* yourself, you will come to understand why I so dearly love it when I hear a white businessman righteously announce, "I would like to hire more blacks, but I just can't find any qualified people out there." Why do I love to hear that? Because then I can respond with the "thud" of the three-pound, 440-page *SuccessGuide Worldwide* landing on his desk and the pronouncement, "Well then, let me introduce you to twenty thousand of my closest friends."

In reality, there are *millions* of highly qualified black professionals and entrepreneurs in this country. I know, because I've recruited quite a few of them for my Underground Railroad of networking professionals. I believe blacks have everything we need right now to begin the final phase of the civil rights movement—our push for economic equality. In 2001 black people spent $590 billion on goods and services. This number continues to grow 3 to 5 percent each year. *You and I* represent the sixteenth largest economy in the industrialized world. And we can build on that. As a God-loving people, we must build upon those who have risen from the underclass into the middle and upper classes. We don't need much, but we do need one another.

As we move forward in a new millennium, we have no time left for blaming, pointing fingers, or the kind of government entitlements that only perpetuate our self-defeating sense of victimization. In the words of Benjamin Hooks, "We need a moratorium on excuses." Trevor Coleman wrote in *Emerge* magazine that "pro-gressive leaders in the black community argue that given the power of Congress, courts and the presidency, it makes no sense for blacks to ignore those entities in their quest for justice." I agree, but I also believe, as do an increasing number of educated blacks, that we must seize control of our own lives and our own futures. The victories forged in the hard-won battle for civil rights should be the icing on the cake, not the cake.

We have talked the talk about gaining independence and controlling our destinies, now we need to walk the walk—a walk; toward excellence, interdependence, and cooperation with one another, but with a healthy competitiveness in the marketplace.

WORKING TOWARD UNITY

Celebrated by more than twenty-five million blacks worldwide each holiday season in December, Kwanzaa strongly advocates economic self-determination for blacks through their own system of supports. As I will show in this book, my own businesses are based on the principles of Kwanzaa. Other business groups such as the National Black MBA Association, the Black Leadership Council, and 100 Black Men/Women are also applying Kwanzaa principles in their efforts to improve their communities by fighting illiteracy and negative self-images among our young. These efforts are important steps toward rescuing our people from crime, drugs, and poverty. Believe me, I know that life.

THE NETWORKING GURU

Let me tell you a little of my own personal history, and my goals for the modern Underground Railroad—which are really my vision and goals for black people. I have been called a "Networking Guru," and although that may be a fairly silly title (you've heard the phrase, "Uneasy lies the head that wears a crown"?), my life *is* an example of the value of networking for success. Perhaps by my relating my story, you will understand why I believe so strongly in the importance and value of black people working together for our mutual success in this nation.

I grew up in Brooklyn, New York, the son of Ida Mae Baldwin and her second husband, Walter Frederick Fraser. My fair-skinned mother, the great-granddaughter of slaves, was a native of Lumpkin, Georgia. My father was of rich black color and a proud native of Georgetown, Guyana, where his family had been wealthy landowners.

After emigrating to London, his family lost most of its savings but retained its pride and proper bearing. Dad was in the British Navy when he jumped ship in New York and began a new life. He was, like most immigrants, virtually penniless.

I was the fifth of six children, and the last one born before my mother was committed to Kings County Mental Hospital in Brooklyn for schizophrenia. My youngest brother was born while Mother was hospitalized at Kings County, where she died thirty-nine years after she had been committed. Because of her illness, my father had to split up our family. He simply could not support us all and care for us while working as a cabdriver by day and a jazz drummer and vibes player at night. We all went to foster homes.

In 1950, at the age of five, I was packed off to a foster home along with my sister Emma, whose light skin was similar to mine, and our youngest brother, Joseph. Our foster parents, Ariah and Frances Morse, were hardworking people whose southern roots had been tempered by the realities of tenement life in Manhattan. My life between the ages of five and eleven was spent at 59 West Ninety-eighth Street—an area that at that time was straight out of *West Side Story*. Gang fights between the blacks of the neighborhood and the Puerto Ricans were common. Because of my fair complexion and Guyana-Lumpkin combo features, I could actually pass for either side—a fact that I occasionally found it necessary to exploit. I learned to be flexible in order to survive the streets of New York.

When I was eleven, my foster family moved to a row house in Queens. My foster father, who had been working in the Brooklyn Navy Yard, took a job driving a cab because of injuries that he sustained at the shipyard. He was a good provider—I ate so much southern-style hominy grits back then, I have trouble looking at them today. My foster father also was a stern taskmaster and disciplinarian, who beat our behinds with a strip of old tire that we called "the black belt" as he held our heads between his legs. To this day, I still remember those "whuppins." He also filled our after-school, weekend, and summer hours with work details in order to keep us out of trouble. I think I sanded and repainted every piece of furniture in our house at least four times. The work ethic was the rule in my foster home. It was not a joyful childhood because of the abusive nature of the Morses' only son, who was much older and mentally unstable. It was an existence in which survival was the basic goal. My psychological scars from that time took years to heal in adulthood. I don't ever remember, for example, having celebrated a birthday in those childhood years. In fact, so little emphasis was placed on holidays or special events that for many years, I thought my birthday was April 1. It is actually May 1.

My foster parents were an older couple, and as they advanced in years, our once-comfortable foster home turned seedy and then decrepit. Roaches moved in. Several years after I moved out, the Morses were evicted. My memory of them is filled with ambivalent emotions. They were more keepers than parents. Ours was not a relationship built on the natural love shared by most parents and children. But they did provide for us for many years, and they did give us the nurturing environment of a two-parent household that so many of today's children lack. In retrospect, I feel a deep appreciation for them. After all, they did teach me that you must earn what you get in life—a valuable lesson in itself.

Fortunately, my teenage years were comforted by the fact that my three elder brothers, Edward, Scotland, and Walter, who were placed together in another foster home, were only a short bus ride away. They were great role models who helped ground me and gave me someone to look up to. They were good-looking, suave, and slick. They dressed well, and to me, were sophisticates. I wanted to emulate them, and to do that, I needed money, which I pursued with great zeal. They had paper routes, shined shoes, and worked in a clothing store. I was an entrepreneur. I had my own house-cleaning service, and my sister Emma and brother Joseph worked for me. I paid them half the rate that I got. I also ran a baby-sitting service that was my first networking operation. I hired boys from around the neighborhood and then I acted as the middleman in finding them baby-sitting work. They benefited and so did I. Soon, I was dressing as slickly as my brothers.

During my senior year in high school, my father finally marshaled enough money to bring us all together under one roof back in the Bedford-Stuyvesant neighborhood of Brooklyn, which was then a lively black community of lawyers, dentists, doctors, and cab-driving drummers. My father was a popular figure who loved to party. He was also a believer in proper values for his children. We were each called upon to contribute our share to the family treasury, so I went to work at Key Foods grocery just around the corner. I had yet to master the art of punctuality, however, and I was fired after establishing a reputation for reporting half the time at the wrong time. It was a necessary lesson that I have never forgotten. I may not operate like clockwork even today, but I'm always doing my best to stay ahead of the second hand.

In my next job, I dared not fail my boss. He was my half brother Benny Evans, who had his own printing company. He paid slave wages to family members, but he instilled us with pride at being part of a family operation. He was a networking mentor for me. He had an infectious enthusiasm for his work, and although he was not particularly well-spoken, he had a sharp mind and a good manner with people. His success implanted in me a desire to one day have the "freedom" of my own business.

At the age of nineteen, I began taking classes at New York University. I worked nights as an executive assistant in mop control for the Port Authority of New York and New Jersey. My specific area of expertise: corridors and floors of La Guardia Airport. It was not to be my most significant job, but my supervisor became an early role model. Mr. Lewis, a large, imposing black man from the West Indies, was maintenance supervisor. He worked that job with the pride and authority of a Wall Street baron, and he inspired his people to work as a team. He was promoted many times over the years, and his manner of leadership was a model for me and dozens of others. Role models can be found in places high and low, I've discovered.

Around that time, I took an apartment with a friend, Jerry Pinckney, who was a union electrician in El Barrio, a predominantly Puerto Rican section of New York. And although I was merely a mop-pusher at the airport, I began dressing as though I were an up-and-coming stockbroker. My model was a neighbor who was a computer programmer for a Fortune 500 company. Don Walker was a black man who had the ultimate bachelor pad, a black Jaguar XKE, and the look of a Madison Avenue executive. He was the first black executive I had ever encountered. He read *The Wall Street Journal* and *The New York Times*.

I wanted to be Don Walker. Or at least the economy-size version. To that end, I bought a sports car, although it was a Triumph TR-4 rather than a Jag. I also took to wearing some mock preppy eyeglasses and carrying the *Times* and the *Journal* into work, along with a big dictionary to help me translate. I enrolled in computer programming school, but discovered I was not programmable. I did, however, succeed in teaching myself ten new words each day, which I learned to pronounce with an accent more commonly heard on Central Park West than in Brooklyn.

I noticed quickly that my more businesslike appearance brought more respect on the street and on the job. People were curious as to why I was mopping floors, and one inquiry led to a job offer in Cleveland, where one of my half sisters, Myra, was working as a nurse. My move to the Midwest might as well have been a trip across the world because, like many New Yorkers of my time, I had never before crossed the Hudson River. I found it unsettling to see farm animals roaming free, without bars or cages to contain them. I could not believe the amount of land allotted to

one home in the countryside. Some farms were bigger than my
Bed-Stuy neighborhood. The deeper into the Midwest I jour-
neyed, the more my world opened up. I had not been much of a
student, but in this place, with all of my past unknown to anyone
but me, I thought I could be whatever I wanted to be.

My job in Cleveland was not really much of a step up from
mop duty, but it helped root me in my new location. It was in the
Cleveland Clinic laundry room, where I worked with honest,
hardworking black folk who became part of an extended family
anchored by my sister. Within a year, I moved to Halle Brothers
Department Store in downtown Cleveland. I started in the basement, fittingly, as a gift wrapper, and moved up to stockboy in the
carpet department.

I worked hard and looked constantly for opportunities to be
promoted, and in doing so, I learned a basic principle of networking: Start wherever the door of opportunity opens, be it in the mail
room or the back room. I see so many young people who want to
start in the front office, if not higher. It doesn't work that way.
Everything good that happened to me during this period was a result of people telling other people good things about my attitude.
I learned the importance of developing good relationships with
my coworkers. If you work hard and well with other people, you
don't always need to job-hunt. Often, the jobs come hunting for
you.

It wasn't all work and no play in Cleveland. Networking is
both a professional and a social tool. As luck would have it, I was
perfectly situated for social networking. My inner-city hotel apartment was in a building located next to a popular nightclub, Leo's
Casino. All of the big rhythm-and-blues stars who played Leo's
stayed at my hotel. Most stayed on my floor and used the communal rest room. Did you know that Ray Charles shaves in the dark?
I saw him.

I became friends with the entertainers and, perhaps more important, the head maitre d', Freddy Arrington. My apartment became a way station for people coming and going from Leo's, and

Freddy, whose palm I greased frequently, became my pass to the front row.

By 1967, my social and business networks were both growing. At that point, I jumped to a job with *Encyclopaedia Britannica*, where I honed my sales skills in the best training ground ever: door-to-door. I was making good money and living fast, loose, and luxuriously for a poor kid from Brooklyn.

My two-part networking program gave rise to two major initiatives during that period. In business, I launched my own encyclopedia sales company. Socially, I began hosting an annual New Year's Eve bash. Both led to bigger and better things for me. While I was working for *Encyclopaedia Britannica*, I read every volume, though it took me three years to do it. One of the things that struck me, quite naturally, was the absence of black history in what was considered the best reference source in the world. Because of my wide social circle among blacks in Cleveland, I became increasingly aware of the importance of self-esteem and historical grounding among blacks of accomplishment. It dawned on me that knowing your roots strengthens you. From my friends, I knew others felt that way, too, and so, I recognized that there was a strong market for material on black history.

That is what drove me to start my first company, Black Educational Development Inc., which marketed several major sources for reference materials on black history, primarily the ten-volume *International Library of Negro Life and History* and the fifty-four-volume *Journal of Negro History*.

My partner, Gene Blackwell, and I packaged these reference books as a black-history learning system. We created our own easy-to-use and graphically attractive study guide with Malcolm X on the cover. It was bold and original. People loved the slick graphics, and many bought the entire set so they could get the study guide free and frame the Malcolm X cover. It was a great marketing tool.

Gene and I sold our reference books door-to-door, and we discovered that our timing was perfect. We rode the crest of the

Black Power movement. You wouldn't know it today, but I sported a full fluffy Afro back then. Black pride and interest in black history were on the upsurge, and there was a ready market for our material. I learned during this period that the black consumer market is vast. And I also learned that I enjoyed selling to that market, especially when I was selling a product that nurtured black self-esteem. Those encyclopedias chronicled the enormous contribution that blacks have made to America and to the world. We were doing well by doing good.

We were, even then, creating a network of blacks interested in the welfare not just of themselves, but of the entire community. In fact, one of our biggest sales boosters was Les Brown, the powerful public speaker and author, who was then a radio station talk show host in Columbus, Ohio. Les's commercials for our product motivated tremendous response. The products themselves seeded my appreciation and understanding of my own black heritage and the enormity of our contributions to this country. This information would serve me well for many years.

I greatly enjoyed having my own business, and it was going quite well. But like many blacks of my generation, I eventually found myself being seduced by large corporations in search of talented young blacks as a response to civil rights legislation and calls for affirmative action. The security of a corporate job was too much to pass up for someone of my background, particularly after I had struck up a relationship with Nora Jean Spencer of Cincinnati, who became my wife in 1973.

Shortly before our marriage, I went to work for Procter & Gamble in Cleveland, which was a pioneering company in terms of cultural diversity and equal opportunity employment. At the time I started, I was one of only a handful of blacks in management at P&G, but this changed rapidly. I was hired as a manager trainee, and I learned a great deal through the corporation's training and management programs. My first boss, Richard Gilchrist, taught me the particularly important lesson that your business life is impacted by your family life, spiritual life, and civic activities.

Richard, who is white but nonetheless was a very dedicated corporate mentor, taught me that maintaining balance among these three aspects of your life was critical to your growth as a person both in the workplace and in your personal life. He taught me that although you can dress for success and swim among the sharks and negotiate to win, ultimately and most important, it is character that counts in the final tally. In the end, people see you for what you are, not for what you pretend to be. Or, as someone told me once, "You can't get the fruits without the roots."

Gilchrist helped me maintain balance in my life. In fact, one of the first things he did after my wedding was instruct me on how to buy a family home with practically no money down. He also got me involved in volunteer work in the community, which Procter & Gamble wisely encourages in its employees. I became active in the United Negro College Fund, which seemed natural to me as someone who had a large network of black friends and contacts.

The 1970s flew by as I became involved in my family, my work, and my community. My two handsome sons, Kyle and Scott, were born. I received several promotions and performance awards for my work in marketing at P&G, where I managed the health and beauty-aids product line. More meaningful, I became an organizer of fund-raising events for the United Negro College Fund, including the Lou Rawls telethon that brought two hundred volunteers together and raised record amounts of money. Because of my community work, I was asked to serve on eight civic boards.

And yet, for all of this activity, early in the 1980s, I realized I had grown bored with corporate life. I felt as though I had hit the infamous "glass ceiling" and that there was not much more for me to accomplish for P&G. I was no longer certain that accomplishing corporate goals satisfied my personal goals. I felt there was something more to be done than make Crest the most popular toothpaste in the country.

I had become a high-profile community volunteer in Cleveland, and that led to my being recruited to be director of marketing and communication for the United Way Services of Cleveland, which was chaired by Cheryle Wills, a remarkable black woman with whom I had worked on several civic projects. The United Way was a benevolent umbrella organization for a myriad of charitable and nonprofit groups. Its professional staff was highly organized and politically astute. My management skills received further honing by its strategists, who demanded results. This was a charity, but it was not a charitable atmosphere. It was sink or swim. At times, I had to tread water, backstroke, and dog paddle just to stay afloat. It was a tough environment, but my volunteer leadership team of Bob Reitman and Vic Gelb were tremendous supporters of my unorthodox marketing styles.

My greatest success with the United Way—and perhaps my biggest failure—occurred on Saturday, September 27, 1986, when a project that I had conceived resulted in a world-record release of 1,453,451 balloons to kick off our annual fund-raising campaign. "Balloonfest 1986" was a major personal success for me because I had coordinated a project that brought fifteen hundred schoolchildren and volunteer workers together for a launch that required fifteen straight hours of preparation. The concept was simple: I wanted to get the next generation excited about United Way and its charitable work. I wanted young people to see that with a community of people, young and old, black, white, and otherwise, you can make the impossible possible. In the months and months of preparation that went into it, my greatest fear was that it would rain. And it did. Murphy's Law ruled, and large cost overruns resulted, which is why I referred to my greatest achievement also as perhaps my biggest failure.

"Balloonfest 86" was a public relations, artistic, and spiritual success, but it didn't raise the necessary funds because of the cost overruns. That is the bottom line when you are in a fund-raising organization, and I realized afterward that perhaps I was more interested in the human capital than the cold hard cash. At least, if I was going to worry about the bottom line, I wanted to be the guy at the top. I felt there had to be more out there; I just wasn't sure what it was.

In three years with United Way, I had learned a great deal dancing across networking lines in the private and public sectors of the workplace. I had also learned that I enjoyed entrepreneurial endeavors in the private sector the most. And I wanted to remain in Cleveland, where my family had become established. I wanted to build something there for my children. So after I carefully reviewed several offers and possibilities, I made a difficult decision: I decided to take a 50 percent pay cut to enter the two-year Ford Dealership Development program.

I was one of only twelve people in the country selected for the program in 1987. My classroom training was at the Ford Marketing Institute in Detroit, and my on-the-job training was done at a dealership in Cleveland, Marshall Ford. I started in the service department wearing a blue uniform, and trained my way up in an instructive but humbling experience guided by Chuck Price and the late Sam Marshall, the veteran dean of car sales in Cleveland, who was willing to share his wisdom.

About midway through my training with Ford, the bottom dropped out of the domestic automobile market, and it became abundantly clear that my better idea had become a bad idea. I began to see that when I graduated from the program, I would face a very depressed market and I would have to leave Cleveland. With this in mind, I quietly began networking and seeking alternative ideas.

The seeds for a new career of my own design were planted in September of 1987, when I cochaired a Networking Forum in Cleveland for Earl Graves and *Black Enterprise* magazine. Over four hundred black professionals came to hear Graves speak on the state of blacks in the business world. Business cards fairly flew across the room in a networking frenzy. It was the first event of its kind in Cleveland, and it sparked something in me.

The Networking Forum reminded me of an exciting time in my life, my New Year's Eve parties and my days as an entrepreneur selling black reference books—my days of doing well by doing good. Earl Graves had always been a visionary and a leader in bringing black professionals together to network, do business, and empower one another economically. On reflection, I found that I had long shared his sense of wanting to strengthen our community. And ever since my days as the head of a neighborhood baby-sitting service, I certainly had always instinctively grasped the power of networking.

The success of the *Black Enterprise* Networking Forum brought many disparate and dormant thoughts to the forefront of my consciousness. I sensed that there must be thousands more black professionals in search of their community. The paper cuts on my hands from flying business cards were also graphic evidence of the enthusiasm among black professionals for networking. And so in the months that followed the energizing networking forum, I began designing my own plan.

At first, it was almost a subconscious process, fleeting thoughts finding one another and clumping together. But when it became more and more apparent that my future as an automobile dealer was not a promising one because of the depressed market, I consciously began developing the concept that would be both my greatest career gamble and my most exhilarating challenge.

In January 1989, I graduated from the Ford program, but I declined to pursue a dealership of my own. It was a scary move. For the first time in twenty years, I had no income, no company car, no benefits. I did have a large mortgage, a very puzzled wife, two growing sons, ideas, dreams, and visions. And I had a start.

A year earlier, I had begun testing my plan by staging the first of a series of monthly networking forums for black professionals in Cleveland. The *Black Enterprise* network forum had been primarily a social affair. Mine was strictly business—a party with a purpose—at least in theory. My idea was to bring in top black speakers of national stature to address a wide variety of topics that would champion personal and professional development throughout the black community. I felt there was a need to encourage interdependence and a greater sense of trust and shared goals among black professionals. I wanted to bring them together on a regular basis to discuss common themes, and to develop a unified agenda for success for all black people.

I staged my first SuccessNet (Success Through Networking) Forum on January 18, 1988. Les Brown was the featured speaker, and the Ford Motor Company, with which I had maintained an amicable relationship, signed on for a two-year sponsorship with an investment of one hundred thousand dollars. The first forum was profitable, brought a great turnout, and convinced me that I was on to something. Even as I completed my final year of training with Ford, I staged monthly forums in Cleveland. SuccessNet became a networker's paradise, not to mention a pretty good place to gaze at the stars. Speakers included Danny Glover, Geoffrey Holder, Susan Taylor, Dr. Alvin Poussaint, Louis Ruckeyser, Carole Simpson, Ron Brown, Tony Brown, John H. Johnson, Denis Waitley, Dennis Kimbro, Wally "Famous" Amos, James Earl Jones, Stedman Graham and, again, Les Brown, to name a few. The forums attracted a wide array of corporate sponsors eager to be the official radio station, airline, newspaper, or hotel for those events, which drew up to fifteen hundred professionals for cocktails, hors d'oeuvres, networking, inspiration, and enlightenment.

Each meeting began with a recitation of a group mantra that went: *"Success lives in Cleveland because Success lives where I live. We must be willing to share our Success and to help others Succeed. Each one must reach one and teach one."* I still use this mantra to this day when I close my dinner speeches.

SuccessNet began as a sideline while I was still in the Ford training program. When I graduated from the program and left Ford's corporate fold, I immediately launched my own corporation—from the extra bedroom in our house. The assets of SuccessSource, Inc. were not ones that most bankers would embrace as strong collateral. I had my "Soul-O-Dex" Rolodex; good friend Gregory Williams, who left his business to join me in my dream; and the monthly bills to inspire me.

In truth, the "Soul-O-Dex" was strong collateral, because it contained the names of some very influential people whom I had

met over the years and with whom I had developed trusting relationships. To finance my new business, I made a private stock offering. And I made it to those people, many of whom were among
the power elite of Cleveland. Eighteen of them were CEOs of major companies. These same people helped me get advertising for
the second product to come out of SuccessSource, the *Success-
Guides.*

I don't want to give the impression that this was a cakewalk,
because it was not. Although I had many wonderful supporters, financially and spiritually, my new business suffered all of the tra-
vails encountered by most minority enterprises—principally, the
inability to get capital for growth. My partner and I worked virtually without salary for several years. More than once, I had to go
to friends for either cash or counsel. But that is why networking is
so important. It provides a foundation of support.

It was during this period that I received some very bad and very
good news from back home in Brooklyn. My youngest brother
Joseph was killed in a drug deal gone bad, and my sister Emma was
completing her course work for a doctorate from Harvard. It was
both a stunning blow and a joyous victory. We had grown up together in the same home, shared values, experiences, and opportunities, yet Joseph's choices led to a life of crime and drugs, and
Emma's choices led to the highest form of educational achievement. It was disparity of results in my own family that provided me
the determination to continue down my new business path and
make SuccessSource work as I had originally envisioned it.

I come from essentially the same background as millions of
other blacks of my generation. And I have learned something that
I believe is of benefit to all people of my race. I have learned that
we have a legacy of success that runs contrary to the media images
of slavery, welfare, crime, and drugs.

SUCCESS RUNS IN OUR RACE

In retrospect, I view 1988 as a turning point in my life, and not just
because of the career switch. What I find striking about that pe-

riod is the fact that although my family's entire financial future and quality of life was at risk due to my business venture, I was not stressed out about it. All of my high-paying, high-visibility corporate jobs had been high-anxiety. Even though I was working within the security of the corporate fold, I had always been stressed about preserving that security. And I was always under pressure to fit into a corporate culture, that for all of its efforts at diversity, was essentially white.

I continue to be a wing-walker by comparison, traipsing on the edge of a deadly fall without a parachute. But I have confidence because I know that my strength does not come from a corporation's ample assets, from a big office or a comfortable pension. It comes from within. And I know the same is true of you and nearly everyone of my race. We are a people with passion and creativity in abundance. The challenge is to channel those assets into a form of social entrepreneurialism that can produce goods and services to fulfill the needs of our community. Technology has dramatically improved within the last decade, but the challenge remains the same. That is why my company, SuccessSource Inc., has evolved into FraserNet, Inc. and FraserNet.com.

Social critic James Atlas says, "A shared pool of knowledge is as important as a common language." That shared pool of knowledge is what I am endeavoring to develop in the black community. When the *SuccessGuides* were conceived, they were a shared pool of black talent in major cities across the country. The first edition of 224 pages was released in January 1989, and it listed the names, titles, addresses, and phone numbers of more than three thousand black professionals, leaders, organizations, businesses, and services in Cleveland. The first printing of five thousand was gobbled up at twenty-five dollars a copy. It brought a strong response from both white and black communities because, for the first time, it was readily apparent what a critical mass of talented black professionals were present in Cleveland back then. Now, more than one hundred thousand copies of the *SuccessGuide Worldwide* are distributed annually.

Today, more than 2.5 million people each year, in fifteen coun-tries, read FraserNet's *SuccessGuide Worldwide*. Let me spell out the vision, mission, core values, and guiding principles that drive FraserNet and its 20,000 global members today:

Vision
To lead a global networking movement that brings together di-verse human resources; to increase opportunities for people of African descent.

Mission
To produce products and services that teach and promote excel-lence and effective networking; to facilitate business-to-business, and business-to-consumer mentoring and role-modeling for peo-ple of African descent.

Guiding Principles
- Put God first
- Foster trust through honesty and integrity
- Give first, share always
- Keep promises to ourselves and one another
- Treat everyone with dignity and respect
- Exceed expectations
- Practice listening as the first duty of love
- Use wealth as a force for good
- Think hard, work smart
- Practice humility as strength of character
- Give thanks in and for all things
- Live authentic lives
- Honor our work as a spiritual practice and as our gift
- Lead by serving

Core Values
- Service to others as the foundation of success
- Learning and growing

- The importance of family and legacy
- Spiritual growth and guidance
- Building wealth honorably
- Being a positive role model
- A strong work ethic and loving what you do
- The importance of our relationships
- Making the investment to succeed
- Measuring success by the generational wealth we transfer

James Baldwin said, "If you know from where you came, there are no limits as to where you can go." My overall goal with FraserNet, Inc. is to go forward while looking back—back to my African roots—and to do well while doing good.

Economic development empowers us because it is an important rail on our Underground Railroad. It enables us to earn, learn, grow, and look after our own while providing meaningful and useful products and services. Economic power gives us the strength to build our self-esteem and fortify our skills. It is the African centered way, and I want to make it also our way. In the following pages, you will learn how you can join the new Underground Railroad to success for modern-day black people.

"The biggest mistake that you can make is thinking you work for someone else. You are the president of your own corporation and you should always try to get your message across."
KEITH CLINKSCALES

Keith Clinkscales has been credited with creating a new voice for urban youth. The former chairman and CEO of Vanguarde Media (VMI) he founded the company in 1999 after serving as president, CEO and co-owner of *VIBE* magazine. Keith says he created VMI because he wanted to "put together a collection of media properties that recognize the true breadth and power of popular culture." Through *Honey, Heart & Soul, Impact Radio, Records & Retail Weekly* and *Savoy*, VMI provided news, trends, and features on urban music, fashion, entertainment, politics, and health; information for young men and women with an urban sensibility that transcended race, class, and religion. Its sister company, Vanguarde Neomedia, published several on-line newsletters, including Impact247.com. VMI also produced the Impact conference; the largest annual gathering of urban entertainment executives and artists in the nation. Keith is now consulting, speaking, and incubating new ideas.

2

It Takes a Village to Raise a Child

It is better to be part of a great whole
than to be the whole of a small part.
— FREDERICK DOUGLASS

L ike many black people, when I first entered the white-dominated corporate world, I did my best to tone down my blackness. I have to laugh now when I remember the internal battle that raged as I would prepare to attend yet another Procter & Gamble formal company dinner. "Do I take my own bottle of hot sauce, or do I leave my cultural tastes at home?"

In reflecting upon those days, I see now that I lived, as many black people do, a dual existence. I ate white when I was around whites. ("Hold the fatback, please.") And I talked white around whites, to the point that I joked I was "bidialectal," speaking white English and black English, depending on whether I was with the brothers or others.

I make light of this duality, but it goes to the heart of a very serious issue that W.E.B. DuBois explored in *The Legacy of John Brown* when he wrote:

It is a peculiar sensation, this double-consciousness, this sense of always looking at one's self through the eyes of others . . . One feels this two-ness—an American, a Negro; two souls, two thoughts, two unreconciled strivings; two warring ideals in one dark body, whose dogged strength alone keeps it from being torn asunder.

Afrocentrist Anthony J. Mensah, a native of Ghana, refers to this "two-ness" as "the schizoid nature of black existence," which, he says, "arises out of the contention that black people in America do not belong to any one functional, coherent, cohesive culture."

Of course, the truth is we belong to one of the most advanced nations in all of history. Tragically, blacks in America have often rejected their own community because they didn't think they could succeed in overcoming racism if they remained linked to the victims of it.

The result of that black flight from our own blackness is evident today in many urban neighborhoods where the exodus of the black middle class has drained hope from the streets. Professor William Julius Wilson of Harvard University holds that "the central problem of the underclass is joblessness reinforced by increasing social isolation in impoverished neighborhoods."

When the poor live only with the poor, they have restricted access to opportunities for jobs, education, and role models. They have no "success network" to plug into. I will point out, however, that there have been several government incentives since 1992 (i.e., housing grants and tax benefits) that have lured middle-class blacks back into inner-city neighborhoods.

Wilson holds, "Neighborhoods plagued by high levels of joblessness are more likely to experience low levels of social organization; the two go hand in hand. High rates of joblessness trigger other neighborhood problems that undermine social organization, ranging from crime, gang violence, and drug trafficking to family breakups and problems in the organization of family life."

The situation is prevalent across the country. In Cleveland, where I live, a Cleveland and Rockefeller Foundation study found that if this trend was not reversed, three fourths of city neighborhoods would be majority-poor by the early part of this century.

Between 1950 and 2000, Cleveland's population went from

915,000 to 478,000. This exodus of primarily the more affluent city residents into the suburbs and outlying communities led to a decline in housing values, deteriorating housing stock, and a disintegration of the support community for the less affluent. As the middle class moved out, the commission found that with them went positive role models and vital connections to employment opportunities so desperately needed by those striving to break the poverty cycle and better their lives. At the same time, much of the capital necessary to support city services and commercial development is drained, to devastating effect, the commission reported:

> Persistent poverty, the kind that endures over many years and with increasing frequency is passed from one generation to another, tends to be found in neighborhoods marked by a deteriorated social infrastructure—that grassroots network of churches, schools, banks, businesses, neighborhood centers, indeed families themselves—which feeds and nourish the life of a small community. Where social support systems have broken down, poverty has become for many a permanent condition.

In a May 2001 analysis by W. Dennis Keating, professor and assistant dean of urban affairs at Cleveland State University, of the Supplement Empowerment Zone program in Cleveland, found that:

> The loss of population reflects the loss of manufacturing jobs, the decline of the central business district, and the general pattern of a suburban exodus from central cities that continues in metropolitan Cleveland (Bier 1994; Hill 1994, 1999). All of these trends have resulted in devastated neighborhoods and high rates of unemployment and proverty, exacerbated by racial tensions (Chandler 1999; Coulton and Chow 1994).

Said another way, many of our young people have nowhere to go and nothing to do. They are looking for jobs, respect, and supervision. I remember when there were Boys Clubs, Christian youth organizations, church activities, Golden Gloves competitions, Boy and Girl Scouts, high school functions, and two-parent families. There were jobs in the neighborhood—safe and stable jobs that also provided the opportunity for young people to learn from mentors and role models. There was an infrastructure in our communities, a network of support and guidance. There was discipline, a dress code, and an ingrained respect for authority whether in the schools or on the streets. Sex, violence, and drugs may have been present, but they were not as pervasive, nor as glorified in the media.

The sense of hopelessness has been further entrenched by government cutbacks in social programs, the breakup of the family structure, and the lack of employment opportunities for even those who have done the right thing and gone on to college.

Our young people in many areas of the country appear to be confused, despondent, and misguided in their values. Their lives have no meaning to them, and as a result, they have no respect for the value of anyone else's life.

I believe that jobs, jobs, and more jobs are, to a large degree, the solution. There should be a much greater emphasis not only on college training but on technical and vocational training. We need to make an investment in this "at risk" generation.

Not every black person can be, or wants to be, a nuclear physicist, president of AOL Time Warner, or an entrepreneur. But every black person must be encouraged to first graduate from high school and then to consider the opportunities that lie beyond that. Our young people need to prepare themselves for the considerable new job opportunities that will await them in the twenty-first century.

After World War II, the Japanese focused on building the finest work force in the world. They did this by stressing and developing programs to train their citizenry in technical and vocational skills. To that end, they succeeded in dominating world production standards in the automotive and electronic industries.

In coming years, the available pool of workers will be largely dominated by blacks and other minorities, whose numbers have increased in far greater increments than other groups. This means opportunity for those who make themselves valuable by obtaining educations and training. This door will be opened for us. But we have to take the initiative and step up to it by setting an agenda and focusing on vocational and technical training.

The black working and middle classes must shore up the infrastructure in their communities. They can do this by networking together. Strong networks give power to the people in them. And power of this sort provides the strength to break out of the poverty cycle. Employers in the private and public sectors must be enlisted in this movement as well, because they control the resources. We must all be part of the solution, and we must all move beyond the myopia of racism.

Author John Williams said, "Whatever future America will have will be directly related to the solving of its racial dilemma, which is a human dilemma."

THE ENEMY WITHIN

While there are racial and societal forces at work on us from the outside, a certain portion of our problem lies within. From the days of our enslavement, many of us bought into the slave mentality. We accepted the white man's pronouncement that we were an inferior race, and even when we came to understand that it was a false pronouncement, it continued to dominate our collective psyches; it was a powerful indoctrination.

The following is an infamous and chilling example of how that mentality was ingrained into our ancestors, and into succeeding generations. It is taken from a speech given by Willie Lynch, from whose name the term *lynching* is derived. Lynch was a British slave owner in the West Indies, probably of Jamaican heritage, who used mind-control techniques on his black slaves and then advo-

cated the use of those manipulative techniques to other slave owners. He was invited to the colony of Virginia in 1712 to teach his
methods to slave owners there, and these are his words as passed
down. I think you will find them haunting:

> Gentlemen: I greet you here on the bank of the James
> River in the year of Our Lord one thousand seven hundred
> and twelve. First, I shall thank you The Gentlemen of the
> Colony of Virginia for bringing me here. I am here to help
> you solve some of your problems with slaves. Your invita-
> tion reached me on my modest plantation in the West In-
> dies where I have experimented with some of the newest
> and still oldest methods for control of slaves. Ancient
> Rome would envy us if my program is implemented. As
> our boat sailed south on the James River, named for our il-
> lustrious King, whose version of the Bible we cherish, I
> saw enough to know that your problem is not unique.
> While Rome used cords of wood as crosses for standing
> human bodies along its old highways in great numbers,
> you are here using the tree and the rope on occasion.
>
> I caught the whiff of a dead slave hanging from a tree
> a couple miles back. You are not only losing valuable stock
> by hangings, you are having uprisings, slaves are running
> away, your crops are sometimes left in the field too long
> for maximum profit, you suffer occasional fires, your ani-
> mals are killed, gentlemen, you know what your problems
> are; I do not need to elaborate. I am not here to enumer-
> ate your problems, I am here to introduce you to a method
> of solving them.
>
> In my bag here, I have a fool proof method for con-
> trolling Black Slaves. I guarantee everyone of you that if
> installed correctly, it will control the slaves for at least 300
> years. My method is simple and members of your family
> and any Overseer can use it.
>
> I have outlined a number of difference(s) among the

slaves; and I take these differences and make them bigger. I use fear, distrust, and envy for control purposes. These methods have worked on my modest plantation in the West Indies and will work throughout the South. Take this simple little list of differences, think about them. On top of my list is "Age" but it is there only because it begins with "A." The second is "Color" or "Shade," there is intelligence, size, sex, size of plantation, status of plantation, attitude of owner, whether the slaves live in the valley, on a hill, East, West, North, or South, have a fine or coarse hair, or is tall or short. Now that you have a list of differences, I shall give you an outline of action but before that, I shall assure you that distrust is stronger than trust and envy is stronger than adulation, respect and admiration.

The Black Slave, after receiving this indoctrination, shall carry on and will become self-refueling and self-generating for hundreds of years, maybe thousands.

Don't forget you must pitch the old black versus the young black and the young black male against the old black male. You must use the dark skin slave vs. the light skin slaves and the light skin slaves vs. the dark skin slaves. You must also have your white servants and overseers distrust all blacks, but it is necessary that your slaves trust and depend on us. They must love, respect and trust only us.

Gentlemen, these Kits are keys to control, use them. Have your wives and children use them, never miss an opportunity. My plan is guaranteed and the good thing about this plan is that if used intensely for one year the slaves themselves will remain perpetually distrustful.

Thank you, gentlemen.

Interestingly, on March 17, 1978, a secret memorandum was issued to the President and his Cabinet as part of a "comprehensive review of current developments in Black Africa from the point of view of their possible impacts on the black movement in the

United States." It was an analysis of the strategic social, economic, and political ramifications made by then-chairman of the National Security Council Zbigniew Brzezinski under Jimmy Carter.

I was provided a copy of this memorandum by the Reverend Walter E. Fauntroy, who, as chairman of the Congressional Black Caucus, joined numerous national black organizations in expressing outrage over this memorandum. Since 1959, Reverend Fauntroy has been pastor of one of Washington, D.C.'s most influential churches. He is the president of the National Black Leadership Roundtable, the national network vehicle of the Congressional Black Caucus, composed of the heads of more than two hundred national black organizations.

It was Brzezinski's position at the time that it was not in the best interest of the United States to allow any part of the U.S. black movement to show outreach and support for the emerging movement in black Africa.

To that end a "range of policy options" was suggested; at least four of those options reflect Willie Lynch's approach to controlling slaves. They were:

- to elaborate and bring into effect a special program designed to perpetuate division in the black movement to neutralize the most active groups of leftist radical organizations representing different social strata of the black community to encourage divisions in black circles.
- to preserve the present climate which inhibits the emergence from within the black leadership of a personality capable of exerting nationwide appeal.
- to work out and realize preventive operations in order to impede durable ties between U.S. black organizations and radical groups in African states.
- to support actions designed to sharpen social stratification in the black community which would lead to the widening and perpetuation of the gap between successful educated blacks and the poor, giving rise to growing antagonism

between different black groups and weakening of the movement as a whole.

Tragically, the infamous Brzezinski memorandum and Lynch's predatory, racist instincts were effective and few of us can deny that the self-defeating mentality that he nurtured among his slaves lives on today. Still, too many blacks prey upon each other, and those who would hold us back watch in delight as the media feeds them with images of conflict within our own families and neighborhoods. All of these preoccupations regarding our differences, plight, and challenges contribute to divisiveness, which makes us all weaker in our battles against racism on the outside. Jealousies within our racial community stifle productive behavior that might benefit us all, and they severely limit our ability to come together for united, positive action in which combined strength and shared resources might elevate our lives. Our enemies delight in our fractured community. They fear unity, trust, and cohesion. We must recognize and resist the insidious "race-lynching" of our own. We have to remove our own hands from the ropes around our own necks before we can begin to effectively battle our common enemies.

For generations, instead of seeking black independence, we sought white acceptance. This self-hatred is obvious even among our own people. Often, light-skinned blacks are considered more attractive than those with the blackest skin colors. We have shunned each other as reminders of our alleged inferiority. And in doing that, we guaranteed our continued enslavement.

In many respects, we lost our sense of tribal community, our self-esteem, and our collective energy. And then we watched in envy, wonder, and growing anger as other cultural groups came into our neighborhoods and, through their elaborate systems of cooperative economics and mutual assistance, surpassed us in economic strength.

The case of Jin Agyuk Kim offers an example of how another cultural group uses its unified economic strength to benefit its people. As the Korean owner of a dry-cleaning business in the Albany Park neighborhood of Chicago, Kim is supported by several large and closely linked networks. One is the Korean Dry Cleaners Association, with more than twelve hundred members. The other is the Korean-American Association, with more than twenty thousand members.

These two groups, as well as several other Korean-based organizations, came to Kim's assistance several years ago when, because of a language misunderstanding at a neighborhood bank, he became irate and found himself struggling with police and security guards. All that Kim wanted was to see his account balance and to make a withdrawal from his account, but there was confusion over just what he wanted. The teller denied his request, said something that he took as an insult ("Have you talked this over with your wife?"), and Kim began objecting loudly.

When police were called, Kim kicked one of them. The police then took him to a mental health center for observation. He was kept there for five days before being released. Although Korean Americans have generally kept a low profile in Chicago, they were outraged by the Kim incident. As one leader put it in news accounts: "Even the earthworm resists when you step on him." This earthworm had more than dirt to throw, however. The bank that had offended the Koreans was located in the heart of their neighborhood and over a million dollars of its assets belonged to Korean-American customers.

More than two hundred protestors appeared outside the bank for several weekends following the Kim incident, and their leaders made it very clear that if apologies were not forthcoming, that million dollars–plus would be very rapidly withdrawn. Although the bank had substantially more in assets, a rapid withdrawal of such a large amount would cause considerable embarrassment. The apologies flowed.

Korean Americans, who have established powerful economic

networks in cities across the country, understand that strength in numbers is one thing, and that strength in dollars is another entirely more powerful weapon.

Now, there certainly have been successful economic boycotts waged by blacks in the past. In fact, Denny's settled many federal lawsuits after black customers said they were denied service or made to wait longer than white customers. Also, in November 1996, oil giant Texaco faced a boycott led by Reverend Jesse Jackson and other civil rights leaders after news reports detailed a taped meeting showing Texaco executives making disparaging comments about a discrimination suit and referring to blacks as "jelly beans." As a result of the boycott, Texaco promised to hire more minorities, triple the number of black-owned service stations, and do more business with minority companies. Texaco settled the discrimination suit for $176 million, a record settlement at that time.

I salute those who brought about the boycotts in Miami and Cincinnati. We need to do much more of this, and we need to become *pro*active, rather than *re*active in our networking for social change. We need to apply our collective economic strength to the next level—cooperative economics. This is the most empowering form of networking for social change in a capitalistic society, because it puts us in the game. We are doing it in isolated groups around the country (I will provide examples throughout this book), and we are doing it increasingly, but we have a long way to go to catch up with other cultural groups.

The Koreans in Chicago, Los Angeles, and other cities form networks that bond their people together economically. Those who first achieve success bankroll those who come behind them. This is evident in Chicago, where Korean Americans have come to dominate the dry-cleaning industry because they help one another get established, and then support one another.

Their networking system is basically the same as that of the Japanese *keiretsu*, or business alliance, which has been the subject of considerable study by American corporate leaders who found themselves chasing the success of Japanese business. Consider what might happen in this country if the top executives of IBM, General Electric, American Express, and Citicorp met regularly to discuss a unified business strategy. Aside from all sorts of antitrust investigations, you would probably see some amazing cooperative economics.

In Japan, there are no antitrust laws, and there, top corporate bosses form mutually beneficial *keiretsu* alliances. They meet regularly to discuss cooperative ventures and share information. It is "a machine that grinds competitors into powder," according to *Fortune* magazine. *Keiretsu* companies in Japan constitute less than 0.1 percent of all companies in Japan, yet they account for 78 percent of the value of all shares on the Tokyo Stock Exchange.

It is not just Asians and Asian Americans who have mastered economic networking. Jamaican Americans, with their tight networks of business-oriented associates, have historically heeded the urgings of leaders such as Marcus Garvey, who encouraged them to become self-reliant and to work for the greater good. In stating the principles of the Universal Negro Improvement Association in 1922, Garvey said, "We are not engaged in domestic politics, in church building or in social uplift work, but we are engaged in nation building."

The president of the Caribbean-American Chamber of Commerce and Industry, in Brooklyn, where nearly a million West Indians have come to live, said in a magazine article that the relative success of these immigrants is due in large part to their "*susu*" networks of friends and family who provide capital for launching businesses.

SEEKING ACCEPTANCE VERSUS EQUALITY

In writing about African Americans as "reluctant entrepreneurs," author Joel Kotkin noted that by 1986, the median income of all West Indian (Caribbean) black families exceeded that of white Americans. "The West Indian experience is the best indication that it is historic and cultural factors, not skin color, that best explain the disinclination toward business among so much of black America—a disinclination that borders on conviction," Kotkin writes.

Why is this? Although it is a theory debated heatedly among blacks, some trace our lack of cooperative economics to slavery, when families were torn apart and blacks were brainwashed into believing in their own inferiority in a white-dominated culture. When black slaves were denied access to education, sometimes killed for trying to learn how to read or write, their self-esteem was further damaged. Some hold that the isolating effect of slavery explains why blacks came to believe that theirs is an individual rather than a collective struggle, and that to associate with other blacks was to align themselves with an inferior partner—an attitude that, sadly, persists in the minds of some black people even today.

Integration, some say, only encouraged this self-defeating self-hatred. Instead of seeking true equality with whites, too many blacks sought acceptance. They fled their own communities to live instead among the whites, because they saw whites as successful and blacks as doomed. This is a manifestation of a self-hatred that many believe is a far greater obstacle to black economic empowerment than racial hatred.

IN SEARCH OF OUR FAMILY

There is a wealth of evidence to show that the black family brought to this country in chains was devastated by slavery. But in recent years, some historians, including Andrew Billingsley, a leading scholar of the African American experience, have uncovered examples of blacks overcoming the divisiveness of slavery and racism. And, as our own scholars explore our history in slavery times and before, in Africa, they discover many examples that show blacks working together for the greater good.

Billingsley and others cite studies showing that large numbers of black families remained intact during slavery, even when parents were owned by different masters. In many cases, scholars argue that the black family became stronger because it extended to include aunts, uncles, cousins and—as we all know—even some folks who were not kin but came to be accepted that way. This extension of the black family actually made it more resilient, flexible, and adaptable, many scholars contend. Free Frank and his family, of whom I wrote in the opening chapter, offer one of the best illustrations that I have come across. Free Frank used his strength to empower his entire family and community.

Whatever the reason for our lack of cooperative economic spirit in the past, I believe that blacks are now quite actively seeking to come together as a people with a unified vision for success. I see the signs everywhere that economic empowerment is the next phase of the civil rights movement, and that Afrocentric networking is the modern equivalent of the Underground Railroad. Blacks of the integration generation who have persevered and succeeded are increasingly coming to see their blackness not as a liability, but as an asset that provides not only psychological strength but economic power.

Freed of the "victim mentality" that has been part of our collective psyche for so long, successful African Americans are turning our sense of style and blackness into the color of opportunity. Let me give you a few other quick examples:

- **FUBU.** FUBU is everywhere—Austria, Canada, Germany, Greece, Japan, Mexico, Panama and the United Kingdom—and expanding. The apparel company has received both congressional and NAACP awards. The company's motto, "It's a new era, about pride and respect in what you wear, and who you are," evolved from what started out as an idea to sell tie-top hats for "easy money." FUBU president Daymond Johns mortgaged his home, and turned half of it into a factory. The other half housed TEAM FUBU (Johns and vice president J. Alexander Martin and cofounders Keith Perrin and Carl Brown). FUBU became the first apparel company awarded a license with the NBA, with authorized usage of all twenty-nine team logos.

• **Karl Kani-Infinity.** With only twenty-six workers, in 1994 Karl Kani caught the attention of national department stores such as Macy's in New York, Marshall Fields in Chicago, and Dayton's in California and Florida. The company produces apparel lines for men, women (including dresses), and boys. His apparel products all bear the Karl Kani logo. Having phenomenal success, Kani subsequently took the company worldwide to England, Germany, and Australia via the Nordstrom department stores. His innovative designs have helped make the hip-hop fashion reach a wider consumer base.

• **Terry Manufacturing.** Owned and managed by brothers, Roy and Rudolph Terry, Terry Manufacturing is now recognized as a leader in automation and computerization that can perform all in-house operations in the areas of design, manufacturing, marketing, sales, and distribution of apparel and related items. Terry's capabilities have grown over the years through experience with distinguished customers such as McDonald's, U.S. Department of Defense, Burger King, Champion, Coca-Cola, ACOG, and many others.

• **Rush Communications.** Russell Simmons has shaped the cutting edge of hip-hop—a creative explosion on par with other African-American art forms (jazz, swing, gospel, blues, rock 'n' roll, soul, and funk). He has immersed hip-hop into every facet of media and pop culture (music, film, television, fashion, and publication), including advertising and the Internet. Russell cofounded Def Jam Recordings—rap's premier label. His hip-hop vision stemmed from two key points: Its appeal could cut across geographic, race, and class boundaries, and it would evolve from musical form to lifestyle expression.

- **Bad Boy Worldwide Entertainment Group (BBWEG).**
Founded by Sean "P. Diddy" Combs, BBWEG is one of the
world's preeminent urban entertainment companies,
encompassing a broad range of businesses including
recording, music publishing, artist management, television
and film production, marketing and advertising, apparel, and
restaurants. Formed in 1994, the flagship company of
BBWEG is Bad Boy Records, whose impressive artist roster
represents millions of records sold worldwide.

MEMORIALIZING BLACK EXCELLENCE

Theories of black economic development first formed during the
Black Power movement of the 1960s and 1970s, and in more recent times have evolved and penetrated into the lives of the working people and professionals of the black middle and upper classes.
In his book *Climbing Jacob's Ladder,* Andrew Billingsley defines the
black upper class as those who "operate at the highest levels of
recognition, impact and respect." I believe black business excellence in particular must now be memorialized, because our contribution to American business and commerce has been and
continues to be significant and unrecognized. Additionally, it is
time black people add to their pantheon of black heroes our business leaders. Today they tend to be our entertainers, athletes, and
social activists.

As founders of the African American Business Hall of Fame
and Museum, we've formally inducted several of the black business giants to include Berry Gordy, Cathy Hughes, Robert L.
Johnson, Clarence Smith and Ed Lewis, Earl G. Graves, Ernesta
Procope, Reginald Lewis, John H. Johnson, Madame C. J. Walker,
and Oprah Winfrey. I conceptualized this idea twelve years ago,
and we celebrated the first induction ceremony during FraserNet's
PowerNetworking Conference 2002, held in Cleveland. Through
SuccessGuide Worldwide, we've honored many of black America's
business giants as well, including Howard Naylor Fitzhugh,
Richard Parson, Magic Johnson, Clarence Avant, Ken Chenault,

Tom Burrell, Byron Lewis, Herman Cain, Quincy Jones, Booker T. Washington, and Dr. Clifton Wharton, Jr.

Granted, those listed above are all prominent, nationally known figures, so I'll offer you a few more for consideration:

- **Bruce Gordon** is president of the Retail Markets Group for Verizon (formerly Bell Atlantic). He began his career at Bell of Pennsylvania as a management trainee and advanced through assignments in personnel, operations, and sales and marketing. Eventually, he was appointed vice president-sales of Bell Atlantic, then served as president-consumer services and vice president-marketing and sales.
- **Dave Bing** (the former Detroit Piston basketball star) is a leading Detroit businessman as founder and CEO of The Bing Group, a specialty steel manufacturer that has sales in excess of $287 million annually.
- **Nathaniel Goldston III** of Atlanta operates the largest minority-owned food service management business in the country.
- **Samuel J. Chisholm** is CEO of the Chisholm/Mingo Group, an advertising, marketing, and public relations company in New York, with sales over $100 million annually.

I could go on, but I rest my case, for now.

The African American Business Hall of Fame and Museum, when constructed, will be a world-class edifice to celebrate historical and contemporary black business achievement and excellence. Race For Success Inc., a 501(c)(3) nonprofit organization, manages the Hall of Fame plus the Center for the Advancement of African American Entrepreneurship. The museum will be the means by which to tell our history of business success in the face of great odds . . . a history that is little known and seldom talked about. Through the museum, future generations will look upon these bronzed black faces and see that success certainly runs in our race. The story of our contribution to the economic development, business, and commerce of America is significant and must be acknowledged by all Americans. We must tell that story with dignity, elegance, and respect.

Without a doubt, there are tens of thousands of highly successful black people, including many black professional men and women, who have achieved outstanding success. And it is these people who are now taking the lead in trying to bring success to others of their race.

The late tennis great Arthur Ashe, a class act all of his life, offered a prime example of this. He once told me that as a youngster in Richmond, Virginia, he was fortunate to have had a group of older black players who formed a junior tennis development program. "The most promising players like myself were able to take advantage of support, both moral and financial, that these senior black players provided, and in that sense, I was assisted greatly by the black community, which pitched in and helped when they could," said the man who broke the color barriers in men's professional tennis and then went on to be ranked the number-one player in the world.

Ashe, who proved himself to be a man of great character, said that he made it a point in his life to remind young people: "In the end, it's going to be your public perception, your moral attitudes, and your formal education that are going to carry you through the rest of your life."

THE RENEWED URBAN VILLAGE

Rather than retiring to their condos or their golf courses, there are thousands and thousands of high-achieving African Americans who are taking time to investigate their cultural histories and to encourage other blacks to do the same. They are reaching back to a tradition rooted in our African heritage, following the proverb for which this chapter is titled: "It takes a village to raise a child."

Although slavery and racism served in many cases to sever or at least strain the ties of family and friendship, and to create a race of people who felt theirs was an individual rather than a collective struggle, there is ample evidence in our past and in our present that it is the nature of black people to work together for the common good. I believe we must deploy our assets to build a new Urban Village in which the boundaries of the inner city are expanded to include the nurturing black middle class so vital to the establishment of a network for success.

Think of this Urban Village as a core community in which you can easily play a role and feel connected. It can be a community of five hundred residents or ten thousand. The important thing is to build relationships and positive programs within this Urban Village. The idea is to revive disintegrating, impoverished neighborhoods so that they become vital, self-nourishing, and productive. The goal is to help our neighborhoods recognize and develop the power within their own people and institutions for the benefit of all who live there.

James Earl Jones addressed the concept of the potential richness of the Urban Village when he spoke at the Fifth Anniversary Celebration for my company. In that sonorous voice, he told the story of Ali Hafed, "the man who would be rich." It seems that Ali Hafed was a man of some wealth, but he was unhappy because he lusted to possess the richness of diamonds, and so he set out from his home to search the world for diamonds. He sold his farm, put his family in the care of friends, and followed the sun. Before long, he had used up his money and his strength in search of diamonds. Finally, despondent over his failure to find them, he threw himself into the sea and disappeared.

After Ali Hafed had disappeared, the man who had purchased his farm went to water his camel one day at a stream, and while the camel drank, the new owner of the farm saw something flash in the waters. He waded in and pulled out a black stone that contained "an eye of light" reflecting all of the hues of the rainbow. The stone was a diamond, and, it turned out, Ali Hafed's former farm was studded with precious stones.

If Ali Hafed had merely stirred the stream on his own farm, he would have found his heart's desire. He would have become hugely rich. The moral of this story is that you can become rich in your own city or neighborhood by looking for the diamonds there, rather than elsewhere in the world. There are diamonds within, if we just pause to look, to scratch the dirt from the precious stone.

There is a movement and black people are beginning to reclaim our neighborhoods! For example, there have been several Community Development Corporations (CDCs—nonprofit organizations formed by residents to revitalize their own neighborhoods) springing up all over the United States. Denise Fairchild of the Local Initiatives Support Corporation in Los Angeles says, "Urban renewal was about displacing residents. Community development is about involving residents . . . Bottom-up planning, bottom-up development, the work of community development is a formula for success."

In New York, the East Brooklyn Congregations (EBC) is an organization comprising over fifty local congregations of all denominations. EBC started the Nehemiah Homes Project, which is financed by loans from member congregations and their parent church organizations. The project has succeeded in building 2,300 affordable, single-family, owner-occupied row houses.

In Miami's Liberty City district, the Tacolcy Economic Development Corporation (TEDC), a local nonprofit group headed by longtime resident and former police officer Otis Pitts, used market research data on what was being spent on food and other services by residents to convince a Winn-Dixie supermarket chain not to abandon the neighborhood. From his research, $2.1 million Edison Plaza Shopping Center followed. With the help of the Ford Foundation, through its Local Initiatives Support Corporation (a national investment organization), five apartment buildings and the Miami-Dade Community College were constructed. From this, the Liberty City Entrepreneurial Education Center was developed.

By concentrating on what resources we have, rather than on those that we lack, we have something to build upon. This more positive approach energizes, rather than saps, our collective energy. The Shorebank Corporation in Chicago has used this approach in poor neighborhoods by identifying and tapping into the energy of small groups of entrepreneurs and helping them develop and grow. Once they've gotten on their feet, these entrepreneurs employ local people who are encouraged to spend their money in their own communities, thus creating more energy and opportunities.

There is no doubt that we have lost much of our ability to see the beauty and power within our own cultural community. This is due to the fact that we have lost touch with our sense of belonging to a cultural community, our sense of tradition. In most cultures, the sense of belonging and tradition, the songs, stories, legends, and heroes, are passed from one generation to the next through rituals in which the elder men and women of a community or tribe impart their knowledge to the young. In some cultures, this is a formal process; in others, it is more subtle. Manute Bol, the seven-foot-six-inch-tall descendant of Zulu warriors who became a professional basketball player, killed a lion with a spear as a young tribesman in Africa as part of his rite of passage into manhood.

Although modern-day black people have little call to take on lions these days, there is a great need for blacks to restore the tradition of passing cultural knowledge and self-esteem on to the next generation. Tragically, in all too many parts of America, the street gang has replaced the family and the community as the source of self-esteem. Gang rituals are the corrupted version of our traditional rites of passage. But in recent years, there has grown a quiet movement for restoring these rites to their positive role in the black community.

THE RITES OF PASSAGE

I became aware of one of an exciting movement in the African-American community—the Rites of Passage—through a very close friend, therapist David Whitaker. As someone who deals often with dysfunctional black families, Dr. Whitaker, along with many others, views this movement as a major step toward building self-esteem and restoring the cohesiveness of the African-American community. I agree.

Based on African culture and traditions, the Rites of Passage movement is a rapidly growing effort designed to build—through self-knowledge—character, self-esteem, and unity among African Americans of all ages and backgrounds. The goal of the Rites of Passage is not to have us all living like African tribesmen here in the United States; it is to instill a sense of perspective, a feel for African culture, and a source of pride in the achievements of the African people.

Many have come to view the Rites of Passage as a way of life, a process of continual growth in which the elders in the black community nurture the young and those who have achieved success assist those endeavoring to join them. The basic premise of the Rites is that every person has a built-in capacity to succeed. In African Americans, that capacity is rooted in our African heritage and principles that date back thousands of years but are still just as applicable and inherently true today.

The Rites provide a process of awakening, helping blacks to make the transition from childhood to adolescence; to early maturity and adulthood; and finally, to the creation of an individual with a deeply rooted sense of self. The building of self-esteem is an especially important goal for those of us who have had lifelong encounters and battles with racism. The Rites teach us to recognize our own beauty, goodness, and power.

In the fall of 1992, Dr. Whitaker invited me to participate in one of the programs run by Paul Hill, Jr., CEO/president of the East End Neighborhood House in Cleveland, an important grass-roots organization involved in Rites of Passage programs for adults and children. The program I participated in is for men, but similar programs for women and young people are also available.

The formal goal of East End's Rites of Passage program is to build a sense of self-worth, to provide moral guidelines, to encourage growth and responsibility, to share and expand upon communal knowledge, and to increase problem-solving and decision-making skills.

My Rites of Passage started on a rain-soaked Friday evening in the inner city of Cleveland. My partner, Gregory Williams, accompanied me. Feeling a bit nervous about the neighborhood, which was made even more ominous by a heavy fog, Gregory and I jumped when a young brother named Raymond came up to the window of our car and asked for our money.

I once fell for a gambit under similar circumstances in my younger and more foolhardy days when I tried to buy a "hot" television set and got burned by the guy who took my money and ran. But my doubts were erased on this occasion when Raymond showed us his printed list of the Rites participants and, with a warm smile, said the only money he wanted was our fee payment for the program we were about to take part in. After we paid, he told us to wait in the car until they were ready for us.

Shortly, all who had assembled in the parking lot were told to form a circle. There were a dozen of us, most in our thirties and forties: lawyers, judges, executives, reformed criminals. I had heard through the grapevine that several people I knew had gone through this program, but none of them had talked to me about it. I spied a few acquaintances who seemed to be as shocked to see me as I was to see them. *This has indeed been a quiet movement*, I thought.

I really had very little previous information on the Rites of Passage movement, and I had some misgivings about what I had gotten into. I wondered if it was one of those militant or nationalistic movements that have always made me somewhat uncomfortable. I was never in a fraternity, but this was beginning to feel like one of those initiation hazings. I nervously cracked a joke as we all assembled, but no one laughed. This was serious stuff, it seemed.

While still assembled in the parking lot, we were joined after a few minutes by a tall, thick man of dark skin color and majestic African features. He was dressed in an African dashiki and wore a *kufe* skullcap. His name was Baba, we were told, and he was an ordained Yoruba priest. In a voice that seemed to come up from the earth, he quietly recited a number of African proverbs and explained the meaning of the rituals we were about to take part in.

He then sprinkled water on the ground to evoke the spiritual aspects of our being. Water, when combined with the earth, symbolizes our physical side. The combination of water and earth produces plant life, which represents the growth that takes place within us, he offered.

The words of the priest were simple but meaningful. As he spoke, we all held hands in a circle, and in that moment, I felt something I had never before experienced. Though they came from differing walks of life, I felt connected to these other black men. The African proverbs spoken by Baba communicated thoughts and ideas that were actually quite profound. They communicated across all socioeconomic lines.

The words were recited in a chant that made me feel connected to the others there—once I got over my feelings of silliness—and to something else not present. Maybe it was my imagination running wild, but these thoughts gave me a chill. It was like hearing stories around the campfire. Only these were *our* stories.

The next experience would prove to be one of the most memorable of my life. We were ordered not to speak at all until we were given permission, and then told to line up by age, which at first seemed to be rather difficult, given the order to be mute. We did it, though, ending up in perfect chronological order, as we would later determine.

I was in the middle, although I was heading for the front until several younger brothers "looked" me back into my rightful position. Next, we were each given a wide circular cloth, black in color, and asked to put it over our heads and around our necks. We were each then instructed to hold the cloth of the person in front as we marched toward the door of the building. It felt like I'd been put in a chain gang as we rather awkwardly snaked our way toward the door of the East End Neighborhood House.

When we stopped in front of the door, we were told to pull the black cloth over our eyes as a blindfold. We were then led, still single file, into the building, each of us placing our right hand on the shoulder of the person in front. We were told not to break this contact at any cost. We walked carefully, but still stumbled a bit. Up some stairs, down again, around corners, through narrow hallways, beneath low ceilings. The air grew dry and then damp again. It was difficult to gauge time, but eventually, we were told to stop, stand, and not speak.

It had been cold outside so we were dressed warmly, and we grew even warmer in this stopping place. It seemed to be the boiler or furnace room of the East End Neighborhood House. I could hear the hum of the motor. I was sweating. We couldn't move, sit, or break the silence as we stood there in the dark and heat.

Five minutes passed, and boredom came. Ten minutes ticked away, and I stifled the urge to make another joke. Twenty-five minutes. I was beginning to get ticked off at this seemingly senseless waiting, and I had to go to the bathroom. Thirty-five minutes, and increasingly, I felt a sense of fear, isolation, and slight panic.

Finally, after about forty minutes, we were led into another room, where our blindfolds were removed and we found Baba playing a beautiful African drum and chanting mournfully. He invoked a sense of the pain our ancestors must have endured while undergoing the middle passage. Suddenly, I was overwhelmed by the realization that what I had just endured was meant to serve as a reminder of that ancestral pain. I was struck by how my mere discomfort was overshadowed by the suffering of those who endured the incredible psychological and physical tortures of human enslavement.

Suddenly, and to my surprise, a new perspective came to me. I saw myself not as an individual struggling alone, but as one linked to an entire race of historic people. It was a very powerful experience, emotionally wrenching, and my eyes filled with tears. The others present also seemed to be very touched. We came together that night. The oldest of our group was given the traditional

African role of elder, and we had to ask his permission each time we spoke, while allowing him generally to offer the last word. It was awkward at first, but as the hours passed, it restored a respect for experience that is part of our nature.

We talked and vented and bonded until one in the morning. We shared our lives and feelings, good and bad. We told of how we dealt with our fears and prejudices and biases. As individuals and then as a group, we addressed a series of soul-searching questions. Who am I? What values, history, traditions, and cultural precepts do I recognize, respect, and practice? Am I really who I think I am? To what extent do I have to understand, internalize, employ, and reflect the cultural authenticity of my people? Am I what I ought to be?

By the time we rose to leave, we were physically spent but mentally invigorated. We went to our own homes and families that night, but we returned early the next day, a Saturday, and spent fifteen hours reestablishing our links to our cultural community, our new Urban Village. We received a fresh indoctrination into all things African: culture, history, and value systems; meditations, symbols, drum playing, group-thinking, and the principles of Kwanzaa. We discussed Afrocentricity versus Eurocentricity, and it was enlightening to examine the differences in the two value systems. I realized that I had been struggling to exist in a Eurocentric world because I was essentially Afrocentric in nature. This was a shocking thing to discover relatively late in my life.

AFROCENTRICITY VERSUS EUROCENTRICITY

The more I came to understand the warring cultural perspectives that influenced my behavior, the more I also realized that I could fully abandon neither of them, not if I was to stay and succeed in the United States. I came to realize that I had to reconcile my existence in both worlds, Afrocentric and Eurocentric, and to develop a new system not just for myself, but for my children and their descendants.

In his book *Coming of Age*, Paul Hill, Jr., writes that the Afrocentric perspective "provides hope in the midst of despair, courage when threatened by terrorism, belief in the midst of doubt, the will to overcome against staggering odds, perseverance despite fatigue, and the strength to hold on when there is little on which to hold."

Afrocentricity is not merely a black thing. Any person or culture can use it; in fact, various components of Afrocentricity are quite evident in several cultures. Here is a brief and, I hope, understandable overview provided to me by Paul Hill, Jr., and David Whitaker, Jr., a lawyer and Ph.D. Both men are authorities on the topic of Afrocentricity.

Eurocentric Worldview: Order is imposed by the stronger force. The stronger force gains the advantage by ordering the universe as it wishes.

Afrocentric Worldview: The universe is active and alive, and the laws of nature reveal its inherent order as well as the Creator's divine laws.

Eurocentric Thinking: Survival of the fittest promotes a drive for mastery and control of nature and the accumulation of possessions.

Afrocentric Thinking: There is a oneness of all things. Life is primary and must reflect a divine nature. Group maintenance, collectiveness, and sharing are essential.

Eurocentric Ethos: Control and mastery of all life.

Afrocentric Ethos: Life is primary, as is the oneness of all things. All things are one with and in harmony with nature.

Eurocentric Cosmology: Humans exist apart and separate from nature in an independent and separate collection of entities that comprise the universe.

Afrocentric Cosmology: The universe originates from the Creator and reflects the interconnectedness and interdependence of all things.

Eurocentric Reality: Worth is measured by utility; therefore, materiality is paramount.

Afrocentric Reality: The Creator provides a spiritual force or essence in all things; therefore, value is inherent in being.

Eurocentric Value: There is a conflict of opposing forces representing a continual struggle, whereby one must prevail over the other.

Afrocentric Value: There is a rhythmic/harmonious interchange of connections (synthesis) and antagonisms (contradictions).

In review then: Afrocentricity reflects the African worldview rooted deep in our culture. When one actually lives according to that view, then he or she becomes *located* Afrocentrically. Even those well-intended African people who behave in the interest of Africans without living from this conceptual base are *oriented* Afrocentrically. Whitaker and Hill have translated this Afrocentric value system into a simpler model, or road map, known as a paradigm, for us to compare the pursuit of the American Dream based on Eurocentric values with the same pursuit based on the Afrocentric values of the Rites of Passage model. This may make the picture clearer for you.

Eurocentric Principles of the American Dream

1. The central theme of the universe is survival of the fittest.
2. Competition is the common denominator that permeates man's interaction with both nature and all other men.
3. Life is "played out" on the various battlefields that man has devised both domestically and internationally.
4. Human value is measured quantitatively: "He who accumulates the most of what costs the most wins, and is thereby the best."
5. The ultimate expression of competition is war; consequently, man's most significant social behavior is expressed in war terms (the war on drugs, on crime, on poverty, etc.).
6. Man's ultimate goal and symbol of accomplishment and worth is to be Number One. The grand illusion of the American

Dream is, thus, that anyone who is focused, educated, and un-relenting can fight his or her way to the top and enjoy the distinction of being Number One.

Afrocentric Principles of the Rites of Passage

1. Man and nature are one.
2. Both man and nature experience cyclical, periodic, and inevitable changes.
3. In nature, these are considered celestial changes. For man, these are considered "life crises."
4. Both nature and man function according to the law of regeneration, in which any system eventually becomes spent and at intervals must be renewed. This process is symbolized by a death-and-rebirth sequence.
5. In nature, this process is monitored by the universe or God. In man, it is monitored by the Rites of Passage.
6. Man's recognition of seasonal change is acknowledgment of his interdependence with nature.
7. "Life crises" are disruptive to both the individual and the community.
8. The Rites assist and serve to cushion the passage from one status to another.
9. Rites involve three essential stages: separation, transition, and incorporation.

The concepts and theories behind Afrocentricity are fairly complex, and the topic really merits more examination. So I have suggested additional reading materials in Appendix E.

A SPIRITUAL CONNECTION

During my introduction into the Rites of Passage, information overload set in by midnight on the second day. The second day of the program drew to a close with a simulated "campfire discussion" led by our taskmaster, Baba. During the discussion, I felt a compelling spiritual connection not only to the other African-

American men present, but to all black people. It came to me that my actions in life, whether good or bad, affected all in my community of black people. *As they go, I go*, I thought.

Such a realization forces a sense of greater responsibility into your consciousness. It affects your actions and decisions in life, because you realize the truth: that you are now accountable to all, and all are equally accountable to you. This thought set the tone of our final discussion that night. Everyone expressed it in his own way, but each was feeling the same weight of shared responsibility and community.

The nature of our community was reflected by our surroundings in the tastefully decorated attic of the East End Neighborhood House. African carving, *kente* cloth, and many scented candles created the mood. I sat on the floor next to a small window that provided a view of the urban landscape. The sirens of police cars, ambulances, and fire engines periodically leaked into the room through that window. The real world was asserting itself in our Afrocentric revelries, reminding us what a challenge faced us outside the walls of this place.

On the final day of my Rites of Passage, I took part in a review of what we had experienced and discussed. We were given a list of books to read on Afrocentrism and the Rites of Passage movement. We played African drums together and bonded as black men with communal interests. It ended with a group photo and warm embraces. I found the experience to be provocative, illuminating, and enriching. It enlightened me by providing me a new perspective from which to live my life. I dedicated myself to living more Afrocentrically, to strive always to pass on my knowledge, my history, and my culture to the next generation and the one behind it.

Anthony J. Mensah, one of the gurus of the Rites of Passage movement, wrote:

> Through reflection on life experiences, the individual arrives at a new sense of self, and/or of community, which evokes a feeling of "I can" or "We can," when others say,

"I can't" or "We can't." Through this reawakening, the individual and/or community gains the ability to fly, or even soar.

Amen, Dr. Mensah. In the days and weeks following my Rites of Passage experience, I found myself contemplating my life and I came to realize that each step in it was a series of *separations* from past experiences, *transition* of new information and ideas, and *incorporation* into various new phases. Once I really learned that about myself, quite honestly, I realized that I was not crazy or wishy-washy, after all. I really was going through life's passages. Some people are suspicious of change, but change is what life is all about.

In effect, what I had done was to "reincarnate" myself and move on to a new level or larger world each time. We all do this in varying ways. These "passages" in life are normal and are to be expected and welcomed. It is how we grow. Growth is most obvious in our children. We can easily observe this as their world expands from the crib to the house to the neighborhood to school and beyond. And like our children, we grow too; less visibly, but it happens. Problems occur when we do not grow, when we become stuck in a rut, or when two people grow apart. This is when we risk shriveling up like a plant in need of water and air and soil.

The Rites of Passage process helps us to understand and endure this dynamic natural process. It also helps us to celebrate it. I have been stuck a few times in my life, but each time, at the right time, someone came into my network and watered my soul, nourishing my spirit with ideas, dreams, and visions. Now I understand; it is my turn to be the nourisher. I am not alone in this newfound understanding, of course. I came across a fellow traveler by the name of Vanessa Gallman, who at the time as an assistant city editor for *The Washington Post* who wrote an essay about the responsibilities of the black middle class:

. . . we have been blessed with a grounding in such values as hard work and the pursuit of excellence. We have had

the best education and the most access to power. If we suc-
cumb to defeatist attitudes and low expectations, there is
little hope for a country so much in need of unifying leadership.

She wrote also of the resentment that successful black professionals feel from younger blacks who sometimes see them as having sold out in order to attain their success. She denies that her
generation of black achievers has sold out.

Our revolution did not play out in the streets, but in corporate offices, the suburbs, government agencies. Our
mission was not to destroy the power structure, but to become part of it. Yet it proved tough to gain influence, and
when we "arrived" there was no plan of action to guide us;
we had to make it up as we went along.

Ms. Gallman continues to have high hopes for her generation.
She sees her peers beginning to coalesce into a new movement of
black nationalism "much more positive than our brief 'Black
Power' period. Good works are always more powerful than anger."
She wrote that her generation has come to view itself as an agent
for change.

But we do not have to give up a good job and fancy clothes
or move back into the crime-ridden inner city to get close
to "the people." A commitment could be as broad as spear-
heading a project to give new life to a poor community, or
as focused as helping someone in the immediate family get
a life. We need now to concentrate on seeing the strength
of trees rather than a monstrous forest of woes.

Rather than bemoaning the incredible challenges posed by
the worst of the conditions oppressing African Americans, she
suggests:

We can act on the condition of one person, one group or one community. That way, we could be a credit to the race and to the country by helping re-instill values and setting high expectations for those who follow. And just maybe, we can find some peace of mind in knowing that we have established a legacy, not just of success, but of service.

I am inspired by blacks such as Vanessa Gallman. And I know there are millions more like her out there looking to become part of the renewed Urban Village. In the chapters that follow, I will show you how to find them, and how to tap into their network of experience and wisdom.

"In having the determination to succeed, I was able to
reap many rewards through networking."
MELLODY HOBSON

Mellody Hobson is president of Ariel Capital Management, Inc., a Chicago-based investment management firm with over $5 billion in assets under management. She oversees the servicing of the firm's corporate, public, and nonprofit institutional clients as well as the marketing of the firm's three publicly traded mutual fund products: Ariel Fund, Ariel Appreciation Fund, and Ariel Premier Bond Fund. As president, Mellody is responsible for firmwide management and strategic planning. She developed an interest in the investment industry after completing summer internships at both Ariel Capital Management, Inc. and T. Rowe Price Associates. Mellody is a regular guest on ABC's *Good Morning America*. Her extensive media experience includes spending three years as a financial reporter on WGN's *Minority Business Report* and also regular appearances on CNN and CNNfn. Mellody is a member of the Board of Trustees of the Ariel Mutual Funds. She also works with a variety of civic and professional institutions, including the Women's Business Development Council; Do Something; the Economic Club of Chicago; and the Commercial Club of Chicago. She says, "When investing, be patient."

3

Perceptions, Reality, and Excellence

Stereotypes are fabricated from fragments of reality,
and it is these fragments that give life, continuity,
and availability for manipulation.
— RALPH ELLISON

I n 1992, while visiting Florida to inspect the damage inflicted by Hurricane Andrew, then First Lady Barbara Bush saw a beautiful young black boy and in full view of national television cameras patted him on the head and told him he would make a good basketball player someday.

Mrs. Bush, a warm and giving person, is not a racist. She had good intentions, but in a subtle way, her words were nearly as destructive as the hurricane. Why is it that she could not see the handsome young black man becoming a good attorney, engineer, or physician? Why should his dreams be limited to the basketball court? Why should our skin color, rather than our intellectual capabilities, our talents, and our drive, determine our futures?

Mrs. Bush was not alone in her subconscious misperceptions about and behavior toward black Americans. In still one of the most extensive surveys ever done on racial attitudes in America, the National Opinion Research Center found in 1992 that eight out of ten white Americans believe we would prefer to live on welfare rather than be self-supporting. The study found that six out of ten white Americans believe blacks are lazy. Five out of ten think we are less intelligent. Six out of ten think we are more violent. Five out of ten think we are less patriotic.

Apparently, there are two dominant images of blacks in America. One is the negative image of poverty, crime, and drugs. The other is positive, but nonetheless a stereotype rooted in ignorance. It holds that blacks can succeed in this country only if they can act, sing, dance, or play a sport. This image has improved somewhat over the last decade but it has not been erased completely. Of the thirty-five million blacks in America, the majority are not lazy or shiftless, poverty-stricken, criminal, or unpatriotic. Nor are the majority of us world-class athletes or great singers. I would have to state, however, that most of us do have great rhythm. And you better believe we can dance.

After nearly four hundred years of building America together, and nearly forty years after the enactment of civil rights laws, it is incredible that so many white Americans still know so little about black Americans. To many of them, we are still either a threat or a burden. This is no accident, of course. An article in *The New York Times* describes an experience of the son of one of the most respected African-American business executives of our generation.

> African American executive Earl Graves, Jr., boarded a commuter train near his suburban home outside New York City and settled into a seat to read the morning paper. When the train arrived at Grand Central Station in Manhattan and Graves walked onto the platform, two police officers grabbed him by the arms and shoved him against a nearby wall as hundreds of commuters streamed in. The officers snatched away Graves' briefcase and frisked him from top to bottom. The police were looking for an African American man approximately 5´10˝ with short hair and a mustache. Graves is 6´4˝ without a mustache, but his color was all that constituted the basis for his being suspected of a crime.

New York psychologist Marshall O. Lee noted the effects of this negative image of black men, as reported in *Essence* magazine:

In the minds of a substantial percentage of the white population, the problems and realities of the black underclass negate not only the striving and accomplishments of the working and professional classes but also the glitter and sparkle of the superstars.

Lee said this thought came to mind after he was startled by the frightened reaction of a white woman on the street when he tried to get closer to her in order to get a better look at a book she was holding. He had seen a black man's face on the book cover and wondered who it was. It was Bill Cosby, and Lee obviously was not. "A white woman reading a book written by an African-American man was terrified that the African-American man standing next to her was going to mug her," he noted.

In his essay, Lee noted also that while whites are certainly guilty of racial prejudices, many black people have fallen prey to the same prejudices. "Black communities also need to battle certain self-destructive tendencies we have internalized that block our advancement," he wrote. Black people have a perception problem in this country, and it is as much a problem of how we perceive ourselves as it is of how others perceive us. Many of us have come to believe that the white man's ice is colder, and in spite of the tremendous strides made in the last thirty-five years—in education and training and greater access to opportunity and wealth—that self-defeating perception has endured.

Having been employed in corporate marketing for twenty years, I know a great deal about the influence that perceptions have upon reality. In the world of advertising, marketing, and communications—according to marketing gurus Al Ries and Jack Trout—the goal of any product or service is to occupy a positive position in the mind of the consumer. The goal of advertising is to manipulate images. Do you know that before advertising wizard Leo Burnett invented the Marlboro Man, Marlboro cigarettes were marketed as an ivory-tipped ladies' cigarette? The female market for Marlboros was poor, so Burnett pulled off what is hailed as a historic feat of image makeover by turning Marlboros into the ultimate macho male smoke, and totally turning around the cigarette's sales performance. This sort of image-manipulation makeover occurs all the time in the world of advertising and marketing.

At Procter & Gamble, one of my duties was to help sell a stronger market position for Crest toothpaste. Today, I can tell you that in truth, therapeutically, Crest is neither particularly better nor any worse than most quality toothpastes on the market. Like all the others, it will clean your teeth and fight cavities, and might even help give you the dazzling smile of Denzel Washington or Halle Berry. But by the time the marketing team at Procter & Gamble got done positioning this great cavity fighter, Crest had become the Bedazzler, the best-selling toothpaste in America. The public perception of Crest that we established through advertising and marketing became the reality. We convinced everyone it was the best, and it became "the best."

Ebony magazine began painting positive pictures of blacks sixty years ago. *Essence* and *Black Enterprise* were the next generation of magazines targeting blacks. Over the past decade, new magazines targeting the black audience have emerged, including *Savoy, Heart & Soul, New Vision Magazine,* and *OURPC.*

USED BUT NOT ABUSED

My years in corporate America taught me that your value and your indispensability are directly related to the corporation's perception of your usefulness. If you find yourself not being utilized, could it mean you are useless? It is my belief that we are all here not to be abused or misused, but to be utilized for the highest purpose.

We have the responsibility to succeed at the highest level to which our talents and abilities will take us. For many black people, that means overcoming racism, drugs, poverty, and what Harvard law professor Chris Edley, Jr., terms "the presumption of incompetence."

If you are black, you know what the concept of presumed

incompetence is. It is what sociologist Dr. Joseph Feagin was referring to when he was quoted in *The New York Times* saying, "Blacks are seen as shoplifters, as unclean, violent and disreputably poor. No matter how influential, a black person cannot escape the stigma of being black even while relaxing or shopping." It is what John Molloy was addressing when he wrote in *The New Dress for Success* that Hispanics and blacks have the most problems with their appearance because society has conditioned us to look on members of both groups as belonging to the lower classes. "Members of both groups," he wrote, "will have difficulty being identified by their successes rather than their backgrounds." It is what the late Arthur Ashe was so tragically alluding to when he said that "being black in America is a greater burden than having AIDS."

Writer Adam Shatz in a *New York Times* book review wrote this about an experience Miles Davis had. "Late in his career, Miles Davis found himself seated beside a Washington matron at a White House dinner. What had he done to be invited? she asked innocently. 'Well, I've changed music four or five times,' he grumbled. 'What have you done of any importance other than be white?' Davis' self-assessment was haughty, but it was only slightly inflated."

Black Enterprise magazine has fought this battle with story after story. "The reality is that, as many of the nation's top black executives have discovered, beyond the glass ceiling there is often a barrier of spiked steel. And the color of our skin . . . is still too often a criterion for whether we or our businesses are deemed creditworthy," wrote editor and publisher Earl G. Graves.

Blacks who join white-dominated law firms know what the concept of presumed incompetence is. We all do. And to tell you the truth, I thought it was something that only blacks had to deal with, until a white friend gave me an example of a situation in which he had to deal with it. "Whenever I walk on the basketball court at the YMCA and I'm the only white guy, it is presumed that I am incompetent until I sink a couple shots," he said.

I wish it were so easy for blacks to dispel notions of their incompetence. Some say we should not care about other's perceptions of us. I maintain that we *should* care, because the impact on us is both subtle and overt.

In a study involving three hundred sixty-eight black adolescents taking a college-prep curriculum at three Illinois high schools, it was found that the most reliable predictor of high grades was a student's belief in his or her own academic ability. The more confidence students had in their ability to handle school assignments, the better their grades.

We *should* care about negative perceptions, because in many cases, the negative images affect our ability to succeed in the workplace, too. We should care also because these negative images have impacted our ability to develop entrepreneurial businesses, and this is often reflected in the difficulties we have in securing loans and other resources to start our own businesses. A study by the Boston Federal Reserve Bank found that blacks are 56 percent more likely to be turned down for loans than whites, and that high-income blacks are turned down more often than low-income whites. In a 2000 study conducted by the Center for Community Change, a housing advocacy group in Washington, D.C., it was concluded that blacks pay higher mortgage costs than whites as well. Race does matter.

We *should* care, because these perceptions have impact on how our children see themselves, and on the kinds of people they select as their heroes. We are raising a generation of children who want to be basketball players and rap singers. We *should* care also because, although we can dress up and be as professional-looking as we can, the negative images cling to all of us and everything we do. We are all in this together.

Bernard Beal, a Stanford MBA and owner of the prestigious Wall Street investment banking firm M R Beal and Associates, said, "If you're not playing the role people think you should, then you're not really seen . . . sometimes you can be invisible if you're out of context." Bernard related one of his favorite anecdotes on this point to *MBE* (*Minority Business Entrepreneur*) magazine.

Beal had gotten a call from a reporter at a prominent business publication who wanted to talk about an innovative product Beal's investment management firm had recently introduced. Beal and his associate, James Francis, agreed to fly down to the nation's capital the next afternoon to do the interview in person. "He was a sharp guy," Beal says of the writer. "He really knew his stuff." They arrived early at the agreed-upon place, a nondescript coffee shop. They noticed the place was rather deserted—an older woman at the only other occupied table, and a few people at the counter. Beal and Francis took a corner booth and waited for the reporter to show up. He never did. After waiting two hours, the pair finally left.

Back in New York and more than a little miffed, Beal got a call from his publicist, who was just then on another line with the reporter, who was angrily protesting that he had been stood up. "But we were there!" Beal insisted. Then the journalist got on the phone. "That's total BS," he sputtered. "I was in that restaurant and waited a half hour past our appointed time, and there was no one in there except an old woman muttering to herself and two black guys sitting in the corner!" At that point, Beal emits one of his hearty guffaws. That was one embarrassed journalist.

A media survey in New York found that although blacks constitute 12 percent of the population, we comprise less than 3 percent of the positive images contained in media advertising but 17 percent of the editorial coverage of crime and violence. This is not a conspiracy, it is a condition. Author Shelby Steele has written: "When a black presents himself in an integrated situation, he knows that his skin alone may bring [black] stereotypes to life in the minds of those he meets and that he, as an individual, may be diminished by his race before he has a chance to reveal a single aspect of his personality." He calls the tension that is thus generated "integration shock."

OUR VIOLENT IMAGE

Perhaps the most dangerous and debilitating stereotype affixed to blacks is the perception that we are more inclined to be violent than other people. In 1992, the black police chief of Washington, D.C., Fred Thomas, pinpointed this problem when he stated on the television news program *Nightline* that a disproportionate amount of crime reported in the media occurs in the inner city, which is predominantly populated with black people. But this is not where the majority of blacks live. When the media focus on these crimes and these criminals day after day, year after year— perhaps because this is the cheapest and easiest way to provide sensational coverage of violence and crime in our society—the criminal acts of a minority of blacks become associated with an entire race of people even though the vast majority of African Americans are nonviolent, contributing members of society.

A Los Angeles TV executive appearing on *Nightline* said that the media find it too expensive to provide editorial balance in their coverage of the black community, and thus, an incomplete picture is presented to a public that seems to be increasingly fascinated by violence and reports of violence. This focus on the most violent aspects of society may be attributable to voyeurism or to the need that some have to feel that violence happens to other people. There is something about human nature that makes us want to compare our troubles with those of others with more serious problems, so that we feel comforted. The media, particularly the ever-growing field of tabloid television shows and increasingly sensational newspapers, have seized on this public fascination with violence with a philosophy of "If it bleeds it leads," meaning that the most explicit, violent, or sensational items receive the most coverage. In analyzing the media's coverage of violence in America, *Nightline* host Ted Koppel noted that the biggest loser in it was the black middle class.

Most blacks agree that this negative image fuels deep frustration, low self-esteem, and ultimately rage among those of us who toil as honest citizens to overcome racism and racial stereotyping.

In New York City, from 1997 to 1998, the NYPD's Street Crimes Unit stopped and frisked 135,000 people, 85 percent of whom were people of color. Only 4,500 persons were ultimately arrested and prosecuted, meaning that over 95 percent of those harassed were innocent. Interestingly, whites who were stopped were significantly more likely to be found with drugs or other contraband, indicating that not only was this policy of racial stops and searches a biased one, but it failed the test as valid crime control on its own merits as well.

Violence is not the answer to our problems, but neither is violence part of our nature as a race of people. The media might do far more good by searching for the positive aspects of the black community than by focusing only on the violence. And by effectively using the power of physical (stand-ins), verbal (telephone), written (e-mail, cards, and letters), and economic (boycott of advertisers) protest we can let the media know what we expect from them.

FIXING THE IMAGE PROBLEM

Think of how powerfully images affect your thinking. When you think of Lexus, you think of quality and prestige. When you think of Volkswagen, you think of small and economical. When you think of Japanese people, you think of teamwork and excellence. When you think of Jews, you think of economic clout. When you think of blacks, you think of poverty, crime, and athletic prowess.

The question you may be asking yourself at this point is: "What does all of this have to do with the power and importance of effective networking?" To answer that question, let me define networking for you. Effective networking is the identification, building, and developing of relationships for the purpose of sharing information and resources. If my image, perception, or paradigm of you is negative—if it holds that you are lazy, shiftless, and prone to violence or otherwise give me the impression that you have limited ability—I am going to be less likely to want to identify you as a meaningful resource. If I don't think you can help me, why should I include you in my network? Negative images, then, greatly impede our willingness and ability to work with each other for the common good. There have been many studies that show how both whites and blacks view the black people through the prism of negative stereotypes. This must change if we are to effectively network, and if we are to thrive as a culture.

What can you do to change this? Here are a few suggestions:

- Support black media, so they can become economically stronger and gain financial and editorial power. *Ebony, Black Enterprise, Savoy, Radio One, Essence, Heart & Soul,* etc., your black community newspapers, and the growing list of other black publications are our first line of defense and offense in the media world. We must use them or lose them. As our economic power grows, we should mount a full-frontal assault on the communications industry. We should infiltrate it with our best and brightest so that we come to control our own community image in marketing, advertising, public relations, television, radio, and newspapers. At the same time, our media must continue to improve the quality of its products and messages. I have seen black media that contributes as much to the erosion of our image and values as some white media does. If we do it, everyone else will think it is okay. I know that sex, violence, and crime sell. But at some point, the line must be drawn, and, if we are to be masters of our own image, it must begin with us. Do not support media that give negative portrayals of blacks as a problem people. Turn off programs that reinforce stereotypes and mock black women under the guise of humor; let the advertisers and network know that you have turned them off. Write letters to the editor castigating newspapers and television stations for negative images of blacks. Encourage them to look instead for positive stories from the black community to balance their coverage.

- Help stage regular events in your community that promote positive portrayals of black people, and then demand that the media cover such events as extensively as they cover crime, poverty, and violence. How about a black history contest? A science competition for black schoolchildren? A neighborhood graffiti cleanup? How about a community book fair such as the one founded by Max Rodriguez and Linda Duggins and put on each year in Harlem, N.Y. Thousands of people attend, along with much of New York's media corps. Let your local newspapers and radio stations know that these are being held.
- Bring positive black role models into your community schools and organizations—weekly or monthly—and invite the media to cover their speeches. If you can pay sixty dollars to hear Mary J. Blige or Maxwell in concert, why not forty dollars to hear the positive and inspiring messages of folks such as Les Brown, Bishop T. D. Jakes, or Susan Taylor? Plant those messages in the minds of your children and the white-controlled media.
- Cultivate your sources in the media. Invite black reporters and editors into your neighborhood and help make them part of your community. Find open-minded white reporters, too, and telephone them with news tips and feature ideas. You might be surprised how eager some of them are to provide a more balanced view; they just don't know how to go about getting it. Look in your local paper, even in the national ones, and engage the regular columnists to editorialize positive messages regarding African-American initiatives in your community. Respond to those editorials that don't depict blacks in positive situations, or those that "miss the mark." Sometimes, you have to take the offensive. Give them access so that they learn how shallow their portrayals really are. If they run a series of stories on gang violence in your neighborhood, invite them back to do stories on an award-winning church

choir, or a community leader who is keeping young people out of gangs and in school. John H. Johnson, chairman of Johnson Publishing, and one of the wealthiest blacks in America, said that "the lack of information will hurt us more than racism." So let's get the positive information flowing.

- Raise the positive profile of black people by volunteering for charities and community groups such as the Boy Scouts, Girl Scouts, United Way, and Big Brothers and Big Sisters. If you want whites to understand blacks better, you have to let them see us in a positive environment. Ignorance is what drives racism. It is easier to vilify and hate people with whom you have never had any contact. But if a black man or woman is on the team, understanding is nourished.

- Support black-owned businesses. If this means spending a dollar or two more, do it! If our community is going to endure and grow, if our children are going to have business role models, then it is worth it. Don't be afraid to make suggestions for improvements to these businesses in order to help them get better and survive. Help them set new standards. Demand excellence, but help show the way. Sometimes it seems there are more whites trying to do business with blacks than there are blacks endeavoring to do business with each other.

- Join black organizations and become active in promoting positive images. Visit inner-city schools regularly, and invite their students to attend your meetings and participate in joint projects. White community groups have done this for years. Target 10 percent of your group's annual budget to create an image campaign for promoting positive reporting in the media. (White organizations spend up to 20 percent to promote excellence within their organizations or professional discipline.) Advertise and lobby for black excellence. I made this suggestion when I delivered the keynote address to the first convention of the Association of Black Insurance Professionals. And wouldn't you know it? They asked me to help them do it. Together, we created an image campaign for their organization. We made a high-quality pictorial collage of black faces—black professionals in the workplace—which we paired with ad copy that read:

EXPERTISE, EXPERIENCE, AND EXCELLENCE
RIGHT IN YOUR NEIGHBORHOOD

The members of the Association of Black Insurance Professionals are committed to excellence. They know insurance. And they know the needs of the communities where they live and work. When you need insurance advice, call on the expertise, experience, and excellence in your neighborhood.

When placed in local publications, the ad drew such a positive response that it was later adopted as a national campaign by the organization. There are more than two hundred fifty national organizations for blacks (see complete list in the Resource Guide section). No others that I am aware of do this sort of positive-image positioning. Could you imagine the cumulative impact this would have on the image of black people if two hundred fifty of our own organizations and their chapters did this across the country?

Some thirty years ago, the United Negro College Fund and its member colleges had an image problem relating to the quality of education in black colleges. Vernon Jordan, then the executive director, used his contacts to call upon the voluntary services of the mega New York ad agency Young & Rubicam and the Advertising Council to help the UNCF solve its problem. The agency developed what became one of the most recognized slogans in advertising: "A mind is a terrible thing to waste." Thanks to this slogan, together with powerful creative execution and free strategic placement of print and electronic ads coordinated by the Advertising Council, the image of member colleges, student enrollment, and fund-raising results improved dramatically over the next decade. It is a well-coordinated campaign, still being utilized.

According to countless polls, the image of the African American has improved, but it's only in a slightly better position today than UNCF was thirty years ago. As I stated in earlier chapters, this is not good for black people or for America. I encourage our national organizational leadership to call on the best black and white ad agencies, and the Advertising Council, to voluntarily co-ordinate a long-term national campaign to help reposition our im-age. Certainly our black professional organizations, fraternities, and sororities, such as the National Bar Association, the National Black MBA Association, and others, have enough collective clout to make a convincing case for the need of this campaign.

By becoming the masters of our own image, we can help raise our image not only among whites, but also among blacks who have bought into negative stereotypes of themselves and their race. Drugs are not the most critical problem for black people. Poverty, unemployment, and crime are the results of what truly ails our community: racism, negative self-esteem, and negative imagery. Carter G. Woodson, the father of black history, said it powerfully years ago:

> If you can control a man's thinking, you do not have to worry about his action. When you determine what a man shall think you do not have to concern yourself about what he will do. If you make a man feel that he is inferior, you do not have to compel him to accept an inferior status, for he will seek it himself. If you make a man think that he is justly an outcast, you do not have to order him to the back door. He will go without being told; and if there is no back door, his very nature will demand one.

CASHING IN ON OUR INTELLECTUAL CAPITAL

The amazing thing is that in spite of the bombardment of these negative images of black people, millions of our generation have experienced great success. We have turned stumbling blocks into our stepping stones. We should continue to seize control of our image and our economy and rehabilitate both. We can do this by better using our established "intellectual capital" to encourage excellence, economic empowerment, and self-help.

Let me define *my* concept of "intellectual capital." It is the estimated dollar value of the formal education and professional training that black people have received over the last three decades. African Americans began to benefit from the civil rights laws enacted in the 1960s. It is the era in which those of us in the integration generation grew up and took advantage of opportunities never dreamed of by previous generations.

In formulating an admittedly rough estimate of what the intellectual capital of black people is, I had my research assistant determine how many classroom hours blacks spent in high schools, colleges, and universities in this country in the last thirty-two years from 1968 to 2000. The figure we came up with was more than 320 billion hours. We then did additional research to find the number of black people in executive, technical, administrative, managerial, supervisory, or professional specialties for the same thirty-two-year period. I calculated the total number of hours of professional training to be about 390 billion hours. When you add the formal education and professional training of blacks together, it comes to 710 billion hours. That means we are the most educated and trained Africans in the history of humankind. Our ancestors would be proud. If you value this education and training at a lowball rate of just ten dollars an hour, it means our intellectual capital is worth more than 7,000,000,000,000 (that's seven *trillion* dollars, folks). Let's call this our investment in America.

The next calculation determined just what kind of return we are getting on our intellectual capital investment. This was done by totaling the value of all the products and services produced by the 823,500 black-owned businesses in America in 1997 (the most recent U.S. Commerce survey). It comes to seventy-one billion dollars. If you then divide our seventy-one billion dollars into the twenty trillion dollars of nonfarm business revenue produced by all American businesses in 1997, it shows we are contributing less than 1 percent of the total nonfarm revenue, or, said another way, we are getting less than a 1 percent return on our intellectual capital investment. This significantly impacts our image, jobs, and businesses for and within our own communities. My argument is: If we were using more of this intellectual capital investment to start and build our own businesses, instead of building other people's businesses (i.e., corporate America), we would get a greater return on our years of education, training, and experience by creating more and bigger businesses, as well as more jobs for black people, and thus greater overall wealth and fulfillment.

COMMUNITY VERSUS INDIVIDUAL SUCCESS

Intellectual capital is nothing more than an empty concept if there is no method for sharing it. Look at a map of the United States, and you will find it littered with once-thriving towns that are dying because they have been cut off from major highways and interstates. Surely there is something of value in each of these towns, but what good is it if there is no connection to anything? It is like money stuffed in a mattress. "Intellectual capital is useless unless it moves. It's no good having some guy who is very wise and sits alone in a room," computer futurist Hugh Macdonald told *Fortune* magazine.

Like goods loaded on trucks and transported on highways, knowledge can be moved on networks, and when knowledge moves, it gains in value, its worth grows exponentially. But to build a network, you have to be willing to share your knowledge. You have to work for the greater good, knowing that by making your community stronger, your strength grows. Individual gain, not the elevation of our entire community, has been the focus for all too many African Americans. I include myself among those who have been so involved in personal struggles that we have neglected those around us. I realized that by failing to think in terms of the community, I actually let down not only the community, but myself and my children. In the total scheme of things, I didn't do as well as I might have, and the community did worse. Out of this realization grew my dream of the new Underground Railroad, a network for African-American success in which those of us who have achieved some measure of prosperity can now work to free others of our race from the bonds of enslaving poverty, and help escort them to financial independence and the freedom to enjoy all the great things this nation has to offer.

Andrew Billingsley, Ph.D., writes: "We are a successful and thriving culture. Yet many successful African-American individuals fall victim to the urge to forget about their group identity and group responsibility and seek only to raise themselves and to vanish into the American mainstream."

This individualism, in which the group welfare is subverted to the individual's, is Eurocentric thinking, not Afrocentric. In Japanese culture, there is no single success, only community/team success. In traditional African culture, there is no single success, only tribal or team success. This is reflected in this phrase from an ancient African proverb: "No one may go in want so long as others have anything to give." This is yet another instance in which we might move forward by going back—back to the traditional way. We do not have the luxury of acting as individuals, of putting our own needs ahead of all others. Society as a whole simply cannot have thirty-five million blacks going it alone, each doing his or her individual thing. Not if we are to succeed as a community of people. Not if our children and their children are to have a better way of life.

EXCELLENCE REDEFINED

To overcome this black failure to leverage our collective resources for the elevation of all, my goal is to help establish excellence as the overriding perception of blacks *and* the *reality* for blacks. Let me make it clear: I want to make a distinction between excellence and personal achievement.

Personal achievement is that which is accomplished by the

individual using his or her unique gifts and talents. We spend the early part of our life trying to identify our gifts. Our capacity for achievement varies according to how well we identify and expand upon those gifts. It is human nature to concentrate on personal achievement as a building block of self-esteem. And while personal achievement among black people has helped us gain individual independence and confidence, so far, it has not significantly contributed to the development of interdependency in our culture. We must fix that!

Excellence, by my definition, is the reinvestment of one's unique gifts or personal achievements back into the community in order to better the human condition within the community. I believe true excellence comes only when you use your talents and gifts to benefit others to a greater extent than you employ those talents for your own personal benefit. An example: Magic Johnson winning the Most Valuable Player trophy is high personal achievement, but it is not excellence, not at least by my measure. The charitable work of Magic Johnson, however, is up to my standard of excellence in the African-American community.

It is my belief also that our generation of African Americans must redefine excellence while maintaining high standards of personal achievement. This is our role and contribution. It is also the next step in our development as a culture. This distinction between personal achievement and excellence is important, because it helps us to think of our excellence in communal terms rather than in personal terms, and this leads to another standard for defining our success. It also encourages black people to create network linkages and to work for the common good of our people.

I believe that we must have networks of:

- Professionals helping professionals
- Businesses helping professionals
- Professionals helping businesses
- Middle-class and upper-class blacks helping the underclass

We must become interdependent, linked together in a common bond of caring and sharing. As long as there is one black person denied an opportunity to grow and move up or denied a quality education, we are all affected. We are all injured. It seems that nearly every culture in America, except black American culture, has grasped this and acted upon it long ago. In my opinion, one of the top priorities for blacks in this new millennium is to find more productive and effective ways in which to reinvest our collective resources back into our own communities, and thus get a better return on our intellectual capital investment. We can begin by starting and building new businesses and more wisely managing our money and enormous purchasing power.

TAPPING OUR OWN ROOTS

We cannot, as some studies have shown, continue to give 95 percent of our nearly six hundred billion dollars in black spending to white businesses and not secure greater employment, supplies, and entrepreneurial opportunities. We cannot score the lowest on SAT scores and expect to be a competent part of this nation's work force in an increasingly technical and demanding workplace. We cannot expect whites to do for us that which we will not do for ourselves. We must move from the bottom of the educational and economic ladder. We must start by mobilizing and motivating the black middle and upper classes to devise an action-oriented economic and educational agenda for the new millenium. We owe our ancestors a better showing. And if we look at, and listen to, their teachings, our ancestors can show us the way.

The celebration of the Kwanzaa holiday and the incorporation of the Seven Principles of Kwanzaa into our daily lives is one example of how we can look to our African heritage and traditions for ways in which to better our lives. Although many of its symbols and terminology are derived from African tradition, Kwanzaa is the creation of African Americans. Black activist Maulana "Ron" Karenga, a Ph.D. in political science and now chairman of the black studies department at California State University in Long

Beach, developed the modern celebration of traditional African values in 1965 to encourage black Americans to develop a greater sense of unity, identity, and purpose. He envisioned it not just as an annual ritual, but as a way of life, a catalyst for social, cultural, and economic progress for the black community.

First celebrated on December 26, 1966, by Karenga and a small gathering of black nationalist men and women, the seven days of Kwanzaa are now observed annually by more than twenty-five million people throughout the United States, Canada, England, the Caribbean, and Africa. Kwanzaa has evolved from a holiday of eating, gift giving, music, and interacting into a political and economic movement in which blacks seek economic self-determination within their cultural community. According to a December 1998 article published by the *World African Network*, an estimated twenty-eight million people celebrate Kwanzaa every year.

The holiday itself is now celebrated not only in private homes, but in small Kwanzaa Holiday Expos that attract thousands of blacks in cities nationwide. In these gatherings, modern African bazaars are created with a backdrop provided by West African *kente* cloth; tribal chants and rhythms from Africa, black America, and the Caribbean; and the exotic scents of traditional African and African-American cooking. The goods offered for sale are produced by blacks for blacks.

The observance of Kwanzaa signals the beginning of the end for those days when blacks fled from their cultural community. We are coming to embrace our heritage. This is exactly what Karenga intended, as he explained in an *Ebony* magazine interview. As a cultural nationalist, he wants to rescue and reconstruct African history and culture and to revitalize African culture in America. Kwanzaa is his method for doing that. "I wanted to stress the need for a reorientation of values, to borrow the collective life-affirming ones from our past and use them to enrich our present," he said. Karenga has called also for black people to "reconstitute themselves by returning to their history, and to build with other pro-gressive people in the world a paradigm for a truer, more just society." You cannot debate his logic or thinking.

THE SEVEN PRINCIPLES OF KWANZAA

Cooperative economics is a key to the elevation of the black community, according to Karenga and many other black people involved in the Kwanzaa and Afrocentrism movements. It is also one of the Seven Principles or *Nguzo Saba* upon which the Kwanzaa holiday is based. Each of the seven days of the week-long holiday is devoted to one of these principles:

Unity *(Umoja)* calls for togetherness and collective action in the family, community, nation, and ethnic group.

Self-determination *(Kujichagulia)* commits us to defining and developing ourselves, instead of being defined and developed by others.

Collective work and responsibility *(Ujima)* encourages us to labor together for the common good while each accepts responsibility for both the successes and failures of the group.

Cooperative economics *(Ujamaa)* promotes the concept of sharing wealth, talents, and resources for the common good.

Purpose *(Nia)* calls for defining goals and motives in terms of what can best benefit the community and family.

Creativity *(Kuumba)* commits us to building rather than destroying, positive action, and a continual search for new and fresh ideas with which to better our lives.

Faith *(Imani)* invests us with belief in ourselves as individuals and as a people, and in our ability and right to control our own destinies.

A NEW AGENDA

Like many black people who have embraced the Kwanzaa holiday and the concept of Afrocentrism, I have tried to incorporate the Seven Principles into my daily life. I believe that our new generation of black professionals, those members of the black middle and upper classes, have a special obligation to do this for our community and our culture. We must come together again and reach across class and income boundaries. I believe that this is vital to our goal of destroying the barriers of institutional racism that affect us all.

It is vital that we tell our stories of excellence and share our resources and values with those in our community who remain locked in the poverty cycle. We must also discourage the media's focus on the 10 percent of our brothers and sisters who struggle while paying relatively little attention to the 90 percent who are making significant contributions to their community, nation, and world. We must focus on our assets and how best to employ them for the good of all black people, rather than continually lamenting the liabilities and looking for where the blame should be placed.

Our goal should be for a lot of us to do a little each, instead of a few of us doing it all. We need to follow the African proverb, "I am because we are; because we are I am." That is why I am suggesting a new agenda for action to facilitate the building of the new Urban Village outlined in previous chapters. The Kwanzaa principles provide us with moral landmarks rooted in our cultural history; the new agenda provides us with an action plan of specific goals and guideposts. It will serve as the track, if you will, for our contemporary Underground Railroad. Over time, I believe this agenda will do for our people what the Jewish agenda did for them after the Holocaust, and what the Japanese agenda did for them after World War II. This is a *black agenda*.

In the following outline, I suggest seven goals and then offer specific action steps for implementing them. Some of you may be doing them already. All of them, I believe, are consistent with our lifestyles and can be implemented in the privacy of our own homes, workplace, and community.

A Black Agenda

1. **Spiritual goal.** To praise and honor our Creator by using our unique qualities and powers to better the human condition.

Action Steps

- Worship and celebrate our religion regularly, whatever your individual beliefs may be.
- Identify our unique qualities.
- Act upon the conviction that one person can make a difference and that you are that person.

2. **Cultural goal.** To understand and celebrate our history and culture and to make them the basis for our values, beliefs, and actions.

Action Steps

- Study our history.
- Share our history with our immediate and extended families.
- Insist on the inclusion of our history wherever history is taught.
- Use our history as a base for building self-esteem and personal affirmation.
- Wear a symbol of our culture whenever possible, and have our cultural symbols in the home, workplace, and place of worship.

3. **Family goal.** To strengthen the bond within our family so that each of us may parent, nurture, and guide our children.

Action Steps

- Resolve any aspect of conflict in our relationships.
- Ensure that every male fulfills the responsibilities of fatherhood.
- Ensure that every female fulfills the responsibilities of motherhood.
- Guide our children toward excellence.
- Reestablish our culture's traditional respect for the wisdom and experience of our elders.

4. **Educational goal.** To take full responsibility for the enforcement of the highest educational and occupational standards at home, in school, and at work.

Action Steps
- Provide for the ongoing education of our families.
- Develop occupational skills that make us vital and invaluable in the workplace.
- Expect high achievement.
- Prepare our children to enjoy learning.
- Increase our involvement in our educational systems.

5. **Economic goal.** To build, support, and reinvest in our businesses so that the ever-increasing quality of our products and services will make others dependent upon us.
Action Steps
- Provide financial support for black-owned businesses and encourage entrepreneurship.
- Patronize those black-owned businesses.
- Support all businesses that invest in our communities.

6. **Community goal.** To share our time and resources where needed and to network and tap *our* resources first.
Action Steps
- Volunteer, mentor, or serve as a role model.
- Use our own resources more effectively.
- Join and pitch in when and where needed.
- Help improve the community in some small way every day.

7. **Youth goal.** To value, implement, and practice the Rites of Passage for young men and women.
Action Steps
- Urge the young men and women under our supervision to go through the Rites of Passage experience.
- Pass an understanding of African and black tradition, history, and culture to our youth.
- Build self-esteem in our young people.
- Serve as an example to our youth by conducting ourselves as caring, responsible, and supportive adults.

- Above all else, convey to our young people that they are part of a proud community, and that their membership in the black community comes with benefits and responsibilities.

THE BIRTH OF THE URBAN VILLAGE

Consider this agenda to be the manifesto for our new Urban Village, the one we are going to build to replace the crumbling and crime-ridden inner-city ghettos, just as we are going to rebuild and revive the lives of the so-called underclass, whom we know to be people of great potential who have until now been cut off from opportunity.

This agenda is intended to end the destruction and to begin the construction. We must acknowledge our problems, but focus on our successes as a means to determine solutions. We must embrace excellence, self-help, education, family, and religion once again. With such an agenda, we can move from the integration generation of the 1960s, 1970s, and 1980s to the business generation for the twenty-first century.

To create the Urban Village, I believe we have to begin building on two fronts. The first building must be done on a human scale, the second on an economic scale. Every week, I pick up a newspaper and read another story that mentions the need for more black role models. The perception from and implication of these stories is that other than the usual athletes and entertainers, there are not enough black role models and mentors out there from whom the young and the struggling African-American population can take guidance.

Leading by Example

The responsibility of role modeling falls squarely on the shoulders of parents first. It is they who shape the foundation of our values, mores, education, and goals. It is our parents who help guide us through our career choices, which lead to career options that beat the odds of failure. With a strong parental presence serving as a guide and a center of balance, our young people stand a far greater chance of overcoming the other obstacles of poverty, crime, drugs, and racism that they may encounter.

Howard A. Peters grew up in the public housing of Memphis, the eldest of five children raised by Johnnie Mae Peters, who was divorced and often worked three jobs. Howard had difficulty in his first two years in school. In fact, he was unable to recite the alphabet at the end of his second-grade term, so he was held back a year. Concerned about her eldest son's schooling, Johnnie Mae Peters got a job in the school cafeteria so she could monitor his progress. His teachers took a special interest in him, and Howard became a good student, a top athlete, and a leader.

Like many men who grew up under similar circumstances, Howard Peters ended up in prison. In fact, he spent most of his adult life in prisons. There is one crucial difference, however. Howard Peters ran prisons. He became the first African-American director of the Illinois Department of Corrections, one of the largest prison systems in the country, with more than thirty thousand inmates, twelve thousand employees, and an annual budget of nearly seven hundred million dollars. Since then Howard has been appointed to the position of Illinois deputy chief of staff and is now serving as the very first secretary of the Department of Human Resources. Both positions were appointments from the governor of the State of Illinois.

What made the difference in Peters's life? His mother, Johnnie Mae, a woman who describes herself even today as "a pusher and shover," and the many other mentors and role models who guided and, in some instances, pushed and shoved Peters through high school, college, and graduate school, and through his career in corrections, where he has established a reputation for innovation and toughness.

Parents, mentors, and role models provide self-esteem, hope, and pride. They instill the message that life's rewards can be won through commitment, hard work, and sacrifice. To build an Urban Village of success stories such as that of Howard A. Peters, we need to extend the parenting outside the nuclear family and throughout the village of our children.

Too many of us who have achieved success have turned our backs on urban America and those who remain mired in the cycle of underclass hopelessness. Too many of us have succumbed to the lazy philosophy that one person could not possibly make a difference in the lives of those who are still searching for a way out. Surely government has both lifted us up and held us down with its ever-shifting social policies, but ultimately, it is up to those black people who have attained success to take on the moral responsibility to reach down and lift up their own. We are responsible for our own success or failure.

In my travels around the country, however, I have seen the beginnings of a movement, a pulling together of our Urban Village. Churches, sororities, fraternities, clubs, and organizations are reaching out. Individuals across the country are daring to be among the too few doing too much, but doing it anyway.

For example, over more than a decade, marketing executive and entrepreneur Julius C. Dorsey, Jr., has made a difference. He served as a role model in an elementary school on Cleveland's West Side. For him, there are two overriding considerations in being a successful role model in the public schools. First, you must have no other reason for being a role model than your sincere interest in children. The second, he puts this way: "I'm not trying to show the children something better. I'm trying to show them something else. The children in my classroom make decisions based on their experience. Learning about another's point of view adds to their perspective and will help them make better decisions. Part of my purpose in the classroom is to offer another perspective, not to teach values."

When acting as a role model, consistency is all-important. You can't just show up now and then. You have to set a regular schedule. And you can't put out varying signals. You have to be there, and you have to care. "Being in the classroom one morning a week means that there is a continuity in the support given to both the teacher and the students," said Julius. "Together, we can connect one learning experience to another."

His initial involvement came in the form of an invitation to speak to an elementary-school class. The outcome was so positive that the principal asked if Julius would come back again. His offer of coming once a week was more than the principal had ever expected. Through his firm, Dorsey and Company, Julius also contributed financially to the classroom. "In every case, the money has been used to make the classroom more comfortable: adding a carpet for the reading area, beanbag chairs, books, and computer software. I'm not in this for the thanks, but the children really do appreciate these improvements."

Julius's role modeling extended beyond this one classroom. He also established the Eleanor and Julius Dorsey, Sr., Education Fund at his alma mater high school in Detroit. The purpose of the fund is to provide scholarships for the "average students," who often are not targeted by recognition but might benefit significantly from some special motivation that recognizes the potential for achievement in their lives. No one believes America's inner-city educational crises are going to be easily addressed. But while many of the politicians and educators and geniuses wring their hands and write articles and convene for meetings, Julius is already making a difference. He's doing it for just two hours a week in the new Urban Village.

Mentoring: A Networking Nudge

The dictionary defines the word *mentor* as a "trusted counselor or guide, a tutor or coach." Being a good mentor means that you endeavor to bring out the best in those you focus on. Here are nine important keys to successful mentoring.

1. Be attentive and listen. Your attention has to be focused during mentoring sessions.
2. Keep your word. Chances are, disappointment has been a big part of the lives of those you are mentoring. You are not allowed to add to those disappointments.

3. Bring something to the party. Have a story to tell, an experience to relate, something intriguing to impart.
4. Nurture the spirit as well as the mind. Mentor the spirit, too. Uplift them.
5. Put yourself in their shoes; try to understand the particular mind-set of the age group and background of those whom you mentor.
6. Cheerlead, encourage, praise, salute. Generally, those who seek mentors have been deprived of positive feedback. One of your biggest jobs is to give that to them.
7. Don't always assume that those whom you are mentoring will get the point. Make sure they understand or see the value in what you are telling and showing them.
8. For youth "at risk," tell them that there are only three priorities that they need to focus on: (a) They must get a high school diploma if they want to be employable in the twenty-first century; (b) They cannot have a criminal record; (c) They must not have any children before they graduate and get a job.
9. For parents, teachers, and professionals engaged in some form of mentoring, I highly recommend reading former U.S. secretary of education William J. Bennett's *The Book of Virtues* and *The Children's Book of Home and Family*, which are full of good stories and poems that communicate sound ideas and insights on self-discipline, responsibility, work, honesty, faith, and other important virtues. I use them in combination with the book *African Proverbs* by Charlotte and Wolf Leslau when I prepare to talk to young people.

A friend once wrote that he likes to compare mentors and the mentoring process to a sequoia tree—that marvel of nature that grows hundreds of feet toward the sky. The sequoia is not only one of the largest living things on earth; it is also one of the oldest. Its long, deep roots spread across the forest floor and help the tree to live for more than a thousand years. Another unique feature of this gentle neighbor is that it gives back to its environment—in fact, it contributes 80 percent more to the forest than it removes.

Mentoring works the same way. As young people receive the benefits of mentoring, they grow and achieve. Their roots go deep into the community and, once established, they give back. As our mentoring programs plant roots firmly in our culture and community, they will bring tangible benefits, but a hundredfold. And like the sequoia tree, our race will continue to grow and prosper.

The Gospel of Equity

There is more than one form of mentoring, and increasingly, across the country, one of the most important types practiced among African Americans has been economic mentoring. A dynamic and exciting movement toward economic self-determination has been building quietly across America in the last ten years. In small towns and major cities, in churches and community organization meetings, what *Time* magazine called "the Gospel of Equity" is being preached by blacks who believe that economic empowerment is possible without government assistance. "Economic development has emerged as the hottest crusade in black America, replacing the emphasis on politics, civil rights, and social programs that marked the previous generation of black activists," wrote *Time*'s Sylvester Monroe, one of our best black journalists.

Behind the growth of the Urban Village and its motto of economic empowerment are groups such as the Brotherhood Crusade Black United Fund in Los Angeles, the Organization for a New Equality (ONE) in Boston, and the 100 Black Men of America. These groups are finding and developing tools for economic reinvestment in our abandoned urban communities. One of their strongest tools is the Community Reinvestment Act of 1977, which requires banks to give back to those who support them. Banks must make loans to individuals or companies in their own neighborhoods, even if the person or group might otherwise be perceived as a poor risk.

The Reverend Charles R. Stith, president, founder, and former national president of ONE in Boston, said this tool enables black people to move on to the next step in the civil rights movement. We have earned the right to ride at the front of the bus; now we are developing the economic power to buy the bus company. Stith's group has used the Community Reinvestment Act to leverage nearly eight hundred million dollars from Boston's financial institutions for black neighborhoods. ONE has created a network of groups in over forty cities to use this same leverage for the rebuilding of the Urban Village.

In recognition of the fact that black people also must learn how to use this economic leverage, ONE conducts seminars and classes in black neighborhoods, teaching people how to obtain credit and understand interest rates, and, in general, how to make money work for their communities.

Another key figure in developing the Urban Village is Danny J. Bakewell, president and CEO of the Brotherhood Crusade in Los Angeles. An experienced banker, real estate developer, and businessman, Bakewell is a strong advocate of cooperative economics and unity for black people. His organization in south-central Los Angeles is supported mostly by voluntary payroll deductions from black workers in federal and local government and the private sector. It has a total annual budget of close to two million dollars, and Bakewell gives his eighty-five-thousand-dollar annual salary back to his organization. "The beauty of it is that we don't have one wonderful white man giving us a million dollars a year," Bakewell told *Time*'s Monroe. "We've got ten thousand black people giving ten dollars, a hundred thousand black people giving us one dollar, and that becomes a spigot that you can't shut off."

On the weekends when I'm at home in Cleveland, I do what I call "weekend mentoring." Each Saturday, from 10:00 A.M. to 3:00 P.M. in one-hour intervals, I dispense free marketing and networking advice to budding entrepreneurs and/or professionals looking for jobs or ideas on how to maximize their skills. Most of these brothers and sisters just need someone to talk to whom they respect, someone to help them think through their ideas and problems. Sometimes I feel like the "Godfather" without the guns and a hidden agenda. Quite frankly, I feel honored and empowered when I'm asked to help.

Our ancestors built pyramids and created a sophisticated culture with its own language, writing, and science at a time when other cultures were living in mud huts. Today, we are the most educated and professionally trained generation of Africans in the history of this planet. Surely we have the network and skills to solve our own problems. It is our responsibility, each of us, to become indispensable in our chosen field, and then to network vertically by reaching down and lifting up those in need of opportunity.

We have the responsibility to serve as beacons of hope for others, to embrace interdependence, and to discard self-centeredness. We must strive to create a new Underground Railroad for the twenty-first century to transport the entire black community and to free them by elevating perceptions, empowering them economically, and encouraging overall excellence!

"I was born to network."
OPRAH WINFREY

Oprah Winfrey is one of the most important figures in popular culture. Her broadcasting career began at WVOL radio in Nashville while she was still in high school. At nineteen, she became the youngest person and the first African-American woman to anchor Nashville's WTVF-TV news. She moved to Baltimore to coanchor the six o'clock news and the local talk show *People Are Talking*. She moved to Chicago to host WLS-TV's morning talk show *AM Chicago*. One year later, it became *The Oprah Winfrey Show*. A year after that, in 1986, *The Oprah Winfrey Show* entered national syndication. Oprah has earned seven Emmy Awards for Outstanding Talk Show Host and nine Emmy Awards for Outstanding Talk Show. She is one of only three women—the others are Lucille Ball and Mary Pickford—to own her own television and film production studios (Harpo, Inc.). As an actress, in 1995 she received both Academy and Golden Globe nominations for her portrayal of "Sofia" in *The Color Purple*. She is the founder of *O, The Oprah Magazine* and *Oxygen Media LLC*, and is an adjunct professor at Northwestern University. Oprah is a very generous philanthropist and child advocate; she initiated the National Child Protection Act, and President Clinton signed the bill, called the "Oprah Bill," into law in 1993. Says Oprah, "My philosophy is that not only are you responsible for your life, but doing the best at this moment puts you in the best place for the next moment."

Part Two

PARTY FOR A PURPOSE: THE POWER OF NETWORKING

4

Entrepreneurship and Networking:
Closing the Wealth Gap

Leap and the net will appear.
There will be a thousand unseen hands
waiting just for you.
—JOSEPH CAMPBELL

Today many people in the black community believe our future lies in creating new businesses and using entrepreneurship as a cornerstone for economic development,
wealth creation, and community building. The twenty-first century
will be the century of entrepreneurship for black people. I believe
one of the major goals of blacks should be that of closing the income and wealth gap in America and other industrialized countries.
Why focus on money now? Not exclusively for the reasons you
may think. My experience tells me on a spiritual level most black
people feel that wealth is not happiness per se. Why do they feel
that? Because many of us know people who have a lot of money yet
are not happy. They are not happy because of a series of bad
choices they've made with their money. I'm not saying that money
is not important to black people—it is; it's right up there with oxygen. However, what we have observed is that wealth for many is
really the highest level of freedom. It's the freedom to have choices
and options in our lives—yes, unlimited choices if possible. Good
choices make us happy because they provide us with the opportunity to choose where we live, work, and play; to choose where our
children go to school; and to choose to have the things that make
our lives more comfortable. It is then the management of our

choices that is the essence of living. In a market-based economy, democratic capitalistic society, the one thing that can provide you more options and choices is wealth . . . money . . . benjamins.

In the 1970s the top 1 percent of Americans held 13 percent of the country's wealth. By 1995, the top 1 percent held 40 percent of the nation's wealth. In 1867 blacks in America controlled less than 2 percent of the nations wealth. In the year 2000 we still controlled less than 2 percent of the nation's wealth. We have made little progress. The rich are still getting richer. We need to participate, and we can participate in wealth-building. As a result of September 11 there were lost jobs and opportunities for everyone, but we felt it the most. September 11 proved once again that when America catches a cold, we catch pneumonia; when America bleeds, we hemorrhage. It is time to shift our thinking to profits, not just paychecks; from getting a job to creating a job. We must have more control over our destinies. To that end, the first critical wealth-building step for any ethnic group is job creation. Why? Because as we invest and build wealth, we can create work and jobs for our people. This is how we can help raise up the poor. This is what many immigrant groups understood and did when they first arrived in this great country. We've seen it among Jews, Hispanics, Asians, Arabs, and East Indians. There are two critical steps to creating jobs: first, our demonstrated excellence in the workplace, and second, small business development or entrepreneurship. Let's consider the first way for a moment.

While entrepreneurship is critically important to the economic development of a people, everyone can't be an entrepreneur. In fact, there are some black folks we've done business with who shouldn't be within one hundred yards of owning a business, and that's okay, because we need people of African descent doing corporate and government business with excellence. This is important, because the ability to effectively compete for public- and private-sector jobs and then perform them "with excellence" helps to change the mislabeled stereotypes of black people. It helps us to demonstrate to the skeptics that we can do more then sing, dance, act, and excel at sports. Most importantly, working in the public and private sector lays the foundation and builds the networks for others to follow behind you to secure similar or better jobs in preparation for going out on our own. Additionally, it protects our strategic interest in the public- and private-sector workplace, because I'm not convinced that if we were not in the halls of government or the boardrooms of corporations contributing to the growth of their businesses the "powers that be" would even be thinking about us or our needs. We need black people everywhere! This step represents the opportunity for the intergenerational transfer of knowledge and even greater opportunity. That was the vision of our parents. They told us to "get a good education and get a good job" so that we could open new doors for future generations. Today the boomer generation is telling its children to "get a good education and *create* a job." Create a job through your demonstrated excellence in the workplace. Create a job for yourself and your children, and if you can, create work and jobs for our people. This is critical in a world that will increasingly depend on cultural minorities and women to work, manage, and lead this and other great countries.

The second way to create jobs is through small business development, by becoming an entrepreneur. As an entrepreneur, you are taking more risks, seizing new opportunities, going through the rigorous training and pitfalls of stepping out on your own. It was Booker T. Washington who said: "No people ever got upon its feet and obtained the respect and confidence of the world which did not lay its foundations in successful business enterprise." Entrepreneurship not only has a profound economic impact on our community, it is also a force that creates social value and a resource for community development. Where "community" exists, it gives its members identity, a sense of belonging, and a measure of security. I am convinced that entrepreneurship cannot only help those who elect to start and grow a business, but can also help those who join entrepreneurs in their effort. Are more blacks doing this? Of course they are—just look at the statistics. They are both encouraging and discouraging.

STARTING MORE BUSINESSES IN THE TWENTY-FIRST CENTURY

The U.S. Department of Commerce's 1997 Survey of Minority-Owned Business Enterprises reported that there were nearly 2.9 million minority-owned businesses in 1997, generating a projected $564 billion in revenue by 1999 and employing nearly 4.3 million workers. Minority businesses have been increasing rapidly, growing 136 percent over the last decade. The growth in revenues has been even more astonishing—626 percent over the last decade, before accounting for inflation. But business activity varies substantially among minority groups. The 1.2 million Hispanic-owned businesses were the most numerous minority-owned enterprises, followed by Asian and Pacific Islander–owned businesses at nearly 832,000, and black-owned businesses at 823,000. While all minority-owned businesses increased 136 percent, the number of Hispanic-owned businesses increased more rapidly from 1987 to 1997 than did other types of minority-owned businesses. The Hispanic growth rate was 184 percent, compared with 120 percent for Asian and Pacific Islander–owned businesses and 94 percent for black-owned businesses.

What is interesting is that minority groups vary significantly with respect to total revenues and average revenue per business. Although Asian and Pacific Islander businesses represented just one third of all minority-owned businesses, they accounted for $307 billion, or 54 percent, of the revenues all minority-owned businesses generated in 1997. Hispanic-owned businesses accounted for a smaller share, at $186 billion or 33 percent of all revenues. Black-owned businesses represented a little over $71 billion or about 13 percent of all revenues. The differences in annual revenue per business are especially striking: $336,000 for Asian-owned businesses, $155,000 for Hispanic-owned businesses, and just $86,000 for black-owned businesses. As you can see, we're at the bottom of every statistic in spite of our 370-year investment in this country. I believe the following statistics are key for sustaining and growing a business. In general, revenues are far higher for businesses with employees than for self-employed individuals without employees. Asians are the most likely to have employees; 266,000, or 32 percent of Asian-owned businesses, had them. This compares with 212,000 or 18 percent of the Hispanic-owned businesses and just 93,000 or slightly over 11 percent of black-owned businesses. Again we've performed the lowest! Here's an interesting point: Among all businesses with employees that were in existence in 1992, 75 percent were still operating in 1996. In other words, businesses with a network of employees stay in business longer.

OVERCOMING THE BUSINESS START-UP BARRIERS

In spite of the myriad of significant new business opportunities for cultural minorities in America, the question that has plagued most social scientists has been, why has there been such a low number of blacks in particular going into business over the last thirty-five years? It is not like entrepreneurialism is new to black people. In spite of the fact that historical racism prevented blacks from gaining access to resources and fair opportunities to develop businesses, blacks in America still found ways to invent things and market goods and services for profit in a segregated society where the majority race would not insure us, bury us, lend us money, portray us fairly in the press, or market things like health and grooming products to us. Make no mistake, entrepreneurial success runs in our race.

As far back as 1798, James Forten, Sr., of Philadelphia owned a successful sail-making company. Thomas Day of Milton, North Carolina, had a successful furniture-making company in 1818. In 1831 John Mashow had a successful shipbuilding firm in Massachusetts. William Lerdesdorff opened the first hotel in San Francisco in 1846, organized the first horse race in 1847, and became the first black millionaire eighteen years before the end of slavery. Black communities and businesses grew and thrived in the 1800s and early 1900s all over the South and West. The famous black Wall Streets of Tulsa, Oklahoma; Durham, North Carolina; and Atlanta, Georgia, were the envy of the majority population. So what happened after the civil rights laws were enacted in 1964? Social scientists have concluded that the following six reasons explain the comparatively low numbers of entrepreneurial blacks:

1. Young blacks have less exposure to entrepreneurial role models; this decreases the pool to draw from. One important avenue for increasing the supply of black entrepreneurs is to increase the pool of young blacks that see themselves as "potential" entrepreneurs. Studies stress that role models, entrepreneurship education, and perceptions about entrepreneurship are extremely important and set the foundation for becoming an entrepreneur long before an individual actually makes the decision to become one. If we are to foster entrepreneurship, we must support and reinforce the perceptions that it is possible, highly regarded, and socially and personally desirable, because it is from our pool of young adults that the supply of entrepreneurs for the twenty-first Century will eventually be drawn.

A recent study by the Gallup Organization on black high school students' attitudes and knowledge with respect to entrepreneurship stated:

- 75 percent rated their knowledge of entrepreneurship as fair to very poor
- the average test score on basic entrepreneurial knowledge was 38 percent
- 84 percent of high school students believe that there should be more entrepreneurship education in schools

- 75 percent of black high school students want to start a business of their own

Add to that, the National Urban League reported in 2001 that more than two thirds of adults surveyed for its annual review of black America said they would like to be entrepreneurs. There is now an important shift back to entrepreneurship in black America.

2. The second reason for low numbers for black entrepreneurs is that there are fewer informal and formal networks for securing key resources and information. Let me explain. Most entrepreneurs don't get their ideas in a vacuum; a new idea usually comes onto the radar screen from someone in their social network. Then, they use others in their network to validate the idea. In other words, recognizing a business opportunity is a social process. Your network—or lack of network—can help or hinder initial idea development. Other important entrepreneurial resources can also be accessed through a network, including capital, labor, and emotional support.

3. Another reason for low entrepreneurial numbers among blacks is lower net worth, fewer assets, or less access to capital. As a result we generally have smaller capital investment, leading to less financial leverage and undercapitalized business and fewer business choices. As my father once told me, "If you've only got a few dollars, you can only do a few things." Historically, this reason has been driven by a lack of education and racist and unfair lending practices in the public and private sector.

4. There is greater influence by the family on the amount of capital a potential entrepreneur chooses to invest in his or her business. The conversation goes something like this with your significant other: "You're gonna do what with our life savings?" Then there is a

one-word negative reference to your race ending in
"Please!" We have become a risk-averse culture due to
fear of loss of our hard-earned and scarce resources.

5. Blacks have fewer years of "hands-on experience" and
business experience . . . we start later. Studies by age
suggest that business ownership comes later for blacks
than for other racial or ethnic groups in American
society. The majority of black business owners are
between the ages of 35 and 44, which is also true of
business ownership in other racial or ethnic groups.
However, only 17 percent of black business owners are
25 to 34 years old, the lowest percentage across groups.
In addition, just 1.8 percent of black business owners are
under 25 years, which again is the lowest percentage
across all groups. In my case it took me 42 years to gain
the educational and business experience to start my
business 14 years ago. But even that was not enough to
thoroughly prepare me for the rigors of entrepreneurship. A business mentor or experience in a family
business would have made a huge difference in my life.

6. The final reason for low numbers of entrepreneurial
blacks is that too many blacks have not put the proper
amount of time into their businesses. Nearly 90 percent
of black-owned businesses have no employees and are
either something the entrepreneur invests in part-time or
sees as a second job.

None of these reasons is impossible to overcome. Understanding them and the effective use of marketing helps.

DOING WELL WHILE DOING GOOD

With the workplace dramatically changing and long-term job security now a thing of the past, blacks must use their education,
skills, and experience to create jobs and seek profits, not just paychecks. We have observed that government is an instrument of

business. Politics/government does not control business; it's the other way around. Thus if we want to have greater control over government and maximize the tax system (which was written by land and business owners) we must have greater impact on the business of America. President Calvin Coolidge told America in the 1920s that "the business of America is business." In 2001 blacks accounted for 4 percent of the 20.8 million nonfarm businesses and 0.4 percent of $18.6 trillion in receipts for all American business. That means we are not a significant factor in business production, we only really matter on the consumption side. It is dangerous to live in a country where you are not significantly contributing to the business of that country. We must fix this as soon as possible. It is now clearer to many blacks in America that the smartest and least risky way to great wealth in America is to be self-employed, and if you stay the course, go through the pain, build the business, and hire more people, the long-term prospects of creating more role models and building greater wealth that can be transferred to future generations is excellent.

In fact, a recent study listed the top five categories of self-made millionaires. They were:

1. 74 percent self-employed. What is interesting to me is that I live on a cul-de-sac street in a very exclusive neighborhood with forty-five six- and seven-figure homes, and nobody is employed by anyone else; everybody is self-employed.
2. 10 percent senior executives. With new government scrutiny and regulations, this will change.
3. 10 percent doctors and lawyers. No surprises here, although with managed care it's become more difficult to gain great wealth.
4. 5 percent salespeople. It's about time black people did more selling than buying. My advice: Find something to sell, even if it's only part-time.
5. 1 percent stock market, inventions, sports, entertainment, and lottery winners combined.

Bottom line: Entrepreneurship is open to anyone willing to take the risks and do the work . . . most of the barriers are now down. In my book *Race for Success: The Ten Best Business Opportunities for Blacks in America* (William Morrow and Company, New York, 1998), I outline and discuss in great detail the ten areas blacks need to focus on for the next several generations if we are to "make a profit and make a difference" or to "do well while doing good." Here is a quick summary of those areas that provide us the most important opportunities:

Education. This $665 billion industry needs more black educators and entrepreneurs. It also needs new and better schools, as well as more preschool and after-school programs. Additionally, teaching our teachers and children how to apply technology to education is critical. These are business opportunities waiting to explode. All of this will develop significantly in the next twenty to thirty years, thus making our schools more globally competitive and more responsive to our country's long-term needs. In cities like Milwaukee, Chicago, Cleveland, and Detroit, blacks have started over two hundred charter and private schools for black children. These schools employ hundreds of black educators, support staff, and suppliers in addition to providing urban kids with a better education. Everybody wins!

Finance and Banking. John Rogers, owner of Ariel Capital Management, a two-billion-dollar black-owned fund management firm in Chicago, is helping blacks invest and multiply their money through selling mutual funds and other stock portfolios. Cleveland-based investment banker Eric Small created a mutual fund product of successful black businesses traded on the stock exchange. Other black bankers, financial advisers, insurance brokers, and stockbrokers are employing similar methods to help blacks more wisely invest, shed debt, and multiply their money. I believe blacks know the banking world; it's now time to expand into the late Reginald Lewis's world of high "corporate" finance.

Small Business Development. At nearly $600 billion in 2002, according to an economic forecast study from the University of

Georgia, black buying power in America ranks among the world's richest economies, larger than the economy of the entire continent of Africa; yet less than 5 percent of this wealth recycles in our own communities. A recent survey of 125th Street in Harlem showed other cultural groups owned 90 percent of all businesses, but we're still the customers. There is tremendous opportunity, as well as a great need, to start and own our neighborhood businesses, both urban and suburban, both retail and manufacturing. Where are the black-theme restaurants? There are over eighteen thousand pizzerias in America, producing $22 billion a year in revenue, employing over one million people. Billions more are being made in Chinese/Japanese restaurants, Greek diners, and Jewish delis. The opportunity to use our culture and business savvy to address the billion-dollar potential of theme restaurants and fast foods is right there in our faces.

Technology. The information superhighway and digital technology are providing new economic opportunities and distribution outlets for our products and services. This is a perfect arena in which to expand our tremendous creativity by developing new software and moving into positions where we can influence and control the content of the Internet and World Wide Web. "Black Planet," "Black Voices," and many other Afrocentric Web sites and on-line services are good examples. Closing the home computer gap between blacks and whites is another major opportunity.

Publishing. Only in the last ten years has publishing discovered the financial power of black writers and reading audiences. Before that, black writers had a difficult time getting published. This was based on three myths: Black people don't read books, black people don't buy books, and white people don't buy books by black writers about black life. After *Savoy*, *Vibes*, and *Heart & Soul* magazines were successfully launched and books by authors such as Maya Angelou, Toni Morrison, Walter Mosley, E. Lynn Harris, and Terry McMillan hit the *New York Times* best-seller list, the industry woke up. Today there are huge new opportunities in all publishing and print media endeavors.

Real Estate Development. Real estate and housing are prime business opportunities for black people. Land is limited, and survey after survey shows that proximity to downtown America is becoming desirable again for both housing and business. Technology and home-based businesses will increase the value of real estate. According to the Washington, D.C.-based Hamilton Securities Group, $2.6 trillion in multifamily and commercial real estate equity and debt will change hands over the next decade. Retro migration back to the city is in. These are our neighborhoods, and we should be the prime developers and contractors of the regentrification of decaying urban America.

Entertainment and Music. Like the sports industry, show business is another place where we have a high profile and also spend a lot of time and money. But when it comes to controlling the product, we're just beginning to get our feet wet. Certain segments (and their offshoots) of the entertainment industry—specifically, film, television, and music—are rapidly becoming arenas of spectacular growth for black people looking to get involved behind the scenes in the many divisions and departments within this multibillion-dollar industry. The hip-hop generation has led the way.

Sports. By any economic standard, black sports stars are earning top money, yet it's obvious we all can't be Tiger Woods. The opportunities in sports are not all "in the field." Former NBA star Isiah Thomas had for years been the only basketball player to invest his money in a team (the Toronto Raptors). In 2002, billionaire founder of BET Robert L. Johnson purchased the Charlotte basketball franchise for $300 million, becoming the first black to have a majority stake in a NBA franchise. That's just the beginning of a change, as a few big-money players are getting together in ways that can really pay off. With these new ventures you can expect the front office staff to become more inclusive of blacks, women, and other races and cultures; the possibilities all the way down the ladder are enormous.

Health Care. This very broad category is expected to increase twice as fast as the rest of the economy. An aging population, as well as medical advancements, is driving the need for health-related occupations. As long as insurance companies and hospitals mandate shorter hospital stays for patients, the increased demand for health care services and those who can provide them will continue. Once more, black people are ideally suited to meet these needs. All trends in health care point toward prevention, wellness, and holistic therapies that integrate mental, physical, and emotional well-being—the hallmarks of our healing traditions. Just as important, black doctors, dentists, scientists, and technologists will be in demand. The needs are great, the opportunities abounding.

Global Commerce. Technology and instant global telecommunications are creating discontent among the 2.5 billion people still living under socialism and communism. People all over the world can now witness the "spoils" of democratic capitalism at work. As governments shift (i.e., Russia and China), hundreds of millions will want the myriad of choices enjoyed by the great democracies of the world. Opportunities to provide these products and services will be opening up all over Africa, Asia, Latin America, Eastern Europe, South and Central America, and the Caribbean.

But the key concepts for new business development must be strategic alliances, joint ventures, and partnerships. No longer can we have eight construction firms in a city with four people each. We've got to come together. We must collaborate or we will shrivel up and die! We have much work to do, but there is plenty of opportunity.

FOUR KEY FACTORS FOR ENTREPRENEURIAL SUCCESS

While the opportunities to start a new business today are unlimited, the entrepreneurial process revolves around four key factors: talent, opportunity, capital, and know-how.

Talent. Talent refers to individuals who recognize market opportunities and then create organizations to take advantage of those opportunities. Entrepreneurs are therefore dreamers who take action. They envision the future and then set out to do something to make it occur. Where there is a pool of talented entrepreneurial individuals, there is the possibility of growth and community development. Research on entrepreneurship shows that those who become entrepreneurs demonstrate a desire to control and direct, a propensity for taking calculated risks, and a problem-solving style. In fact, the most often-quoted reason for becoming an entrepreneur is not to get a lot of money but rather to be one's own boss and to control one's own destiny.

Opportunity. Entrepreneurs recognize and pursue opportunities. An opportunity is customer-driven. It is rooted in meeting a real need in the marketplace, or solving a real problem. Effective entrepreneurs understand the environment of their target market. They know the concerns, worries, and problems of their customers and provide real solutions to real needs—not perceived or assumed needs. They can sense opportunity. In the process of seizing opportunity, they sometimes find out that they can be good at something that they did not expect to be good at. I'm reminded of the story of the boy who took his ball and bat in the backyard to practice his hitting. He told himself that he would be the greatest hitter of all time; he tossed the ball in the air, swung, and missed. He picked the ball up, told himself that he would have a longer hitting streak than Joe DiMaggio, tossed the ball in the air, swung, and missed again. He picked the ball up one more time, told himself that he would hit more home runs than Babe Ruth and Henry Aaron combined, tossed the ball in the air, and missed a third time. Then, he picked up the ball, thought for a moment, and exclaimed, "Wow, what a pitcher!"

Capital. This may be the most elusive factor in the entrepreneurial process. The elusiveness stems from the diverse nature of money and its sources of supply. Yet, capital is a critical element for every entrepreneurial venture. Because most start-up entrepreneurs use personal funds, their funds are quite limited and the search for capital then becomes more challenging, complex, and uncertain and at times very frustrating. One entrepreneur was so frustrated with his search for money that he went into a church to pray to God for help. While he was kneeling in the pew, he heard a deep voice from above say, "Do not give up hope." The entrepreneur asked, "Is that You, God?" "Yes," came the reply, "it is I, the Lord." The entrepreneur said, "Lord, I've been trying to raise a million dollars for what seems like a million years." The Lord said, "Remember, a million years to you is like a second to me." "What's a million dollars like, Lord?" asked the entrepreneur. "A million dollars to you is like a penny to me," he responded. "Then could I have one of your pennies, Lord?" the entrepreneur asked. "Yes," said the Lord. "In a second!" Money is hard to find, but it will find you if you are prepared, passionate, and committed. Tennis great Arthur Ashe summed it up nicely. "Start where you are, work with what you have, do what you can."

Know-How. This may be the most critical factor in ensuring the continued success of an entrepreneurial venture. Every entrepreneur must develop and/or acquire the skill and expertise to run an enterprise. This involves the practical but essential ability to manage change, personally and organizationally. Personal know-how requires skills such as leading, communicating, listening, negotiating, and team building. Organizational know-how involves learning about business books such as marketing, finance, accounting, and business planning. Importantly, entrepreneurs also gain know-how through their ability to utilize networks. Research on the sociology of entrepreneurship has shown that entrepreneurs learn from social relationships that expand their access to information, resources, and support. A particularly powerful influence on your decision to start a company is the presence of role models or mentors who through their own entrepreneurial activities present good examples for would-be entrepreneurs. Entrepreneurship is an equal opportunity process. You don't need to be degreed, certified, or accredited, although it will help greatly. Passion is the enthusiasm, joy, and zeal that come from the energetic and relentless pursuit of a worthy and uplifting purpose. In the entrepreneur, it is described as drive—the determined, optimistic, and persistent desire to succeed at one's own venture. It is the "fire in the belly" that makes the impossible possible. "Getting ahead in a difficult business or profession requires avid faith in yourself. That is why some people with mediocre talent but with great inner drive go much further than people with vastly superior talent!" says the internationally acclaimed actress Sophia Loren.

Entrepreneurship is embedded in networks of continuing social relations. The more extensive his web of relationships in the community, the more the entrepreneur is likely to have access to opportunities and the greater chance of solving problems quickly and, ultimately, the greater chance of success for the venture. Finally, it's important to understand that you cannot do these things in a vacuum. Work diligently on cultivating friends, and relationships, at work, at home, and in the community. I often tell people that the key to success is directly related to your willingness to ask people for help, and whomever you are asking for help is your network, your infrastructure of support. Therefore, spend a lot of time building your friendships, and relationships; it is critical to your success in business and life.

RECIPROCITY: LEVERAGING OUR PURCHASING POWER

As you embark on the goal of creating work and jobs for our people, and closing the wealth gap through entrepreneurship, you will need to understand one other thing. We need to learn how to use and leverage our powerful purchasing power with companies that have demonstrated their support and commitment to the betterment of our community. Companies such as IBM, Coke, Pepsi, Anheuser-Busch and Ford have demonstrated a deep commitment to black people. Theirs is not a new, "Johnny come lately" marketing ploy.

If there were an historical and modern-day model for today's Fortune 500, it would be Ford Motor Company. It was through the leadership of Henry Ford that the company was and continues to be one of a handful of industrial-based companies committed to economic empowerment and upward mobility for all of America's people; especially those who have been left out and disenfranchised. It was Henry Ford in the early 1900s who helped lay the foundation for a solid immigrant and minority working class. His visionary idea of $5 a day, guaranteed wages, was available to anyone willing to do the work. This helped to start the great northern migration of blacks. Many baby boomer parents left sharecropping and low-wage jobs in the South to join in this new northern industrial revolution. Henry Ford was not afraid to embrace and support the disenfranchised. Was he perfect? Absolutely not. Did he make a difference when few others were willing to risk their businesses and images? Yes he did. That legacy remains to this day.

Today however, what is most significant is that Ford Motor Company spends more working with minority businesses than any other company in the world: $3.5 billion in 2000 and $3.1 billion in 2001, which is a larger dollar amount than the gross national product of some small island nations. Ford minority suppliers have created more than 39,000 jobs in our communities. Today Ford has one of the largest groups of minority employees, professionals, and management in corporate America. It also has the largest group of minority auto dealers in America, and is actively seeking more. *Fortune* magazine called it one of the Top 50 Places for blacks, Hispanics, and Asians to work. They are the models for corporations around the world. Many, like McDonald's, General Motors, and DaimlerChrysler, are making important strides in supplier, employment, and ownership diversity. It is companies like these we must support now and in the future, while at the same time continuing to seek reciprocity for our investment in them. Said another way, if they are not supporting the things that are important to us, don't support them.

TEN STEPS TO STARTING DOWN YOUR ENTREPRENEURIAL PATH

1. *Do what you love;* passion and purpose, not profits, are the fuel that drives the small business engine forward.

2. *Save your money to fuel your dreams*—"Save your money and your money will save you"; "Live below your means, invest the rest." You will need capital to get started in your business.

3. *Prepare yourself;* know your business backward and forward before you take the plunge.

4. *Enter a new field with growth potential;* the competition is less established.

5. *Read;* scour the business sections of your local bookstores for books on functional subjects such as marketing, planning, and minority business enterprises (MBEs).

6. *Check out local universities and colleges* to find those that offer free or low-cost business consulting and planning services.

7. *Increase your visibility.* Let people know you exist. Business is not for shrinking violets.

8. *Consider joint ventures* . . . strategic alliances and partnerships with existing enterprises. Sometimes it's better to purchase an existing business than to start one from scratch.

9. *Join or contact a minority business organization,* black chamber of commerce, and/or the National Minority Supplier Development Council, a private-sector institution that provides access to capital for minority businesses in the United States. These are good networks set up to help you start and grow your business.

10. *Be creative when looking for potential clients.* Don't forget your former employer—always leave on good terms. Bottom line: Network, network, and network some more.

TEN REASONS FOR DOING BUSINESS WITH MINORITIES

Joseph R. Hudson, who is president of the Hudson Strategic Group, a management consulting firm in Atlanta, Georgia, offers his "Ten Best Reasons to Do Business with Minorities," which I wholeheartedly endorse for whites, but *also* for blacks themselves:

1. *The number of qualified minority firms is increasing.* The U.S. Chamber of Commerce, in 1997 (the latest report released), stated the number of minority-owned businesses in the United States increased by 136 percent to 2.9 million businesses, employing 4.3 million people and generating a projected $564 billion in revenue by 1999. Minority businesses are increasing faster than white-owned businesses.

2. *Minority firms are more competitive.* With increased opportunities to sell their goods and services to corporations, minority businesses become more competitive. A survey by the National Minority Supplier Development Council showed that 86 percent of corporations demand quality, and that 75 percent of minority suppliers are working harder to provide it.

3. *Minority firms improve the economic viability of communities.* When corporations do business with minority companies, those companies create jobs, which in turn helps increase the overall social and economic viability of minority communities.

4. *Minority firms help expand the consumer base.* Because they help create wealth in communities, strong minority companies also are the key to expanding the consumer base. That is one reason why Ford increased its minority economic development efforts. Research showed that the black community alone accounted for more than $30 billion in new and used car sales in 2001. Ford concluded that if it were able to secure one incremental percentage point in the auto market by increasing its business with minority firms, the associated economic benefit to Ford would be an estimated $40 million a year.

5. *Minority firms reinforce corporate responsibility.* According to Hudson, this reason is best illustrated by the vision and commitment of corporations like Disney. In late 1982, then-chairman of the board Carl Walker formalized the company's minority business enterprise program. Before then, Disney did less than one million dollars in business with minority-owned companies.

6. *It's the right thing to do.* Faced with increasing global competition, it has become the right thing to do for corporations to

develop suppliers they can count on—and that includes minority vendors.

7. *The cost of not doing may exceed the cost of doing.* Some corporations report that they have saved money when they switched to minority vendors. Why? In part because new vendors may not have the same expenses as older, more established vendors, and therefore, may be able to offer goods and services at lower prices, Hudson believes. Minority businesses, which tend to be smaller and newer, certainly fit into that category.

8. *Minority organizations are corporate allies.* Minority business organizations such as the Atlanta Business League, the National Minority Supplier Development Council, and black chambers of commerce have long been allies of major corporations. And major corporations have played an important role in the development of these groups by assigning their corporate employees to serve on the organizations' boards and special committees. Through these networking relationships, the employees, their corporations, and the black business groups have all benefited, according to Hudson.

9. *The competition is doing it.* Admittedly, Ford's interest in the minority market share may stem in part from the interest of its competitors in that same market. General Motors, DaimlerChrysler, and Toyota all have minority enterprise development programs. Even if every corporation in an industry doesn't realize the intrinsic benefits of helping to develop minority businesses, they certainly can recognize the benefits from a competitive standpoint, according to Hudson.

10. *It makes good press.* The UniWorld Group, one of our nation's premier African-American ad agencies, believes that credible minority economic development efforts offer corporations significant marketing opportunities. A good track record on minority business development also helps corporations—black and white—enhance their overall public image and defend against advocacy group attacks.

"Networking is one of the keys to success."
TERESA HAIRSTON

Teresa Hairston is the founder and CEO of Horizon Concepts, Inc., parent company of *Gospel Today* and *Gospel Industry Today* magazines. She is also a founding member of the national industry organization known as the United Industry Council, and founder of the Gospel Heritage Foundation, which is an organization dedicated to the preservation and perpetuation of Gospel heritage. Teresa's formative years were filled with music and she pursued her first employment opportunity at age seven as a church musician. Her service to churches continued for the next thirty years. Soon after relocating to New York City, Teresa assumed the position of national director of promotions for Savoy Records. Teresa worked with legends such as James Cleveland and Albertina Walker, among many others. During her time at Savoy, she began to generate a small newsletter for the company. With Savoy's okay, Teresa began production of the newsletter, *Gospel Score,* independently from the company. A year later, *Gospel Score* wasn't proving successful. But, giving God the credit for her perseverance, she turned the newsletter into a magazine, and it succeeded.

5

Getting Together to Get Ahead

When spiderwebs unite, they can tie up a lion.
— ETHIOPIAN PROVERB

arolyn Watts Allen and her husband, Robert, both African-American professionals, had lived in Cleveland Heights, a culturally diverse upper-middle-class suburb of Cleveland, for ten years. Although they had attained what many only dream of, the Allens were city lovers who often found themselves discussing the possibility of one day moving back. Their philosophy is that successful blacks should be part of the rejuvenation of the traditional black urban neighborhoods. "Our motivation was to live out that philosophy and maybe help start a trend," said Carolyn. "We discovered that there were others already out there wanting to do the same thing."

Their dreamy "someday" discussions about one day leading a return migration to the city were jolted into immediacy and reality when then Cleveland mayor Michael R. White asked Carolyn to become the city's public-safety director in charge of both the police and fire departments. City law required that if Carolyn accepted the position, she had to live within the city limits. She took the job and met the residency requirement initially by renting a house in a city neighborhood with her husband.

After Carolyn had settled into her new position, she and her husband, a research technician for NASA, took their bearings and decided that what they would really like would be to build their own house and make a social statement at the same time. Their dream was to build not just one house, but an entire new neighborhood to which couples who shared their desire for a community would be drawn. They wanted to be part of the rejuvenation of Cleveland—a role in which professional blacks have been significant players.

And so, the Allens built a network that could well serve as a model. At first, they contacted friends: a lawyer, a pastor, and other middle- and upper-middle-class blacks in their circle. Eventually, by tapping into friends and friends of friends, they pulled together sixty-seven potential house builders.

As a model for their project, they focused on the home of a police district commander, William Tell, who was noted for being the only man of his rank who lived within the district he commanded. Tell's new, large house in the poverty-stricken Hough neighborhood had become a symbol of urban renewal and black gentrification in Cleveland's inner city. For $147,000, the police commander had constructed a three-thousand-square-foot house on three quarters of an acre. This was value that anyone could recognize.

The obvious presence of the high-ranking police official in the neighborhood had also caught the attention of would-be criminals in the area. The Hough neighborhood had one of the lowest crime rates in the city. With the diminished crime, city services improved. This attracted other urban pioneers, including those in the Allens' network.

Realizing that commitment was essential, the network required an initial nonrefundable twenty-five-dollar fee for those interested in the project and, later, a five-hundred-dollar refundable fee for the right to partake in development decisions. In the end, twenty families signed on for what became known as the Renaissance Project.

Many of those involved in this network were natives of the inner city who had joined the black exodus to the suburbs but wanted to go back. Others were lured by the economic advantages of both cheaper housing costs and proximity to their jobs in the city. All of them were interested in the social implications and impact of the Renaissance Project. They hoped to inspire those who were already in the inner city to share their excitement.

These network members, then, shared common interests and goals. They also shared concerns about the move back into the city, particularly when it came to the school system; but all were devoted to the idea of improving it by taking an active role from within.

With the power of their network, the Renaissance Project managed to ease financial concerns over the risk of urban pioneering by soliciting an incentive package from the city. They received a fifteen-year abatement on city property taxes; a $20,000 loan that had to be paid back only if the individual moved; and low mortgage rates that provided monthly payments as low as $725 on a $150,000 house with a 20 percent down payment. This partnership of public and private interests is but one example of the innovative programs of Mayor Michael White, who while in office endeavored to rebuild Cleveland's neighborhoods.

The Renaissance Project included at least twenty new houses built around a private park and recreation area financed by the homeowners, a diverse group that included two teachers, two clergy members, two U.S. mail carriers, a construction worker, several city employees, a chemical engineer, and an FBI agent. When completed in the fall of 1994, their model Urban Village featured a tennis court, a half basketball court, a children's playground, a jogging trail, and a picnic area. The houses face outward toward the existing neighborhood residences, not inward and away from them.

The Renaissance Project network members did well while doing good, and their dreams became reality, all because they realized the value of working together toward a shared interest. "Two thirds of the people who came into the group were friends or friends of friends, and the others were recruited by the local housing development corporation, Hough Area Partners in Progress," Carolyn told me. "Robert and I got this started, but we have people who have hung with it for three years and made it work."

Their successful networking project to return to the city and rejuvenate a neighborhood has been both a social statement and a "spiritual experience," she said, adding, "We have a real belief that by working together and building in this community, we are going to give hope to a lot of people. We want to do away with the philosophy that success means getting away from your own people. We want people to stay and be part of this neighborhood and give hope and inspiration to other black people. We also want other black professionals to recognize that there are blacks working hard to make the city viable, and we want them to give some thought to being part of the rejuvenation. We know that blacks who have moved to the suburbs talk about returning, just as we did. And we want them to put their money where their mouths are and be part of the solution. By doing this, we are saying this neighborhood is not desolate, it is worth saving. We are giving hope." Today, the Renaissance Project has helped to totally revitalize housing, education, and commerce in the once-riot-torn Hough community.

SHARING THE WEALTH BY NETWORKING

This is a classic example of networking for social change. The Renaissance Project network grew out of the Allens' frustration with the erosion of the old Urban Village in Cleveland. Government programs had failed them. So, powered by an idea and possessed of information, they built a network that overcame the failures of government. What an exciting and empowering thing it is to make the world better with an idea and a network to enact it. The Allens and the other black folks involved in the Renaissance Project were not afraid to share their ideas, dreams, and resources with one another by networking. They are high achievers and big thinkers who are elevating the lives of many blacks through their network. This is vital to black people, because we have traditionally been excluded from the resources controlled by the white majority. Unity and collective work are essential to our emergence as a race whose stereotype is success. This requires interaction. It requires the construction of strongly rooted and mutually beneficial relationships.

Networking is the means to attain a goal, whether it is an immediate goal or a long-term project that may span decades. In the African tribes of our ancestors, individuals with unique talents and abilities worked together for the common good of the tribe. Sometimes, that required sublimating the individual's self-interest in favor of the general welfare of the group, but the members of the tribe were willing to do that because it was the way of their culture. Networking expert Marilyn Ferguson, author of *The Aquarian Conspiracy*, lists conferences, phone calls, air travel, books, phantom organizations, papers, pamphleteering, photocopying, lectures, workshops, parties, grapevines, mutual friends, summit meetings, coalitions, tapes, and newsletters all as forms of networking. To this list I would of course add the phenomena of e-mail, list servers, electronic bulletin boards, and the World Wide Web. She notes also that networking is the twenty-first-century version of the ancient tribe, and that it will be the tool for the next step in human evolution. "The function of most networks is mutual support and enrichment, empowerment of the individual, and cooperation to effect change," she has written.

The Renaissance Project is an outstanding example of networking, and although black people are increasingly embracing networking, I still find in far too many of our people a "scarcity mentality" versus an "abundance mentality." Those with the scarcity mentality believe that the resources that they have, be it ideas, money, or opportunity, will disappear if they share them with others. In Chapter 10, you will hear blacks express their frustration over trying to network with other blacks who seem to feel that to share knowledge is to give up wealth. This attitude, while somewhat understandable for a people who have had to struggle so long and so hard, obviously inhibits our ability to network as a cultural community. The abundance mentality provides us with a psychological confidence that says there is plenty for all of us and that therefore if we share and enrich one another today, we will all flourish and be continually enriched by the totality of our knowledge.

How do you network? Say you have fifty business acquaintances—people you know well enough to call upon for information or a favor. Now, in all likelihood, each of those fifty acquaintances has at least fifty contacts, too, which means that your extended network now spans across twenty-five hundred people. Take this step two more times, and you now have an electronic organizer stocked with more than six million contacts. With this sort of network, you have power. You could probably even get through to the White House. Maybe even to Oprah.

When I give this example in my speaking engagements, white people in the audience usually nod in agreement, while blacks generally exhibit skepticism. I believe this is due to the fact that black people have traditionally failed to grasp the value of networking in their lives and careers. This is a serious and costly mistake. It could mean the difference between success and failure in the workplace; between a comfortable existence and a life of struggle.

In preceding chapters, I have illustrated how other cultural communities—Koreans, Japanese, and Jews—have embraced networking, while blacks have been slow to grasp and employ this valuable tool. There have been some notable exceptions, of course. John H. Johnson and other black business pioneers developed early grassroots network systems that not only led to their own success, but also inspired many others to seek the riches within their own culture. Earl Graves, publisher of *Black Enterprise* magazine, can rightfully claim to be one of the leaders of the modern networking movement among black business professionals. A man of vision, he developed, marketed, and produced black America's first formalized networking forums around the country, and brought together thousands of black professionals, introducing them to the networking concept.

As one of those inspired by these Afrocentric networking pioneers, I can now see the spawning of the next generation of black networking professionals and entrepreneurs. There are thousands and thousands of young, well-educated, highly motivated black men and women eager to make a contribution to America and to their own cultural community. In the past, blacks have networked through our churches, social clubs, and close-knit neighborhoods. But those networks, while valuable for their moral support and positive reinforcement, are by themselves no longer powerful enough to serve our increasingly sophisticated needs. We need networks that provide job information and opportunities in the marketplace. What is needed today is a much wider network to supply information, support, and expertise. As America's acceptance of diversity proceeds, the opportunities expand, and we must be ready to capitalize on them.

From the days of smoke signals to the present age of the Internet, people have shared what they have to meet mutual goals. The word *network* has been traced back to the sixteenth century, and referred to the use of fishing nets. We are still fishing, but now for information, resources, and support.

THE SUCCESS NETWORK FOR YOU

I believe one of the keys to success is directly tied to your willingness to ask people for help. Whomever you're asking for help is in fact your network, your infrastructure of support.

I am going to provide you with some guidelines and tools for plugging into any network that interests you. But remember to think Afrocentrically when you network. It is vital that you join in this movement, which many see as the logical continuation of the civil rights movement. *The Wall Street Journal* carried a front-page story describing the scope of the emerging black business networks:

> . . . the goal of the newer networks is to overcome the isolation and frustration of working in predominantly white, male-dominated corporations. As a result of these special channels, blacks are getting a faster start, vying for better

jobs and finding emotional encouragement from black colleagues even as they develop and maintain similar valuable ties with white colleagues and classmates.

I agree. It is *vitally* important for black professionals and entrepreneurs to network with blacks and with whites. After all, what is one of our main reasons for networking? It is to gain access to resources. That is the key. The more people you know, the more potential access to resources you command. Whites still control the great majority of all resources, but many more blacks are now strategically placed to gain greater access to a broader range of these resources, and this is why blacks must be gainfully employed in all sectors of the workplace. But networking with whites doesn't mean you can't think Afrocentrically.

The Seven Principles of Kwanzaa listed in chapter 3 are based on Afrocentric thought and perfectly suited for application to our community network. Here is how you can apply them.

Unity: Black people will first look within their own community when seeking information, resources, and influence in their professional and personal lives.

Self-determination: By learning both to network within the black community and to link up with those outside it, we will work to redefine our image in terms of success and achievement.

Collective work and responsibility: Black people will accept that ours is a collective rather than an individual struggle, and that we all bear responsibility to elevate the lives of all of our people.

Cooperative economics: Members of the network with financial resources will work to build an economic base that nurtures the black community, creating businesses, jobs, and hope.

Purpose: Black people will network within their own culture to collectively build upon our historical achievements through careful and thoughtful planning.

Creativity: Network members pledge to strive always to seek new methods for encouraging creativity and beauty within their community by nurturing the talent within it.

Faith: Black people will network within their race with the shared conviction that theirs is a righteous and ultimately victorious cause, because they are a race of successful people beloved by themselves and their Creator.

GETTING TOGETHER TO GET AHEAD

The point is often made that networking is a process or series of actions, not some static object. The important aspect of the growing national network of black professionals and entrepreneurs is not the network itself, but the process of establishing the links in it and the communication it facilitates among blacks dedicated to improving the lives of everyone in their cultural community.

Our Afrocentric network is designed to foster self-help, to encourage the exchange of information, and to lead to a change in both the image and the reality of the black community. It can serve to link you, through the blacks you know, to those whom they know in an ever-expanding pyramid of communications. The intent is to rebuild our community by reestablishing the link between those who have succeeded and those still striving for success. It is a tool for beating the system that has isolated us from one another. It is a key to clout, to money, to know-how, to self-confidence and self-esteem. It is also a license to ask for help when you need it, as well as a resource that helps you know whom to ask and how to ask for it. It allows you to help by serving as a resource for one another, and particularly for those who are less fortunate. In sum, it is getting together to get ahead.

How do you network? You already know the answer to that. In fact, whether you realize it or not, you already have a network of some kind. How many people do you know? Everyone you know is part of your personal network.

When you contact someone you know for assistance or information or just to communicate a thought or emotion, you are networking. When you call up a friend and ask her where to buy fresh vegetables, you are networking in a very elementary way. When you telephone a business associate and ask where that person goes for marketing information, you are networking in a very similar manner, but for a more sophisticated type of information.

Network Check

For a quick check of your network, follow these five steps:

1. Write down the names of people you regularly call for any type of information. To help your memory, check your address book, PDA business card file, or office directory. Don't forget your family, friends, and colleagues.
2. Next to people's names, write down what sort of information they have that you value. Also note the names of those people they know whom you would like to have as a resource.
3. Now write down information that you need but don't have access to. Put down the names of anyone you think might have that information.
4. Next to your own name, write down the information or contacts you have that might be valuable to other people.
5. Congratulations! You are primed and ready to network for success!

A network can be thought of as something quite simple or quite complex, depending on your perception of it. Think of a tree. Is a tree merely a source of shade, or is it a complex organism that can provide lumber, pulp, or firewood? Shelter, food, even great art can come from a tree if it is understood and put to use properly. Your network has an equally useful and diverse applicability. You can nurture your network, too, or let it just stand unused. It is up to you.

It has become an axiom of networking that it is not what you know, or even whom you know that is always important. What is really important is how well *you* are known. A strong network gets your name and what you do spread around out there. You can have all the talent and intelligence and drive in the world, but unless you can find the right outlet for it, you are just another suit on the sidewalk. A strong network connects you to opportunity and sets you up for success.

Why has an appreciation for the value of networking eluded so many black people? I believe the problem lies in our shared history, and I believe the solution does, too. Distrust and low self-esteem are the legacy of slavery and racial discrimination. As a child, I was told by my foster parents that "a nigga ain't shit" and that "you can't trust white folks." That narrowed my boyhood network considerably. The bottom line was, "Don't look for help, do it on your own." That mentality pulls the plug on networking for many black people.

When even blacks are raised to believe that other blacks are ignorant and useless, a powerless race of people is guaranteed. Although we have made enormous strides and have attained levels of success undreamed of by our parents and grandparents, this taint of ineptitude lingers over us and cripples our ability to network effectively. It is said that if something doesn't change, the hip-hop generation will be the first generation that will not do better than its parents.

Could it be that our lack of networking savvy is due to the fact that those of us who have "made it" view the reliance upon other black people as a sign of weakness, as some sort of intellectual welfare? Might it be that because of this perception, we want nothing to do with networking among our own people? Are we afraid to ask questions and reach out for assistance because we are inherently insecure and fear letting others know that we occasionally need a helping hand?

Harvard Medical School professor and former consultant to *The Bill Cosby Show*, Dr. Alvin Poussaint told me: "I think there is an issue of trust among blacks. To work and network together you have to have positive feelings about each other. If you feel blacks aren't worth much or that black identification will bring you down, then you can't network seriously. To do that, you have to believe that the group you are networking with is worthwhile, and also that it has power. Why would anyone identify with a group that has no power?"

Many blacks are unwilling to confront this deep self-doubt. Instead, they avoid the problem. They avoid establishing relationships with both whites and blacks. I believe that we can break free of this psychological bondage. I want you to believe it as well.

NETWORKING FOR ACCESS AND SUCCESS

The resurgence of black entrepreneurs and the emergence of black corporate professionals on the American economic scene has brought the whole issue of networking among our people to the forefront. In the past, we have used our churches, our social clubs, and community and professional organizations as platforms for civil rights initiatives and as sanctuaries from the pressures of living and working in a white-dominated environment. These organizations also offered moral support and positive reinforcement to soothe our ingrained sense of isolation and intimidation. They have not been effectively used, however, as networks for economic development. It wasn't so much that people did not want to help. It was just that they were not in a position to help. Now they are. That is why I believe our shared history is also an asset. We all know what struggle is, we all know the sting of racist insults and the debilitating impact of negative stereotypes. But many of us have succeeded anyway, and now it is time for us to come together so that more of us rise up and succeed. "Now people are realizing there is power in unity, and strength in networking," agreed Dr. Poussaint. "I think as we develop more self-esteem and a greater political awareness of our sense of community, then networking will increase."

Between 1964 and 2000, the number of blacks in professional, technical, and business ownership positions increased dramatically. From under a half-million across the country, our numbers rose to nearly nine million. We are in *business*. And now we need to get down *to* business, and we must stop doing the old-fashioned Negro "bidnit thang." With more of us on the professional career ladder or launching our own entrepreneurial endeavors, the demands of the workplace mean that we now require support systems that are geared to career, personal, and business development. Social contacts won't do. A copycat of the old-boy, white-boy network won't cut it. We need to become a community again. A community that believes in its own potential for success.

Networking is perhaps the most user-friendly method for gathering information. In *Megatrends,* John Naisbitt notes that a firm specializing in obtaining information from the government for corporate clients, Washington Researchers, estimates that it takes seven phone calls to find the specific information it needs from most government agencies. Naisbitt notes that many networkers claim they can reach anyone in the world with only six interactions, and the real pros boast that they can reach anyone in the United States with only two or three knocks on the network door.

Every time you talk on the telephone or e-mail or send someone your business information, you are networking. When you give someone your business card, you are networking. It boils down to finding the people you need to know in order to help you both to accomplish your goals. How do you tap the right people? That is what makes networking so exciting and so interesting. You never know when a casual business acquaintance may become the link in an important chain that will help you land a big contract or get you the job you have always wanted. Professional resource guides such as *SuccessGuide Worldwide: The Networking Guide to Black Resources* add thousands of names to the list of people you can call upon. The National Association of Black MBAs and the Hispanic Chamber of Commerce produce such guides to increase networking among their membership. Consider such guides to be your industrial-strength Soul-O-Dexes.

BUILDING MUTUALLY BENEFICIAL RELATIONSHIPS

Nothing breaks a good networking connection faster than abuse of it. When I have a specific job or goal and it requires plugging into a network connection, I am always careful to respect what that connection can or cannot do. It is important never to put someone on the spot. That is why it is vital to build mutually beneficial relationships, not just contacts. You cannot ask someone for more than they can reasonably and comfortably give. And you must be willing to give as well as receive. What you give may be different from what you receive, but over time, I have found that the law of increasing returns often is triggered once you become involved in the networking process.

My friend Eleanor Hayes was a popular weekend news anchor in Cleveland, and she and her station's general manager, Virgil Dominic, have long supported the African-American community, so I gave them a free half-page color advertisement in my *Success-Guide*. My goodwill gesture was done without any hidden agenda or selfish motive. I just liked what their station, WJW-TV 8, was doing for our people. To my surprise, however, the good feelings seemed to be mutual. My business became the subject of a thirty-second public service announcement that ran nearly fifty times during a three-week period on WJW. Now the value of the free advertisement I provided them was about twenty-three hundred dollars. The value of a thirty-second spot run that frequently on their television station is about one hundred thousand dollars. That is an example of the unexpected results of networking.

There is a quote that is often associated with the networking process. It is from an old proverb that goes: "If you want to be prosperous for a year, grow grain. If you want to be prosperous for ten years, grow trees. If you want to be prosperous for a lifetime, grow people." When I write of networks, I am referring, of course, to people—a whole array of people in your vast field of assorted relationships.

Being sensitive to other people is a key to successful networking, and I am sure some people skills can be taught. We all need to be reminded occasionally of a few basic rules to building and maintaining relationships. I have two sets of rules for maintaining my networks. One set deals with honoring the people in my network, the other with honoring the network itself. I call them my FraserNet Maintenance Rules, one set for nurturing those in your network, and the second for nurturing the network itself. First, the people rules.

1. *See the knots, not the net.* Individual people are the knots that hold your network together. You have to see them as individuals and deal with them on a personal level. When you contact someone in your network, approach him or her from the position of what is important to that person, not to you. Those two positions could be very different.

To build a strong networking relationship, you have to know a person well enough to understand what his or her values, goals, and agenda are. Most people project their own desires and perspective onto other people. Most often, this is a mistake. Maybe you don't need to walk a mile in the other person's shoes, but you do need at least to stand in his or her footprints for a minute or two before you attempt to network. Is the individual most concerned with money? with power? with principles? with relationships? These are important things to consider before tapping your relationship with anyone in your network.

2. *Be up front, up front.* One of the biggest mistakes network rookies make is assuming that their network partners know what they want. You have to make it clear from the start what you expect from your networking relationships. By doing this up front, you will save yourself a lot of misunderstandings and ill feelings later. No hidden agendas allowed!

Just as you cannot judge people based on your

experiences and perceptions, you cannot expect them to
know what you expect, unless you make it clear to them.
Do you expect your network partners to respond to every
note or telephone message immediately? Do you expect
them to act as references every time you apply for a job?
If so, let them know. It isn't always easy to be
straightforward, but it is better to be open in the
beginning than risk a damaged network later.

3. *Be the host, not the guest.* In the course of networking,
it is all too easy to act like a guest rather than a host, to
make demands rather than tending to the concerns of
others. Make a special effort to inquire about the health
and welfare and family members of your individual
networking contacts. Be sincere, not brusque about it.
You don't have to remember every birthday or anniversary, of course, but make notes on conversations so that
the next time you talk, you can follow up. How was that
vacation? Is the new dog working out? Is your wife
feeling better now? Has the baby learned to walk yet?
The simple personal touch, if heartfelt, can strengthen
network ties more than any favors or gifts you might
offer. I will cover this in greater detail in later chapters.

4. *Don't make promises you can't keep, but keep the ones you
make.* Mutual trust is vital to networking relationships,
and there is no quicker way to destroy it than by failing
to honor your commitments. Understand that it is often
difficult for people to call upon others for information or
assistance.

As often as we tell ourselves that networking is an
honorable and widespread method, there is always that
nagging little bit of insecurity about calling upon someone
else for help. And if the person you ask for help does not
deliver it, then you are unlikely to call upon that person
again or respond to his or her calls. Remember that when
someone in your network calls upon you for help, it is

probably ten times more important to them than it is to you. So honor their request and your commitment to the network relationship by showing integrity.

5. *'Fess up when you mess up.* You have to be a strong person to admit when you have wronged someone else. And if you want to maintain a strong network, you have to be able to admit when you have overburdened a connection or failed to fulfill your end of the networking agreement. So 'fess up when you mess up. A policy of admitting your errors will strengthen your network. A policy of ignoring your errors will eventually result in your becoming a one-person network.

NETWORK NURTURING

The network itself is dynamic and ever-changing. The care of it is as challenging as caring for a child. You cannot establish a network and then expect it to operate on its own. In my years of network-ing, I have come up with eight important principles that I think are the keys to nurturing your network. As you read through these principles, consider how you can apply them to your own business or personal life.

1. *Be a good parent to your network.* What are two of the first things a new parent learns? Patience and commitment. You can't leave your network "Home Alone." You have to guide it and nurture it. Nobody else is going to baby-sit it for you. You have to keep in touch with your network partners and keep the lines of communication flowing with two-way information.

2. *No network abuse.* How do you abuse a network? By using it for the wrong purposes. You may reap rewards down the road, but networking is not like going to the instant cash machine. Do not use networking forums as sales meetings. You are not selling a product at these functions; you are building relationships. Remember, networks are for mutual exchanges. You are supposed to be giving as much as you are getting.

3. *Stay loose.* Your network may bring home some strange characters now and then, but remember, to grow, you have to be receptive to new approaches. Even those contacts or situations that you consider of negligible networking value can surprise you.

4. *Be a good provider.* Be on the lookout for opportunities for others in your network as well as for yourself. If you only call your network contacts to further *your* self-interests, you'll soon find that your calls are not taken. On the other hand, remember that networking opportunities often crop up in the most unexpected places.

Keep your business cards updated and handy, and wherever you go, remember that opportunity awaits. I read a profile of a young movie star in which someone disparaged him as dull-minded by saying, "He doesn't bring much to the party." Always take something to the party, and be gracious about sharing it.

5. *Don't play favorites in your network.* If you are going to gather information, you are going to need all sorts of sources. Often, the chambermaid knows more of the nitty-gritty than the vice chairman for hotel management. So develop networking partners of all stripes, and be considerate toward all of them.

6. *Communicate with your network.* If you need help, ask for it. You cannot be a network churchmouse afraid to show your needs. You belong to a network because you want to use its expanded resources. So do it.

7. *Don't push your network too hard.* A child who is forced to do something or pushed into areas in which he or she has no real interest will eventually rebel, or inevitably be unhappy. Your network is the same way. Don't ask the people in it to give what they do not have, or do not want to give. If you do, don't expect them to be available for your next call.

8. *Show appreciation.* Don't treat your fellow networkers as if they are hired hands. Show your appreciation for their help and advice. Follow up with thank-you notes or small gifts, and let them know that their assistance made a difference for you.

THE BIG FOUR OF NETWORKING

At any given time, you may need to use your network of business and personal contacts to solve a specific problem, meet a deadline, or accomplish an important project. I have found it helpful to categorize different types of networking that I do in order to clarify my goals and to determine which people to contact in a given situation. As I have done this over the years, four distinct categories of networking have become apparent to me. They are:

1. Networking for information
2. Networking for influence
3. Networking for resources
4. Networking for good

It is helpful to recognize these four categories and to keep in mind when you are preparing for a networking event or opportunity. Always go into it knowing what you have to offer and what you hope to get out of it. This is known as establishing the quid pro quo. Here is a quick introduction to each category.

Networking for Information

Each of us retains an enormous amount of information that we have collected in our travels, our daily lives, and our professional experience. The quantity and variety of this information are as individual and unique as we are. This gives us that magic buzzword: expertise. What you need to remember in your battle to establish yourself in the workplace is that everyone you meet has his or her own wealth of knowledge—even you.

Networking for information includes seeking information relative to job searching. You know, 70 percent of jobs are filled not through massive national searches for talent, but through word-of-mouth networking. Top managers consider these jobs too important to fill without some inside information on the applicant. My position at Procter & Gamble, for example, came about as a result of a word-of-mouth recommendation from another African-American executive search firm with inside contacts. My credentials and skills got me the job, but I never would have been considered without the timely word and influence of a key contact who understood the importance of networking.

Networking for Influence
In the context of this category, I translate *influence* to mean access to key people. The next best thing to knowing someone with the power to help you is knowing someone who knows that person. Think of networking as a jumble of circles like the Olympic symbol. Where those circles connect is where networking is done between two different people with a mutual interest and need that links them.

Knowing a person with ability to link you to what you need to reach your goal—this is critical to your success. It is particularly important in volunteer organizations when specific projects can only be accomplished through the goodwill of highly influential people who, in turn, share common resources—either personnel, finances, or goods and services. Perhaps a case study from my own experience will help illustrate the importance of networking for influence.

One year as I was planning the schedule for the SuccessNet speaker's program, it occurred to me that it would be valuable to have Donald Petersen, then the chairman and chief executive officer of the Ford Motor Company, come to Cleveland to speak on the subject of productivity and world competition. Bear in mind that Mr. Petersen had never been to Cleveland for a public speaking engagement. The traditional "old boys' network" had either never been able to get him to this city—where at that time Ford employed over seventeen thousand people—or had never tried. How could SuccessNet, as a black professional organization in Cleveland, expect to reach a top executive in Detroit?

I had already developed a compelling case to lure Mr. Petersen to Cleveland by showing him the benefit a visit would have for *him*. I had my strategy, but I was in need of that key first move. It turned out to be as simple as a couple of good meals.

The regional manager of Ford's urban programs happened to be a black female. I asked Helen Love to lunch. And at the lunch, I talked to her about the idea of bringing her chief executive officer to Cleveland. She liked the idea, and as a believer in the power of networking for the success of her cultural community, she gave me a ticket to my next stop on the new Underground Railroad. She introduced me to another contact, a black woman who was strategically positioned to move me even closer to my goal. I took her to lunch, too. She liked the idea, so she handed me a ticket to one of her contacts, Mr. Petersen's executive assistant. We joined forces to take the executive assistant, a white male, to lunch. I pitched him and he pitched my idea to Mr. Petersen. The result was that Ford's CEO made one of his first public appearances in Cleveland as a guest of the SuccessNet Forum.

Complex? Not really. It was simply a matter of using a network of like-minded people with influence to achieve a goal. Of course, my proposal fit in with Ford's goals and objectives at that time, which involved raising the corporate profile in the black marketplace, but that was no coincidence. I made the effort to determine what their goals were, and I tailored my approach to them. My problem was how to get my idea on Mr. Petersen's desk. I solved that problem by networking for influence. Please note. *No money changed hands.* Money was not the carrot that would have attracted someone such as the CEO of Ford. Fitting into Ford's plan was the key, and getting my plan to Mr. Petersen turned it in the lock.

Networking for Resources

At some point in your career, you may need resources of some kind: investors for a new business, human resources, advertising, event sponsorship, products, or services. Again, the human resources are especially important in volunteer organizations, where free help is vital to a project's success. Knowing where to go for the resources you need is vital. Be sure, however, to make *reasonable* demands on the people in your network.

In 1989, when I was asked to be the cochairman of the inauguration committee for Cleveland's mayor-elect Mike White, I was given one key instruction: Stay within the budget. The budget was minuscule. My son's birthday party had a bigger budget. So we had to go after donations. I needed not just financial donations, but donated resources as well, in order to have enough for a first-class inauguration.

One point that needs to be established here is that you never ask someone for more than that person can afford to give. Be considerate of their situation as well as your own. In the end, we found all that we needed to make the mayor's inauguration a memorable event, and we didn't break the back of anybody's budget. We built goodwill, and we actually raised money that we donated to a worthy cause, which brings me to another form of networking that you need to be aware of—networking for good.

Networking for Good

One of the most productive and effective ways I have found to network is through volunteerism. I learned this, of course, after becoming involved in a number of worthwhile organizations. My motive was to help a cause, and I found that my networking skills were vital. And do you know what else I discovered in my hundreds of hours of volunteer work? I realized that networking for good very often proved to be good for my business network as well. The people I met through volunteerism often shared the same vision and sense of mission regarding our charitable work. At the same time, they brought to the table a wide variety of skills, important positions, and a desire to help others. I continue to volunteer, and my goal has remained the same: to give and to help others. I never anticipate that I will receive something tangible in return for volunteer work, but the fact is that I always do receive much more than I give, both in personal satisfaction and in productive relationships.

So, my advice: Volunteer because you want to help, and bear in mind that you will meet people with similar motives but with diverse skills and backgrounds. You will come together with people for a common purpose: to share, to learn, and to leverage collective resources. You will often have special exposure to resources, both human and physical, which you would not otherwise have.

While working on several projects for the United Way and the United Negro College Fund, I met high-level professionals with strong skills in publishing and advertising. My relationships with them helped me when I established my own publishing company. They knew me and trusted me by that time, and they were willing to do whatever it took to help me get established. That is networking at its highest level. John Glover, a longtime friend and networking mentor then an executive with UNCF, gave me my volunteer mantra twenty years ago upon signing me up as a volunteer for his organization. He said, "George, you got to give until it hurts, then give until it feels good. If you're not givin' you're not gettin'." I've never forgotten this advice, and it has served me well.

National Networking Month

I have a suggestion. Why not our own month? This month could be nationally recognized as the time of the year for promoting all types of networking. This is the month in which individuals and businesses can establish, reestablish, confirm, and affirm professional relationships. After all, networking is the identification and building of relationships for the purpose of sharing information, opportunities, and resources.

National Networking Month should be celebrated in January. This is an ideal time of the year because it represents a new beginning. It is the time of year when many of us resolve to improve our lives by implementing positive change. This often comes in the form of "New Year's Resolutions" such as quitting an addictive behavior, exercising, managing money better, and taking many other proactive measures that are geared to improve the quality of one's life.

Isn't networking an ideal way to improve the quality of life for everyone? It certainly is! Networking fosters a sense of pride, accomplishment, and unity. It allows individuals to unite for a common goal—success. It builds new partnerships and refurbishes existing structures. As the old adage states, "A chain is only as strong as its weakest link." Networking links people and ideas.

National Networking Month is the time of year when each of us can define our personal agendas for the new year. It is a time for action, not reaction. How does one celebrate National Networking Month? Is there a tree that we decorate? Is there a special meal that is prepared? Not exactly! However, metaphorically, the tree that we decorate is the oak tree known as our career, and the meal is the nourishment that we give that career through networking.

This month can be "celebrated" in a number of different ways.

- Create a networking event for your organization.
- Attend a variety of networking events in your community.
- Contact associates to say thank you.
- Ask several new individuals out to lunch and start building a relationship.
- Call as many people as you can in your PDA or organizer during this month.

- Volunteer for a new charitable organization.
- Set a goal and introduce your business/services to a set number of new individuals.
- Update your Networking Goals and Agenda.
- Send congratulation card/notes to new businesses in your area.
- Local chambers of commerce, clubs, organizations, and churches can extend invitations to new members.
- Use the power of e-mail to spread your message.

Many times we wish to contact a company or an associate but we just don't have a reason. Well, now you have a reason. National Networking Month is a perfect time to reach out and touch those who have helped you succeed. It is a time to pat someone on the back for being a part of the human family.

Whether it's creating new business contacts, acknowledging existing relationships, or doing charitable work, it is incumbent upon each of us to participate during this time of year. Although it's officially known as National Networking Month, in order to achieve the success we desire each of us will have to celebrate networking for the full twelve months of each year.

Each of us has something to share. If we do not use those gifts, as Les Brown is fond of noting, we risk taking our talents to our graves without ever using them. If others do not call upon us to share our gifts, then we are not marketing ourselves effectively, or perhaps, we are putting out negative signals. The only way to build a network is to advertise that you are available as a source yourself. Be willing to share your gifts.

*"Networking must be mutual, and you have to be cognizant
of the fact that if you are asking someone for his or her time,
then you must approach that person in a manner that will
make him or her want to do something for you."*
WILLIE JOLLEY

Willie Jolley is president and CEO of Willie Jolley Productions International, a communications firm covering such topics as Youth and Adult Motivation, Leadership, Self-Development, Empowerment, and Team Building and Success. Willie has released two best-selling books: *It Only Takes a Minute to Change Your Life* and *A Setback Is a Setup for a Comeback*. He hosts the *Willey Jolley's PBS Youth Empowerment Special* and is the host of "The Magnificent Motivational Minute," seen on The Success Channel on the Primestar Network and heard daily on the radio. Toastmasters International has named him the Outstanding Motivational/Inspirational Speaker of the Year. Willie also earned the National Speakers Association's Certified Speaking Professional Award, held by less than 7 percent of speakers in America. Says Jolley, "The best way to build your future is to build yourself. And the best way to build your organization is to build your people."

6

Make Networking Work for You

*The foremost enemy of the Negro
intelligentsia has been isolation.*
— LORRAINE HANSBERRY

While working at a Black Expo in Cleveland, I ran into Lynn Feaster, a young woman who had once come to me with several other eager young black entrepreneurs seeking advice on starting their own businesses. Lynn was starting her own travel agency. I had attempted to support her in her business and she, in turn, had supported my SuccessSource endeavors. She and I had maintained contact over the ensuing years.

When we happened to meet again recently, she reminded me of how I had encouraged her in the early days of her business. And since I had a booth at the Black Expo, she purchased some of the products we were selling and asked if we could get together soon so she could bring me up-to-date on a new opportunity that she was involved in that I might also find interesting. I happily agreed to meet with this go-getting, natural-born networker.

Just a few days after our chance encounter, she called to set up an appointment. On the telephone, she was charming and quick to the point. "I have come across a significant opportunity that could result in thousands, if not millions of dollars for my business, your business, and the city of Cleveland." She had my attention. "But I need some help and advice. Would it be possible to see you soon to discuss it?"

With an approach like that, could there be any doubt that I would meet with her? "Of course," I said, and of course, I meant it. We met, and as it turned out, she had not overstated her case. The opportunity was as important for me as it was for her. She brought a group of close friends—her support network—to the meeting and outlined her immediate needs to me. Once a television-commercial writer, she had been awarded a multimillion-dollar contract to start a pilot program for a black-oriented home shopping network. She needed an office space within two days so that she could meet some critical deadlines. I listened carefully to her proposal and then agreed to help.

On Lynn's behalf, I went to Saad Khayat, a prominent attorney who owns several small office buildings and apartment complexes. I had not known Saad long, but I was helping him put together a group of black people for another business venture. We had an established networking relationship that I wanted to expand to include Lynn. When I called, Saad was pleasant and open. I explained the situation briefly and simply asked if he could meet with Lynn to hear her proposal and possibly help her meet her immediate needs. He thanked me and offered that he had been looking for a tenant for a small office building that he owned. Saad said that if I recommended Lynn as a tenant, then that was all he needed. He and Lynn met, and several days later, she was moving into her new office space in his building.

As soon as she was set up, Lynn called to thank me for my assistance in establishing her new business. I then called Saad and thanked him for helping Lynn and he, in turn, was grateful to me for helping him find a reliable new tenant. By the way, I've mentioned how her proposal would eventually prove to be nearly as rewarding for me as for Lynn. Well, she offered me twenty-five minutes of free time to advertise my products. Now, that is how effective networking works! Everybody felt good about the process. Nobody was asked to do something beyond his or her means. Everybody gained something. In this case, it was win-win, and win again.

Networking works when you fully understand that there is *inherent value* in every human being and every human relationship regardless of one's title or position. Only when we mature enough to stop *prejudging* people as to their worthiness of our assistance can we truly give without expectation. When you give first, without expectation, you are networking for the benefit of others, and therefore the law of increasing returns will reward you tenfold. There are no exceptions to this law. Had the people in my life prejudged me because I lived in publicly subsidized tenement housing or because I mopped floors at La Guardia Airport, I would never have had the assistance I needed to fully blossom and maximize my full human potential. Neither would most black people. This is the spiritual and philosophical underpinning of effective networking.

Networking works when you understand that there is very little that you can do or have in life without working with other people. Therefore, you work diligently on building and developing your infrastructure of human resources.

Networking works when you understand that the whole is greater than the sum of its parts. Networks must be built upon a foundation of established relationships, first of all, but they can extend beyond. Building that essential foundation, however, takes time. You must have an established rapport with your key core of networking contacts.

Networking works when you can comfortably and successfully match needs and resources. Creating the win-win situation is the optimum, and although it may not always be exactly an even exchange, often things work out that way in the long run.

If, at first glance, you do not appear to have an established network base of close friends and contacts, you need not despair. You probably do have the necessary foundation, but you simply have not yet recognized your friends and other associates as the base of your network. As adults, on average we each know at least five hundred to seven hundred people on a casual or social basis. If you multiply that number of contacts by the number of people each of them knows, then your extended network of secondary contacts—friends of friends, colleagues of colleagues—is mind-boggling.

There have been many studies to document the power of the extended network, but one of the most renowned is that of sociologist Mark Granovetter. Entitled "The Strength of Weak Ties," it was presented in the *American Journal of Sociology*. He found that acquaintances are more likely than family or friends to give individuals direct information and to recommend opportunities to them. These acquaintances, he found, are often only two or three contacts away. With the right interpersonal skills, which I will present in the next chapter, you can be successful in attracting their assistance, even though you do not have personal relationships with them.

Perhaps most important to making networking work is showing appreciation for the contributions of your fellow networkers. Remember how your mother labored to ingrain gratitude in you? ("Now, say 'Thank you.' ") Well, as usual, your mother knew best. Expressing gratitude is positive reinforcement. It works. I make a point to thank people just for making a call for me or sending me some special article they think I might be interested in. All of this takes time, but it is time invested toward a larger reward.

If you read the account of Lynn's networking again, you will notice that each of the elements I just outlined came into play. And that is why her effort bore fruit. Your average day should be full of interactions and networking such as this.

DEFINING YOUR NETWORKING GOALS

"If you don't know where you are going, any road will take you there." This age-old saying is certainly true as it applies to networking. The first step in building a network is to discipline yourself to sit down and think about your short-term and long-term goals. Then you determine your agenda, which is your tactical plan for achieving your goals. I will offer more on determining your agenda in a later chapter.

You are never too young to write down your goals. Nor can you be too old. When my son Scott, for instance, was not even thirteen years of age he was already a veteran networker who had a solid fix on his goals. One of his first networks was a group of friends, relatives, and neighborhood contacts whose help he called upon each fall to raise money through the sale of candy bars for his annual school projects. So successful was Scott in door-to-door sales and tapping into Mom and Dad's network that, unlike most teenagers, he looked forward to reaching the advanced age of sixteen not so that he could drive a car, but so he could get a part-time job in order to raise money for his own personal projects.

It is important to have a vision of where you are going, and a driving sense of mission about getting there. Stop now and think for a few minutes about where you would like to be in one year, five years, ten years, and twenty years. What will your job be? Where will you live? Who will be sharing your life? What will your standing be in the community? What will be your greatest achievement?

Stephen R. Covey, author of *The Seven Habits of Highly Effective People: Restoring the Character Ethic*, has written that you should always "begin with the end in mind." Effective networkers have a personal vision. They know where they want to go even though they may not know, at first, how they are going to get there. From my days of selling encyclopedias on black history, I always knew that I wanted one day to have a business that was Afrocentrically centered, even though the term *Afrocentric* had not yet been coined. Of course, I had absolutely no idea how I was going to bring that about. But with that personal vision always in mind, I eventually found my way along the erratic path. I am still finding my way, but the journey, as difficult as it may sometimes be, is one that continually thrills and fulfills me.

As the president of J. T. Tillman's Nationwide Insurance Agency in Cincinnati, Jerald Tillman saw the need for a networking organization for blacks in the insurance industry. So he started one. He is founder and president of the Ohio Association of

Insurance Professionals, which in just ten years has grown to eleven hundred members nationally and is now called the National African-American Insurance Association.

Jerald says that "the value of networking to me is developing mutually beneficial relationships that result in positive growth for all parties involved."

A graduate of Miami University of Ohio, where he was a strong safety on the football team and a founding member of the campus chapter of Alpha Phi Alpha fraternity, Jerald says networking among fellow insurance professionals in the state has allowed him to offer a greater breadth of service to his clients while also encouraging "a tremendous flow of ideas" among black people in the insurance industry in Ohio. "We meet annually to discuss issues such as national health insurance, redlining, and basic insurance and social issues," he says. "The objective is to become an advocate group for black people involved in the insurance industry, but we also operate many public service programs. My main motivation is the pride I have in the black talent across this country and in our history as a successful people in spite of the difficulties we have faced."

SETTING GOALS

It is a basic exercise in any endeavor, but it is as vital in networking as in grocery shopping to make yourself sit down and list your goals on paper. By writing down your goals and dreams, you give them life in the same way that this book came to life only in the writing. Without goals, your networking may be aimless and nonproductive. Without direction, you may encounter only frustration. It is okay to set general long-term goals, but it is best to set specific goals for the short term.

Understanding and executing all of the principles and recommended guides to success will not help you unless you define long-term and short-term goals, and use the skills and principles of effective networking to attain them. Here are a few sample goals to help you get started:

- I'd like to get a new job this year.
- I'd like to change my career next year.
- I'd like to get on the board of the local NAACP.
- I'd like to raise my visibility in the community by volunteering for the United Way.
- I'd like to become known as an expert in my field.
- I'd like to start my own business.
- I'd like to make new friends in my field.
- I'd like to increase the size of my business by 20 percent in the next twelve months.
- I'd like to find a good physician, dentist, or attorney for my network.
- I'd like to date a single black professional who shares my interests.

How many more goals can you think of that fit your specific needs and aspirations? Remember that as you grow and evolve, you must continue to modify, evaluate, and retool your goals. I review my short-term goals monthly and my long-term goals annually. I now have two long-term goals, one to write my third book and another to build our annual PowerNetworking Conference to be the largest conference in black America. I expect to accomplish each goal within the next five years. My years at Procter & Gamble taught me that goals should be specific, measurable, achievable, and compatible with the overall goals of the company. What this really amounted to was the age-old formula of *what, where, why, who, when,* and *how*. These are precisely the questions I asked myself and incorporated into my business plan when I created the concept of my company, FraserNet, Inc.

I asked myself:

What are my immediate goals for the first three to six months, my short-term goals for the first nine months to one year, and my long-term goals for the first year to five years?

Where will the best market develop for my idea?

Why are these goals important, and am I truly committed to them?
Who are the people I can recruit to help me, and how can they help me?
When do I realistically expect to achieve my goals?
How will I know I have achieved them?

You can begin the work of building and cultivating your network once you are clear on your goals and committed to them. Commitment is a key, because your commitment will drive your planning, enthusiasm, and presentation to your potential network.

YOUR NETWORK HUGGERS AND SHAKERS

I have observed, and other experts in networking have also noted, that there are usually two types of people in your network: the *huggers* and the *shakers*. The huggers are the core of your network. They help you get through life by providing a foundation of support, stability, and emotional balance. Loved ones, close friends, colleagues, and extended family make up this critical group. You must pay a great deal of attention to the huggers, because without them, you could easily slide backward upon encountering difficulty en route to your goals. Many of us get tangled up in the "busy-ness" of business and neglect the huggers. When we do, eventually, the emotional alarms go off. We begin to feel rootless and off-balance. The huggers help us find our balance again.

These individuals in my network provide very specific support for me. Some keep me focused on God; some on family; some on health and exercise. Some keep my ego in check (a big job, some might say) by challenging me and forcing me to face important questions. Some make me laugh and ease the stress. Most give me love. My life would be very different and basically unfulfilled without them. There are other huggers who are at the backbone of my network, because they are key to getting my work done. Often, they are experts in some particular field.

There are people who serve in all of these same capacities

within your network, and you need to identify them in order to become an effective networker. In my case, they also include those professionals on whom I can count to do their jobs well: photographers, writers, proofreaders, and computer experts—all people I am inclined to hug because they make my professional life so much easier.

The key people I have noted above are part of a mutually beneficial network base. They keep you rooted and working, but they do not necessarily motivate or lift you to continually expanding levels of achievement. That role is held by the *shakers* in your network, the people who shake you out of complacency and push you forward in your personal and professional lives. Within this group are three subgroups: the mentors, the role models, and the connectors.

The Mentors

Mentors act as trusted advisers. They share wisdom and resources. Carole Hoover was a key shaker in my Underground Railroad. She shook me when I got off track. She shook me until I got locomoting again. A black woman of stature and charm, she is the president and chief executive officer of Hoover Milstein, a newly formed partnership between Hoover and New York businessman and entrepreneur Howard Milstein. She is well connected in community, government, political, and social circles.

Carole also has a successful small business of her own, and she serves on the board of several major corporations. She was one of my most important mentors. She has helped propel me toward my entrepreneurial career goals, sometimes with a gentle nudge, sometimes with a well-aimed kick. She has provided me access to high-level corporate executives and politicians, and opened opportunities for my company to secure new business. Mentors are catalysts who move networkers from one phase to the next. I've found that, on average, successful networkers encounter at least three major mentors during their careers. Tommy Dortch, the charismatic leader of 100 Black Men of America, told me one of

his first mentors was social activist Julian Bond, then Mayor Andrew Young, and then his last boss, Senator Sam Nunn. That's
quite a lineup. How can you fail with a guidance system like that!

The Role Models

Role models are people you wish to emulate, personally or professionally, or as entrepreneurs, regardless of your age or station in
life. I naturally try to use black people as my role models, because
we often share similar backgrounds. I look for those who have
overcome the same obstacles that I must overcome. Role models
are generally watched from afar, as opposed to mentors, who usually are intimates or at least much closer to you. Although the pattern can vary, mentors usually select you, while you select your
role models.

I have always been careful in selecting my role models, however. Former NBA star Charles Barkley made quite a stir when
he said he is not a proper role model: "Just because I dunk a basketball doesn't mean I should raise your children." I agree.
Barkley believes parents should be role models for their own children. My father was my first role model. I admired his sense of
humor and charismatic personality. My foster father was less col-
orful, but I have tried to emulate his work ethic and his sense of
excellence. My older brother Walter had a sense of style and
fashion that I admired, and my brother Edward's communications skills are still models for my own life. As I mentioned in the
first chapter, my first manager at Procter & Gamble, Richard
Gilchrist, was both a mentor and role model for my professional
development and demeanor. Pictures of these people and their
values are still firmly planted in my brain. Today, the role models
in my network like Earl G. Graves are as varied and as important
to me as ever.

The Connectors

Connectors are friends who have friends and resources and are
ready, willing, and able to share them. These are the shakers who

force you to move on and up. They are creative, smart, and resourceful, and get special satisfaction out of matchmaking and problem-solving. The late John Kennedy was a prominent attorney in Atlanta. An African American, he was very well connected in the legal world. I was introduced to him by a mutual friend, Rebecca Franklin. Within a relatively short period of time, John and I discovered that we had friends in common in several major cities. We, in turn, became good friends. As a result of our friendship and his impressive credentials, I decided to feature John and his firm in the Atlanta edition of the *SuccessGuide*. In turn, John has connected me to a long list of important contacts across the country.

Some time back, I needed to reach the well-known personal-injury attorney Willie Gary, an African American who is one of the wealthiest and most successful lawyers in America. He has appeared on *Oprah* and as the subject of the CBS Evening News' "Eye on America." He made national news for pledging ten million dollars to Shaw University in Raleigh, North Carolina. John Kennedy made the initial call on my behalf, and set up a trip to Florida so I could meet Gary to talk about a mutually beneficial opportunity.

When I needed to meet someone important in Atlanta and I didn't have a direct contact, John would make a call to plug me in to his network. John, then, was a connector, a friend, and an important part of my national network. With just a few key figures like John, you, too, can be connected to a nationwide network.

Turn to Exercise 6 in Appendix A and list your huggers, shakers, mentors, and role models, or potential mentors and role models, along with what it is that you admire about them.

NETWORK NEMESES

Are there any people you should make it a point *not* to network with? Certainly your network can include people who are not close friends and even people whom you may not particularly care for. What is important is having mutually beneficial goals. It is also important, however, that you share basic standards and respect for each other. I would advise you to exclude those individuals whom you do not trust or respect, or who you feel will be strictly a one-way connection, what some call "network mongrels," Doberman-like opportunists posing as earnest puppies.

You may also want to avoid people whose personal style conflicts with yours. If you are low-key and like to work behind the scenes, you may not feel comfortable networking with highly aggressive individuals, although in some instances, their aggressiveness might work in your favor. You have to be the judge of whether you can make it work. I would also advise you to be cautious about networking with people whom you do not know well, particularly if you are going to be called upon to recommend them to others. I have had some embarrassing experiences with "newcomers" whom I embraced and recommended without thoroughly checking them out. If another networking contact whom you know well recommends this person wholeheartedly, go ahead and check the person's credentials anyway. If you find yourself in an uncomfortable situation in this regard, try to set up a lunch meeting or at least an extended telephone conversation in order to shore up the networking connection.

Every now and then, you might have to clean up your network, remove the dead wood and contacts that have lost their vitality. It is sometimes a painful process, but it's as necessary as pruning the dead limbs off a favorite tree. Sometimes the cleanup can be done simply by cutting off contact; other times, it must be done in a more formal way. You can simply say in honesty that the relationship has not been fruitful, and that you have moved on in your life.

NETWORKING TOOLS

Here is some of the best news you are going to get about networking: It doesn't cost much. For a small investment in a PDA (Personal Digital Assistant), which can cost a little more than you would spend on a school starter set for a first-grader, you will have all the tools you need for networking. A PDA can be purchased for a little over a hundred dollars, unless, of course, you decide to go with the "power networking" PDA, which can cost as much as five hundred dollars.

Have Card, Will Network

You may not be surprised to learn that my favorite television character in the late 1950s was Paladin, the fast-draw gunslinger from the Old West who handed out business cards that said, HAVE GUN, WILL TRAVEL. Now that was some get-right-down-to-it networking. The business card is, in fact, still a primary networking tool. Its importance cannot be overstated. Your face may be forgotten, but your business card lingers in the Rolodex or PDA. I can't tell you how many times I've received telephone calls and obtained business from someone who just happened to be flipping through his or her Rolodex or organizer and, coming upon my information, realized that the time was right to call upon my services. It happens all the time.

If you are an entrepreneur, it is vital that you have business cards printed up even if you are still working a day job and moonlighting in your field of choice. A business card brings a higher degree of credibility. It says that you are serious about your venture. A standard order of five hundred business cards can cost less than twenty dollars, so this initial investment in your business career is minimal, and the returns on that small investment can be incredible. Wally "Famous" Amos has an oversize business card with his logo. It looks like a miniposter, and when he was still in the cookie business, no matter where he put it down, it was so large that people couldn't help but see his name and logo. Because of its advertising appeal, he got orders for his cookies just by setting the big business card down on tables, resulting in thousands of dollars in business.

Here are a few tips on how to maximize the potential of your business cards, and also your name tags at networking forums such as conventions and seminars. Remember, these name tags should be considered stick-on business cards.

1. *Your business card is your most visible company representative.* Make sure it is easy to read, appealing, and attractive. It is a relatively inexpensive item, so don't cut corners on it. Forgo the leased Mercedes and get a Lincoln or even a Taurus if you have to, but spend the money on the right design, color, shape, and message for your business.

Your business card should describe your business or position in the simplest terms. Your name, telephone number, and e-mail address should be the most prominently displayed information so people don't have to become squinting gawkers to find out how to contact you. You've seen that breed at gatherings, haven't you? They look like nearsighted Big Birds trying to find a worm in the brush pile.

Another of my pet peeves is the business card with an exotic company name that offers absolutely nothing to suggest what this business can do for its customers. "Symbiosis, Inc." could be a chemical company or a Moluccan terrorist network, for all I know. I also find it exasperating when a business card has no address, area code, or zip code. How many conversations are launched by the fact that you have mutual knowledge of a city or state? "Oh, so you're based in Atlanta? I hear that it's beautiful. Do you ever get into Savannah? Do you know Barbara Wilson? What exactly is your product?"

Get the address on your business card. And do not turn your business card into a sales gimmick with free coupons on the back. Tacky, tacky, tacky. The business card is a means to an end, not the end in itself—unless you turn it into a *dead* end.

2. *Business cards are not a replacement for meaningful conversation.* I have encountered people who do the "grunt, shake, and shove." They *grunt* a greeting, *shake* your hand, and *shove* a business card at you before then walking off to stalk their next victim. For these card sharks, I have this message: "Don't call me. I won't call you."

You network by building a rapport, finding a common interest and a mutually beneficial relationship. That takes time, work, and effort. Grunting, shaking, and shoving won't cut it, folks. Remember your goal, yes; but remember that goals are achieved step-by-step (that is the agenda). You build relationships first. The network is built on relationships, not on your self-interests. Success is built upon the network foundation. Think of what you might miss by failing to establish relationships because you are so intent on getting your name out. It's like the farmer who just throws out seeds and never does anything to nourish the soil around them. Come harvest time, his wagons will have nothing to haul home. I'll offer more detailed tips on network conversations in the next chapter.

3. *Always carry more than enough business cards, and put them where you can gracefully and assuredly draw them out.* This is a basic point, but an important one. Doing the business-card fumble does not leave a strong impression of competence. Think of James Bond producing his cigarette lighter for a seductive lady. Play Sade in your head. Be a *smooth operator.*

Networking guru Mel Kauffman says that if you take twenty seconds to find your business card, in a year's time, you will have fumbled away hundreds of new contacts. Time is money, especially in networking, where research has shown that 10 percent of those you meet become your clients.

4. *Develop a business-card filing system for your walking file cabinet—you.* Put incoming cards in one pocket, and your outgoing cards in another. (And please find a third location for your handkerchief.) This separation of the incoming and outgoing cards prevents you from committing one of the more embarrassing networking faux pas: giving someone else's card away instead of your own. Not smooth. Not smooth at all.

5. *Make notes.* Whether it's in the electronic organizer or directly on the business card, record things to spark your memory of the person later when you come upon the card. When you have exchanged business cards with a new acquaintance, jot a note to yourself on the back of the card summarizing that person's area of expertise or an unusual personal characteristic: "reconditions fax machines"; "scuba dives in the Caribbean"; "president of a company that makes printing ink"; "director of council of small enterprises"; or "light, hazel eyes."

Someday you might need a secondhand fax machine, or want to take a scuba-diving vacation, or need information about printing ink or medical insurance for your small business. An organized business network will make your search easier, and a lot more productive. Having the name of the person's spouse and the name or names of any children is helpful for personalizing conversations. Gratuitous use of family names can seem insincere or phony, however, so avoid false intimacy.

Note on the card where you met the person; whether any promises were made about sharing information; what things you have in common; who mutual friends might be. Always keep in mind that the network needs nurturing.

A networker extraordinaire, public relations whiz Terrie Williams notes birthdays, wedding anniversaries, and other special occasions of those in her files.

6. *Cover for others.* I've advised you to make sure you always have enough business cards, but I have also found it useful always to carry a few blank business cards with lines for name, company, business title, address, and phone numbers. I do this for the people I encounter who have run out of business cards. When you are quick on the draw to relieve someone of their embarrassment for having no cards, you win their gratitude. They remember that sort of grace. And it also saves you from having to write information on paper napkins, matchbook covers, or bar coasters.

7. *Follow through, follow through, follow through.* Let fellow networkers know you want to be a player. You know how important the follow-through is in shooting a basketball, making a golf swing, or hitting a tennis ball. It is even more vital in networking.

You must let people know you care greatly about cultivating them as resources. You don't have to slather them with praise, shine their shoes, or build a temple in their honor; but let them know you value their skills and knowledge. And then, let them know what you know, and even more important, let them know how much you want to *share* that information with them. The bottom line is: Keep in touch. One way of doing that is to keep in mind a person's interests, and to mail that person pertinent articles, cartoons, and business leads that you may come across.

8. *Consider name tags to be your stick-on business cards.* In this case, your *firm's* name should not only be at the top, but it should also be two times as large as *your* name. Both should be in block letters that are easy to read from ten feet away.

Savvy networkers first seek out professions or industries that are relevant to their own, or are financially important to them. Your name becomes important only after that relevance is established. Place your name tag on your right lapel. This places your firm name in the networker's line of sight and quickens the verbal response opportunity.

9. *Carry prepared name tags.* I once arrived at a networking gathering only to be handed a preprinted name tag that read, JOE FRAZIER, SUCCESSSORCERER INK. Well, maybe that didn't actually happen, but I have had nightmares of it happening. Because so many gatherings provide improperly prepared name tags, I recommend you carry several prepared name tags in your coat pocket in order to be sure that you always have a correct one to wear.

This also saves you from having to wear the dreaded HELLO, MY NAME IS . . . name tag. To my way of thinking, such abominations are the double-knit leisure suit of name tags. This is a tag for Tupperware parties, not professional gatherings. And from a practical standpoint, this type of name tag does not leave room for your company name to be displayed first, which slows the networking process considerably.

10. *Think Afrocentrically when you are out there swapping cards.* Stay centered and self-assured in who you are and what *you* bring to the party. Before you go to such an event, review the Afrocentric networking principles on page 63 in Chapter 2. And walk tall.

Organizing Your Business-Card File

If you become an avid networker, you will collect hundreds of business cards. But all of those cards are as worthless as so much pocket lint unless you organize them in a useful filing system. The retrieval system you design will ultimately determine how effective your networking will be.

You do not want to spend hours looking for a key contact because you cannot find his or her business card. So you must devise a system that allows you easy access to names, numbers, categories, and simple updating. A good networker will add between twenty-five and one hundred new business cards per month. Keep the information on those cards updated: Note changes in titles, phone numbers, and addresses. Review your files weekly to jog your memory and help you keep in contact with old and new network partners.

Here are a few suggestions for business-card filing systems:

1. *The PDA (Personal Digital Assistant) system:* This is my favorite system personally. I have a state-of-the-art PDA with plenty of RAM and memory. It holds over ten thousand digital records (business-card information). I can access almost anyone I want using several different cues or criteria. I confess to having difficulty remembering names initially—blame it on advancing years. The PDA helps me to access my key contacts in a variety of ways (i.e., profession, city, first or last name) instantly.

SuccessTip: Because most of my contacts are black, I make sure that I note when someone is of another race. That way, I make sure to use black resources first whenever possible.

2. *The computerized card file.* This more high-tech system of filing your business cards offers maximum flexibility. On the computer, you can code for organizations, professions, clubs, industries, name, gender, eye color, or personal scent—nearly any category you can imagine. It is great for sorting, listing, and mailing capabilities if your business is that well equipped technically. I have a computer database system that I use to produce a quarterly, twelve-page printout of my key network contacts. And I can carry this around airports much more easily than hauling my beloved, but bulky Soul-O-Dex. We use Microsoft Access to do this, and there are other, similar contact management programs available.

3. *The notebook file.* This is for the well-organized detail person. Many sophisticated networkers record all conversations including name, date, event, contact results, and follow-ups in their "handwritten" notebooks, which they carry everywhere.

4. *A 3-by-5-inch card system.* It is a little "old school," but salesmen seem to like this system. All information is handwritten and filed by last name. This is also good for recording details about contacts.

STARTING YOUR OWN NETWORKING EVENT

As the founder of Cleveland's first monthly networking events, called SuccessNet, I was often approached by ambitious black professionals interested in starting networking affairs in their communities or particular fields of interest. I began the SuccessNet events in 1988 because I saw a need to bring Cleveland's emerging black entrepreneurs and professional community together regularly to network, to share, to learn, and to encourage the effective leveraging of our collective resources.

I was careful to take measures so that SuccessNet gatherings never turned into a party or meat market atmosphere. They were social gatherings, but they were business-oriented. Of course, that is not to say that many "warm" relationships didn't result. I still believe every city in America could benefit from similar networking opportunities for black professionals and business owners. Here are a few SuccessTips on how you can start your own.

1. *Form a small group.* Recruit no more than seven movers and shakers from the black business community, and set up your organization as a for-profit venture. It is important to be a profit-seeking group for several reasons, particularly because profits provide an incentive to persevere over the long haul. Many nonprofit groups fail because they lack those incentives. SuccessNet events, for example, were profitable from the very beginning, which helped a great deal to motivate my staff and me to continue with them even in hard times.

2. *Sell your potential partners in this venture on the networking concept.* Adopt a name. Create a logo, letterhead, Web site business and e-mail address, phone number, and electronic mailbox, doing it all with black-owned businesses whenever possible. This not only follows our Afrocentric principles; it also helps get the word out that something new and exciting is in the works for your community.

3. *Find a sponsor.* Major corporations recognize the buying power of the middle-class and upper-class black community. Ford, Continental Airlines, and BP America have been my business sponsors over the years. Coca-Cola and Pepsi-Cola, Budweiser, local banks, utilities, and other Fortune 500 companies are frequent sponsors of black-oriented events and conferences. Your local radio stations, hotels, newspapers, airlines, clubs, and organizations will also be eager to be a "supporting sponsor." You will need to give most major sponsors six months to a year's lead time to approve participation.

4. *Establish a date and regular time for the monthly events.* I have found Tuesdays, Wednesdays, and Thursdays to be the best-attended days for such events. Generally I scheduled them for right after work in a convenient downtown location. I don't recommend staging events during the summer. It is just too difficult to combat vacation times. I do not recommend having deejays, live bands, or dancing. A professional decorum should be encouraged.

5. *Find a place to have the forums.* Often an upscale soul food restaurant and bar or a local hotel will be willing to be a supporting sponsor and provide a ballroom or meeting room free, in exchange for advertising, bar receipts, and catering.

6. *Select your speakers well in advance, anywhere from six months to a year before the date of the event.* The top professional speakers need a lot of lead time. The key to making this kind of networking event memorable and successful is your choice of speakers and topics. The rule of thumb: Use a speaker with "marquee appeal" (a famous local or national name); or create a really provocative title for your topic (for example, "Why Are Black Businesses Failing?"), then build a credible panel or speaker around it. Both strategies work well. Over the last ten years I have hired more than two hundred nationally known speakers. I heard more than four hundred speakers (there are more than a thousand on the circuit), and I listened to over two thousand hours of audiotapes. I informally polled hundreds of people about who is best; fifty names continued to be mentioned. In Appendix C, I list those many consider to be the most influential fifty black speakers working today. Most of them charge $7,500. My criteria for this informal research take into consideration: my opinion; other people's opinions; and the speaker's charisma, passion, vision, message, commitment, name recognition, history, accessibility, and overall ability to move a crowd to its feet. This is "The Fabulous 50"; when they show up you will have an audience, when they talk people listen. All of them inspire and motivate.

7. *Secure mailing lists.* Obtain lists from black-oriented clubs, organizations, businesses, and professional groups by offering free tickets, part of the proceeds, or co-sponsorship. E-mail blasts to targeted groups can be very effective.

8. *Promote your event.* Use the Internet, direct mail, sponsored radio and newspaper advertising, public service announcements, flyers—and the grapevine.

9. *Project attendance figures; then set a cover charge.* You'll need to cover the cost of the speaker. Cheese-and-fruit hors d'oeuvres should be available only one hour before and one hour after the event. Order enough food for only 60 percent of the anticipated crowd. One of the biggest—and most expensive—mistakes is ordering too much food. Have a cash bar only.

10. *Get a popular local figure.* Perhaps you can book a dynamic business leader or a local television figure to be the master of ceremonies.

11. *Establish a format.* Provide name tags; collect business cards; furnish blank business cards; have a question-and-answer period; and offer door prizes from black businesses.

12. *If you cannot get a sponsor to cover at least the cost of a first-rate speaker, don't hold the event.* Do not depend on door sales.

PLANNING AND NETWORKING AT AWARDS CEREMONIES

I have a complaint about the difficulty of networking at black awards ceremonies and banquet dinners that I have attended over the years. They never begin or end on time. I am not the only one who finds this extremely frustrating, not to mention time-wasting. I often put in twelve-hour days, and it is too much to ask of my attention span to require me to sit through dinners that run four or more hours. This cuts deeply into my networking opportunities. I have planned and coordinated nearly as many events as I have attended over the years, and so I have a few suggestions as to how you might put together your own awards or testimonial banquet, and how to keep the people coming back year after year.

The Fifth Anniversary Celebration of my company was one of the most important events I'd put together until that moment. It presented particular difficulties because of the fifty-five dignitaries and honorees in the program. But, surprise: It started promptly at 6:30 P.M., after a one-hour cocktail reception, and those who attended were on their way home by 9:00 P.M. I accomplished this without the benefit of either a whip or a gun—at least, not a loaded gun. And so, here is how I did it, and how you can do it.

First of all, here is the program for that evening and the time allotted for each part of the program.

PROGRAM

		Time Allotted in Minutes
Welcome	George C. Fraser	2
Invocation	the Reverend Allison Phillips	3
Proclamation	Governor George Vonovich	10
Dinner		45
Introductory Remarks	George C. Fraser	7
Black Excellence Video		7
Keynote Address	James Earl Jones	15
Hall of Fame Induction	James Earl Jones	15
Award Presentations		
Top People to Watch	Julius C. Dorsey	10
Top Achievers	Carole Hoover	10
Entrepreneurial Excellence and Remarks	Mayor Michael R. White	20
Closing Remarks	George C. Fraser	3
Benediction	the Reverend Allison Phillips	2

Total time: 2 hours 29 minutes

To pull off the unusual feat of staging a black event on time, we stuck to our tight schedule like marines on a mission. We did not allow our fifty-five honorees of the evening to make acceptance speeches, thereby eliminating the usual homages to mothers, fathers, grandmothers, and second cousins twice removed.

A twenty-second script was read to musical accompaniment to highlight each person's achievements. People came up, received their awards, and then stood onstage while others in their category were called forward, thus allowing each of them some time in the spotlight, without giving any of them the microphone. Photographs of the honorees were taken after the event, so those who wanted to network could do so, and those who wanted to go home to their beds were free to go on their way.

Here are a few more of my SuccessTips for getting folks in,

then getting them fed, feted, and out the door before the season changes.

- *Insist* that your dais guests arrive at least a half hour before the official starting time. Keep them in a VIP room, well stocked with refreshments. Don't wait for high-level speakers (unless among them is the keynote speaker), whose hectic schedules seldom allow them to show up on time.
- Start on time! It should not matter whether there are fifty or five hundred people in the room. If you establish this as your policy, they will get the hint sometime before the twenty-fifth anniversary of your event. Generally, the early parts of any program are perfunctory anyway, so your guests won't miss all that much. And if they complain, show them the official starting time on their invitations. If you are having a reception prior to the program, make sure it is in a room near to the location of the main event. Shut the bar down ten to twenty minutes before the program is to start. This will either move people quickly into the main room, or trigger a demonstration.
- Plan and script the program so that it lasts no longer than two and a half hours. If it goes longer than the movie *Titanic*, you've gone too long. This includes the meal, entertainment, awards, and recognition and keynote speech, which I recommend you limit to under forty-five minutes. Lunches and breakfasts should be shorter, of course.
- Write out a full, detailed script of all speaking parts as if you were staging a play. This is the key to a timely event. Most organizations will not take the time to do this, but without a detailed script, your event will most assuredly run over and over and over. Script dais introductions for the master of ceremonies. Script awards and recognition introductions to be given by guest presenters. Script all

remarks and comments by the emcee and all presenters
(allow them no more than two minutes each), with the
exception of the keynote speech. Leave a five-minute
cushion for political dignitaries to ad-lib for the voters. You
don't need to script benedictions and invocations, but allow
only three to five minutes for each.

- If your staff is not writing the remarks for a guest, ask the
  guest for a copy of his or her remarks and insist that the
  speech fit *your* time frame. Be particularly careful when
  turning the microphone over to a minister or a politician—
  two groups that include many gifted orators, very few of
  whom are known to actively practice brevity.
- Six to eight speakers plus a keynote speaker should be the
  limit. Any higher number runs the risk of causing mass
  hysteria, or at least all sorts of digestive disorders, among
  your guests, triggering a black exodus.
- If you have more than six award winners or honorees, *do
  not let them speak!* This is not the Oscars, and even the
  Oscars have become a major snore because of long-winded,
  politically correct posturing by the award winners. Let
  them grin, grab, and go. Ask your audience to hold their
  applause to the last honoree, knowing full well that
  Grandma is going to break that rule when her
  granddaughter appears. For six or fewer award winners,
  insist on an acceptance speech scripted for under three
  minutes—about four hundred words. Put a timer on the
  podium and crank up the music when they run overtime.
- Save all photo opportunities until after the program or off
  the dais. Your nonphotogenic guests will be highly
  appreciative of being spared the flash.
- Walk through a rehearsal at least once and talk through it
  several times with your staff, including technicians, kitchen
  managers, and waiters.
- Preset your meal with salads and desserts, if at all possible.
  Each time a course is served, time and noise and confusion

are added. If you cannot preset the dessert, start the program during the dessert. No more than fifty minutes should be allowed for the meal before the substantive part of the program begins.

• It is an African tradition to have the keynote address before the meal. This gives everyone something to talk about during the meal. Be sure you have something just as interesting planned for after the meal; otherwise, don't count on them sticking around to digest it.

Implementing these suggestions will not only shorten and facilitate your event, it will also give networkers more time to socialize, make new contacts, and learn new information. Avid networkers, as well as most other people, prefer not to sit for three to four hours while others do all the talking.

NETWORKING IN ACTION

At this very moment, you are holding in your hands an excellent example of networking in action. So I thought I'd end this chapter on the nitty-gritty details of networking to tell you how the principles that I am presenting came into play in the creation of this book. The story illustrates how following some very simple networking principles can lead to rather extraordinary developments.

Mel and Sheryl London are famous cookbook authors who have been writing successful books for years. They have a home on Fire Island in New York. They are neighbors and friends of Sherry Winston, a jazz flutist who also spends her summers on Fire Island. I met Sherry when I was the keynote speaker for the national conference of the National Association of Market Developers, a group of black professionals in sales and marketing. I am a jazz enthusiast, so Sherry and I swapped—my *SuccessGuides* for several of her CDs. Sherry showed the *SuccessGuide* to her neighbor Mel London, and she and Mel proposed that I write a book about the concepts behind *SuccessGuide* and networking in the African-American community.

Now, that is just the first phase of the networking that went into the creation of this book. Sherry set up a dinner meeting so Mel and I could discuss this idea when I came to New York. Within a month, I was back in town, and we discussed the project at an elegant restaurant in Greenwich Village. Mel and his wife are very creative, and they offered all sorts of tips, ideas, and advice on how to write the book. Their enthusiasm was contagious, and, at least in my mind, I was a best-selling author before dessert. I even made an outline for the book right there on my dinner napkin. They were encouraging me to reach for another level. And then they connected me to their own network by setting up a meeting with their agent, Madeleine Morel, a British woman working in New York with the Barbara Lowenstein and Associates agency.

If you have had any exposure to the publishing world, you will already have realized just how powerful networking can be. One of the most difficult things for an aspiring author to accomplish is to get a good agent to even take a look at your proposal. But because of the recommendation of the Londons, I had an immediate in. Madeleine agreed to meet me for lunch. She was warm and friendly, but straightforward when we met about a month later. Who is George Fraser? What does he have to offer the publishing world? Can he tell it and sell it?

The significance of that meeting struck me as she put those questions to me, but as best I could, I told it and sold it to her. And the power of networking was so evidently at work in our getting together that she recognized the value of what I had to offer. She liked the proposal, and she arranged a meeting for me with the high-powered Barbara Lowenstein, one of the top literary agents in New York. Barbara has made something of a specialty out of scouting for African Americans with the potential to write commercially viable books for the black market. My proposal for a book on black people networking for success fit her focus.

Because of the network I had built with Sherry and Mel and Sheryl, and then Madeleine and Barbara, I penetrated the difficult publishing market, and a few weeks later, this guy from Cleveland landed a major book contract. Now, writing a book had been one of my goals, but I had it on my five-year plan. Thanks to network connections, I reached that goal four years ahead of schedule. Being prepared, I was ready when the opportunity presented itself.

But you can't rest on your laurels in this networking business. I shared the wealth. Following the Afrocentric principles that I believe in so strongly, I plugged others into this newly developed network, and as a result, my friend public-television talk show host and multimedia man Tony Brown hooked up with the same agent and he, too, landed a book contract. Tony had long been planning to write a book, but he also discovered that a network connection can make things happen much more quickly. Over the years we've been able to plug others into this new and exciting network link.

Effective networkers must make themselves useful, knowledgeable, and helpful to others. In this post–Internet boom economy, where layoffs and lockouts are becoming all too common, you have to become indispensable. You can do that by building your skills, sharing those skills, and then making them available and accessible through networking.

*"Networking is so important. Until we start working
together and supporting each other and providing
opportunities for our children, we will continue to be an
endangered species. We absolutely must change our way
of thinking about and dealing with each other as black people."*
MARILYN FRENCH HUBBARD

Marilyn French Hubbard believes there is a link between health, wealth, and spirituality and that true leaders are those who lead by serving others. She is an author (*Sisters Are Cashing In*), lecturer, consultant, facilitator, trainer, and business coach. She brings her Christian beliefs to teach individuals how to bring joy into their lives by discovering their God-given gifts, careers, or ministries. She coaches business leaders and organizations to embrace diversity and build high-performance teams. She has served as an adviser to Michigan governors and mayors and to the administrations of Presidents Clinton, Bush, Reagan, and Carter. Marilyn is the founder of the National Association of Black Women Entrepreneurs, a 5,000-member international network for entrepreneurial and enterprising women. She did the initial research and development for the Detroit Self-Employment Project, the pioneering program to move welfare recipients from public dependency to business ownership. Marilyn is part of the senior leadership team and is the corporate vice president for organization and community partnerships with the Henry Ford Health System in Detroit.

7

The Art of Network Conversation

*In order to have a conversation with
someone, you must reveal yourself.*
— JAMES BALDWIN

You are at a big networking event, perhaps a national conference or award ceremony teeming with many potential business contacts. You see someone you would like to make part of your network. You walk up and say, "Hi, how are you doing?" The person looks at you blankly and replies, "Fine."

You go to the weather. "How do you like all this rain?" The blank look thickens into the Great Wall of China. "I don't," dribbles the response.

Okay, you think, *let's go right to the introduction.* "My name is Susan Brown and I'm with RJR Nabisco." You then stick your hand out. Mr. Great Wall shakes it with all of the enthusiasm of a man meeting his embalmer. Without another word, he turns and follows his nose out of your orbit.

Has this ever happened to you? If it has, it is because you did not plan what you wanted to say, or you did not say what you had planned. Either way, you missed making a networking connection. Not everybody has a gift for making small talk. It has been said that if former President Richard M. Nixon, who was awkward in one-on-one situations, had been more skilled at small talk, he might have been a much more popular and successful leader. There is a perhaps apocryphal story of Nixon struggling to establish camaraderie with a TV network reporter, whom he must have considered a playboy type, by inquiring, "Well, have you forni-cated lately?" So much for establishing rapport. There has been much talk about how both Presidents Bill Clinton and George W. Bush are very effective networkers. They have mastered the art of sincere, relevant small talk, firm handshakes, penetrating stares, and infectious smiles. I've met President Clinton—twice; the ru-mors were very accurate. I'll never forget the moment, and I still like him to this day.

If personal charm doesn't come to you naturally in conversa-tion, you have to work at it. Your opening banter in networking situations is the verbal version of the foot in the door for door-to-door salesmen. Believe me, as a former encyclopedia sales-man, I know what it feels like to have the door slammed on your foot.

Most people you encounter in networking situations will be more courteous than Mr. Great Wall, but the secret of effective networking is to develop and use your people skills to penetrate ei-ther the wall of disinterest or the equally unsettling veil of insin-cere courtesy. You do this by giving your target reasons why he or she should want to know you better, whether it's because you are fun to be around, knowledgeable, or a potentially valuable contact.

The key to engaging strangers in conversation is the key also to effective networking: You have to establish a common ground or a sense of mutual purpose. When you boil it down, the initial phase of networking—making contact—is nothing more than small talk, just as you might converse with anyone you meet at a sporting event, a church gathering, or around the whist table. But in this case, your talk is not simply small talk, it is very important talk. It has a definite purpose.

One of my favorite stories from the networking front came from limousine service operator Oscar Smith, also known in Louisburg, North Carolina, as "Oscar the Limo Doctor." A mas-ter of the network opportunity, Oscar told *Black Enterprise* maga-zine that he never fails to take advantage of his "captive audience."

"People often ask my opinion on local restaurants, sights, and entertainment. Once they discover I'm resourceful and trustworthy, they not only give me repeat business, but they throw additional business my way," he said.

If you are as serious about networking for success as Oscar the Limo Doctor, you don't have time for idle chitchat. When you are aggressively seeking success, you are constantly *working* to widen *the net* of your business contacts in order to attain career success. You don't have time to sit around and shoot the breeze with the boys and girls at the office. Notice that the real achievers don't do it. That's why they are achievers and the others are still the boys and the girls.

PEOPLE SKILLS AND NETWORKING

People skills—or, as they are known in modern business jargon, interpersonal skills—are simply your ability to get along with people you don't know well. You don't need people skills at a family reunion, obviously, unless it isn't *your* family's reunion. In the working world, you do need people skills, unless you are the night watchman and want to *stay* the night watchman. Fred Pryor, who conducts business seminars across the country and on-line, says that the primary reason some people succeed at networking in the workplace is that they have a higher level of interpersonal skills than those who fail. By the way, I highly recommend Fred's seminars to you should they come to your town. In fact, I advise you to take advantage of any opportunity to enhance your people skills, whether through readings, seminars, or videos. These are vital tools for successful networking, and it takes study and practice to become skilled.

The first things I look for when networking or interviewing a prospective employee are the following six people skills:

1. Effective listening skills
2. Strong communication skills
3. Inquisitiveness

4. Self-assurance
5. Well-groomed and tasteful appearance
6. Sincere desire to help others and to share expertise

All-Ears All-Stars: Listening Skills

Clarence Smith, retired president of *Essence* magazine, is one of the most effective listeners in the publishing business, which is probably why he was a leader in the industry and one of the most effective print-advertising sales executives in business. I remember a meeting I had with him in a local bar around the corner from his office. In spite of his vast experience and knowledge of the advertising world, he patiently listened to my presentation without interruption.

He concentrated on me. He probed. He clarified. He helped me develop my ideas further. He became involved, asked good follow-up questions, and then provided me with expert advice regarding my plan. We made a small barter deal on a handshake, and parted with good feelings. I know that I left the meeting feeling as if I had talked with a man who cared about and understood what I was saying.

Clarence is an All-Ears All-Star, who apparently took to heart that same admonition that many of our mothers and fathers gave us: "God gave you two ears and only one mouth so that you'd listen twice as much as you talk." Because of his excellence and contributions to the African-American community and the American economy, he was among the first inductees into the African American Business Hall of Fame and Museum, which I founded in 2001.

Men can learn something from women about listening. I know far too many men who think listening involves merely waiting for their turn to talk. This must go back to the days of telling hunting tales around the campfire in the cave, each caveman trying to one-up the other in order to improve his standing in the tribe. Well, that dinosaur is dead, my friends. To get ahead in the global tribe, you have to absorb information as well as spew it out.

Women are generally excellent listeners, because they are better at tuning in to other people. They are often not as self-absorbed as men. They relate to other individuals rather than relating to the individual's experiences. Sometimes, men think women listen too well, I'm afraid, because they are excellent at reminding us when we contradict ourselves.

When you don't listen attentively, you cheat not only the speaker, but yourself. This is the information age, and that is information flowing past your ears. To be an effective networker, you have to listen to everything that is being said and everything that is *not* being said. Listen with your brain, not just your ears. And remember that you have to listen with your body, as well. You can't fold your arms and lean back. That says, "I would rather be doing something else." You have to put energy into listening.

Jim Moore was a manager with General Electric. His tall frame moves with grace and confidence at gatherings. His brown face is expressive, with a diamond-mine smile and kindly eyes. When he speaks at networking functions, his voice plays in the bass keys. He could recite the Yellow Pages, and his energy, enthusiasm, and body language would command your attention. Jim has the nonverbal and the verbal skills of networking mastered. This is charisma in action.

Here are a few tips to tune up all three parts of your networking apparatus—your ears, your brain, and your body language:

- Focus on the speaker. Maintain eye contact.
- Don't fold your arms or lean back. Keep your arms to your side, and try to lean toward the speaker to demonstrate your interest.
- Keep an open mind. Don't challenge until you've heard it all. Take mental notes.
- Identify areas of mutual interest.
- Watch for hidden clues to feelings and meanings displayed through body language.

Voicing Your Talents: Communication Skills

Remember that your voice is a tool and an instrument. I advise anyone who is truly interested in improving himself or herself to consider getting professional training from a speech or voice coach. A clear, enunciated speech pattern can transform you. I am lucky to have known and worked with the actor James Earl Jones, who has one of the greatest voices and deliveries in the media today. His is a gift, but it is one that he worked incredibly hard to develop. Until he told about it in his autobiography *Voices and Silences*, very few people knew that he was a stutterer as a child, and still stutters to a slight extent in conversation. He recorded a seven-minute script for a multimedia presentation put together for my company's fifth anniversary celebration, but he took more than an hour to get it the way he wanted it. He is the master of his voice.

With the help of Anne Baber, author of *Great Connections*, here are a few voice tips to add polish to your presentation:

- Practice lowering your voice so as not to sound whiny. A slightly lower voice can communicate confidence and authority. Ever notice how you first answer the telephone when it rings? The alertness and tonal quality of that phone voice is just about what you need to use in networking conversation.
- Emphasize key words in your delivery by varying your tone. Use a tape recorder for practice and read a favorite poem by Maya Angelou or a passage from James Baldwin. You'll be pleasantly surprised at how you can "play" your voice to convey more emotion and excitement.
- Make it a point to listen to masterful speakers such as Susan Taylor, Dr. Michael Eric Dyson, or Les Brown. Study their methods for investing their words with power and meaning.
- Your delivery should move along at a speed somewhere between rap and romantic ballad—one hundred fifty to two

hundred words per minute. At this speed, you can be well understood and still move through the message swiftly.

Inquiring Minds Want to Know: Inquisitiveness

Some of the most effective networkers I know are those with highly developed questioning techniques. Not surprisingly, one of these is my best friend of thirty-five years, Corky Williams, who is skilled at asking the right questions in the right manner for any occasion.

Corky is careful to limit his interrogations to the courtroom, but he uses some of the same techniques in his daily life. He listens well in order to get information that may be useful. He asks questions carefully, because he knows that good questions further his networking agenda and his goals to achieve success. Good questions also help you to:

- Build information
- Move conversation along by providing feedback
- Demonstrate your analytical skills
- Clarify your needs to the speaker
- Introduce new ideas and perspectives
- Help others to feel that you value their knowledge

It is a basic premise of lawyers that you never ask a question in the courtroom unless you already know the answer. Of course, lawyers don't always stick to that, and neither can you, but if possible, you should plan ahead and *do your homework before a networking event or meeting with someone,* so that you have a good idea of what sort of questions you will need to ask. One way to prepare yourself is to write down your agenda for such meetings. Having an agenda in mind will help you to ask questions that move you closer to your goals.

SuccessTip: Keep in mind at all times one of the primary rules of networking. It is permissible to use other people and their skills and knowledge in networking to further your agenda and goals, but only if you are open about your intentions, and only if you give something back in return.

When you ask good questions, people are clear about the purpose of your networking. People also enjoy the verbal engagement and exchange of interesting and meaningful sharing of information. If you have trouble thinking of questions, I suggest following the standard rule that reporters follow when they are seeking basic information for a story. The first things they always get are: Who? What? When? Where? Why? and How? Then they build on that basic foundation of information.

Here are a few suggestions for questions that can open up an informative conversation:

- How did you get started in your business?
- Why did you go into this line of business?
- What do you hope to get out of this meeting?
- When do you enjoy your work the most?
- Where do you do your best business?
- Who is your best source of information?

Self-Assurance Assures Others

Have you ever met someone who seems to drag a giant anchor marked INSECURE around with him? Well, most people upon encountering someone like that move away quickly, lest that anchor drag them down, too. You must learn self-assurance in order to be an effective networker, because you can never get others to believe in you if you don't believe in yourself. And the bad news is that learning self-assurance is not easy. In fact, it is a very tricky thing, because there is always the danger of going too far and coming off as arrogant and self-absorbed.

Assertiveness is not aggressiveness. It is being comfortable with who you are. It is liking yourself enough to share yourself with others comfortably.

I know a woman who rarely has a good first impression of anyone she meets, although she often changes her view of people later. My reading on her is that she is not comfortable with herself, so she has difficulty accepting other people. She is afraid they won't like her, so her answer is to be slow in accepting others until they demonstrate clearly that they have accepted her. This is a tortuous and neurotic way of dealing with the world, particularly in business, where you don't get a lot of opportunities to build relationships over time. First impressions mean a lot. You can't go into a networking meeting with a chip on your shoulder or feeling that someone is probably going to offend you.

Self-assured people are comfortable with themselves and others. If you are into Zen, you think of this as being centered. You find something you like about yourself, and you center your self-image on that admirable and solid quality, building from there. Okay, so you are a slob; don't build your self-image on that. Build it on the fact that you are also compassionate toward others.

Self-assurance gives you the power to be assertive without being overly aggressive. Assertive people often get what they are after, but they don't walk all over others to do it. They are successful while still being concerned about others, which is one of the keys to effective networking.

Self-assured people have these qualities that are very helpful in successful networking:

- They ask for help and don't apologize for it.
- They offer help whenever and wherever they can.
- They initiate conversations.
- They take pride in their appearance.
- They accept responsibility for their own successes or failures.
- They are not offended by rejection, because they realize that everyone has his or her own agenda.
- They are eager to lead, share opinions, and exchange ideas.
- They don't compare themselves with others.
- They speak clearly and with authority.
- They do not seek approval for their opinions and ideas.

Dennis Kimbro, coauthor of *Think and Grow Rich: A Black Choice*, is one of the most self-assured interviewers and networkers in the African-American community. His skills have enabled him to interview and plumb the minds of some of the most successful black Americans, including John H. Johnson and A. G. Gaston, a pioneering entrepreneur in the insurance industry. Dennis's engaging persona, presence, and warmth charm others into opening up to him. He is a fine example of a man whose self-assurance inspires confidence in others. When speaking with him, the thought comes to you: *If this intelligent and charming guy finds me interesting, then I must have something worthwhile to say.*

The ability to give other people self-confidence is a rare and great talent, and in conversation, it is a talent that often rewards you tenfold for everything you give out.

The Look of Success: Good Grooming

Your visual "package" is as important in the initial stages of networking as all of that information and talent wrapped up inside. John Molloy, author of *Dress for Success*, writes that 90 percent of how you present yourself is visual. Your appearance and demeanor communicate who you are, your level of self-assurance, and your ability to interact.

Your ability to present yourself as a professional determines whether or not people are drawn to you or compelled to flee. Have you ever noticed how a gathering gravitates away from those who are obviously out-of-place, while it tends to move toward and surround those who shine? There is nothing wrong with asserting your own unique fashion sense, as long as you don't mind being the topic of conversation rather than the leader of it. A tip that I've heard often is that you should dress for the position that you one day hope to attain. That is pretty much what I began doing when I was still a janitor but wanted to be an executive. Sure, my briefcase contained nothing more than *The New York Times*, my dictionary, and a cheese sandwich, but they didn't know that on the subway.

More than grooming and clothing goes into your personal presentation. Your manners, your posture, your eye contact and verbal skills all come into play. Networking meetings are out of necessity quick hits—and smoking, drinking too much, talking while you are eating, making sarcastic comments, or displaying any other improper behavior can leave a lasting bad impression. That said, relax and enjoy yourself at networking meetings. You'll never make a good impression if you are stressed out.

The Willingness to Share

Regardless of your station or position in life, each of us has something to share with others, a gift to give, a role to play. Though he has only a high school education and speaks in a strong black dialect, Wilbur Black is a successful beauty-salon owner. He wears lavender loafers to match the lavender strips in his double-breasted suit. His jewelry—four gold and diamond rings and a gold bracelet—lends him the glitz of a Vegas headliner. But believe me, Wilbur is a rare gem. He is the organizer of a local networking event called SHARE, which stands for Successful Hair Designers Annual Resource Expo.

Wilbur's goal is to focus on business education for salon owners and the need for them to purchase their products and services from black-owned businesses. Wilbur has the sincere desire to share his knowledge, resources, and leadership with others. His sharing empowers others, and in turn, it helps his business, his industry, and ultimately, him.

When you empower someone, you are doing no more than helping that person realize that basic human need to be of value and significance in this world. To do that, you must have a fundamental love of other people; you have to understand the value of each individual; and you have to listen to others with an open mind. The more you listen, the more value you communicate to others. The more value you communicate, the more others feel empowered and drawn to you. The more they are drawn to you, the more they will do for you, which in turn multiplies your efforts toward a specific set of goals.

This is how good organizations function. And the leaders of those organizations are exceptional at empowering others to reach common goals. Skillful networkers are constantly looking for ways to be helpful, and finding the value and good in people. They expect no direct compensation. Without exception, the law of increasing returns dictates that they will be repaid tenfold over time.

With these six people skills, your path toward effective networking will be paved with success.

WHAT IS YOUR AGENDA?

Say what? You don't believe that you have an agenda? Well, I don't believe that you don't have an agenda. In fact, I am sure that you do have one, but perhaps you have not yet identified it. As you may recall, I noted earlier that your agenda is the method by which you reach your goals. Without an agenda, you are like a ship without a rudder, a traveler without a map.

How many times have you looked at a person moving around a room or coming at you with his or her sights set on your forehead, and asked yourself cynically, *I wonder what his (or her) agenda is?* To network effectively, you must identify your own agenda, your goals, your dreams and ideas—whatever you wish to accomplish in the limited time you have on this planet.

Every now and then, I talk with someone who just blathers on and on without saying anything. There is no focus or sense of purpose to the conversation. He or she has a shotgun approach, so that person never makes a direct hit with me. To make a connection, you have to be direct and to the point. I would advise you to narrow your immediate goals to the critical objectives that will advance you toward your ultimate goal. I wanted to write a book. A shotgun approach to that goal would have been to send a proposal to every agent and publisher in New York, and to talk to everyone I met about what I wanted to do. Instead, I took the direct approach. I talked to a friend who had a friend who knew an agent and arranged a meeting. The very real result of that direct approach is in your hands.

Without a sense of purpose or a well-defined agenda, you might as well not attend a networking function. It's like going hunting with an unloaded gun. You'll never bag your game. You have to know where you are going before you can ask for help getting there. I have never been tempted to pick up a hitchhiker holding up a sign that says "?"

Agendas don't have to be complicated or grandiose. In fact, they should be the opposite—concise and workable. You probably won't get to be president of a company if you don't have a step-by-step agenda. Agendas are like the spray of a hose: The more focused they are, the more power they have. With a focused agenda in mind, you can concentrate your energy, enthusiasm, and excitement to a more powerful degree.

Have you ever noticed how excited and creative you get when you really go after something you want? My mind goes into overtime in those situations. I find myself solving the minor problems in my sleep, because my focus is so intense, even my dreams become energized. And when you are that energized, you draw people to you who empower you further.

One way in which you can get yourself energized is to view every networking encounter as an opportunity to discover silver and gold—the treasure both within yourself and within those you meet. Your mind-set and your approach to life define your agenda. You really do have to seize every moment, enjoy every day, and find something of merit in every person you encounter. The clichés of the human potential movement are clichés only to those who choose to ignore the basic truths they communicate. I truly believe that if you expect the best from people and give them your best, everyone wins in the end. I have never seen even one exception to this rule in all of my work in public, corporate, and entrepreneurial business.

Here are a few strategies for setting your agenda and focusing on it:

- List those things you have to offer: your expertise, talents, ideas, resources, etc.
- List the things you would like to obtain. These are your goals; for example: an education, a new job, a new house, a new car, a publisher, new recipes, a girlfriend, a computer, a board appointment, etc.
- Set priorities for your agenda and go public with them. If you can't articulate your agenda and goals to others, then you have not defined them well enough. And once you are able to articulate them, it helps to get the word out that you are looking for that new job, or new clients, or whatever happens to be your goal.

There is nothing wrong with having an agenda and letting people know what it is. I find it offensive, however, when people have hidden agendas. How can you deal with someone in business if that person is not straightforward in communicating what he or she wants? And I find it equally unsettling when people expect me to come to their assistance but refuse to share any of their knowledge or talents with me. Author Stephen Covey, who was quoted in the previous chapter, writes that "you can't expect to take anything out of the bank if you don't put something in it." Build your bank account through networking give and take. Bank on meeting your agenda through networking.

OVERCOMING FEARS AND DOUBTS

Effective networking cannot be done until you overcome any awkwardness you may feel when meeting new people. This is no time to have to face the old bugaboos of insecurity, shyness, or timidity. Negative self-images are a particular problem among black people, though certainly, not all of us lack self-confidence.

It is vital that you overcome this negative thinking, not only for your career development but also for your personal growth and happiness. You can't stand back and be scenery for other people's lives. You have to become engaged in life and take life on.

There are all sorts of motivational and self-help books and tapes out there, although very few deal specifically with networking situations. So here are a few basic tips for overcoming your inhibitions and negative thinking when it comes to networking for success.

The Great Entrance

Zora Neale Hurston once wrote of a character, "He walked like he knew where he was going." Vanity is not a great attribute to carry into a networking situation, but confidence and self-assuredness are. In networking, you have to carry yourself with confidence if you want others to feel confident about you. For example, Hosiah Huggins, Jr., is CEO of Zebraa Communications, a technology consulting firm. When he was a relative newcomer to the political scene in Washington, one of the toughest towns in the world for breaking into the circles of power, Hosiah quickly became one of that city's important networkers. His secret? He talks to himself, not like some babbling street person, but yes—he does talk to himself. He calls it positive self-talk.

In effect, he gives himself a pep talk before entering a roomful of strangers. *This is going to be great, because I'll get a chance to meet some key people I've been trying to contact,* he'll say to himself. *I bet I will uncover new opportunities.*

Pepped up and empowered by these positive thoughts, Hosiah enters into networking encounters with a dazzling smile and a *Let's Make a Deal* demeanor. You'd never know it, but he is inherently a shy person. But he overcomes his phobia with relative ease. He knows that self-confidence inspires others to approach you. If you slink into a room, most people will slink away.

Opening Lines

Here are a few guidelines to follow so that you can walk into any networking occasion ready to grip and rip.

- Psych yourself up by remembering this is fun. It is dynamic. You are doing something about attaining your goals. Take a roll call of your talents and knowledge. Pump yourself up.
- Start your conversation with a simple but enthusiastic greeting. Make good eye contact. Remember that firm handshake. You'd be surprised how many times I still come across someone with a limp-rag grip. Then again, don't get too carried away. I've had a few people, men and women, clamp me in a knuckle-crusher.
- Your enthusiasm should be obvious in your demeanor, although you don't have to jump up and down like a puppy in search of a treat. Practice your greeting until you are comfortable with it and it doesn't sound rehearsed or phony. I practice mine on my sons, Kyle and Scott. They let me know if I'm coming across like Robo-Networker.
- Be succinct when you introduce yourself, especially in that initial contact with a person. Before you go, prepare a thirty-second script that covers who you are, the company you are with, and what you are looking for. Practice your script until it sounds smooth and natural. Your goal is to set up a convenient time to talk further. The fatal error most networkers make is being too wordy. If you want to make a good and lasting impression, be quick and to the point. I suggest using the "match" test to burn this philosophy into your brain, or at least your finger: Strike a match and hold it while you practice your introduction. If the match burns too close to your fingers before you finish, then your script is too long-winded for a networking occasion. (If your entire hand is consumed, however, you might consider a career in politics.)

Here is the script that I normally follow at networking meetings:

> Hi, I'm George Fraser from Cleveland, Ohio. I'm CEO of FraserNet, Inc., and publisher of *SuccessGuide Worldwide: The Networking Guide to Black Resources*. I help people network and find the resources they need to succeed personally and professionally. One resource I use is the PowerNetworking Conference, which I founded. I'm always on the lookout for people who are interested in building a network of contacts in the black community. What brought you here today?

Would you believe I can get all that out without so much as scorching a fingernail? My introduction accomplishes several things. It tells you who I am, where I am from, what I do, why I do it, how I can help you, and finally, it gives you, the person I've approached, the opportunity to provide me with the same information about yourself. There is also enough information in my introduction to trigger follow-up questions and lead to an engaging conversation. All of this in just thirty seconds of burn-free soliloquy.

Fifteen Ways to Break the Ice Without Creating a Chill

You are primed, pumped, and ready to rock. You've got your introduction down; you know your agenda for the long and short terms; you're looking good, feeling good. Now, remember, you don't just charge up to a person or a group and start firing at will. Wait for a break in the conversation, or for someone to turn to you for a comment or introduction. And be ready to think on your feet.

Here are some sample conversational openers to get you thinking nimbly:

- As the owner of a business, what do you find to be the two or three greatest challenges you face?

- What exactly do you do in your job day-to-day?
- What are the most interesting aspects of your work?
- In your educational training, what were the most useful things you learned?
- How do you relieve the stress of your work?
- What do you hope to get out of this meeting?
- How did you get into your line of work?
- What books have you read that have been helpful in your career?
- Tell me about your family.
- Who are your role models?
- When did you decide on this career path?
- What is it about your work that excites you?
- How has your year been?
- What is your goal for next year?
- Where would you most like to live and work?

And One Instant Freeze

In putting these examples together, I was reminded of a line I heard a not-so-nimble fellow use on a woman in a bar one night. This is not recommended for public use, but I still find it amusing. "Hi, I'm Darrell," the fellow said. "How do you like me so far?"

Needless to say, I advise you to stay away from opening lines that could lead to dead ends or a punch in the nose. Questions that require only one-word answers are a bad idea, too. Make them personal without being nosy. It's okay to ask about someone's family, but not someone's love life. Generic questions about the weather or sports are generally perceived as the terrain of dullards and a waste of time—unless, of course, a tornado has just gone through, or you're talking to Kobe Bryant. The best opening questions are those that encourage people to speak about themselves, or their work, passions, family, or experiences. A sincere compliment or declaration of appreciation will always be well received. False praise never rings true, *you gorgeous thing you*. (See?)

Group Encounters

"Enter and sign in, please." That's a line from the old television show *What's My Line?*, in which a group of blindfolded panelists had to guess the occupation of a guest within a short time frame. Networking affairs are something like that. When you enter them, people always seem to be clustered in groups, trying to guess the importance of people as they come in, gauging whether or not each individual is worth their time and effort. This can be intimidating if you are the individual walking into the room under scrutiny. How do you approach these groups?

Here are a few suggestions and rules of etiquette for group encounters at networking meetings:

- Again, think positively. *This looks like an interesting group; I bet I'll learn something here.* Remember that groups of people always welcome someone who brings fresh energy to the group. Be alert to the dynamic of the group. Are they rolling on a topic, or are they in need of a new direction?
- Check the body language of the group. Do they appear receptive to new people, or are they clustered close together in a huddle? Avoid entering into discussions in which the participants are standing within two feet of one another, talking intently, or obviously emotional.
- To enter a group, make eye contact with a listener or the speaker, and when necessary, touch the shoulder or an arm of a participant to signal that you'd like to enter the conversation. Like a batter who takes the first pitch to get a feel for the pitcher, don't start swinging with your comments right away. Get a feel for the flow and the topic. I generally wait for a lull and then introduce myself and ask a well-considered question of the last speaker or the person next to me. If the conversation needs recharging, I'll pop one of my opening lines: "Hi, I'm George Fraser with FraserNet, from Cleveland. Are there any other Midwesterners here?"
- If you enter a group only to find the conversation is not

one you'd care to join—say, they are discussing their secret admiration for Timothy McVeigh or the best place to have their money laundered—you can politely excuse yourself to get a drink, some food, or a 357-magnum Super-Soaker, and then go off to find a more welcoming group.

- A very effective tactic for starting a group of your own is to look for the smiling face of a loner and strike up a conversation. Remember, this is not the lonely hearts club. Most of the people at networking affairs are looking to make contact.

REMEMBERING WHAT'S-HIS-NAME

I can network until the cows come home and the rooster crows. I can pick up the telephone and get a lunch with the Dalai Lama in just three calls. But I can't remember names for the life of me. It is, I confess, my only flaw. Well, my staff might have a few to add to that. But in order to do better, I often turn to advice from memory expert Henry . . . uh, Harvey . . . uh, Harry! That's it, Harry Lorayne, whose tips I've incorporated below.

- Repeat the person's name immediately following the introduction. Use it in a short sentence: "Great meeting you, Susan."
- Think of a personal connection: *That's my father's name. That's the name of my high school science teacher's eldest son.*
- Visualize a picture: If you meet someone named Bob at a Halloween party, visualize him bobbing for apples. (If you meet someone named Igor, run!)
- Ask the person to spell his or her name: "Is that Fraser with an S or a Z?"
- Ask the origins of the name: "*Aisha*—that's an unusual name. Does it have special meaning?"
- Compliment the person, if appropriate, using his or her name: "Barbara, I understand you started a new business downtown. Congratulations."

- Help people remember your name with a unique statement: "I'm *George*, like the president. *Fraser*, like the boxer, except I can't take a punch."

You Forgot It Already?

How do you handle it when, just three minutes after being introduced to someone, you are called upon to use his or her name and you can't come up with it? Don't wait for your memory to save you, because under such pressure, it probably won't come up with the name until about three in the morning, when you will shoot up in bed and shriek at the top of your lungs, "Khalalia Mfumbotuma! That's it! Why couldn't I remember that?" Here are some tips when memory fails.

- Look for a name tag. (Well, miracles do happen.)
- Don't guess. In this case, two Wongs won't make a Wright.
- Do try to remember the exact circumstances of the original introduction. This might trigger old Mister Memory.
- Ask for a business card. Brilliant!
- Reintroduce yourself, using your full name. Often, people will merely think you are senile, and go ahead and reintroduce themselves.
- Ask an associate to introduce himself or herself, and get the mystery name on the sly.
- If all else fails, rely on honesty. I know, it may be difficult, but 'fess up and say: "I've had a memory lapse, probably due to overexposure to tortilla dip. Please tell me your name again."

THE ETIQUETTE OF INTRODUCTIONS

Miss Manners, an expert in etiquette, says that the general rule is to introduce the name of the higher-ranking person first, or the person you most want to honor first.

- When introducing women, rank prevails over gender. If the man is your boss, introduce him first. If he is a peer, introduce the woman first: "Michael Jones, I'd like you to meet Jane Walker. Jane Walker, this is Michael Jones. Michael is the manager of our department."
- When introducing a customer to business associates, treat the customer as a superior to honor the relationship. Say the customer's name first: "Gregory Williams, I'd like you to meet Josh Archer. Josh, this is Gregory Williams. Josh, Greg just purchased our new XL Computer system. Josh is responsible for our customer service department."
- When introducing a superior to a subordinate, use the superior's name first: "Jim Moore, I'd like you to meet Millicent Lee. Millicent, this is Jim Moore. Jim is our new director of marketing." Use the first name only if you are on a first-name basis.
- When introducing peers to each other, use either name first.
- When introducing older people to younger people, you can ignore age, but being old-fashioned myself, I use the older person's name first.
- When introducing persons with no business status, such as introducing your parents to a peer, say your parents' names first to honor them. If you are outranked by a colleague, say the colleague's name first. In this case, rank over honor.

When making introductions, always show enthusiasm. Let people know you are glad to meet them, and make sure you stand up for all introductions, except when seated in a restaurant or when circumstances make standing awkward (while getting a massage, while in the bathtub, while seated in your car).

RULES AND TOOLS OF CONVERSATION

Two of the rudest things you can do in a group conversation are: interrupt a person who is speaking; and, give a long-winded monologue. Both are conversation killers. I was at a family gathering once when a neighbor—a stockbroker known for his self-absorption—wandered over, helped himself to the buffet, and then sat down amid a group of people he did not know and announced, "Well, stock prices in Japan just went to hell." Understandably, they looked at him as if he were the brother from another planet.

People who do such things are rude bores and probably egomaniacs, quite likely both. The same goes for people who dominate conversations to the exclusion of all others. Martin Luther King's "I Have a Dream" speech and Abraham Lincoln's "Gettysburg Address" each took less than ten minutes to deliver. So, don't ever become so enamored with the sound of your own voice or the brilliance of your own ideas that you drive away everyone around you.

Networking affairs are not places for going into detail on the finer points of your laser printer. Save that for the sales meetings. If you can't answer a question or describe your latest five-speed turbo widget in under two minutes, save it for the follow-up. Even nonstop humorous monologues wear thin. Long-winded jokes are even worse, and there is no place for blue or sexist humor at a networking meeting. Save it for the back room. In fact, I'd suggest that you not tell jokes at all in networking situations. The best humor springs from real-life situations, and if you can tell a funny story about yourself or your family that fits into the conversational flow, fine. Most "jokes," however, do little more than interrupt the flow of networking conversation, and all too often, they are told at someone's expense.

On the occasion when I encounter a monologist, I slip in a quick question when he or she pauses to draw a breath. Thank goodness, everyone has to breathe.

Effective networking can only take place when there is a dialogue, or when the conversation includes several people. If all you talk about is yourself, then prepare to have a one-man network, which is about as effective as a one-hand clap.

Remember these good conversation rules:

• Never talk for more than three or four minutes without including someone else in the conversation.

• Ask relevant questions of other speakers and listen to their answers.

• Encourage others to get involved by asking: "Do you have any questions about this?"

• Acknowledge new people and invite them into the conversation.

• Interrupt only when there is a give-and-take flow going.

• Don't make gender or status-based power plays in conversation, or talk condescendingly.

Conversational Common Ground

After introductions have been made, the opening question shifts the emphasis from who you are to what you are interested in, and the quest begins for the common ground from which everyone in the conversational group can participate comfortably. If you've been on a topic for five minutes and you see that not everyone is comfortable with it, switch to something new, or move to another group.

Here are a few strategies for moving conversation along:

• Follow up on the answer to your opening question. As the person responds to your question, listen carefully for clues to expand the topic. Don't be afraid to jump around or change the topic quickly.

• Ask questions to get more information and dig deeper, but don't turn into The Interrogator. Ask nicely.

• Remember, people are normally flattered by sincere interest expressed by others, and they feel most comfortable talking about things they know well.

• Relax and let the topics from your experiences and immediate environment flow. The brain has an amazing capacity to recall and associate words with personal experience. The key to relaxing in conversation with strangers is to tell yourself how enjoyable it is to meet and share experiences with new people. Remember, there is gold lurking in those networking contacts.

• B. L. Ochman, editor of the now defunct public relations newletter *PRINK*, offers these conversational tips:

Never say:
I didn't understand.
I don't follow you.
I disagree.
What you're trying to say is . . .

Instead:
Let me see if I understand. Are you saying that . . . ?
That's certainly valid. Would another way to look at that be . . . ?
From what you've told me, the question seems to be . . . ?

• Your goals and agenda will drive your conversation, and if you keep those objectives in mind at all times, you will eventually find someone at each networking event who will move you closer to your goals.

Closing the Conversation: A Four-Point Technique to Exiting Gracefully

When the conversation starts to fizzle, or the eyes of the participants begin to wander, it's time to exit gracefully. Announcing a sudden bodily urge is not considered graceful, but there are ways to go about it. Many find it stressful and cop out by just disappearing into the night. Others lie: "I'll be right back." You don't want to do that, because it can cause hurt feelings. And it is rude. Here is a technique for making a polite withdrawal: Be honest but don't be cruel; tell your conversational partner or partners that you feel it is time to move on, but excuse yourself tactfully. I don't suggest saying, "You bore me," or "I'm boring you, so it is time for me to leave." Instead, here are some closing statements that should help you slip away without causing hard feelings.

- I need to see a few more people before I leave.
- I want to go over and meet the speaker.
- I promised to meet with my colleague before she leaves.
- I'm going to continue circulating so I can meet some others.
- I'm looking to meet some new clients, so I think I'll move on.

It might help ease the moment if you remember to show appreciation for the time and conversation you've been having, and if you note something that your conversational partner said that was particularly helpful. Be genuine and don't overdo it with false praise. Here are a few examples:

- Your enthusiasm is infectious. I look forward to being infected again.
- Your business is fascinating. It's been great talking with you about it.
- It's nice to meet someone so committed to his work.
- You sure lead an interesting life. It's been fun hearing about your adventures.

In leaving a group or an individual, don't kiss your conversational partner off with false promises of "I'll call you for lunch sometime," or "Let's get together." It's insulting. But if you sincerely want to get together, set a specific time for discussing it. Such as:

- I'll contact you Wednesday morning to set up a luncheon.
- I'll get a copy of the material we discussed in the mail to you tomorrow.

- I'll have my marketing director, Jim, call you Thursday with that information.
- Please make sure you send me your brochure.

Finally, shake hands and move on after making sure you've exchanged business cards. Don't overload people with bulky material; send it to them later. Exit gracefully. A good exit is as important as a good entrance. And so, I'm going to exit this chapter gracefully. Right now.

*"There is power and unity and strength in networking.
I think networking is always relevant. And I think it is particularly
relevant for blacks because of our feelings of isolation."*
WILLIE GARY

Willie Gary is a renowned attorney who has gained international recognition as a leading trial advocate, public speaker, and philanthropist. He opened the first black law firm in Martin County, Florida. Willie's scope of interest goes beyond the courtroom. He has given millions to his alma mater and gives $20,000 scholarships annually to deserving students from his hometown of Indiantown, Florida. He funded a day care center for a disadvantaged neighborhood and he donates the use of his eighteen-seat Gulfstream II jet to fly critically ill cancer patients to U.S. treatment centers. In 1995, he won one of the largest jury verdicts in U.S. history—a $500 million damages settlement resulting from a clash between two funeral service companies. He's a member of the National and American Bar Associations, American Trial Lawyers, Florida Academy of Trial Lawyers, Martin and St. Lucie County Bar Associations, and the Million Dollar Verdict Club. Says Gary, "Don't 'make it' and catch amnesia. We all have an obligation to be about more than our own agendas. We have an obligation to be more than about just making money or seeking the limelight."

8

Networking for a Purpose

Remember that our cause is one,
and that we must help each other,
if we would succeed.
— FREDERICK DOUGLASS

For many weeks, the northern California city of Walnut Creek had been plagued by burglaries along a popular jogging trail through an affluent condo community. These crimes were unique, because the burglar who committed them was also known for grabbing the backsides of female joggers while he apparently staked out his intended victims. He was thus known as the "Trail Side Grabber."

Detective George Willis of the Walnut Creek Police Department had compiled a thick file in his investigation of the Trail Side Grabber. More than eighty burglaries and assaults were thought to have been committed by the Grabber, who seemed to be getting more and more sexually aggressive with each new incident.

Officer Willis, an African American, took his file on the Grabber to a weekly networking meeting of city and county burglary detectives. Known as the Central County Burglary Investigators Group, it had proven so effective over the years that detectives specializing in youth crimes, armed robberies, and other categories of police work had used it as a model for their networking groups. The purpose was to share information on area crimes with other police agencies in hopes of helping one another—a classic professional networking group.

At the meeting, Detective Willis asked the other officers if any of them had come across a criminal matching the description of this man. A detective from a nearby community said he had dealt with a criminal of similar description, who had been convicted and sent to prison for burglary but recently had been paroled.

Based on the name and other information provided by his networking contact, Detective Willis went to work, tracked down the parolee, and, thanks to his network, nabbed the Grabber within a few days.

Often, we have knowledge or information or expertise that, when shared with others, becomes even more valuable to us. This expertise has the sort of "collective value" referred to in the principles of Kwanzaa. The information in Detective Willis's file was not enough to get him the Grabber. But when placed collectively with the information held by his networking contact, it was more than enough to lead to an arrest and conviction.

This chapter will show you how to use and expand upon your information base by networking for a specific purpose, be it for a job, for customers or clients, or for career advancement.

As I've stressed in other chapters, everyone should have an established goal and an agenda for networking to obtain that goal. Your agenda is dictated by your goals. Your ability to expand on your own expertise—the area in which you have specific information—by networking to build a wide range of contacts and enduring professional relationships may ultimately determine whether you get what you want out of life.

This chapter will stress the importance of recognizing not only that your own expertise is valuable as networking capital, but that other black professionals are also sources of knowledge and information that must be cultivated. Black people must make it a priority to show unity by sharing information through our own Underground Railroad of Afrocentric networks. But, as in the example of Detective Willis, you must also network with others who have information valuable to you.

According to Joel Kotkin, author of *Tribes: How Race, Religion, and Identity Determine Success in the New Global Economy*, there are five global tribes—Jews, Japanese, Chinese, Indians, and British—that share three basic characteristics that have helped them to achieve economic success in the twentieth century and beyond:

1. A **strong ethnic identity** with a sense of mutual dependence and emphasis on family structure
2. A **global network** based on tribal trust that allows the group to function collectively
3. A **passion for technology** and a belief in scientific progress

I'm afraid that we are only batting one for three in this arena. Surely, many black people share a passion for education and a growing appreciation for the value of technical knowledge. I know that it is certainly a dominant topic in my household and among my peers. All of us stress education to our children and we tell them that the pursuit of technical expertise is vital.

But our ethnic identity and our global networks have been slow to evolve. The Black Power movement flared up in the 1960s, but diminished greatly over the next twenty years as most of us accepted integration, bought into the melting-pot concept, and attempted to blend into the Eurocentric culture. Many of us did well, but not enough of us did well enough. The Afrocentrism movement signals the reemergence of our ethnic identity and the widespread desire of black people to achieve more, for more of our people. The vast array of Afrocentric networking groups across the country—associations of black lawyers, psychologists, beauticians, engineers, data processors—manifests our strong desire to get ahead by getting together. By networking, I believe we can put it *all* together.

I agree with Kotkin that global networks based on tribal trust are one of the best ways for black people to wield their collective resources. If black people are going to succeed, they must reach out to one another and to those who are willing to help. This includes reaching out to the motherland of Africa, where many of our people are looking for assistance in their struggle for economic development. It is a great opportunity and also our responsibility to lend our resources, clout, and intellectual capital to those African people, as some African Americans such as the Reverend Leon Sullivan and Randall Robinson have done through TransAfrica. By our building bridges back to Africa, our people on both sides will benefit.

Networking, unfortunately, is not a skill taught formally in schools. So, I have compiled some strategies and tactics for you to employ as you network in order to get what you want out of life. You will be surprised how responsive people can be when they are approached in a professional manner. Remember, when your skills are put to a purpose, results occur. And remember also to think black first, and then expand your outreach from there, because if you start networking first with those with whom you are most comfortable, then you have built a strong base.

NETWORKING FOR A JOB

Employment counselors agree that more than 70 percent of all jobs are found through the networking process. You can add to that old saying "It's not what you know, it's who you know" the following: "And it's who *they* know, too."

The arithmetic is quite amazing when you think about it. If you have just fifty people in your network, you can reach more than six million people by the fourth-generation contact—the friends of friends of friends of friends. If you remember the concept of "the strength of weak ties" covered in Chapter 5, you'll recall that social scientists have found that acquaintances are more likely than family or friends to give individuals direct information and to recommend them for opportunities. That is the power of an extended network when you are job-hunting.

The so-called hidden job market, which represents 70 to 80 percent of the available positions of significance or importance, can primarily be accessed by word-of-mouth networking. The fact is that employers would rather hire someone they know or someone that one of their trusted employees recommends highly. If you read about a job in the newspaper, it is generally for a few reasons: The law requires that it be advertised; it is a highly specialized position; nobody in the company wanted it; nor could any employee think of anyone who might want it.

Your ability to find a job, then, is directly related to how good your network is at the time you start to job-hunt. Caution: If you didn't start networking long before you started looking for a job, you are in for a rocky road. Without an established network, you will have to reach out to four or five times as many people to even begin to get some leads. Networking is a long-term process. It is not a quick-fix, 911 call for help. "Hello? Sorry, the career-rescue squad is on another call."

By effectively networking *throughout* your career—that means from your school days onward—you'll build a support base that can easily provide you with everything you need for the job hunt: word of job openings before they happen, inside information on new opportunities, and a group of friends and colleagues willing to open doors for you. Keep in mind, this network is a two-way street. You must have a lifelong policy of being prepared to help others if you expect them to be there for you one day.

You should also keep in mind that you should never tap into your network before you have prepared yourself adequately. Paul, a longtime associate of mine, cornered me at a social event and told me he was about to be laid off from his radio station, and he needed a job. Taking him seriously, I asked him what in particular he was looking for. He said he would take anything. "I just need some income to take care of the basics until I can find a good job," he said. But when I asked him what it was that he really wanted to do, he obviously had not thought it out. He was networking ineffectively, because he was going at it out of desperation and fear. That is not the way to do it.

Paul's groping approach caused me to pull back from really networking hard for him because, first of all, who in my network has a job opening for someone looking for "just anything to tide me over"? And second, Paul was a great radio personality. He had been at the top nearly all of his career. Where was his own network of contacts inside the broadcasting business?

I didn't hang Paul out to dry, however. I did tell him that he needed to take inventory and to get more serious about relocating in his field of expertise. When he did so and came up with a specific plan and agenda, I successfully connected him with a radio station in the South, where he really wanted to locate.

A point to keep in mind is that if you have been fired or laid off or "downsized," it has a depressing psychological effect that you may not even notice or feel consciously, but it will manifest itself in your behavior. The best way to overcome that is to put aside thoughts of where you were and invest your positive energies in where you are going. Consider it an opportunity rather than a setback. And don't feel that you have to take a step back in your career. Do whatever you can to keep moving up. You don't want to land in a job that you hate. Life is too short for that.

Taking Inventory

Here are a few important things to think through when networking for a job:

- What are my skills and strengths?
- What industry is my focus?
- Where, geographically, do I want to work? (Would I be willing to relocate several times to get where I want to be?)
- What level of position am I qualified for?
- How much do I *have* to earn to meet my responsibilities?
- How much would I like to earn?
- Would I take a pay cut to learn a new skill or industry?

Once you have carefully answered these questions, then you can begin to formulate your networking strategy. I stress *carefully*, because you don't want to abuse your network by shooting for positions that you are not qualified for or, in reality, are unwilling to take. There is a trust inherent in the networking process, and it is unfair to violate it or to force someone else to violate it.

Another friend, Jack, whom I met early in my career, was a very talented writer working in a newspaper market that was well below his ultimate reach. About every two years, he would get antsy and call me, saying that he was ready to move up. Like a good networking partner, I'd make some calls, get some people interested in him, and open the door to his moving up. And always, Jack would then decide that he was better off where he was. That is an abuse of network trust.

It was good for his ego to know that his talents were valued in a bigger market, but it was damaging to my reputation because, in the end, this guy whom I had championed didn't come through.

People in your network trust that if you recommend or refer someone, she or he must be qualified *and* serious about making a move. Your endorsement, if you are regarded as a serious networker, gives the person you recommend a competitive advantage over other candidates. This often results in better job opportunities at higher starting salaries. But if your recommended candidate backs out, that diminishes your effectiveness in the future, and hurts the chances of your future recommendations. Eventually, when Jack called and voiced a desire to move up, I no longer took him seriously. I couldn't afford to keep straining the lines of trust that I'd worked so hard to establish in my network.

Make a List of Contacts

Start with a comprehensive list of everyone in your desired field. Think of black people first, because of the cultural and sociological connection, but don't limit it to any one group. Use professional directories (might I suggest *SuccessGuides*?), the Internet, newspaper clippings, and specialized publications for leads to people in your field.

Next—and this is the fun but tough part—list everyone you can think of in your extended network. It doesn't matter who they are or what they do. This can include immediate family, other relatives, your hairstylist, postman, or professor, club members, alumni group members, grocers, physicians, former customers, supervisors, employees, etc. You don't have to risk your ego by telling them you are desperate for work. Tell them you are "looking for new opportunities."

Telephone or contact each person on this list, giving each your positive pitch and asking for contacts or referrals. Your goal is to get one hundred and fifty names. Then follow each referral using a simple thirty-second introductory statement, spoken with enthusiasm. Here is a format suggested by Howard Armstrong, a training and telephone scripting expert:

Good morning, Ms. Smith! My name is Tom Allen. You don't know me, but it appears that we have an acquaintance in common—Pete Harris. The other day, I was telling Pete that I was part of a recent downsizing at the XYZ company, and to reenter the job market, I had to do a considerable amount of research and networking in the insurance field. He suggested that I get in touch with you. Is this a convenient time for you to talk?

Another suggested format:

Good morning, Mr. Adams. The reason for my calling you is that while I was in for a checkup with my physician, Dr. Jones [your referral], she suggested that I call you. You see, I am currently conducting informal informational interviews around the construction industry. When she learned of my area of interest, she suggested that I give you a call. Is this a convenient time for you to talk?

Each of these examples provides you with a basis for starting your conversation on a professional level. Remember, your enthusiasm should be high (regardless of how many calls you've made earlier). You will have established rapport by mentioning your referrals early; you will have flattered your referral by recognizing his or her expertise in your field; and finally, you will have put the contact at ease by stating clearly that you are doing research and gathering information, rather than hitting him or her up for a job.

Putting It in Writing

At some point in your job search, you will probably be asked to provide a résumé. The natural thing to do is to write a cover letter and attach it. Your ability to write an effective letter will be one of the most powerful and revealing aspects of your communications skills. I receive countless letters and résumés, many of which are so badly done that they practically jump out of my hands into the circular file on the floor beside my desk. The next person to see them is the janitor.

These poorly done résumés are often handwritten, full of misspelled names and words, and composed like junior-high theme papers. I will also never be able to understand why some people think the best form to follow is to write of themselves as if they are God's gift to the professional world. No one wants to hire The Ego That Ate Manhattan and then try to fit it into the staff. Save the ego trips for—well, I don't know where they belong, but they don't belong on a résumé.

When I get a badly prepared résumé, I am chagrined, because the applicant has not only embarrassed himself, but also eliminated himself from consideration. Your job may not require any writing skills, but you will be judged by your ability to communicate, and that résumé and cover letter are vital first impressions. The quality of your education shows not just *on* your résumé, but in the quality of its preparation, as well.

Make no mistake; people will judge you by your writing skills. When you commit something to paper, you are drawing a picture of yourself. It is your image, and it will be permanently implanted in the mind of the person who receives it.

The best advice I have read on applying for a job was written by Kenneth Roman and Joel Raphaelson in their book *Writing*

That Works, to which advertising guru David Ogilvy contributed his insights. I have borrowed from them and added a few touches of my own to come up with five important points:

1. *Spell all names correctly.* It is astonishing how often job applicants misspell the names of the companies and people they hope to work for. When this happens, the rest of your application might as well be thrown out the window. "What? Can't even get my name right? How serious can this applicant be? How thorough would this person's work be?"

2. *Be specific about the position you are applying for.* Don't say, "Whatever you've got, I'll take it." Make it clear at the start of your cover letter that there is a specific position or area in which you are interested, and also state where you learned of the opening: from a want ad, a network contact, their Web site, or a general job site such as monster.com.

3. *List your qualifications in a straightforward manner.* "Able to leap tall buildings in a single bound" is not a believable or honest attribute, unless, of course, the cape and tights fit. I've received résumés with superhero abstractions such as "Ambition mixed with a striving for excellence is my strongest asset." Okay, but can you use PageMaker, or program a computer, or oversee a staff of twenty people?

4. *Be personal, direct, and natural.* You may be desperate, and the interviewer may be the person holding your future in hand. But you are both human beings, and you should write as one individual to another. Be businesslike and courteous, but not stiff and impersonal. Don't try to dazzle anyone with your sparkling personality, but do allow your personality to come through. Write it as you would say it in person. The more the letter sounds like you, the more it will stand apart from your competitors'.

A journalist friend of mine was once hired for a reporting job by one of the best newspapers in the country. Though there were hundreds of applicants with impressive credentials—including several who had the inside track because of personal ties to the hiring newspaper—the editor who hired my friend told him, "I took the stack of résumés home and was reading them in bed, and I was just about to fall asleep because they were all so dull. But you woke me up. You obviously weren't trying to write like anyone else." So be yourself, because if you have to play a role in a job, you won't like it—or last in it very long, anyway.

5. *Propose a specific next step.* Close your letter with a clear and precise statement of how you wish to proceed toward an interview. Avoid the written equivalent of mumbling and shuffling your feet toward the door: "Hoping to hear from you soon. Thank you for your time and consideration. I'm looking forward to the opportunity of discussing a position with you."

Relieve your prospective employer of having to decide what to do next. Take charge of the process by offering a next move such as: "I'll call your office Wednesday afternoon to see if you'd like me to come in for an interview," or "I'm free for an interview every morning until eight forty-five, and Thursday after two-thirty. I'll call your office on Wednesday afternoon to find out if you would like to get together during one of those times."

At this stage, a phone-call contact makes things easy for the person at the other end. If you don't call him, he has to go to the trouble of calling you or writing to you. The idea is to make it as simple as you possibly can for your prospective employer to set up an appointment at a time that is convenient for both of you.

Come On Strong

Never bargain or job-hunt from a position of weakness. Soar like an eagle, even when you are feeling like a wounded pigeon. Don't tell anyone that you are desperate and willing to take anything you can find. That desperation turns people off. Be confident in your abilities, and pitch your assets, not your deficits. Here are a few ways to let your networking contact know that you are in the market for career opportunities:

- I have strong contacts in the media, and a successful public relations background. I'd like to work with a company that values and includes public relations in its overall strategic planning.
- I can supervise a small office very efficiently for a company that might be just starting a new department.
- My college education and summer jobs in journalism provided me the training and experiences needed to hit the ground running in an entry-level copy-writing position.

Present Yourself as a Problem-Solver

Your education, training, and/or on-the-job experiences have all presented you with problems that you have had to solve. When you discuss your qualifications with network contacts or job interviewers, focus on how you have employed all of your natural and learned skills to solve problems in the workplace. This gives positive reinforcement that you are less likely to *cause* problems than to *solve* them.

Position Yourself as an Expert

Advertising expert David Ogilvy defines positioning as "what the product does and who it is for." Marketing executive Jack Trout says that positioning is "occupying a position in the mind of the consumer." The concept of positioning is also very important in the world of networking. Establishing a reputation for expertise takes time and strategy. Give information freely, send articles written by you or about you, and volunteer your expertise in a particular field. The process begins with your first contact, and is cultivated over a long period of time. Work on establishing expertise in your field. Let your contacts get to know you for your expertise, so when job or business opportunities come up, they will think of you first.

Go to the Mountain

Moses went to the mountain to get the Commandments; you should go to your networking contacts in the field you have chosen for tips, facts, ideas, and insights on how to get a job. In *Live Your Dreams*, public speaker Les Brown writes of how he relentlessly followed the nation's best public speakers when he was trying to develop his own public speaking career. Ask established professionals in the field of your choice how they broke into it. Decide which method is best for you, and follow it. Vendors and suppliers also generally have a feel for where the opportunities lie in a particular field, so find out who they are and ask them, too. People who work in related fields also often have good inside information. Accountants tend to know tax attorneys. Construction engineers know architects. Computer suppliers know corporate office managers. Journalists know public relations people.

JOB HUNTING FOR THE NEW COLLEGE GRADUATE

During the Internet boom, college seniors in many fields were actively pursued by recruiters, who descended in droves on campuses and competed for the top students. Those were the glory days, and, sadly for more recent grads, they are gone, gone, gone.

These days, the number of entry-level job positions is down considerably, and the recruiters make far fewer trips to campuses. The days of the job-offer carnival have given way to the cold, cruel circus of job hunting. Under these circumstances, your networking should have started with contacts from summer jobs, part-time jobs, professors, coaches, roommates, and fellow students. Having the opportunity to get an advanced education, be it college or technical training, puts you at an advantage in the process of building your network. For the most part, you will be in the company of people who have similar values and goals. Most will be receptive to helping you find your way in the job market. Extend your contacts to alumni groups, fraternity or sorority members, or team members—whether the debate team or football team. Expand your reach also to your family, friends, minister and church acquaintances, and neighbors. Remember, when you put the word out to them that they have their own network of friends, it encourages them to put the word out on the extended party line.

As a student, you are at a stage in life where building a productive network should begin in earnest. Your prospects may be bright, but sooner or later on down the line, you are going to need a network of trusted people. Nobody goes it alone, at least not successfully. Be receptive to others and help them when you can with their careers. When your time comes, you will be pleasantly surprised at how the troops rally for you. And remember that any prospective employer will be impressed by someone with a network of supporters, because people skills are vital in almost any job.

As I write this, I think of my niece Aisha, who majored in marketing at Florida A&M University. Her grades were good, and she had a winning personality. Aisha didn't coast through her college days. She built a network that serves her well to this day. She kept her friends and family informed about her grades and her activities on and off campus. This put those of us who formed her support network in a position to talk knowledgeably and enthusiastically about her to contacts in the workplace who were responsible for recruitment. This helped our contacts in the pre-recruiting process, and it definitely helped Aisha's prospects for the future.

Not that she needed all that much help—she volunteered for several campus and civic organizations; she worked part-time on campus; she held summer jobs that related to her area of career interest, including an internship for State Farm Insurance, which was then known as a great place to work but a difficult place to get into. As a result of her work, Aisha got a job offer from State Farm after she graduated.

While still a student, Aisha often used this short introduction in exploring her career options. "I'm Aisha Fraser from Shaker Heights, Ohio, and I attend Florida A&M University's school of business and industry. I'm a junior majoring in business administration. I understand that your firm is offering summer internships; could you tell me a little more about your program?" Not bad, Aisha, not bad at all.

Here are a few examples of things you can do to build your network in preparation for graduation:

Volunteer to Earn and Learn

One thing I believe benefited Aisha is that because of her campus activities, she had earned the respect of a wide number of people. Volunteer work is a very good way to meet the movers and shakers before you become a mover and shaker yourself. I can't tell you how much I have benefited from the contacts I made while volunteering for the United Negro College Fund and working for the United Way, because my efforts were observed by the board members of those charities, most of whom were executives and presidents of dozens of major corporations. My volunteer work also put me in contact with many businesses that would later be major advertisers in my publications.

Volunteer work provides you with the opportunity to learn a great deal about how the world works. Their causes may be benevolent and their tax status may be nonprofit, but volunteer organizations generally employ some of the best and most influential executives and marketing people in the business. Often, they operate on lean administrative budgets, so the volunteers have the opportunity to step in and do a lot of work. That is experience that will eventually mean greater salary opportunities later, if you try to soak up as much information and experience as you can.

Another particularly valuable part of volunteer work is that you can use the organization and its board members as references, if you believe you have impressed them with your work. The names of a few community leaders and business chiefs can add considerable heft to the résumé of a recent graduate.

The key is to treat volunteer work as a job, because although you may get paid nothing at all, there are substantial rewards. You never know who is watching, but in charitable groups, it can very easily be your future employer, or at least, a future networking contact.

Before you volunteer for an organization, make sure you know what you are getting into. One of my associates once joined a men's public service organization only to discover that most of the members were more interested in drinking and carousing than in doing good for the community. As one of his first projects for the group, he staged a candidates' night, asking local political candidates to come in and speak before the group. Several members came to the affair after a visit to happy hour, and their behavior so embarrassed my associate that he subsequently left the organization.

So before you sign on, ask people you know in an organization if they enjoy their work for it. Read the organization's annual report and newsletters. It might be a good idea to attend a meeting or two as a guest, and introduce yourself to the group's leaders. Look for hidden agendas in the group's activities. Is it a public service orientation, or is it an excuse to get out of the house?

Market Yourself Wisely

You may have "aced" Black History 101 or World Geography 401, but that is not what you want to note on your résumé because, in most cases, individual college courses do not carry much weight in the real world. It's the whole package that employers are concerned about. Experience, people skills, personal appearance, reliability, diligence, honesty, leadership—these are major factors in your marketability. Being editor of your college newspaper or captain of the debate team indicates strong writing or communication skills, but it also denotes leadership capabilities.

Create Your Own Networking Card

Just because you are not yet in business doesn't mean you can't have a business card. You do *have* business already, don't you? Sure you do; the business of trying to get hired. I recommend that you create a simple networking card with your name, address, e-mail, and telephone number on it. The various software packages available today will make it easy for you to create a very professional-looking card. On the card, list your most marketable skills. Be modest now, but straightforward. Go at this as though you have your own company, and describe what you do based on the skills and experience that you have. Aisha could have put on her networking card, "specializing in research and marketing for the insurance industry." This addresses her marketing degree and her research experience from her summer job with State Farm Insurance. Although the networking card is no replacement for a well-prepared résumé, it is convenient and fast, and demonstrates thoughtfulness, uniqueness, and professionalism.

KEEP THE NETWORK PLUGGED IN

Far too many people neglect their job-hunting network once they have accomplished the mission of finding employment. Big mistake, my friends, particularly in an uncertain economy in which even companies that are doing well tend to slash and burn just to keep the stockholders happy. There is no such thing as job security anymore, so you cannot afford to pull the plug on your job-hunting network. Stay in touch. Send greetings and helpful newspaper articles, and make a couple of phone calls or send a few e-mails a day just to networking contacts. And always make a sincere effort to help those who contact you for assistance in finding a job. Believe me, there may well come a day when one of those people will be in a position to help you in return, and even if that doesn't happen, the pleasure of helping someone get his or her life back on track is a great feeling.

NETWORKING FOR CUSTOMERS OR CLIENTS

Networking is one of the most effective ways to develop and cultivate relationships that can help produce clients or customers for your business. Whether we admit it or not, those of us in business tend to see every acquaintance or contact as a potential customer. There is nothing predatory or wrong about that, if you follow five basic rules when networking for this particular purpose.

1. *Build relationships first.* This is one of the cardinal rules of effective networking. Asking someone to purchase your product or service before you've established a relationship beyond small talk is just plain rude and will result in rejection. Unless you answer the phones at the Home Shopping Network, open envelopes at a mail-order catalogue firm, or work the checkout line at a grocery store, you probably need to put some serious effort into building customer relationships beyond merely taking orders for your products or services. All good and productive business relationships develop over time.

2. *Be a source of ideas, information, and inspiration.* One of my business's suppliers, Stephen, has a business repairing and selling new and used copy machine equipment. Stephen is always willing to share trade secrets on how to make repairs and perform basic maintenance on our office copy machine at no cost. This saves us hours of downtime and repair expense. He keeps his friends updated with the latest product information, and provides them with inside tips on how to purchase new and used copy equipment at prices close to cost.

Stephen is also always recommending the products and services of his customers, and offering ideas or words of inspiration. Although his business is relatively new, his reputation as the person to call for "your copy machine repair needs" has grown quickly. Stephen has built his reputation and his business by giving his network of contacts ideas, information, and inspiration without demanding anything in return. The truth is that Stephen probably expects that his well-tended network will bring him customer loyalty, and in that regard, I believe his expectations are valid.

3. *Soft-pedal the hard sell.* In networking for customers, I am an advocate of the soft sell over the hard sell. Soft-selling entails getting information to identify problems in a friendly, conversational tone, then devising solutions using the ideas and information that you are willing to share.

Tom, a graphic designer, describes his business as "helping to make people look good on paper." He spends his networking time brainstorming with his customers on how they can improve their business cards and other graphic images used to represent their firms. One of Tom's favorite questions is, "If you could wave a magic wand, how would you enhance your graphic image today?" The answers often open up conversations that result in more business for Tom. But he never presses, nor does he attempt to close a deal on the spot. He simply arranges for a more convenient time and place to expand the discussion and, ultimately, the size of the sale.

The key concept here is, when networking for business, never make the hard sell. Instead of trying to make money, solve problems and know that later, the cash will flow your way. Of course, if you find yourself giving away more than you are getting back, you might have to reassess your style of problem-solving.

4. *Use your successes to build success.* Pam is a public relations executive for a small firm, and when she networks for clients, she calls upon a wealth of anecdotal success stories that, when presented in her humorous fashion, showcase her problem-solving skills. She was once asked by an executive at a cocktail party how she would have dealt with the WorldCom financial disaster if she had had that public relations challenge. Although she had never had to face such a great disaster, Pam had done public relations for companies involved in embarrassing situations. With anecdotes from those experiences, she responded so professionally that the impressed executive later had her signed to a thirty-thousand-dollar retainer with his firm. A year later, that led to a larger contract with a local arts organization that had the executive on its board.

Parading out your success stories just to impress people in casual conversation is bad form. But incorporating them into relevant conversations in your soft-sell pitches to potential clients is wise. It is a great way to be remembered for your skills.

5. *Once you've done a good job, ask for referrals.* One of the most effective ways to get new customers through networking is the referral from satisfied customers. When you have delivered on your promise to do a good job or provide good service, then you get referrals, sometimes without even asking for them.

The degree to which you succeed in receiving referrals from past customers depends, of course, on how satisfied they were with your product. But it can also depend upon your approach. Even if you have delivered a good product or service, the customer simply may not think to recommend you to others unless you diplomatically ask for his or her referral.

You don't want to do this until you have earned a customer's respect, however. You don't want to put the customer in the position of feeling obligated or put upon. And you don't want him or her to feel like he or she is doing you a favor, either. When asking for a referral, let your customer know that you would like to provide the same opportunity for quality service to his or her friends and associates. This position of mutual benefit creates the optimal win-win situation, and just may open a floodgate of referrals.

If you find yourself having difficulty cracking a new market, a letter of referral or recommendation from a past client can work wonders in opening doors. If you have a client who is particularly good as a reference, a personal call or e-mail to the new target client might work well. I also suggest that you set up a series of one-on-one breakfasts and lunches with individuals in the new market in an effort to build relationships before you really get down to the nitty-gritty of selling.

NETWORKING FOR CAREER SUCCESS

In today's highly competitive job market, working hard at your assigned tasks is not enough to guarantee success over the long term. Ask all those former Enron employees standing in the unemployment lines. Specialization was wonderful in the days of full employment, but today, you have to be indispensable, you have to know so much about how your company works that your employer simply cannot afford to lose you. That kind of knowledge comes only through skilled networking. Your ability to access information, make sound career decisions, maneuver effectively, and play the corporate political game will depend greatly on who you know, who knows you, and who your networking contacts themselves know.

Attracting mentors, role models, and sponsors to help you will depend greatly on your people skills and your strategic networking ability. Just doing a good job is not enough to keep your job, and definitely not enough to ensure that you will move up the ladder. The higher you go, the more important networking skills are to your success. Here are some guidelines for networking your way to career success.

Office Politics

One Webster's dictionary defines politics as "having practical wisdom and prudence." That definition in itself is a revelation to those of us who have come to perceive politics as a dirty game between competing interest groups; something negative, then, cynical and conniving. "Practical wisdom and prudence"? Perhaps the dark side of human nature has tarnished politics in our minds, but clearly, politics is part of our lives, not just in government, but in the workplace. Whenever and wherever groups of people organize to get things done, politics comes into play. In a group, each person's ability to influence decisions by demonstrating his or her wisdom and prudence provides that individual with a platform from which to assert leadership and control.

Psychologists tell us that the three basic human needs in any group dynamic are structure, organization, and proper environment. Remember, politics is a group dynamic. In other words, politics cannot be overlooked, even though I'm sure we have all heard someone say, "I stay out of office politics." If that is truly the case, that person might as well stay out of the office.

When I refer to networking and office politics, I am not referring to the common connotation of back-biting and infighting. I am simply referring to the very wise and prudent policy of staying as informed as possible about matters pertaining to your business, and staying in communication with as many of your coworkers and associates as possible, up and down the line of authority.

Engaging in office politics as part of networking simply means employing these six strategies:

1. *Join groups or organizations to gain recognition for your skills.* In order to advance your career goals, this is a great way to develop and showcase your speaking, writing, and leadership skills.

You want to be perceived as a producer, a doer, a self-motivator who solves problems rather than creates them.

A friend of mine received one of the highest compliments in his corporation when an executive attempting to lure him to another division said that his only fear was that my friend's current boss "will never let go of anyone as productive as you." That's what you want to hear— corporate chiefs fighting over you.

If you are perceived as a valuable commodity in the workplace, you will attract mentors. You can raise your visibility by getting involved in group leadership, and in speaking, training, and writing for publications related to your work. If people feel you are a rising star, they will want to mentor you for selfish reasons, too. That is all right, as long as you recognize it and take it for what it is. You will probably need three or four mentors at least in your career climb, so make the best of all of them, and make it a priority to seek out good and valuable people as your supervisors, because these good people generally take their most valued workers up the ladder with them.

2. *Use informal meetings to network.* Breakfasts, lunches, social and sport events, and conferences offer good opportunities to network with key people in your organization and related organizations. Such settings provide a comfortable way for people to get to know you in a one-on-one context.

3. *Seek mentors or sponsors to hone your skills and expand your access to key people.* These contacts within the workplace can also provide you with access to important and timely information such as unwritten rules related to the organization's culture, and informal but important grapevine rumor, gossip, and speculations. Many consider the office grapevine a vital source of unofficial information. Studies have found that three-fourths of organizational gossip and rumor is based on fact. Being tuned to the grapevine, and even being a nonmalicious contributor to its flow of unofficial information, can be a

key to getting news of opportunities and developments
before the thundering herds hear it. At its lowest form,
the grapevine can become nothing more than an outlet
for gossipmongers. But if you tune in to a higher
frequency, it can be more like your own private CNN,
broadcasting vital news from *your* world twenty-four
hours a day.

4. *Act as a mentor or sponsor in order to build your own team
and network.* Those whom you mentor will one day
become your cheerleading section, and who knows what
positions they may soar to down the road. Les Brown
struggled for years to build his one-man speaker's bureau
into a million-dollar business. During his difficult years, I
was in a position to provide him with speaking
opportunities and occasional advice and motivation
regarding his marketing challenges. While I was not the
only person to help him, he has shown his gratitude, and
today, he is in a position to help me and he has. My time
and effort on his behalf were done out of friendship, but
they were also certainly wise networking investments.
Every business and organization has people in need of
assistance in their struggle to succeed. Help them,
recommend them for opportunities, and teach them what
you know. The law of increasing returns holds that you
will be rewarded tenfold.

5. *Network with colleagues at the next level.* In your career
climb, model your skills, dress, and behavior patterns on
colleagues an echelon above you. Most organizational
cultures have an image they cultivate. Those who move
up in those organizations generally fit into and
understand that image. Sticking out to be different or to
get attention will only make people shy away from you.
Work on blending into the image, but labor also to stand
out in your performance. What really matters is your
contribution. You may be a thorn among roses, but if

your division leads all the others, the roses will soon be studying the thorn's theories.

The issue of acceptance and appreciation of the workplace's diverse cultural blend has taken some of the starch out of image-conscious organizations. Corporate law firms allow their attorneys to dress more casually. But wearing a skullcap to a corporate meeting might still be considered a little "out there." Of course proper grooming is important, but I would think hard about the latest hip-hop hairstyle. If you work in a place where the emphasis is on creativity, style, and culture, go for it. Remember, business is a battlefield and you must wear the proper uniform so your fellow soldiers know that you are on their side.

6. *Network with key sources to make sure you are in the formal and informal information loop.* Beyond the contributors to the grapevine are those who produce and control the flow of information: Web sites, reports, bulletins, announcements, newsletters, brochures, etc. Everyone from department heads and Web site editors to the mailroom clerk is privy to certain fresh information. Networking with them keeps you informed and on top of the information flow about new projects and directions. This gives you a headstart in devising your strategies to stay in front of the pack.

NETWORKING AT CONVENTIONS AND CONFERENCES

Writer Tang Nivri took a few well-deserved shots at the sad state of black conferencing in an *Emerge* magazine article entitled "Being Seen at Negro Conventions." In the article, he wrote:

Negroes routinely get together to eat chicken, drink vodka, chase women, play cards and make plans to do it all again next year. The convention is now little more than a chance for Negroes to get together to blow a lot of very hot air into the eyes and ears of anybody caught in the room at the time. . . .

Amen, I say, to Mr. Nivri's comically right-on observations, which, by the way, are equally applicable to many white affairs as well. Black folks do need to clean up their collective act. I attend at least one hundred conventions and conferences each year, and I am amazed at how little attention and serious effort black people put into networking during what should be among the most fruitful and meaningful opportunities on their calendars.

The annual National Urban League Convention is a classic example of a well-planned and strongly supported event that provides black professionals with a multitude of opportunities to network. On any given day, the plenary sessions, special events, and exhibit halls are packed with corporate vendors and their top executives passing out freebies. Many black businesses participate and sell their products. The most knowledgeable and skillful speakers in the country and world are recruited for these gatherings, from the President of the United States to the president of the Black Entertainment Network. If you are looking for ideas, customers, suppliers, job opportunities, or networking contacts, this is one of the best places to be. But all too many go only to grab a bag of free goodies and some good times without seizing the opportunity to engage in meaningful networking. I have become convinced that most people don't really know what to do with themselves at these gatherings, and so they opt to party or to indulge the vice of their choice. To help remedy this problem I created the annual Power-Networking Conference. Its goal is to teach and train black people in the principles, strategies, and tactics of effective networking.

Here are eleven SuccessTips we teach at the conference for handling yourself at major events:

1. *Choose the event wisely.* Getting into conventions, expositions, and large meetings can be costly and time-consuming. Know who is likely to be there and why they are there. You don't want to bust in on a highly technical training conference for Microsoft employees. You won't be welcome, and you'll probably feel as if they are speaking a foreign language. But you might want to make an appearance at a convention of African-American computer programmers.

2. *Make yourself available to speak on subjects within your range of expertise.* There is nothing like being at the head table to draw attention. Believe it or not, people are looking for those in the know.

3. *Volunteer to help out, if you have the time and flexibility.* If you are out of work, it can only help. And if you have a job, your boss and potential bosses might be impressed by your enthusiasm and energy.

4. *Consider setting up your own booth space.* Now, don't do this if the only thing you are handing out is your business card. But if you have something to sell, a product or an idea, you have to get it out there. Ask any book dealer about the difference in sales between a book that is just crammed on a shelf with dozens of others and a book that is displayed with the full cover showing.

5. *Remember the convention's objective.* The true purpose of a convention is to educate, to communicate, and to motivate. If you can return home with some benefit from each of these functions, your time and money will have been well spent.

6. *Set your networking agenda.* It should enable you to:

- Meet key people in your field and related fields
- Be motivated by new ideas and perspectives
- Acquire new skills, knowledge, and information from experts
- Explore your marketability
- Heighten your professional profile among peers

- Identify potential customers
- Spend some leisure time relaxing and renewing your creative juices

7. *Outline your schedule on paper.* Prepare for the convention by writing down and carrying a list of things to do and people to meet during your stay. Start by reviewing a copy of the program guide and circling sessions you plan to attend and questions you would like answered. List speakers, peers, and colleagues you plan to meet. Take the time to inventory your needs and wants and what you are willing to do or give in exchange. Make contact with key people prior to the conference, and set up breakfasts, lunches, dinners, cocktails, or common seating at special events or sessions. Arrange early to relax or socialize with special customers or contacts. Keep some of your time open and flexible, and don't overcommit or overschedule. Usually, two or three special meetings per day is plenty. Understand also that a number of new opportunities will crop up each day, and you will want to leave time open to capitalize on them.

8. *Attend only sessions that provide new information and stimulate your thinking.* Sit near an exit and head for the door if the speaker numbs your butt rather than excites your brain. Don't be afraid to ask questions. This is a good way to attract the attention of people who share your interests, and you'd be surprised at how many fruitful conversations and networking contacts can result. Make sure you introduce yourself to the best speakers after they've made their presentations. Some of my most valuable networking is done down in front of the podium at this time. Speakers are like everyone else; they enjoy feedback, especially positive feedback, and often, they are happy to set up meetings or telephone discussions if you show an interest.

9. *Work the room.* Attend the luncheons, dinners, and workshops. In most cases, conventions and exhibitions last two to five days. Identify the person in charge, and build rapport. He or she will know where you can make the most contacts relative to your interests. Visit all of the booths and get to know the people on the floor of the event. Don't zip around like a water bug. Take your time. Stay in control. Build the network.

10. *Practice your networking skills aggressively.* Don't be afraid to introduce yourself. Ask questions. Ask for business cards. Set up appointments. This is a good time to experiment with questions, ideas, opinions, and methods of handling situations that you might normally not be willing to try on your home turf. Most of those who attend conventions are open and friendly and hoping to achieve the same results. This is the time to go for the gold, but remain professional in your demeanor. There are too many valuable contacts out there to risk tarnishing your reputation.

11. *When it is over, follow up on the contacts you made.* Send notes, e-mails, or brochures. Make calls. Review and then file away your program book full of notes to use as a year-round reference and as a planning guide for the next year's convention agenda. Convention manuals can also serve as idea generators for your organization's next conference.

NETWORKING FOR INFORMATION

Information moves so fast and so far and wide today that, as John Naisbitt, author of *Megatrends*, notes, the race now goes to "those with the best information first."

Communications experts tell us that the pool of knowledge now doubles every two years. No wonder our brains seem to be on overload. And we'd better stock up on brain food, brothers and sisters, because revolutionary technological advances such as the World Wide Web promise to make the flow of information even more swift.

The key to keeping pace in your work and intellectual life is having access to the *right* information, the pertinent facts, the news that *you* can use, and the resources and the support that *you* need.

That is what networking for information is all about: having access to the *specific* material that you need. My Soul-O-Dex is chock-full of the names of people with expertise in everything from law to dairy farming. Every project that I undertake, every problem that I tackle, every major decision that I face, usually results in my tapping into experts, who are like my living encyclopedias or how-to books. From my networking contacts, I've learned how to repair bicycles, cook, write, speak, and do countless other things. And believe it or not, sometimes people come to me for help.

Ron is a public transportation executive who was elected chairman of a small local foundation. His objective was to expand the financial base of the foundation, and to hire a full-time professional to assist him in running the operation. Alex, a mutual friend of Ron's and mine, suggested Ron discuss his plans with me because of my experience in this area. We met for forty-five minutes, and I presented him with three different plans to carry out his goals. Ron left our meeting feeling that his time and networking had been well spent. He eventually implemented one of my suggested plans.

Ron knew what he needed. He asked the right questions. He made contacts within his network and found someone with the experience to help him. Information is like an electrical cord. Unless it is plugged into an outlet, it has no power, no value. What information do you possess or have access to that could be of value to your fellow networkers? I am afraid that it is typical of black people to feel that they have little information of value to others. This poor self-image is a problem that we are beginning to overcome, but it still impedes the ability of many blacks to network with others of their race.

Networking for information requires a positive and confident mind-set and only a few simple steps that will make you more productive. The mind-set is, "At any given time the people in my network are ready, willing, and able to provide the information I need to help solve my problem." You can feel comfortable with that, because that is why people consent to be in your network.

Once you've got that mind-set ingrained, here are a few simple steps to follow when networking for information:

- Identify the problem and determine exactly what information you need to devise a solution to it.
- Write down the questions before you seek the answers. Make sure you have a clear understanding of what it is you need, when you need it, and all of the other related facts and issues. This will help organize your thinking and avoid repeated callbacks to cover something else.
- Review your own Soul-O-Dex, if you prefer, for networking contacts most likely to have the information you seek, or to see if your contacts know someone who has it. Don't ask your contacts for confidential information that they are usually paid for.
- Pick up your telephone, make your contact, be warm and succinct. Ask your questions and then listen. After you've asked any other questions, give your thanks, hang up, and then take whatever action you decide is necessary based on the information you have gathered.
- Follow up with a telephone call or a thank-you note to your networking contact. If the information led to a significant result, let the contact know.
- If you don't have a networking contact with the desired information, try the research or reference departments of libraries or government offices. I use my contacts with

related professional groups, clubs, and organizations. I also use telephone contacts, e-mail, snail mail, and requests to magazines, authors, and college professors specializing in the areas in which I'm interested. I have found that there are very few secrets. Almost everything you need to know has been written about in a book, newspaper, or magazine article.

NETWORKING FOR BOARD APPOINTMENTS

At one point in time I served on nine civic and educational boards: a chamber of commerce, a visitors and convention bureau, a university, a bicentennial commission, a museum, a state building authority, a scholarship fund, a citywide leadership group, and a small foundation. One was a gubernatorial appointment (Republican) and one was a mayoral appointment (Democrat). How is that for good politics? Today, because of business and travel demands, I serve on only two boards. These were all, by the way, nonpaying positions. Paid corporate positions are rare, and getting those positions requires all of the above qualifications as well as the right connections: who you know and who knows you. And if you have to ask to be selected, you don't qualify.

My board appointments have put me shoulder-to-shoulder with the power elite and city fathers of the Cleveland community. This has enabled me to access resources that would not otherwise be available to me in the task of raising money to start my business; be privy to the inner workings and plans for my city; influence decisions that impact black students, education, and business; and be invited as a VIP to the best parties, dinners, and events in town, just to mention a few rewards.

In recent years, with the growth of my new business and my hectic travel and speaking schedule, I have not had the time to fully participate and serve with great distinction, but I have still reaped enormous benefits from the visibility and associations. The question I am asked so often is: "How do you network to be selected to these illustrious boards?" The secret lies in understanding why anyone would select you in the first place. What do corporations and charitable groups and universities look for in selecting their board members? From my experience, the following criteria come into play when selecting a board member:

- *Public service track record.* Are you a selfless doer, who has served with distinction on other boards or important committees over the years?
- *Influence in the community.* Do you have a successful business or professional position or a high-profile reputation that puts you in a position to influence the movers and shakers?
- *Wealth.* While it's not what has landed *me* on any boards, it is an attribute that definitely enhances one's profile in the community and brings power.
- *Positive profile.* This is the "Mother Teresa" factor. You don't necessarily need great wealth or influence; if your reputation for good works and high moral character is strong enough, this alone can bring invitations to certain board seats.
- *Political savvy.* Are you politically active? Do you publically support candidates?
- *Belonging to a racial minority and possessing any of the above qualifications.* Examples of prominent black people in this category who serve on many boards are Andrew Young, Bob Johnson, Earl Graves, Vernon Jordan, Quincy Jones, Dr. Johnnetta Cole, Dr. Andrew Brimmer, Dr. Alvin Poussaint, and Hugh Price.

Don't be offended by being offered a *minority position* on a board. Be energized by it. Being a minority-slot selection to a board is a foot in the door. It is your opportunity to make a difference. Just don't forget how and why you are there. If you are not serving black interests while fulfilling your responsibility to the organization, you are just another "spook who sits by the door."

Keep in mind that a raised clenched fist and angry posturing are not necessary in this situation. I have seen blacks in these vaulted board positions respond in two ways. Some try so hard to be neutral and avoid their blackness that they fade into the beige-toned decorating and act in a manner that would make Uncle Tom blush. Others disrupt and posture to no effect other than to call attention to themselves and to make the other board members wish they had never made the effort to include minority representation. Neither serves the purpose of our black community.

People on boards are generally powerful individuals who bristle at anything that they consider to be intimidation. They are better influenced by quiet leadership and tactful suggestions. You have to be comfortable with power to sit on a board, and you have to know when to work for a consensus, when to pick your battles, and when to stand up and say, "Enough!"

On nonprofit boards you will be expected to contribute intellectually and financially. That is why you were selected, after all. And in all likelihood, you will not be paid. If you are fortunate enough to be selected for a corporate board, however, you will be paid handsomely in cash and perks. Some political board appointments pay as well. All board appointments should be viewed as a great way to build your network contacts, and as a method for contributing to your community's improvement.

Here, then, are a few ideas for positioning yourself to gain these powerful and influential board positions.

- *Volunteer.* Begin at church, at work, in the community, and in your alumni groups. There are no shortages of volunteer positions out there, but you have to pick those in which your special talents can best be applied, and those in which you have the time to become actively involved. Remember,

volunteer work generally means less time with your own
family, unless they can participate, too.

- **Step forward.** Once you have volunteered, don't be a mere
  drone or just another face in the crowd. Offer to head
  committees; suggest new directions and fund-raising ideas.
- **Build relationships.** Work on your interpersonal skills
  inside the volunteer organization. Test your leadership
  abilities and build a network of contacts that may later help
  you achieve your goal of attaining board positions.

Steve Minter, the brilliant and retired executive director of the
prestigious Cleveland Foundation, serves on a number of prestigious boards, including Goodyear and Rubbermaid. Steve says
that to be selected for these high-powered, high-paying boards is
all about "chemistry, fit, and timing." He tells the story of how he
was selected for his first corporate board, Ohio Bell, now SBC
Ameritech. Shortly after being selected as director of the Cleveland Foundation, he got a call from Ed Bell, president of Ohio
Bell, to go to lunch. They talked, Ed liked what he heard and felt,
and he announced to Steve that he had been selected to serve.
Steve knew one reason he was asked was because of his prestigious
position; he soon found out the other two reasons when he showed
up to his first board meeting and met Howard Fort. Fort was the
lone black on the board and was about to retire. Howard had
known Steve when he was just a kid, but Steve had not remembered Howard. When Steve's name was brought up as a possible
replacement for Howard, obviously Howard gave it an enthusiastic two thumbs up. Howard retired, and Steve replaced him as the
lone black. When Howard then retired from the Goodyear board,
guess what? Steve replaced him again. While he served on the
Goodyear board, Steve met Stan Gault, then president of Rubbermaid. Steve was soon asked to join the Rubbermaid board. When
relationships and networks meet sound qualifications, good chemistry, and perfect timing, a chain reaction occurs—Steve will tes-
tify to that.

NETWORK MARKETING

Network marketing is a legitimate part of what has been called the distribution revolution in this country. Marketing expert Bob Brewster has written: "A wide variety of products are now being carried direct to the consumer by a massive army of individual entrepreneurs." This technique is known as network marketing or multilevel marketing, MLM.

In lieu of spending huge sums of money on advertising, retail sales promotion, and other traditional forms of marketing, companies such as Amway, Avon, U.S. Health Advisors, Pre-Paid Legal, ACN, and MATAH (one of the few black-owned companies in the business) have created multiproduct and multicategory lines that reach you right where you live. They are networked into your home through your friends, peers, colleagues, and neighbors. The product is distributed to you more efficiently; therefore, the company saves money, you save money, and the networkers make money.

The network marketing process has stablized but it has suffered growing pains and abuse. Its public image was poor, and at one point in time it turned off many who could potentially profit and benefit from one of America's last "low-cost" entrepreneurial opportunities. Much has improved in the process since its early beginnings in the 1950s. I believe network marketing provides those blacks who truly enjoy and excel at sales and networking the opportunity to build a second income or substantial primary income for a small investment, usually less than five hundred dollars. Good networkers can pick entire categories or catalogues of products to sell.

With network marketing, the road to financial independence does not have to depend on securing a second mortgage or borrowing from every relative and friend. This process does not work if you don't work, no matter what the quality of the product is. And it is not easy. If it were easy, why would the manufacturers need you? It requires everything any other business demands. I believe in networking marketing, particularly as an economic opportunity for black people who aspire to own their own businesses.

Network marketing is something the small investor and the budding entrepreneur should consider. New products, new companies, and new opportunities will grow in the years to come—but pick prudently and wisely. Look at the company's products, its management, and its track record. Talk to others in your network. Get a sense of whether they are eager to have the product. Don't waste your time if you are not seriously committed to working at it regardless of how small the investment is.

NETWORKING VERSUS NECK-WORKING

Finally, I would like to address a topic that comes up nearly every time I call for questions from the audience when I give a speech or workshop about networking. It is the question generally asked by women, but sometimes by men: "How do you keep sex out of the networking process? How do you come on strong as a networker without appearing to come on strong sexually? And how do you pull the plug on someone who starts 'neck-working' when you were simply networking?"

It was spring in Atlanta. The dogwoods were blooming and a National Conference on Black Entrepreneurialism was buzzing with black movers and shakers and networkers. The elegant black-tie opening cocktail party at the Marriott Marquis was under way, with beautiful and successful people turned out by the hundreds.

As the reception progressed, one of the brothers in a small "quality circle" of networkers noticed a bevy of beauties approaching. Eyebrows arching, he signaled a few males in his group by slightly lifting his head in their direction. As the women drew closer, the neck-working warm-up dance was well under way. If the women had circled behind them, there surely would have been a few disks ruptured or vertebrae snapped.

The braver brothers offered a few greetings, most of them polite, but at least some inappropriately overexuberant "Hi, ladies!"

escaped. The men fanned out and joined the women, enlarging the networking circle, or so the women had thought.

When it became obvious, perhaps by their leering, or maybe by their less-than-businesslike conversation, that the men were neck-working rather than networking, the women went on the offensive. These were not shrinking violets. These were self-assured, intelligent, and assertive sisters who have survived and succeeded in a world that discriminates against both their sex and their color. In other words, these were *seasoned* warriors of the world.

Before they could put their tongues back in their mouths, the neck-working men found themselves undergoing a severe tongue-lashing lecture on male chauvinism, feminism, and the glorification of sex and violence toward women in the media. In a very precise way, the sisters dropped smart bombs on the brothers, who had forgotten their surroundings and their manners.

The message from the women was this: When networking in a business environment, it is not appropriate to flirt. Flirting, and all of its more salacious forms, is unprofessional, crass, and, ultimately, a turn-off. Smart women want to be treated accordingly. Aim at the brain and you are more likely to hit the heart, if that is your target.

Most professionals understand and adhere to a networking decorum. But some brothers, even those who have been educated at top schools and trained in the best corporations, revert to street manners when it comes to the opposite sex. These sometimes unconscious behavior patterns may not be maliciously intended, but they are generally perceived that way by women who regard their careers as serious and their sex lives as private. So what follows is a basic primer to remind us of what is acceptable and unacceptable, what is neck-working rather than networking.

Body language is one of the strongest forms of flirting. Here are a few examples of what is generally viewed as improper body language for a business-networking forum. There are exceptions to every rule, of course, but if you find yourself displaying behavior that others deem inappropriate, take the hint, and then take a cold shower.

Item: A woman is in danger of being taken as a "neck-worker" or flirt if she:

- Encourages discussion and smiles, even though the topic is inappropriate and contains sexual innuendo or double entendres
- Strokes or fondles her hair during conversation
- Isolates contact to one person by holding on to an arm or a hand
- Gazes into a man's eyes beyond short intervals
- Lowers her head and peers through or bats her eyelashes
- Stands within the other person's "space" and/or touches shoulders or hips or anything north or south
- Engages in flattery that goes beyond the normal "nice suit" or "great Pocket Planner"
- Touches in a proprietary manner, adjusting the man's clothing or picking lint from it
- Holds a man's hand long after the handshake
- Wears inappropriately low-cut or otherwise revealing attire to a business-oriented event

Item: A man may be guilty of "neck-working" behavior when he:

- Does any of the above
- Makes repeated contacts with the same person without any clear or appropriate purpose
- Sits closer than needed for conversation
- Uses inappropriate forms of address such as *honey, baby, sweetheart*
- Is oversolicitous about the woman's comfort, jumping up to bring her a drink or to get her coat

Suggestion: A woman can put a stop to a neck-working man's inappropriate behavior if she:

- Ignores it if it is relatively harmless
- Changes the topic and steers it back to dry business
- Uses deflective humor: "Are you networking or neck-working? If it's the latter, you're sticking your neck out too far."
- Walks away, or turns away from the neck-worker

The following is an example of how a woman might diplomatically handle a persistent neck-worker.

Female: Hi, my name is Constance Hill, and I'm the senior vice president of marketing at the Peterson Group.
Male: Hi, Constance, I'm Jeffrey Engel, and I'm an account manager at *Escapade* magazine. Um, um, um—you sure look good, girl.
Female: Thank you, Jeffrey. Tell me a little about your job at *Escapade*. What is a typical day like for you?
Male: Are you staying here at the convention hotel?
Female: Why do you ask?
Male: I'm staying here, and I thought it might be nice to catch you for a drink later.
Female: That is nice of you, Jeffrey, but you still haven't told me about your job. *Escapade* is such a hip magazine. Tell me a little bit about the environment there for minorities.
Male: What are you doing later?
Female: I'd love to hear more about your job. Who knows—we might be able to help each other on a business level someday.
Male: My place or yours?
Female: You know, Jeffrey, I could be very helpful to you in your ad placement. I have several plum corporations as clients at the Peterson Group. What are your ad rates, so I know what I am dealing with?

Male: This conversation is making me thirsty, baby.

Female: Jeffrey, would you excuse me, please? I see one of my colleagues across the room, and I have some very important business to discuss with him. Perhaps we can speak on the telephone about your ad rates someday soon. It has been . . . *challenging* talking with you. Good-bye.

"Networking does work.
I am a real witness to that."
DAMON DASH

Damon Dash is the CEO of Roc-A-Fella records, and along with Jay-Z and Kareem "Biggs" Burke has created Roc-A-Fella Enterprises. The company creates music and films that further define the "street life" of urban youth through hip-hop. There's also Roc-A-Fella Center, an on-line operation that sells an array of products, including Roc-A-Wear apparel and Roc-A-Fella Sports. As with most hip-hop franchises, their philosophy and business concepts evolve around a culture that is in defiance of the "structured" mainstream music and film industries. Through Roc-A-Fella Enterprises, Dash and his partners have added to the $5 billion hip-hop industry, which includes music, apparel, films, television and radio, and video games. Says Dash, "I'm not going to let anyone tell me what to do. It's our music and we're going to do it our way."

Part Three

CREATING A SUCCESS STEREOTYPE

9

Networking as a Way of Life

Whoever works without knowledge works uselessly.
— AFRICAN PROVERB

O nce you have embraced networking not only as a method of reaching your goals, but also as a way of life, opportunities leap out at you. Jim Chance is president of a design, engineering, and project-management firm that handles hazardous waste cleanups—Environmental Data Consultants of Yonkers, New York. Chance once attended a regional meeting of the National Black MBA Association of Boston, where he was seated at a table with Yvonne McCants of Somerville, New Jersey. They talked casually and, as good networkers, exchanged business cards. Not long afterward, Yvonne passed on Chance's business card to an associate who, she learned, was developing an information and tracking system for hazardous materials. And, as it turned out, those two "Chance" occurrences resulted in opportunity. Chance got a contract.

In a world where access to information is vital, success of almost any kind is based on networks and partnerships. Even a successful athlete in an individual sport such as track and field must rely on trainers and coaches and a network of support. Wherever you find success, you will find people working together toward shared goals.

If you have learned anything so far in this book, it is that, in spite of media portrayals and racial stereotypes, there are millions of highly successful black people out there committed to success.

Each individual is the center of a network. No one individual is more important than any of the others who feed their talents and knowledge into the network. The problem in the past has been how to bring our people together into a global network to serve the agenda of our entire race. We know that global networking begins with an understanding of how powerful and important each person is.

There is no success that I can point to in my lifetime that was not the result of working with and through people. My network, linked to the networks of others, has produced many successes over the last twenty-five years. I have never met a successful person who did not have the same experience with networking. From my own networking experiences and those of others, I have identified some common threads and guideposts for effective networking. I call them the "Fraser Guidelines" simply because that is an easy name for me to remember. You can call them anything you want. The important thing is to review them and put them into action for your benefit and the betterment of your community of family, friends, neighbors, and networkers.

What is the hardest-working thing you know? Think about it for a second. The answer is *nature*. Nature works without fanfare, quietly, effortlessly, and in harmony with all things. When you wake up in the morning, its job is already done. Nature makes no speeches, issues no press releases, and proclaims no victories; it just gets the job done for the benefit of humankind based on a simple set of universal laws and principles.

It is my belief that if we work with a common set of networking principles, we can take another step toward serving a common agenda, our collective success as a people. I am hopeful that if you and I follow these guidelines, millions of other black people will join us on this new Underground Railroad toward economic liberation and freedom.

THE FRASER GUIDELINES FOR
EFFECTIVE NETWORKING

1. Make a commitment to network and make it a way of life. Take a vow, marry the networking concept, and be faithful to it in sickness and in health.

I believe you have to become wedded to networking to make it succeed as part of your life. The greatest challenge you must overcome is the "I can't afford the time" mind-set. (It is said that Robinson Crusoe was the only one who could get anything done by Friday.) The same self-defeating attitude blocks those who need to lose weight or improve their level of education. If you are committed, you understand that you can't afford not to find the time. You will not and cannot succeed in a vacuum.

Networking, like all important movements, is a process, not a program. You do a little bit each day, every day, and you keep at it, building it over time. I actually had someone say to me once, "I tried networking at an event last week. It didn't work." Ha! That's like saying, "I tried marriage one day." There is a beginning to the networking process, but no end. You have to be patient, be determined, and be visible to make it work over the long haul. You have to learn it and teach it by example.

Networking is both an art and a science. It is fun, productive, and politically correct, and it will lead you to a more fulfilling and interesting life. Peggy Winston was an energetic college graduate with an MBA from Hampton University. After college, she was recruited by several banking firms in northeastern and midwestern cities. Each recruiter was attracted by her strong academic credentials. She worked for many years in the financial sector, but decided to enter the complex and rapidly changing field of communications. She became a

compliance officer with a communications engineering
and consulting firm, specializing in obtaining
telecommunications technology licenses from the Federal
Communications Commission. Although her position
was created to ensure the accuracy and integrity of FCC
applications, Peggy was ultimately hired because of her
academic record and her people skills. She was the right
person with the right skills at the right time.

After several months on the job, Peggy discovered
that the black community had been left out of all
previous FCC licensing processes. She was determined to
educate, inform, and include the black community in the
FCC's licensing for IVDS, which is commonly referred
to as "interactive television," a form of communication
which industry experts had forecasted to be a trillion-
dollar industry within a decade or two. Forecasters said
that someday you will be able to order furniture, balance
your checkbook, buy groceries, plan trips, and conduct
all sorts of everyday business electronically. They were
partially right. Today on-line shopping using the Internet
is very popular. The ability to access the Internet through
your television is a convergence technology that is now
on the rise. IVDS is still evolving and will reemerge as a
role player in this technological revolution. (The Home
Shopping Network, on which viewers look at merchan-
dise and then order it by phone, is considered to be a
precursor to interactive television.)

Peggy felt that the black community could participate
in one of two ways. They could either pay some vendor a
monthly fee (like they do for cable TV) for use of the
service once it was piped into their homes, or they could
position themselves to *be* the vendor and collect the
monthly fee from customers.

Now, a lot of investors with "inside" and specialized
information made considerable sums of money in past

lotteries for rights to similar FCC-controlled licenses in wireless cable, cellular telephones, and personal pagers. Peggy saw this as an opportunity for black people to take part in a venture that was potentially very lucrative, although not without some risk. It was also the perfect opportunity to exercise her networking skills. Unfortunately, as she quickly discovered, her networking skills were unrefined. She tackled the job with enthusiasm but without a strong network in place. Without a well-connected person involved to help her to overcome her own lack of a client base, she had little success. She wrote letters and made telephone calls for a few weeks but came away without creating much enthusiasm among African Americans for the licensing opportunity.

Peggy simply was not getting the information to the right people, namely, those black people with the cash resources and patience to take risks that could lead to considerable gains over the long term. Peggy became impatient. She developed bad feelings about networking with black people, much like men who don't know how to approach women can develop negative feelings about them. She came to believe that blacks were unsophisticated about nontraditional investment opportunities, but, in truth, what she needed was a more sophisticated approach to the more sophisticated target audience she was attempting to serve.

Fortunately for Peggy, one of the contacts she made was Bob Lanier, the publisher of the local *Black Pages*, a Yellow Pages directory for black businesses. Bob took an interest in the investment opportunity. He also realized that Peggy needed some more contacts and more coaching in effective networking, so he had her get in touch with me, after he had filled me in a bit on her dilemma. Our initial half-hour conversation was more akin to a therapy session than a business or networking meeting. Peggy was basically puzzled about how to connect in this environment. She was a treasure hunter without a map.

In our first telephone discussion, I presented Peggy with several networking strategies such as letters of recommendation, personal calls on her behalf, group meetings to explain the business opportunity, and a series of one-on-one breakfasts and lunches.

After I met with Peggy and talked with her several more times, our networking relationship flourished. She learned quickly, and she had many networking skills that were only in need of nurturing and refinement. What she really needed was a greater *commitment* to the process of networking. As it turned out, Peggy recruited many black people within my network—myself included—for her interactive television investment opportunity. But, more important, she became committed to the *process* of networking. She came to understand that simply because you have a goal or a product, you cannot expect the world to fall at your feet. Moreover, she learned that "where there is great difficulty there is also great opportunity." She said: "You need determination, skills, and patience to develop a network that eventually will help deliver you to your goals, whatever they may be. You need unfaltering commitment."

Understand the importance of what took place in this instance. Because Peggy eventually got assistance and guidance, she succeeded in her goal of bringing more black people together around an investment opportunity with long-term potential.

If Peggy had not gotten help and direction, she would have been like the man who was standing in the river dying of thirst. If she had walked away in frustration, convinced that her own people were not sophisticated enough for such a venture—when, in fact, *she* only needed to refine her own networking skills and reach out to her target market—we all would have lost out, just as we have been losing out on economic opportunities for decades in this country. As I've stressed throughout this book, networking is not a mere buzz word. It is a very real and practical method of creating opportunities for our people.

That is why I regard networking as so vital. That is why I call it the Underground Railroad to success. And that is why I preach that we have to become committed to the process of networking to make this work.

2. Set achievable goals. Say your goal is to create your own business importing authentic African art for sale to the black community. Your *vision*, however, is to do well by doing good, that is, to earn a comfortable income while building pride among African Americans in their heritage. If once you start your business you discover that you are unable to make a connection with African artists who do quality work, then you must reconsider this goal, because it does not fit your vision of doing well by doing good. Time to rethink the goal and perhaps look for another, more high-quality product line that will fulfill your vision.

To achieve anything in life, you must have goals, and you must go after them with your eyes open. Writing your goals down is a time-tested method for making them real in your mind and the minds of those you need to help you along the way. Networking goals should be specific, measurable, achievable, and compatible with your vision for your life. Once you have established what your goals are and written them down with daily steps toward achieving them (for example, "Today I will make six phone calls toward my goal of finding a source of high-quality African art"), it is then up to you to go after them with all of your determination. And remember, networking is about building relationships first, so do not strain the fibers of friendship by demanding too much too soon.

Ken Ferguson is an expert in karate and runs a small martial arts school for young people. His business is located in a working-class suburb of Cleveland, the very neighborhood where Ken has lived most of his life. He has been active in the local business association for many years. In this neighborhood, Ken has a reputation as a steady, hardworking family man who loves children. He teaches in his karate school part-time, but his long-term goals are to turn it into a full-time business and also to become active in city politics.

Ken has been developing his political skills within the business association by serving on and chairing various committees. Recently, he was nominated to lead the entire association, but he expressed concerns about the responsibility and the time required. His close friends were called upon to remind him of his vision to become a city leader. They encouraged him to take the association chairmanship and to regard it as one goal toward his vision. They assured him it would enhance his profile in the community and broaden his base of support.

Ken was uncomfortable at first, because he did not want to be seen as an opportunist using one position to launch himself to the next. But once he refocused on his vision and accepted the greater role in his community and became comfortable in it, his leadership qualities blossomed. He has become a masterful organizer and networker. Now, hundreds more people are among his supporters. If his vision remains clear, his network should be strong enough to take him where he wants to go.

3. Always be prepared to network. In fact, network around the clock. "I would rather be prepared and not have an opportunity than to have an opportunity and not be prepared," said Whitney Young, the late president of the National Urban League.

This Fraser Guideline is my version of the Boy Scout motto, "Be prepared." Most networking conversations start with small talk, and most small talk centers on what is happening in the world. Advice columnist Ann Landers once noted: "People with great minds talk about ideas. People with average minds talk about events. People with small minds talk about other people." To talk about ideas, you have to read newspapers and books, watch the evening news, and subscribe to thought-provoking magazines that give you an overview of the world. This is common sense, but I am frequently amazed at how people become so wrapped up in their own daily struggles that they pay no attention to the world around them. Your struggle might be made easier if you understand the influences working on you from the outside.

Scan your newspapers for stories that have a bearing on your world, or that simply catch your interest. Save those that particularly interest you, and send or e-mail copies to people in your network of these stories and others that are specific to their interests.

When you go to a networking event, be prepared with a plentiful supply of business cards, pens, a small notebook, and a well-thought-out agenda for the affair. Make sure you understand just what the meeting is about, whether it is formal or informal, educational or social. Take the attitude that you are a host, not a guest, and treat people accordingly. Follow the tried-and-true five-P's philosophy: *Prior preparation prevents poor performance*. Rehearse your self-introduction (the thirty-second version; save anything else for your Nobel Prize acceptance speech).

Cynthia Jones is a graphic designer with her own well-respected firm in Atlanta. Always impeccably dressed, she is a walking billboard of good taste in design, color, and coordination. She exudes confidence and warmth. I met Cynthia at Dartmouth College during an extensive executive training program we were taking for minority business owners. Knowing that there would be successful black businesspeople from all over the country participating, I bent the event to my purpose a bit by getting permission to have three cases of my *SuccessGuides* and my business brochures shipped to the college.

During the early-evening cocktail hour, the college provided me a small area to display my products. I gave out free copies of my networking guide and secured several important leads for future business deals. Everyone else handed out business cards, too, with the exception of Cynthia, who had come armed with an elaborate portfolio of her graphic design work. Like me, Cynthia had foreseen that this affair was an outstanding networking opportunity. In attendance were serious business owners and entrepreneurs who were not the least bit shy about doing business on the spot. In fact, it was like a gathering of the gladiators, and most of the gladiators were eager to flex their business muscles in front of the competition.

Cynthia came by my small display during the event, and as a graphic designer, she made a professional inspection of my *SuccessGuides* and brochures. She was complimentary and charming while at the same time asking me very specific and probing questions concerning my design, layout, style, and content objectives for my product. She listened closely to my responses, asked insightful follow-up questions, and then responded in turn by offering her suggestions as to how I might enhance the appearance of my product. She then offered to show me her portfolio for my inspection and critique. It was a beautiful, leather-bound showcase, and her work offered further proof that she knew what she was talking about and that she had the talent to practice what she preached.

We exchanged business cards that evening, and within the next year, Cynthia got the contract to design the next edition of my *SuccessGuides*. Like a good Scout, she was prepared.

4. Give first, expect nothing in return. It is better to give to the network than to receive.

John Glover, former executive director of the Cleveland chapter of the United Negro College Fund, recruited me into UNCF to be one of his key volunteers. He has his own version of this networking guideline; it bears repeating: "Give until it hurts, and then give until it feels good." No one starts networking for purely unselfish reasons. It wouldn't be human to expect to get nothing from networking, but the best attitude you can bring to the process is to network because you are helping others. I cannot overstress my belief that you have to build relationships before you try to sell anything. Once you get into the habit of giving and break through that threshold of selfishness, then your networking and your life will take on more fulfilling and gratifying meaning.

Michael Lewellen was the urban and minority affairs manager for Nike. He was partly responsible for helping Nike develop and execute its exceptional community outreach programs. I met Mike at the annual National Urban League Conference, where he was diligently working a booth, passing out posters and pens and corporate goodwill. When I struck up a conversation, we clicked immediately. He invited me to attend a special reception Nike was having later that evening, and I, in turn, learned that he did not have a ticket to a concert to be held that night in conjunction with the conference. It was a hot ticket because the bill included several of black America's top R&B acts. I had a hundred-dollar VIP seat that had come with the convention package I had purchased. I asked Mike to do me a favor and take my seat, because I wasn't sure if I would be able to make it. He was very appreciative. Later that evening, as it turned out, I was able to attend, and I found another seat through a network connection. It was a great concert, and a rewarding one.

Several weeks later, I received a beautiful pair of Nike shoes in the mail and a thank-you note from Mike. And not long after that, his ad agency reviewed the merits of *SuccessGuide*, and Nike placed a two-page color advertisement—a five-figure purchase. Giving Mike my concert ticket had not been a calculated move on my part. I liked him and I wanted him to enjoy the concert. I expected nothing in return, other than a continued friendship and perhaps a networking relationship that would grow. I'm sure Mike felt the same way when he invited me to the Nike reception. And I'm sure he felt that he was getting good value when his agency placed the ad in *SuccessGuide*, otherwise he would not have done it.

But so far, there has been considerable mutual benefit from our budding relationship. The way to nourish that relationship is to stay in touch, to send notes and articles of interest, and to be alert to each other's needs and concerns. We have established a networking bond based on mutual respect and trust, and that is ultimately the goal of any business relationship as well.

5. Build rapport, don't sell. Never make demands of a network connection until you have made sure it is a solid one secured by trust and good communication. Building a strong line of communication is the key to developing good rapport. There is nothing wrong with utilizing that rapport at some point for future sales opportunities, but don't make *selling* the only reason you include a person in your network. People tend to pick up on a sales agenda very quickly, and most will be turned off if it is overaggressive or premature. Remember, the goal of networking is to build relationships for the purpose of sharing ideas, information, opportunities, and resources. If you are in sales, naturally you will have a network that is devoted to that purpose, but it should never be the sole purpose of your larger network.

Securing the late Ron Brown, then chairman of the Democratic Party, for a speaking engagement took me two years of rapport-building and persistence. Working with and through his chief of communications at that time, Joe Louis Barrow, son of the legendary fighter Joe Louis, I had attempted several times to schedule Brown, but frankly, I don't think he considered it a priority in his politically sensitive agenda. I made several visits to Washington to meet Barrow, but it wasn't until I got invited to a power meeting of political heavyweights in Cleveland prior to the 1992 presidential campaign and met Brown personally that I was able to establish a solid connection with him.

I worked hard on shoring up that connection, and within a year, Ron agreed to speak to a SuccessNet audience. His presentation was brilliant, and his predictions and observations for the campaign proved to be dead-on and visionary. He said the Democrats would regain the White House against all odds.

The point here is that I had to build rapport and a strong line of communication before I could make that network line to Ron Brown work. But then it worked quite well.

6. Be an active listener. An "All-Ears All-Star." This could be the Golden Rule of networking. Simply said, most people don't listen, they only prepare themselves to talk. So if you are really listening, you will stand out from the crowd. Listening requires more than keeping your fingers out of your ears. It requires patience, eye contact, alertness, empathy, body language, and a sense of humor. Good questions are always a sign of a good listener.

Shifting eyes and head means either the person has a nervous tic or is a lousy listener. Then there is the affliction I call *SAD*, which stands for Self-Absorption Disorder. Some people are only tuned to their own wavelength, which must be a pretty monotonous channel when so many others have the whole world to tune in. You've probably known people like this. You tell them what you consider to be a fairly interesting story and their response is to completely ignore what you just said and launch into an unrelated story about themselves. SAD, but true. It is a matter of respect to listen with your ears and your heart. And if you are to achieve any success through networking, you have to listen thoroughly to what others are saying.

When my son Scott was twelve years old, he had a highly developed sense of humor and good listening skills, as evidenced in a response he made to me after he'd put in a day's work at my office during the summer. He had worked diligently for six hours packing shipping cartons for a UPS pickup. At the end of the day, proud of his work, he marched into my office, plopped down in a chair facing my desk, and informed me he had successfully completed his job. Since we had not discussed or agreed upon a fee for services earlier, he began negotiations tactfully: "Dad, I'm finished with the job you assigned me. I believe I've done a good job that will meet your satisfaction. How much do I get paid?"

I thought a minute and replied, "Scott, I really appreciate the work you have done and had hoped you would make a small sacrifice for the company by volunteering your services until the business resolves its short-term petty-cash dilemma."

Scott's smile diminished as he listened intently, then he thought for a minute and came back with a classic win-win response. "I certainly understand your problem, Dad [empathy], but there are a few things I need for school that could save you some money [mutual benefit], so I'll charge you only five dollars for the *sacrifice* and three dollars for the *dilemma*! That's only eight dollars for a day's work. Would that be *fair* [sense of humor]?" I have to admit, my son got me. I laughed aloud and then gave him a twenty-dollar bill. I was raising the world's greatest salesman and one heck of a networker. He even collected business cards and had his own business card, which he passed out to build up a network of connections to help him raise money for school projects. *His* networking book, *Son of Success Runs in Our Race*, should be out within a couple years. Watch for it.

7. Treat everyone with dignity, respect, and courtesy. Honor your networkers. I have presidents and plumbers in my network. They are all equal in my Soul-O-Dex. I can promise you that there are times when the plumber is more important than the president, especially when there is a pipe leaking somewhere in the network's plumbing. The moral here is to treat everyone as an equal and to prejudge no one. Information, resources, and referrals are more important than titles. Be flexible and keep an open mind. Return your phone calls and don't ever forget where you came from, because your friends and family surely won't.

Here are a few examples of how great networking connections came from the most unexpected contacts:

- One of the largest orders in my company's history came from a twenty-year-old wearing a *Malcolm X* cap, whom I met at a football game. Turns out his father was a senior purchasing agent for a major library system. Ring! Ring! Ring!
- In what began as a casual conversation with Mack Clemmons, a veteran public relations agent in Cleveland, I found myself delivering a passionate speech about the value of networking among black people. I guess I triggered something in Mack's mind, because he told his friend Tony Brown in New York about me, and the next thing I knew, I was delivering the same passionate speech on Tony's public television show. Ring! Ring! Ring!
- While staying at the Omni International Hotel, I struck up a conversation with the bell captain in an elevator. He asked me what I did. I told him and gave him a copy of the *SuccessGuide*. Later in the day, I received a call from the manager of the hotel's gift shop saying they would like to distribute the *SuccessGuide* in the exclusive hotel gift shop. Ring! Ring! Ring!
- While planning a New Year's Eve party, I realized I was in desperate need of some suitable music. I contacted an acquaintance who owned a nightclub. We talked music first, then we talked business. Today he is my partner. Ring! Ring! Ring!

8. Think race and culture first. Network from the roots up. Just as cultural networking is practiced by other groups such as the Jews, Jamaicans, Chinese, Japanese, Koreans, Arabs, Irish, and others, black people should always look within their own cultural community for networking contacts and then move out from there to expand their base to include anyone who embraces them and wishes to share information, ideas, and resources, remembering that white males still control the vast majority of resources in this country. Nonetheless, networking begins at home because those closest to you are most likely to share your cultural agenda, and black people are most likely to be sensitive to your needs and to understand the challenges you face.

Black people have a long way to go to build the sort of network that many other cultural groups have established over decades and decades. But I believe we are moving in the right direction, and in the next chapter, I will provide some outstanding examples of black networks doing positive things for our community.

On the other hand, I was distressed several years ago to read a *USA Today* survey of one thousand black consumers in which nearly 60 percent said *it did not matter* if blacks were employed where they shopped. This is not only irresponsible thinking, it is extremely self-destructive. Consider that nearly every social scientist proclaims stable employment to be the foundation on which strong families and individual self-esteem are built. Consider that other surveys have shown that blacks are still are laid off in numbers disproportionate to other groups. How could such a high percentage of blacks be so disengaged from their own fates and livelihoods that they would respond to a survey by saying it does not matter if other blacks are employed in the places they patronize? In this day and age, this fact astounds me. Black psychologist and family therapist Dr. Dave Whitaker says that black children during their formative years are not instilled with a communal sense of supporting their own people. Believe me, children in other cultures, such as the Jewish community or the Asian community, learn this at a very young age! So should our children.

We must network to increase awareness that we have to do more to leverage the five hundred and ninety billion dollars in black buying power; the seven and a half trillion dollars in black education and training; and the incredible power of a black community that includes about nine million people in professional, technical, and entrepreneurial positions. If developed to its potential, this network of black economic and human resources can be a powerful tool to be applied to the many problems faced by members of our race.

I have a suggestion as to how you might wield your own economic clout. Anytime I need or want to purchase something, I begin with my network of black contacts. I am not always successful in finding someone with the right skills at the right place at the right time, but believe me, I am constantly amazed at the quantity and quality of valuable resources out there in the black community. Sometimes, however, my contacts in the black community lead me to network connections who are not black, but are sensitive and supportive and can provide valuable resources to help me get done what I need to get done when I need it done. The economic impact of leveraging and recycling our collective black wealth can be staggering.

To show you what I mean, I have tallied up my own personal and company expenditures for a year.

Roughly one quarter of my household expenditures and a third of my business's expenditures were invested in the black community that year. How about yours? My goal is to increase each category of trade done with black businesses by 5 percent each year for the next five years.

If the ten million black households reinvested one quarter of their average annual household income of $27,910 back into black businesses and professional services, in one year, the dollar value of the products and services of 823,000 black businesses in America would double. Additionally, it would create an estimated one million new jobs per year. If those of us in business targeted just 30 percent of all expenditures to go to other black businesses and a black payroll, another fifteen billion dollars would recycle back into our community each year!

Buying Black-on-Black

How about a *black-on-black set-aside program* for us? We have worked hard to secure local, regional, and federal government set-aside programs and Equal Employment Opportunity Commission guidelines for major corporations. Why not teach by example, and voluntarily implement our own program through focused personal and business spending?

Another benefit to this strategy would be the pressure it would put on black-owned businesses to improve and expand the products and services they provide our community. The potential of increased revenues would provide incentives and working capital to grow their businesses, create jobs, and improve the quality of their products and services. This would address one of the most frequent complaints blacks use as a reason for not supporting their own. This is a circular problem: Lack of support means reduced revenues; reduced revenues limits growth and improved quality and service; which results in lack of support.

If you find that the black businesses that you would like to patronize are not competitive, let them know. By patronizing black-owned businesses, we can make the difference often in whether they make it or not. We need to do whatever we can to ensure their success so that our children and grandchildren will grow up in an environment populated by high-achieving, successful black people. At some juncture, each side of the problem must take responsibility for its role, act on it, and stop pointing fingers.

A good example of black-on-black buying was offered in a *Black Enterprise* magazine article about two black former pro football adversaries, Mel Farr and Charlie Johnson. Johnson, a former defensive tackle, is president of Active Transportation, in Louisville, Kentucky. Farr, a former running back, at the time owned four auto dealerships, including Mel Farr Ford in Oak Park, Michigan. When Johnson needed twenty-five new car-hauling trucks for his business, he decided to do some black-on-black buying. He invited Farr to bid on the deal, and the result was a $1.5 million sale—the largest single deal ever done by Farr's automotive group. "Those companies that can help other companies get on stable ground should do it," Johnson said.

Harriet Michel, president of the National Minority Supplier Development Council, which I cite for its economic empowerment networking in Appendix B, said that black-on-black buying does not have to be limited to big-ticket deals. "If we could get all minority businesses to use minority suppliers, we'd see a lot more business for minority firms," she said.

Selective Buying Using Reciprocity

I believe we should also leverage our buying power in dealing with major companies that produce products and services in highly competitive categories. We should support those who support us. The questions I ask before I buy are:

- Does this company employ black people in proportion to our 13 percent of the United States population?
- Does its advertising talk to me?
- Are there black people featured in its advertisements?
- Does it place ads in black media?
- How do its ads portray blacks? As jocks? Victims?

Entertainers? Sex objects? Threats? Professionals? Family-oriented? Churchgoing? Law-abiding?
• Has this company been active in sponsoring events or programs beneficial to the black community?
• Do they support our institutions of education and/or organizations?

I know this may sound like a lot to consider before buying a new car or ordering new office furniture, but it really doesn't take that much time if your awareness has been heightened, which is what I am attempting to do here. The collective impact of targeted spending could mean thousands of jobs and billions of dollars in return to our Urban Village. This is not an economic boycott. It is *selective buying* in the competitive marketplace.

How much leverage does the black community have? Ken Smikle of *Target Market News* provides these figures to show how much blacks spend annually in specific areas:

SPENDING BY AFRICAN AMERICANS

Category	2001
Housing and household products, furnishings	$143.3 billion
Food, beverages, and tobacco	$60.9 billion
Cars and trucks	$30.1 billion
Clothing and personal care	$27.5 billion
Health care	$14.5 billion
Entertainment, books, and travel	$8.2 billion

Many of the companies producing these products and services have demonstrated strong outreach and commitment to the African-American community, but many of them have not. Token advertising and marketing budgets coupled with token black-management representation in the workplace are generally clear signs that our buying power is taken for granted. Recent employment figures still demonstrate we are the first fired and last hired in good times and in bad times.

9. Keep the Help Line open. Ask for help and give help when asked. The primary purpose of your network is to provide assistance and provide you with assistance. Assuming you have built a strong network built on positive relationships, the next step is to use your network efficiently. Take an inventory of your network, as I did when putting the dedication page of this book together, and I am sure you too will feel empowered by the breadth of the resources that exist for you.

Remember, however, that your network is there to be used, not abused. If your network is not being used, it's useless. I go to my network for help when I need investors for my business; when I needed a source of information; when I need constructive criticism; when I want to help someone find a job; when I need to raise money for a charitable group.

Networking is not a complicated process. We complicate it when we have to overcome our own psychological barriers and poor self-esteem. You have to be able to admit that you need help, and that involves throwing the ego out the window sometimes. If you have that sort of ego, it deserves to be thrown out the window.

10. Give thanks to your network. Praise, thanks, and thoughtfulness are three of the great lubricants and complements of life. It is human nature to want to be recognized for your good deeds and friendship. Regardless of what people tell you or how embarrassed they may appear to be when complimented, psychologically, they love the warm fuzzies—don't we all? Timing is important, and you have to know when to lay it on thick and when to make it just a sincere veneer. Short notes, small gifts, interesting and relevant newspaper or magazine articles are all ways to demonstrate thoughtfulness and to keep you in the forefront of someone's mind. I go through my Soul-O-Dex every month and pick five to ten key contacts to call just to keep the network ties strong, and also to catch up on what is going on in the lives of those individuals. I limit these calls to friends I have not been in touch with for some time. It's a nice break in the day, and in general takes no more than a total of one hour out of my monthly work schedule.

A key act of thoughtfulness is returning telephone calls and replying to e-mails as soon as possible. If you can't do it yourself, you should have an assistant or someone close to you do it for you. When you make calls, let people know the best time to return them so as to avoid mind-grating games of telephone tag. These courtesies demonstrate your respect for the networking relationship.

NETWORKING DOS AND DON'TS

Over thirty-five years, I have observed all sorts of behavior on the networking circuit—some of it good, some bad, some funny, and some resoundingly ugly. As a result, I have compiled a substantial list of networking Dos and Don'ts. It is a list that grows with every fresh networking experience.

Here are the Dos.

- Do keep your sense of humor, especially while reading this list.
- Do stay up-to-date on current events. ("What? *Enron went bankrupt?*")
- Do bring a pen and plenty of business cards. ("Mind if I write my name and phone number on your hand?")
- Do return telephone calls within twenty-four hours. ("When did Mr. Jackson die? He just called me six months ago.")
- Do listen and respond when people talk to you. ("I'm

sorry, what did you say about jackasses mating downtown? Oh, jackets made in Hong Kong!")
• Do mind your personal hygiene and grooming.
• Do inform anyone whose name you have given out to a networking contact. ("Hello, Mr. Simpson—this is the FBI. George Fraser gave us your name—mind if we come in?")
• Do give a firm handshake, one that establishes that you are a vital human being, while still leaving all of the shakee's bones intact.
• Do bring cash. In fact, don't leave home without it, because the bartenders and parking-lot attendant do not accept any major credit cards or personal checks.
• Do plan ahead for networking events, checking who is going to be there, and why you are going. Web sites are good sources for this.
• Do say thank you for networking assistance.
• Do follow through on promises. ("Gee, Shirley, I forgot all about picking your boss up at the Apollo Theater last night.")
• Do leave before the lights are turned off.
• Do speak standard English.
• Do keep one hand free for meeting folks.
• Do thank and say good-bye to the host or hostess before leaving a network event. That is, if you want to be invited back.
• Do write a thirty-second self-introduction for networking events. (Avoid: "Well, I started out as a small black child in a middle-class family. Then, shortly after birth . . .")
• Do accept compliments graciously. Say thank you without explanation.
• Do make at least one banker and one lawyer part of your network.
• Do confirm all appointments before going.
• Do know what you are going to say before you say it.

- Do RSVP when an RSVP is requested.
- Do fly first class when you can, in order to make good contacts.
- Do bring your admission tickets.
- Do get to the point quickly.

And now, the Don'ts.
- Don't smoke in public.
- Don't chew gum, either.
- Don't show up if you've just gotten real bad press.
- Don't ask people if you can "pick their brains."
- Don't send a résumé without calling first.
- Don't say, "I know you don't remember me."
- Don't make anyone guess your name. Say it first.
- Don't misrepresent yourself.
- Don't try to sell at a networking event.
- Don't talk while you eat. Or vice-versa.
- Don't hog a VIP's time.
- Don't flirt.
- Don't show cleavage.
- Don't talk when the speaker is talking. Particularly if the speaker is a former All-Pro.
- Don't forget your table manners.
- Don't overfill your hors d'oeuvre plate.
- Don't hold multiple conversations within the group. Unless, of course, you have multiple personalities.
- Don't give one-word answers to questions. Two is not much of an improvement.
- Don't pass out business cards indiscriminately.
- Don't be late. Start a trend: Arrive on time.
- Don't tell dirty or racist jokes.
- Don't limit the conversation to male or female topics only. Mix it up.
- Don't be long-winded. Short gusts are much more effective.

- Don't abuse your body; a sharp body enhances a sharp mind.
- Don't interrupt.
- Don't gossip about people or make negative comments.
- Don't ask for free advice from paid professionals. Unless you want to be presented with a bill the next day.
- Don't take yourself too seriously. You may be the only one who does.
- Don't say, "I'll call you," or, "Let's get together," if you don't mean it. And I mean this.
- Don't cancel when you can reschedule.
- Don't be afraid to go to events alone. Being alone often invites a crowd.
- Don't wear outlandish hairdos. Patti LaBelle has her own network.
- Don't misspell names, titles, or companies when corresponding. The secret to success is in the details.

TEN TIPS FOR WHITES SEEKING TO NETWORK WITH BLACKS

1. *Avoid generalizing about an entire race of people.* Get to know black people better as individuals so that you learn not to accept stereotypes of an entire race as the truth.

2. *Avoid assuming we have homogeneous tastes or that we all know each other.* We are as diverse as the white community in our backgrounds, education, and socioeconomic strata. I don't know Ice-T. Nor have I ever slam-dunked.

3. *Go to black events.* Yes, enter our world. Volunteer to serve on the boards of major black organizations. Increase your exposure so that you might increase your understanding.

4. *Be careful of faint praise such as "I wish there were more blacks like you."* A more acceptable, and far wiser, statement would be: "I know that there are thousands of

African Americans like you. Can you help me get in touch with more of them?"

5. *Be a realist.* Acknowledge that you are not color-blind and that, like everyone, you are susceptible to media stereotypes of African Americans, but make the effort to go beyond those images.

6. *Do your best to avoid tokenism when inviting blacks to participate in events.* We are finely tuned to sense a lack of sincerity, so put the invitation in writing, and then follow up with telephone calls and personal requests. You will get better results also if you invite more than one of us.

7. *Try something different: Mentor an African American so that you might better understand our culture and our work ethic.* By extending the mentorship socially, you may come to better understand the nuances of communicating with people of our race.

8. *Count us in.* One of the fastest-growing target markets in America is the black middle and upper class, which includes over two million African-American households earning more than fifty thousand dollars a year. If you want our disposable income and our respect, you must market to us with advertising that includes blacks and shows that you understand our culture and our needs. Black-owned advertising agencies and media are particularly well suited to reach our lucrative markets.

9. *Under no circumstances should you tell a racially based joke.* You may get a courtesy chuckle or two, but you will soon find yourself standing alone and your image tarnished forever.

10. *And please, avoid saying, "You people" and "Some of my best friends are black."* This is a clear sign that you are trying to hide your white guilt.

Ellis Cose, author of *The Envy of the World: On Being a Black Man in America*, wrote:

It may very well be that the civil rights debate has been so distorted by strategies designed to engender guilt that many whites, as a form of self-defense, have come to define any act of decency toward blacks as an act of expiation. If an end to such strategies—and indeed an end to white guilt—would result in a more intelligent dialogue, I, for one, am all for wiping the slate clean. Let us decide, from here on out, that no one need feel guilty about the sins of the past.

Mr. Cose presents us with a profound and interesting challenge.

*"No one, black or white, succeeds on his own;
you have to be part of a network."*
CHERYL BROUSSARD

Cheryl Broussard is CEO of Cheryl Broussard & Co., Inc., an Oakland, California–based financial and small business consulting firm. The company conducts consulting and informational seminars on topics ranging from financial and estate planning to money empowerment. Broussard is the author of two best-sellers: *Sister CEO: The Black Woman's Guide to Starting Your Own Business,* and *The Black Woman's Guide to Financial Independence: Smart Ways to Take Charge of Your Money, Build Wealth, and Achieve Financial Security.* She periodically writes a fiscal fitness column in *Heart & Soul* magazine and is the cohost of *Ebony Money Power,* an *Ebony* magazine video. Her articles have been featured in such publications as *Black Enterprise* and *USA Today.* Says Broussard, "I see entrepreneurship as really the wave of the future . . . Those big corporations are going to be tightening their belts. And when they're tightening their belts that means they're going to be letting some people go. And that could be an opportunity for you."

10

Networks at Work

There are two ways of exerting one's strength:
one is pushing down, the other is pulling up.
— BOOKER T. WASHINGTON

I n the first chapter, I wrote of Free Frank McWorter as a person who exemplified the spirit of this book, an uncelebrated and common man uncommonly devoted to the betterment not just of himself, but of all those of his race. If I had to select a modern-day example of such a person, Paul G. Watkins would certainly be a top candidate.

Like Free Frank, who was little known in his day, Paul has generally gone quietly about his mission of working to elevate the lives of the black community. He is an excellent example of a man who networks unselfishly for the betterment of his race. And I believe his dedication is nothing short of heroic.

Throughout this book, I have told you why I think it is vital for blacks to network together for their common good. I have provided many illustrations of how, in spite of media images to the contrary, we are historically a race of successful people, and how we have always been a successful people, even when in chains. To encourage you to strive for a greater and more widespread success among our people into the next millennium, I have given you networking guidelines, practical tips, agendas, and Afrocentric principles to follow—principles derived from the ancient and proud culture of our tribal ancestors, one of the most highly developed civilizations in ancient history.

In this chapter, I will provide several outstanding examples of Afrocentric networks at work. Some of the networks are comprised of like-minded individuals; some are networks of charitable, religious, or service groups; and some are private business organizations—social entrepreneurs if you will—joined together to have a great impact for good in their communities via this new form of the Underground Railroad.

NETWORKING FOR ECONOMIC EMPOWERMENT

I'll begin with Paul G. Watkins, whom I first learned of from an article in *Black Enterprise*. Paul retired after thirty years as a supervisor in the automotive maintenance division of the city of Philadelphia. He lives modestly in the suburb of Flourtown, where he has become a networking guru for other blacks of modest means who are aggressively working for their own economic empowerment.

Since his retirement, Paul has devoted himself to helping other blacks form investment clubs in which members pool financial resources, information, and knowledge for the economic benefit of all. He lives the Afrocentric Networking Principles, modeled on the Seven Principles of Kwanzaa, that call for unity, self-determination, collective work and responsibility, and cooperative economics.

Investment clubs are an increasingly popular form of economic self-determination for black people across the United States, and, interestingly, these clubs share a lot with our ancestral culture in which all property and information were pooled unselfishly for the greater good of the tribal group.

"When I first started in investment clubs, one of the things I found was that people were willing to share whatever information they had. That was refreshing for me, a new experience, so then I started doing the same thing," Paul said. Once he discovered that sense of cooperative economics in investment clubs, he found it addictive. But networking is a very positive, healthy, and invigorating addiction. Through his own investments in utilities and other stocks, Paul has made enough money to finance additional investments in real estate and other areas. He has found, however, that his favorite investment is in the economic welfare of his black brothers and sisters. Paul told me: "One of the criticisms I have heard over the years is that the members of the black community who move ahead don't ever bother to look back. That is something I don't want to be guilty of. I am pretty set financially—at least, if I don't live too long—but now my goal is to give something back."

There are more than one hundred fifty blacks in the ten investment clubs that Paul has launched over the years. Jessie Pinder is one of those who has benefited greatly from networking with Paul. A surgical technician, she was recently divorced when she asked for his help in starting up an investment club. She felt that although her own financial resources were limited, she could expand her investment opportunities by pooling resources with like-minded black people.

Under Paul's guidance, Jessie contacted a half-dozen business associates, friends, neighbors, and other African Americans and set up a meeting in which Paul explained that an investment club is neither a pyramid scheme nor a get-rich-quick program. Each club requires members to invest a set amount of money each month. That money is then invested in stocks, bonds, mutual funds, or other areas, according to the wishes of the group.

As Paul preaches, investment clubs should be regarded as long-term propositions—at least one thousand of the more than more than nine thousand investment clubs registered with the National Association of Investment Corporation (NAIC) have been together for more than thirty years. Those are the kind of numbers that get Paul Watkins hopped up. "I'm still excited every time I speak to a group of people interested in starting a club. I'm afraid I've probably talked some people to death and lost a few friends because of it, but when you get on a roll, sometimes you have to go with it. I'm keyed up about this, and I just hope that it rubs off on other people," he said.

Wise investment of collective wealth is a key to the spread of success throughout the black community, according to Paul, who is doing his share to see that happen. "Blacks have a problem with economics, in my opinion. We seem to have addressed every other area of concern—equal opportunity, civil rights—but economics is the last great project for us to master as a people," he said. Paul believes that too many blacks have taken on the victim mentality. They feel victimized by a system that seems to hold them in poverty, and rather than trying to learn to master that system and break out of the poverty cycle, they give up. "We have a problem. We don't like how capitalism functions, so we don't investigate how it works in order to gain an advantage over it," he said. "If you look ahead, you don't see the situation improving. We are not keeping in step with other ethnic groups. If we think of ourselves as victims, we will continue to lose ground."

Paul believes that in a capitalistic society, the only real strength that any ethnic group can wield is economic strength. With economic muscle comes political power and the ability to force social change, he said. "Asking for something is one thing, but demanding it is another. To make demands you must have something to trade, and that is where we come up short as an ethnic group."

Cooperative economic strength is the way to remedy that disadvantage, he believes: "We need to find ways to keep our money in our community so that it benefits our own people. Too many blacks start thinking about how to spend their money as soon as they start making any. I know, because that is what I used to do. But now I have seen what can be done by hanging on to it and investing it."

So have those he has helped get into investment clubs. Paul, who was on the board of the NAIC's Delaware Valley Council, assisted Jessie Pinder in forming the Sure Safe Way Investment Club in Philadelphia. She recruited sixteen members ranging from a twenty-six-year-old nurse to a fifty-six-year-old minister. They began with a pledge to invest just twenty dollars a month each. Their portfolio grew into the thousands of dollars, as did their individual knowledge of sound investment principles.

Jessie said that investment and stock guides once read like Greek to her, but after Paul helped her understand material provided by the NAIC, she and her investment network partners learned to read corporate annual reports and prospectuses to gauge the potential value of their investment opportunities.

Paul does not just attend a couple meetings and then leave his clubs to flail about the dense world of investments on their own. He sets high standards and tight restrictions and then monitors their work. The Visions Investment Club that he founded in 1990 does not commit to buying any stock until one of its twenty-five members makes a presentation that covers the prospective company's ten-year performance as well as a five-year earnings projection.

This careful policy has resulted in some impressive rewards. From 1990 to 1993 the group's twenty-thousand-dollar portfolio had an average return of 11 percent. "Investment clubs are definitely rewarding, and for me, the greatest rewards come in seeing someone take hold of what I'm trying to impart to them and do something positive with it," said Paul. One of Paul's favorite examples of the value of networking for economic empowerment is a young woman who is a member of the first investment club he launched. "When she started, she had two or three dozen credit cards that were charged up to the limit," Paul said. "Now she has no credit cards, and she has her own stock portfolio. When you see someone like that take a hold of the principles you are trying to impart, it makes up for all the headaches. That is the reward in this work for me—when you see someone lift himself or herself up because of the environment you have created."

Part of what drives Paul Watkins to continually work for economic empowerment in the black community—even though he is financially comfortable himself—is his feeling that blacks of his generation could have done more to economically empower the next generation. He concludes: "I have some guilt feelings about it. I obeyed the laws and paid my bills and raised my son, but I still feel guilty because so much was not done to improve the lives of all of our people. We are one community, and the fault falls on everybody. That is what keeps me pushing."

ONE HUNDRED MULTIPLIED BY MILLIONS

Warren Valdry and Paul Watkins are kindred souls. As past president of One Hundred Black Men of Los Angeles, a consortium of upper-middle-class black professionals dedicated to putting something back into the community, Valdry read a report in 1985 that disturbed him. It showed that less than 4 percent of California's annual twenty-three thousand black high school graduates had the grade average and college prep courses necessary to attend the state's public university system. "I felt it was unacceptable to have that many kids falling through the cracks," he said.

Being a black man who believes in the power of self-determination, unity, and collective work and responsibility, Valdry decided to find a solution to the problem. The result is the Young Black Scholars (YBS) program. Valdry worked with teachers in Los Angeles County to identify two thousand black high school freshmen who showed promise. Then he built a support network of black professionals to provide afternoon and weekend tutoring workshops in writing, algebra, and taking standardized tests. To further motivate the kids, the YBS held a yearly Slam-Dunk Awards Dinner at which guests included Bill Cosby and Sidney Poitier.

By 2001, nearly three thousand of the Young Black Scholars graduated from high schools; of those, 65 percent had earned a B or better average. Most are now attending 133 different colleges and universities around the country, some of which have YBS support groups. And YBS has continued to launch programs for other classes of freshmen.

The Wall Street Journal reported several years ago: "Most

blacks can't even be considered for highly skilled jobs because they don't have enough education. Only 13.1 percent of blacks in the workforce have college degrees compared with 24.6 percent of whites and 38.6 percent of Asians, according to the 1990 Census." The 2000 Census shows that we have gained ground (over 15 percent have a college degree), but we still have a ways to go.

One Hundred Black Men of Los Angeles is doing something about that by networking for the success of young blacks. The Los Angeles organization is one of more than ninety chapters of One Hundred Black Men around the world, representing over ten thousand African-American business and professional men (there are also chapters of One Hundred Black Women nationwide). The Los Angeles chapter footed the original $250,000 cost of the program, which has since attracted the support of state, corporate, and philanthropic sponsors. Valdry is convinced that forming academic support and motivational groups is more important than merely finding college funds for black urban youth. "Dammit," he told *Fortune* magazine, "don't just have another scholarship fundraiser. Get their minds ready."

CREATING ECONOMIC INROADS

That same philosophy of preparing today's youth to be tomorrow's leaders is reflected in the networking of Inroads, a St. Louis–based program designed to put blacks, Hispanics, and Native Americans on a fast track to positions of power and influence in the business world. Described as "part college, part career, and part boot camp," Inroads was founded in 1970 by the late Frank Carr, a Chicago publishing executive who became a Catholic priest at age sixty-four. The program trains, tutors, and generally grooms high-achieving minority youths—80 percent of them black—for business internships with Fortune 1000 companies including IBM, AT&T, Microsoft, Merrill Lynch, Exxon Mobil, and other giants.

Carr, who took inspiration from being present in 1963 during the Reverend Martin Luther King, Jr.'s historic "I Have a Dream" speech in Washington, believed that minority students had as much talent and managerial potential as any other population group, and that there was a need for a training and facilitating organization to help the private sector find and develop this untapped pool of talent for the corporate world.

High school and college students with grade points of 3.0 or better are selected for Inroads programs operated in thirty-nine cities. Inroads participants are given additional and intensive instruction in mathematics, science, and English, along with specialized career counseling—everything from calculus to table manners.

Inroads college students are assigned year-round counselors who monitor their course load and provide assistance. Participants are also required to do community service with such groups as the Salvation Army. Most program participants work through their summer vacations and on weekends. Few have time left to go out for sports or other time-consuming extracurricular activities. For every one hundred high school students who sign up, twenty-five drop out before graduation. The survival standards are tougher than at nearly any college, according to Inroads officials. Former Inroads president Reginald Dickson wrote in the *Harvard Business Review:*

We don't just help them into jobs, we prepare them to succeed. We *insist* that they succeed, and we put the burden for succeeding squarely on their shoulders. We require sacrifice, commitment, resiliency, and hard, hard work from our young people, but we supply business with college graduates who consistently give companies what they need in terms of intelligence, education, commitment, and business experience.

Dickson, who is in private enterprise in St. Louis, added that Inroads does its work without federal or state support. "Our organizational strategy puts business ahead of philanthropy. We're not do-gooders who have targeted business. We're businesspeople with a social agenda."

About seven hundred fifty businesses act as sponsors for about five thousand collegians from the Inroads program each year by giving them summer jobs and training. The businesses pay about thirty-five hundred dollars to Inroads for the interns. "In return, we give them the finest minority youth we can find, mold, and deliver," wrote Dickson. A major by-product of all this is the creation of a critical mass of professionals in technical areas of business, many of whom choose to go into business for themselves. "What the students get in return for all this sacrifice is a foothold on the corporate ladder and, in many cases, a boost up," Dickson adds.

The young people in the Inroads program do not enter the business world with a victim's mentality. They enter it with the confidence that they are the cream of the crop. Dickson wrote:

> The blacks and Hispanics in the Inroads program are not saying, "We're victims; you owe us a free opportunity." They're saying, "We're talented, we can make our way, we can help you compete. Just give us some training and some tools." And, on their side, the white businesspeople are saying, "We want to hire these bright people, but we're not paying reparations for past injustices, we're paying compensation for present value. This isn't blood money. This is business."

Of five thousand minority youths who go through the Inroads program each year, dozens and dozens go on to become owners, partners, and presidents of their own companies. One of these was Randy Crump. Randy is an outstanding example not only of the sort of high-quality people who come out of the Inroads program, but also of how the benefits of Inroads multiply exponentially because of what the program instills in its participants.

The son of a laborer and a cleaning lady, Crump was one of the first Milwaukee-area young people recruited for the Inroads program. Highly motivated and a top student, he was already majoring in electrical engineering at Marquette University when Inroads found him and, he told me, greatly expanded his horizons.

"Through Inroads, I developed the idea that I could have my own business someday," he said. "I am a tremendous supporter of the Inroads concept that there is an amazing amount of talent among not only blacks but Hispanics and Native Americans as well, and that by tapping into it you can run any corporation or business in America."

Upon graduation, Randy went to work with the Eaton Corporation, which had been his Inroads sponsor, but within a short time he left to create his own firm, assembling and distributing industrial apparatus and automation equipment. Cannily, he retained Eaton as a major client. Then, in 1992, Randy enacted a plan that grew out of the culturally diverse environment fostered by Inroads. He launched another company, but he did it by tapping into the experience—and financial support—of nine other blacks from yet another Afrocentric network, the Milwaukee alumni association of Alpha Phi Alpha fraternity. As the oldest predominantly black Greek-letter organization in America, Alpha Phi Alpha is one vast Afrocentric network of incredible potential, with 125,000 active members and 750 chapters in forty-eight states, the Caribbean, Africa, Europe, and Asia.

As a man of considerable vision, Randy Crump recognized the potential of this international Underground Railroad of black talent and brain power. He said: "Years ago, I had envisioned having a company owned by Inroads' alums from various disciplines. I have done it, but instead of tapping Inroads alumni, I enlisted fraternity brothers from Alpha Phi Alpha. When you start a business, you need to know that the people involved are serious about what you are doing, and I have seen these people toil over community issues and projects for the alumni association. I have seen them put a lot of sweat into making things happen, and I knew these men could do the same with a business. I wanted people who were not afraid to work, people who have imagination, and people who are willing to wait for the fruits of their labor to mature."

As it turned out, the wait has not been long at all, according to Crump. Begun in March of 1992, ElecTech had one million dollars in sales in its first year. "It has been an extremely profitable endeavor already," Crump said. ElecTech is a custom engineering firm that takes on "engineering challenges" from other companies and then designs, builds, and installs systems to meet the challenge. Although not all of his partners are involved in the day-to-day operation of ElecTech, they do lend their expertise when called upon. That amounts to a considerable range of expertise, since the group includes a federal bank examiner and a banker, an electrical contractor, a human-resources expert, an industrial engineer, a computer-aided designer, a microprocessing engineer, a marketing expert, and Crump himself, who noted, "We have one opening on our board, and we are looking for a lawyer."

Crump said that in difficult financial times when black people tend to be laid off in greater numbers than others, it is of no little comfort to his board members to know that their talents are welcome at ElecTech. In fact, one of the board members—the banker—became the company's administrator after he was laid off, Crump said.

The company has grown. "Our goal is not to have a completely black organization, but we do want to have the significant portion of our work force be from minority backgrounds," he said, noting that ElecTech is willing to train people with no electronic-engineering experience for assembly and installation positions.

Crump believes in reaching out to elevate the lives of the black community, and he especially believes in the power of networking to accomplish that. He says: "In today's climate of downsizing, minority business start-ups are definitely the way to go. And I advise blacks who are in large corporations to always question whether their employers are doing enough business with minority firms and vendors. I believe that those minorities in large corporations now are the key to the future of minority-owned business."

PREACHING ECONOMIC REDEMPTION

Individuals and farsighted benevolent organizations have discovered the power and the glory in Afrocentric networking economic empowerment. And so have black churches. These traditional centers of leadership and power in our communities have also begun to wield the sword of cooperative economics and collective work and responsibility in their neighborhoods. An outstanding example of this is the work of the Reverend James Perkins and his Greater Christ Baptist Church on Detroit's Lower East Side.

In the mid-1980s, word began spreading that the long-abandoned storefronts across the street from the church were being used as crack houses. Reverend Perkins viewed this development as "an opportunity to see redemption at work in the community." He told me: "I saw these abandoned buildings and the crack dealers in a spiritual sense as the reality of evil. I saw it as an opportunity to prove that God is powerful enough to use us to redeem our community and stretch the concept of redemption beyond individual morality. And when we redeemed the buildings and put them to a productive use, that was a resurrection—our community came back from the dead."

The minister brought this spiritual redemption about by very practical and financially astute means. He developed a plan to purchase the abandoned buildings across the street by tapping into his congregation's credit-union fund. "Our notion of economic development is not to go to some bank and ask for a loan. We believe in being your own bank, borrowing from yourself, and paying yourself interest," he said. He received permission from his congregation to borrow sixty thousand dollars from their credit union, and he then purchased the crime-ridden, eyesore buildings across the street. His next move was a brilliant one in which he spun gold out of rotted wood and crumbling brick. He leased the land to the Burger King Corporation, which built a restaurant on it and hired young people from the neighborhood to work there. Now the restaurant is putting money into the community, *and* paying rent to the church's credit union on a substantial twenty-year lease.

The Reverend James Perkins did not stop his networking for community redemption there. Nor did he rest on his laurels. Shortly after the Burger King deal was completed, he and his congregation founded an educational center to assist neighborhood young people in getting their high school diplomas and employment-skills training. One of his most satisfying projects was a church-operated academy for black males, offering classes from kindergarten through the third grade. "Mainly the idea is to give these young fellows a solid grounding in academics and to give them socialization skills and teach them Christian values and principles—to give them a new and more positive sense of manhood because, unfortunately, the image in this community seems to be self-destructive—dropping out of school and getting involved in street and criminal lifestyle," the minister said.

On an economic front, he and his congregation had formed a network with four other area church congregations called People Organized to Work for Economic Recovery (POWER). Their plan was to expand on the same neighborhood redemption work accomplished when Reverend Perkins knocked out the crack houses and put up a Burger King. The network of churches had just started looking at a plan to pool their financial resources to replace another eyesore commercial area with a new shopping mall. "This network was spurred by our desire to increase economic development in our community, and by our realizing that we can do more together than as individual congregations. If we can each get our congregations interested, then the network of churches can lead the way." Reverend Perkins asserts: "I think it is very important to network. I think part of the reason many blacks don't network is that they bought into the 'American dream' notion that encourages you to achieve as an individual. But I don't understand the American dream as ever having been intended for black people. I don't think it was the intent for black people to be the co-equals of white people. We have to define our own sense of mission as a people in this land by taking charge of our own destiny and building up our own communities. For instance, I've suggested that black lawyers in Detroit should come into the black neighborhoods and locate their law firms here, instead of renting expensive space in the Renaissance Center or other downtown buildings. In that way, they could serve as role models for the youths of the community, and they would also have a built-in clientele."

Black churches across the country have caught the same spirit of self-determination. Like the Reverend James Perkins's church, many are focusing as much on economic redemption as on spiritual redemption, and they are doing it by networking. The Metropolitan Missionary Baptist Church and the Reverend William Hartsfield in Kansas City, Missouri, fought to build a symbol of hope on the site of an abandoned hospital in its neighborhood—a shopping mall and sixty units of moderate-income housing. This was accomplished by some very aggressive networking for resources on the part of Reverend Hartsfield. Aware that economic development was not his area of expertise, the minister went for help to the Community Development Corporation of Kansas City. The development corporation put together the plan for the eight-million-dollar shopping center. By working together they have now realized their dream.

In a similar move, the Bethel AME Church in Birmingham, Alabama, cosponsored construction of seven new low-income homes in the city's ravaged Ensley neighborhood. The Allen AME church in Queens, New York, brought shops, high-rise senior citizens' housing, and a church-run school into an impoverished neighborhood. Black churches, which nationwide have more than twenty-five million members with weekly collections of ten million dollars, have discovered that by networking together, they can accomplish what government programs have failed to do. The same has become increasingly true of blacks in private enterprise, who more and more are looking back to see what they can do to improve the lives of those still striving for success.

PRIVATE ENTERPRISE DOES PUBLIC GOOD

Individuals, churches, service groups, and charitable organizations *can* make a difference in their communities, and as evidenced by what you've read so far in this chapter, they do. But private enterprise still has the real clout and the more immediately available resources to contribute, not just to the tax base and the economy, but also to the uplifting of entire communities.

Social Entrepreneurialism

Husband-and-wife team Lee Bowes and Peter Cove—both of whom are white—are social entrepreneurs who run a business that profits everyone, even the taxpayer. Their twenty-person firm, America Works, Inc., in New York City, with offices in Hartford and Indianapolis, has assisted more than four thousand former welfare recipients, the overwhelming majority of whom are black women, in New York, Connecticut, and Indiana. A government-funded audit of the program found that 85 percent of those who were assisted by America Works were still on the job one year after being placed.

America Works operates on the belief that most people do not want to be on welfare, but they need positive incentives to motivate them to get off. "Motivation is a function of opportunity, and if opportunity is presented, people are motivated. That is true for all of us," said Bowes.

America Works works this way: Welfare recipients are screened, given orientation and training, and then sent on job interviews after learning the basics of how to dress and act in the workplace. They are also taught elementary word-processing and basic computing skills. After being placed in a company, the clients are allowed to remain on welfare and Medicaid for four months, during which they receive the minimum wage from their employer through America Works. This removes the fear of losing welfare payments if something goes wrong, Bowes said. The hiring company does not provide any benefits for the first four months and pays only an hourly rate equivalent to what the job will pay to America Works.

During that trial period, representatives from America Works act as go-betweens and counselors to help the client become efficient and self-sufficient in the workplace. America Works arranges for day care, schedules welfare caseworker meetings, even picks up welfare checks to ease the sometimes jarring transition from public assistance to private employment.

After four months, those clients who succeed in the jobs they are placed in go off public aid and receive full wages and benefits. The average starting salary is fifteen thousand dollars, according to America Works, which receives a placement fee from the state that ranges from four thousand to fifty-three hundred dollars. The America Works representatives receive commissions based on the number of people they position in jobs successfully, and they stay in touch with their clients' supervisors for a year or so.

The hiring company receives a tax credit and saves as much as four thousand dollars over the fees it might pay to a conventional placement firm, explains Lee Bowes, who has a Ph.D. in social work and has conducted extensive research in how the jobs are obtained. And, she said, the overwhelming number of jobs are obtained through networking.

"There is a fallacy that based on background skills and qualifications you will get hired. When you look at it more closely, the way you get employed is through networks," she said. "Most company and business managers say they avoid going through their own human-resource department when looking for employees, because they believe they are the worst source of employees. The labor market operates largely through networks."

Networks are the primary source of job information for both Harvard grads and those without formal training or college degrees. And it is particularly true for the working poor, said Bowes, who wrote a book on employment methods entitled, *No One Need Apply*. She asserts: "Most training programs for the poor are set up on the assumption that if you get trained, you will go out and find a job. But that doesn't work. A tremendous amount of money goes into job-training programs for the poor, but these programs just cycle people through and then back out into unemployment, because they are based on wrong assumptions on how the market operates. Job-training programs don't work unless someone is helping the trainees get networked into jobs."

When black neighborhoods contained blue-collar, white-collar, and other ranges of employed blacks, there were established and efficient networks for people to find jobs. But with the erosion of those networks due to the exodus of the black middle and upper classes, the remaining "underclass" has been isolated from the network that once might have provided jobs that would have helped pull them out of poverty. A few weeks or months of job-skills training cannot replace these networks, she said. "These are people whose self-esteem is destroyed; they've been told they are rotten people, and then they are told to get a job by calling potential employers on the telephone. That is not the way people get jobs," said Bowes. "You have to overcome the isolation. You need to build job links and create networks through associations, schools, internships, and other means."

Successful Blacks Reaching Back

Fannie Watson, fifty-three, made gift baskets and sold them to Kmart for resale. Ben Washington had a wholesale pharmaceuticals company in Chicago. Both of these African-American entrepreneurs ran into a wall when they went to their bankers to finance large orders early in their business histories. And both eventually benefited from a policy of cooperative economics practiced by the National Minority Supplier Development Council, comprised of minority businesses that have achieved success and now are willing to go back and extend a hand to others.

Fannie Watson had a business that is actually a "Basket Case." The daughter of a Detroit steelworker, and a networker of no little skill, Fannie began making gift baskets in the basement of her mother's home in the early 1980s. In her wide circle of friends, the baskets became popular gifts, and when one friend suggested that she try to get Kmart, which is based in Detroit, to sell her baskets in her local store, she was just bold enough to load a bunch in a shopping cart and take them to the huge discount chain's head-quarters in search of a buyer. The buyer told her he liked the baskets, but they were too expensive. "I know how to make cheap baskets, too," Fannie replied. The buyer, who was notoriously tough, said suppliers didn't get more than one shot at making a presentation to Kmart. But Fannie told him she would be back in a week to take a second, cheaper shot, and she was. The buyer ordered four thousand, "and he has become like my godfather," said Fannie.

In no time at all, however, Fannie Watson was a Basket Case, literally and figuratively. At first, after getting the order for four thousand of her baskets, she cried with joy. Then she cried in fear at the realization that the basement basket factory at her mother's house was not exactly set up for that size order. "When the buyer told me how many he wanted, I started crying. He said, 'Isn't that what you came out here for?' I said, 'Yes, but I didn't think you would do it!' "

Even though Fannie knew a great many of Detroit's movers and shakers through her years of political and volunteer work, the local bankers didn't know her well enough to front the money she needed to gear up for mass basket production. Like many black entrepreneurs, she faced the dilemma of having a great product and a ready market, but no ready source of financial backing. Lady luck was in Fannie's basket, however. A long-standing lawsuit, arising out of an accident in which Fannie had severely injured herself, was resolved just as she was getting desperate for a source of financing. The fifty-thousand-dollar settlement enabled her to finance production so she could meet Kmart's initial order.

But neither she nor her new company were ready for Kmart's follow-up order—for forty-five thousand more gift baskets. After a brief panic attack, the irrepressible Fannie hit the banks again.

But again, she hit the wall. Even with proof of her order, she could not find financing. Since it appeared unlikely that the legal system would come up with another surprise settlement, things looked bleak for Basket Case, which is the name she gave her business. But this time, a business banking network with considerable clout came to the rescue.

As a member of the National Minority Supplier Development Council (NMSDC), Fannie discovered, she was eligible for consideration of a loan from the Business Consortium Fund (BCF), a financial institution closely aligned with NMSDC, a financial institution, operating in the private sector, that provides access to capital for minority business enterprises throughout the United States. "The purpose of public and private minority business programs is to spur economic development, to create new jobs and new taxes, but few programs have been able to report significant tangible benefits for the communities they serve. One clear exception is the Business Consortium Fund and the National Minority Supplier Development Council," wrote *Atlanta Tribune*'s then–guest columnist Joseph R. Hudson, president of the Hudson Group.

Since 1987, the BCF has helped to create 7,000 new jobs nationwide by providing almost $170 million in loan guarantees more than 750 to minority-owned businesses. In fiscal 2002, BCF provided $6.1 million in loans and guarantees. Founded in 1987, the BCF is a unique partnership of NMSDC corporations, local banks, and regional minority supplier development councils. Its goal is to help minority business owners overcome the greatest obstacle to success, lack of support from financial institutions. Robert Woodson, president of the National Center for Neighborhood Enterprise, told *Fortune* magazine: "We don't need more minority contractor set-asides. Our communities don't need to be treated as cesspools of pathology to be rescued by more social programs. We need infusions of capital to help us develop our potential as producers." The BCF can lend or guarantee up to 75 percent of loans, for up to $750,000 and $562,000 respectively, from participating banks. With that show of support for minority businesses, financial institutions are much more inclined to make the sort of loans that allow struggling black entrepreneurs to survive and thrive. "The BCF is a partnership that creates a winning situation for everyone involved," Hudson wrote.

Fannie Watson is a winner in large part because of her networking assistance from the BCF. "Without the consortium, I don't know if I would have been able to continue this," she said. Over the years, the BCF has guaranteed loans to Fannie Watson of nearly $375,000 to help her meet the demand for her product, which has generated annual sales of around a half-million dollars consistently in past years. Kmart alone had ordered as many as one hundred thousand baskets a year from Basket Case, which employed about twenty workers during peak times.

The BCF success story of Benjamin Polote and The Polote Corporation, a construction company located in Savannah, Georgia, is even more impressive than that of Fannie Watson. Polote was a high school graduate from the projects who had both street smarts and a good business sense. His established business was already doing about $8 million a year, and employing sixty-eight people, when he received a $6 million contract from AT&T to build communications huts all across the south. The new AT&T business did not come to him easily, but rather as a result of some well-placed strategic relationships. The new contract was a great business opportunity, but he couldn't get the financing. His thirty-one-year-old small business had gone through the usual ups and downs, culminating in a Chapter 11 reorganization in 1987. Up to that point he had a stellar credit and work record. Tough times and a few poor decisions quickly changed his circumstances and the standard, conservative southern banking institutions wouldn't give him a break or touch him with a ten-foot pole. He struggled to keep things going. In 1999 Polote attended Rev. Jesse Jackson's Wall Street Project Conference in New York, where he made a pitch for some corporate business and met Winston Smith, then deputy director of diversity for AT&T. Winston, a serious advocate for minority businesses, liked Benjamin's passion, intellect, and courage and asked him to serve on AT&T's Diversity Board. In spite of tough times for Benjamin, he agreed to give him some time, with no strings attached. Within a year, Ben not only secured a $6 million contract, he met several key executives involved in BCF who led him to Robert Emerson, a senior executive at BCF with a heart of gold and the mind of a seasoned financier. Ben said, "Every moment I spent with BCF and Robert was focused on how to say yes to my financing needs versus the banks, who looked for every way to say no."

In November of 2001, in partnership with the New York National Bank (NYNB), BCF provided the Polote Corporation a $750,000 loan at 1 1/2 percent above prime. "I cannot praise them enough; they truly, truly helped my company when no other financial institution would dare to take a chance on me," Ben said. Another interesting networking twist came into play. The New York National Bank's 25 percent stake in the loan had to be fully collateralized. Benjamin didn't have it, but his former employee of eight years Pat Mathis did. She had already stepped out on her own to form the Pat Mathis Construction Company. Pat not only had the $187,500, she was willing to put the money up in the form of a CD to secure NYNB's portion. Since then Ben has not only successfully serviced his debt and completed the AT&T project with excellence, but his business has thrived, employing more people and providing 80 percent of the subcontract work to other minority-owned businesses.

Getting Together to Get It Together

Another network of organizations banded together to positively influence the black community is the Consortium of African American Organizations, with which I am intimately familiar since its home turf is my own, Cleveland. This midwestern city is emerging as a Rust Belt success story, in large part due to a very vibrant and aggressive network of black professionals, leaders, and entrepreneurs. Cleveland was the first major city to have a black mayor, and it has a rich and diverse history of black leadership. I'm proud of that, and I am even more proud of the fact that Cleveland's black professional leaders are setting an example of unity, cooperative economics, and self-determination in their neighborhoods and community.

A prime example of this is the Consortium of African American Organizations, which is comprised of nineteen charger black professional organizations. The nineteen are: African American Chamber of Commerce of Northeast Ohio; African American Faculty & Staff of Case Western Reserve University; the Black Data Processing Associates; the Black Professionals Association; Blacks in Government; Blacks in Management; Cleveland African American Library Association; Cleveland State University Black Alumni Organization; Cleveland Woman's Council of the National Association of Real Estate Brokers; Forest City Dental Society; Kappa Alpha Psi Fraternity Inc; Minority Link Inc; National Alliance of Market Developers; National Association of Black Accountants; National Black MBA Association; the National Society of Black Engineers; National Technical Association; the President's Council; and the Urban Financial Services Coalition.

I list all of these groups because I think it gives a good feel for the breadth and depth of the African-American success story in Cleveland. All of these organizations work for the betterment of the community, both black and white, but by uniting into the consortium, they can use their collective strength to do even more. The overall goal of consortium is economic empowerment. The members work to establish and grow businesses, provide professional development and leadership empowerment for its 10,000 members, act as mentors in Cleveland schools, and address community concerns with a unified voice. The founder and head of the consortium, Connie Atkins, says, "This is a unique coalition of nineteen African-American professional organizations mobilized to promote economic growth in the African-American community by three means: by encouraging African-Americans to stay and live in Cleveland's urban areas to increase the purchasing power and skill-level base in the city; by providing job referrals and business leads; and by providing a variety of benefits to empower our members in three critical areas: entrepreneurial, wealth building, and leadership."

IN CONCLUSION: NETWORKING FOR THE SUCCESS OF ALL

The wonderful networking stories that you have just read serve as examples of the ideas and ideals I have presented throughout this book. Because space was limited, I could only bring you a few stories, but there are thousands more—perhaps yours, or those of friends and family in your town. Effective networking is not only important, it is critical to the very lifeblood of the black community's future in this country, and all others where black people gather to live and grow.

As we reach out to create a global network linking all people of the African Diaspora, from Africa to South America, from North America to the Caribbean, over time, millions more must and will join us in this powerful chain of human excellence. But those of us who choose to effectively network are the models, we are the beacons of hope, we are the ones chosen to carry the legacy of our once-great civilization. From the chains of slavery and a psychological holocaust endured by few cultures in the history of humankind, we are rising once again. In the words of the acclaimed poet Maya Angelou: "You may crush me down like ashes, but still again I rise."

We have come from our bellies as we lay wedged into slave ships; then risen to our knees as we scrubbed floors to feed our children; then moved from the crouch of the invisible man to, finally, the winning stance of Martin's Nobel Prize acceptance speech, fully risen. We have used our God-given powers of creativity, endurance, intelligence, and forgiveness to move us into the next phase. We are dreamers and we are doers, but we must not be lulled to sleep by our progress. We must be diligent as we build and grow.

This is not an individual task; it is a collective one. Therefore, we must think through and act upon our agenda; our resources and personal achievement must be translated into an excellence that improves the human condition. Our thinking and values must embrace the Afrocentric principles of cooperation, not competition; community, not just the individual. To achieve this, we must reach out to one another and build a new Urban Village where the bridges to those less fortunate are crossed in greater numbers by those of us who have so much to give. Yes, your network, our network, are all part of the new Underground Railroad quietly moving information and resources into just the right places, like the king stalking the chessboard looking for the "checkmate."

Our reemergence will occur because our collective consciousness is slowly being awakened to the importance of "we versus I." You read of this consciousness and see it every day of your life; maybe now you will recognize it! There is hope, because you and your dreams for abundance in our community exist. In some special way, we are all linked to your dream, because we all dream the same dreams. Success does run in our race, and this book, as well as thousands of others before it, document this. Our commitment to continue this legacy is tied to our commitment to the Kwanzaa principles of collective work and responsibility. A New Agenda will help us carry out the ideas that many fertile minds have laid before us. Our commitment must parallel those of the great dynasties—be they cultures or great companies. John Welch, Jr., the visionary leader of General Electric, captured in his "commitment to diversity" speech to his shareholders the essence of our twenty-first-century challenge:

"The companies that find a way to **engage every mind . . .** harness every volt of passionate energy . . . bring excitement to the lives of their people . . . and **break every artificial barrier** between people . . . will be the companies that win in the twenty-first century and beyond." (Emphasis added.)

This is a bold vision that must be shared by all those who impact our daily lives. But for our purposes, if we change the word *companies* to *cultures* or *communities*, you will have an important plan and a powerful vision. So let's chart our own course and stay that course!

Until our paths cross again, let's stay connected.

"You don't have to be an entrepreneur to support black entrepreneurs.
All of us must support black entrepreneurs because they are the ones
who will employ black people. They can make the greatest difference
to the economic viability of the black community."
Bruce Gordon

Bruce Gordon was born in Camden, New Jersey. He is president of the Retail Markets Group for Verizon (formerly Bell Atlantic). He began his career at Bell of Pennsylvania as a management trainee and advanced through assignments in personnel, operations, and sales and marketing. Eventually, he was appointed vice president of sales of Bell Atlantic before serving as president of consumer services and vice president of marketing and sales. Prior to the Bell Atlantic–GTE merger, he was group president-Enterprise Business, one of six groups reporting to the Office of the Chairman. Before Bell Atlantic merged with NYNEX, Bruce was group president of Consumer and Small Business Services of Bell Atlantic's Network Services Inc. *Black Enterprise* named him "1998 Executive of the Year." He is a member of several organizations that include Gettysburg College; Alvin Ailey Dance Theater Foundation; the Executive Leadership Council; and he is national chairman of the National Eagle Leadership Institute.

Appendix A

The FraserNet Workbook

Very few people are born with all the skills it takes to be an effective networker. Networking requires a combination of both practical and interpersonal skills learned and developed over time. As with anything else, practice makes perfect.

To help you practice and plot your networking course of action, I have provided the following exercises. They begin by taking inventory of your resources and then plotting how you can best use them as your own Underground Railroad, not only to benefit your personal agenda, but also to be put to work for the betterment of your community and your world.

This appendix is designed to help you write out and think through the elements that go into effective networking. The exercises may take some time to complete, but it will be time well spent, because it will bring you into focus on your goals and the talents you already have, and those that you need to develop and hone.

I urge you to take your time and do all of the exercises. I think you will find it worth the investment of your energies.

Exercise 1: Identify Your Network

On the dedication pages of this book, I listed my complete inventory of networking contacts. It took me nearly eight hours to compile this list of people whom I know and people who know me. Friends and family are included, so are close acquaintances and colleagues, all of them people who are willing to assist me because they know I am willing to assist them.

Listed below are several categories to consider when identifying your own network. On sheets of paper, list the names of as many contacts as you can in each category. Refer to address books, club directories, Christmas lists, birthday lists—anything to help you identify your network. You may think of other categories, which you can add under the *Others* heading (and you'll want to leave more space for names in each category than we're able to provide here).

MY NETWORK

Family	Colleagues	Neighbors
Classmates	**Professionals**	**Community**
Friends	**Club/church associates**	**Interest groups**
Others	**Others**	**Others**

Exercise 2: Evaluate Your Networking Skills
Are you an effective networker? What areas would you like to improve, and what are you doing about it?

Listed below are skills for effective networking. Check those items in which you feel you need improvement.

——— Asking open-ended questions
——— Concentrating on what others are saying
——— Showing sincere interest in others
——— Keeping an open mind to what is being said
——— Sharing your opinions and views
——— Asking for help
——— Offering assistance
——— Being knowledgeable in a particular area
——— Letting others know who you are
——— Dressing to convey you are serious about your goals
——— Using your body language in conjunction with your words
——— Sharing your knowledge and expertise

Write one thing you can do now for each skill you would like to improve.

_____

_____

_____

_____

_____

_____

Exercise 3: Improve Your Networking Skills

Like anything else, networking takes practice. List the last four times you had the opportunity to network. Include the names of those you networked with, the information or resources you shared or received, and finally, what the result was.

NETWORK HISTORY

Name	Occasion	Information Exchanged	Result
1. _____	_____	_____	_____
2. _____	_____	_____	_____
3. _____	_____	_____	_____
4. _____	_____	_____	_____

Now, what would you have done differently in each situation to make yourself a more effective networker?

1. _____

2. _____

3. _____

4. _____

Exercise 4: Identify Networking Opportunities

Seize the moment. Start immediately to make something happen in your life or the life of someone in your network. Think back to the activities over the last few weeks and months and list the opportunities you have had to network. Think about what you might have accomplished in each situation. Be sure to list the networking opportunities that are not so obvious, such as riding the elevator each day from the main floor to your office, or opportunities that may arise at church, or on the bus or train, etc.

NETWORKING OPPORTUNITIES

Daily

_____

_____

_____

Weekly

_____

_____

_____

Special Activities

_____

_____

_____

Exercise 5: List Your Personal and Professional Goals

By putting your goals down in writing, you begin to determine what it is you really want, and by setting an agenda, you begin to map out how you are going to achieve your goals. Goals should be set for the short term (up to one year) and long term (up to five years). Remember, just because you have written them down doesn't mean you can't change them as you grow as a person.

List statements that describe your short- and long-term goals. Here are a few samples:

- I would like to get a new job at a higher salary next year.
- I would like to become an officer or a board member in a large volunteer organization.
- I would like to find a mentor in the workplace.

MY TOP GOALS

Short-term	Long-term
_____	_____
_____	_____
_____	_____
_____	_____

List the five immediate actions you will take to reach your goals:

1. _____
2. _____
3. _____
4. _____
5. _____

Exercise 6: Identify Your Huggers and Shakers

Huggers and shakers are the core of your network. Huggers provide support, stability, and emotional balance. Loved ones, close friends, colleagues, and extended family make up this critical group. Shakers keep you motivated or lift you to continually expanding levels of achievement. These mentors, role models, and connectors shake you out of complacency and push you forward in your personal and professional life.

Using the following charts, it is now time for you to classify the people in your network.

Huggers   **Mentors**

_____   _____

_____   _____

_____   _____

_____   **Role Models**

_____   _____

_____   _____

_____   _____

Shakers   **Connectors**

_____   _____

_____   _____

_____   _____

Shakers exhibit many qualities that are important to us. What do you admire about your shakers, and why are they helpful to you?

_____

_____

_____

Exercise 7: Review of Mentoring Activities

Mentors are those who have a significant impact on your life both professionally and/or personally. They act as trusted advisers and share their wisdom. The interesting thing about mentoring is that we usually experience it from both sides: as mentor and mentee. We all mentor at some level in our lives by passing on our knowledge, skills, advice, and counsel to those we select to help. Mentoring requires a deeper and longer commitment to the individual than role modeling. Expanding our mentoring to the inner city is the next challenge for the black community.

Review by checking off your mentoring activities to include what others have done for you and what you have done for others.

Mentoring	Given	Gotten
Provide opportunity for growth		
Address negative attitudes or behavior		
Assist in career development		
Guide through organizational politics		
Provide critical support		
Provide coaching		
Present new challenges and ideas		
Share critical knowledge		
Set high-achievement goals		
Provide support and encouragement		
Promote professionalism		
Teach by example		
Help increase self-esteem and confidence		
Offer friendship		
Provide advice/counsel in personal matters		
Provide words of wisdom		

Exercise 8: Review of Role-Model Attributes

Role modeling is different from mentoring. It is generally less formal. There are two different kinds of role models: the parental role model, and those role models whom you select. Often, people look at someone from afar and say, "I'd like to be like that person." They model their behavior from afar. It could even be a situation where you've never spoken with a selected model—you've just read about her or him. I've had role models who don't know me from Adam, but I have admired them from afar for years and have read about them or followed their lives.

Mentors select you, but you select your role models. A lot of people confuse the two. A mentor is a much more involved relationship, a much deeper commitment.

List people whom you have selected or would like to use as your role models, and then list what attributes you admire about them.

ROLE MODELS

Name	Attributes

Exercise 9: Create a Networking Plan

A networking plan is a little like a business plan or road map. It is a simple outline of the key components we discussed earlier. Writing out a networking plan for the first ten to twenty opportunities will get you in the habit of doing it and making this process of planning second nature. It will become automatic.

Plan your next networking opportunity by completing the following outline:

Occasion: _____

Goal: _____

Agenda: _____

Key contacts: _____

Preparation: _____

Personal script: _____

Conversation openers: _____

Information and resources to share: _____

_____

_____

Information and resources to obtain: _____

_____

_____

Follow-up: _____

_____

_____

_____

_____

Exercise 10: Write Your Self-Introduction Script

Remember the Bill Withers song lyric, "Who are you and what are you to me"? That powerful message is delivered in less than fifty words. You should try to do the same with your self-introduction. Keep it short, informative, and relevant to the networking situation.

In the space provided below, write an introduction for yourself. Remember, your introduction should cover who you are, the company you are with, what you do, and what your agenda is. Your script should be approximately thirty seconds in duration and a maximum of seventy-five words. Here is an example:

"Hi, I'm George Fraser from Cleveland, Ohio. I'm president of FraserNet, Inc., and publisher of *SuccessGuide Worldwide: The Networking Guide to Black Resources.* I help people network and find the resources they need to succeed personally and professionally. I'm always on the lookout for people who are interested in building a network of contacts in the black community. What brought you here today?"

Write your own self-introduction script here:

_____

_____

_____

_____

_____

_____

_____

_____

Exercise 11: List Your Information Sources

Being prepared not only means having the right tools (business cards, pen, etc.), it also means preparing yourself to be conversant on current events and up-to-date on developments in your own discipline. Reading your local newspaper and watching television news will not provide you with adequate information on global affairs.

Listed in the left-hand column are information sources that I think would benefit you in your networking conversations. In the right-hand column, list those that you currently utilize.

INFORMATION SOURCES

Suggested Sources	Current Sources
Daily (minimum)	**Daily**
Local newspaper	_____
Local and national news	_____
One hour reading a book or professional	_____
journal, listening to a tape/CD related to your	_____
work, or visiting your favorite Web site	_____
Weekly (minimum)	**Weekly**
Jet and/or black newspaper	_____
The Wall Street Journal (three days weekly)	_____
The New York Times, Sunday edition	_____
Time, Newsweek, or *U.S. News*	_____
Monthly (minimum)	**Monthly**
Ebony	_____
Essence	_____
Savoy	_____
Black Enterprise	_____
Upscale	_____
Heart & Soul	_____
A local black monthly magazine	_____

Fortune, BusinessWeek, or *Forbes* _____

Trade publication or professional journal _____

Inc, Entrepreneur, or *Fast Company* _____

Annually (minimum)   **Annually**

SuccessGuide Worldwide _____

Six to ten books related to your field and to _____

    national events (read popular novels _____

    for pleasure and conversation.) _____

    Think about what information sources you might add.

Exercise 12: Create Conversation Openers

This is a real "stopper" for many new networkers. They just don't know how to open a conversation with something other than, "How about this weather we're having?" It really is not that difficult to come up with some good opening lines.

Imagine that you are at a function with a mix of people. You will need a variety of conversation openers in order to start networking. Use the chart below as a guide to help you prepare for a networking event. Examples are included.

Ask a Question   **Example**

About the function
> What do you hope to get out of this meeting?

About a current event
> What are the two major issues in the President's new proposal before Congress?

About business or career interests
> How did you get into this business?

Solicit Opinions

About the function
> What do you think of the speaker's new book?

About a current event
> What do you think of the President's proposal?

About business or career interests
> What was your greatest challenge in this job?

State an Interesting Fact

About the function
> The speaker has just published a new book.

About a current event
> The new proposal will positively affect blacks.

About business or career interests
> The first three to five years of a new business are critical.

Exercise 13: Prepare Good Questions

Good questions are always an indication of good listening skills. Being "in the moment" of conversation will trigger ideas and follow-up questions, but . . . always consider your agenda first, before asking questions. By planning your questions beforehand, you will have a better chance of obtaining the information you want. Remember, always ask open-ended questions that require more than a simple yes or no.

Select one of your agenda items and write three questions that will help you gather the desired information.

AGENDA FOR THIS MEETING

_____

_____

_____

_____

QUESTIONS TO ASK TO FURTHER MY AGENDA

_____

_____

_____

_____

Exercise 14: List Your Networking Agenda

Balance is the key here. The balance between what you expect to give and what you expect to receive should always be tilted toward giving more than you get. Why? Because this is part of our spiritual teachings. It is the spirit of our ancestral culture. You must give to your network and then know that the wheel will turn someday to you.

List those items that you have to offer to your network contacts, and then list the things that you may one day need from your network. An example is included in each category.

THINGS I HAVE TO OFFER (RE: INFORMATION ON CAREER TRAINING)

_____

_____

_____

_____

THINGS I WOULD LIKE TO RECEIVE (RE: INFORMATION ON INTERACTIVE TELEVISION MARKETS)

_____

_____

_____

_____

Exercise 15: Self-Assurance Checkup

Find some things that you like about yourself, and center your self-image on those admirable qualities. Don't make the mistake of accentuating the negative aspects of your character or appearance. Look within for the positive aspects and list below the qualities that you like most about yourself. An example is included in each category.

THINGS I LIKE ABOUT MYSELF
(RE: A GOOD SENSE OF HUMOR)

_____

_____

_____

_____

THINGS OTHERS LIKE ABOUT ME
(RE: I AM AN EMPATHETIC LISTENER.)

_____

_____

_____

_____

ATTITUDES ABOUT WORK

Positive

_____

_____

_____

How can I capitalize on them?

_____

_____

_____

Negative

_____

_____

_____

How can I overcome them?

_____

_____

_____

Exercise 16: Take Inventory of Your Skills

Giving is the secret of successful networking. List below the talents and knowledge that you have to offer. You'll find this a very empowering exercise, and it may help give you the confidence you need to enter into mutually beneficial networking relationships.

Listed below are several categories to consider when taking inventory of who you are, what you have done, and what you know. List as many items as you can in each category. An example is included in each.

PERSONAL INVENTORY

Work Experience
(computer analyst)

_____

_____

_____

Expertise
(Web design)

_____

_____

_____

Cultural Experience
(Rites of Passage)

_____

_____

_____

Education/Training
(BA, Management Information
Systems)

_____

_____

_____

Community Work
(mentoring)

_____

_____

_____

Organizations
(NAACP, 100 Black Men of America)

_____

_____

_____

Other skills, experience, specialized knowledge, etc.

_____

_____

_____

Exercise 17: Network to Achieve Organizational Goals

Do you belong to a black organization (social, civic, fraternity, sorority, professional)? If not, why not? If *yes*, how are you helping this organization to achieve its goals using effective networking techniques?

Think of an organization that you are actively involved in and fill in the following information.

Name of organization

_____

_____

_____

_____

The goals this organization is trying to reach

_____

_____

_____

_____

How I am networking to help this organization achieve its goals?

_____

_____

_____

_____

Exercise 18: Personal Goals for Community Reinvestment
Black-on-black set-asides are a form of community reinvestment.
Allocating at least 10 percent of your annual household income to
reinvest in black business and professional services is one way to
help recycle our dollars. Most black households spend less than 5
percent a year in black businesses.

List those black businesses and services that have proven they
can provide you with value, quality, and the service you deserve—
and make sure you utilize them for future purchases. Set an annual
goal and increase this goal each year by at least 5 percentage
points.

List several black businesses and professionals that you can do
business with and make purchases from to meet your community
reinvestment goal.

Companies   **Estimated Annual Expenditures**

_____   _____

_____   _____

_____   _____

_____   _____

Professionals   **Estimated Annual Expenditures**

_____   _____

_____   _____

_____   _____

Exercise 19: Selective Buying Review

There are many major corporations in the marketplace that demonstrate a strong outreach to our community. You see black people in their ads, you see their ads in our publications, and they sponsor events and special programs. They have a large work force that includes blacks in a variety of responsible and productive positions. In general, they have a high profile and a good image in our community. They truly deserve our support; it's called reciprocity!

List those companies that come to mind. If you don't know the company, list the brand. Send me your list, and I will publish the top twenty vote-getters in future editions of the *SuccessGuide*. Send your suggestions to FraserNet, Inc., 2940 Noble Road, Cleveland, Ohio 44121.

BUYING GUIDE

Company Name   **Brand Name**

_____   _____

_____   _____

_____   _____

_____   _____

_____   _____

_____   _____

_____   _____

_____   _____

Exercise 20: List Your Personal Networking Dos and Don'ts
This will help you stay on top of those little habits that you wish
to change, adopt, or refine. For example, I continually tell myself,
"Don't forget people's names."

List your most important networking Dos and Don'ts.

Dos   **Don'ts**

_____   _____

_____   _____

_____   _____

_____   _____

_____   _____

_____   _____

_____   _____

Appendix B

The Thirty Best Places to Network

Event	Date	Agenda	Estimated Attendance	Booths & Displays	Workshops	VIPs & Receptions	Entertainment	Keynote Speakers	Networking Opportunities	Overall Rating	Comments
100 Black Men of America Inc. 404-688-5100	June	Scholarship, Mentoring	2,000	**	**	***	***	***	****	****	The talented tenth meet to discuss change
Alpha Phi Alpha Fraternity Inc. 410 554-0040	August	Community Service & Education	3,000	*	**	**	*	**	***	***	Great fraternizing
Black Enterprise Entrep. Conf. 800-543-3786	May	Networking, Business	1,500	***	***	***	**	****	***	****	Best & brightest teach the rest
Black Enterprise/ Golf & Tennis... 800-209-7229	August	Social Networking	1,500	*	**	***	**	NA	****	****	Movers and shakers on the links
Blacks in Government 202-667-3280	August	Personal Growth & Development	2,000	*	***	**	*	***	***	**	Big meets new opportunities
Bronner Brothers 770-953-4247	July	Beauty Care	75,000	****	***	**	**	**	***	***	Beauty and the best
Congressional Black Caucus... 202-675-6730	September	Public Policy	5,000	***	***	****	****	****	****	****	Power networking and power parties
Delta Sigma Theta Sorority... 202-986-2400	July	Social/Civic Responsibilities	5,000	**	***	***	**	**	***	***	Black women nurture & share
Executive Leadership ... Dinner 773-651-8008	April	Corporate Policy	1,500	NA	NA	***	**	***	***	***	Power dinner
MOBE/Marketing Opp. In B&E 773-651-8008	April	Entertainment Technology	700	*	***	***	*	***	***	***	Changing ... TCB in entertainment & technology

Event	Date	Agenda	Estimated Attendance	Booths & Displays	Workshops	VIPs & Receptions	Entertainment	Keynote Speakers	Networking Opportunities	Overall Ratings	Comments
Nat. Alli. Black ... (NABSE) 202-483-1549	November	Education of Black Children	2,500	***	***	***	*	***	***	***	Educators educate each other
Nat. Alli. Market Dev. (NAMD) 908-561-4062	April	Target Marketing	500	*	***	**	*	***	***	***	The hookup for the latest marketing trends
Nat. Assoc. ... Colored People 410-358-8900	July	Civil Rights	10,000	***	***	****	***	****	****	****	The power speakers convene
Nat. Assoc. of Black Journalist 301-445-7100	August	Media & Communications	2,500	***	***	***	***	****	****	****	Power communicators strategize
Nat. Assoc. Investment Cos. 202-289-4336	October	Investment Strategies	300	NA	***	**	NA	***	***	***	Opportunity meets big money
Nat. Assoc. Black Tele. Prof. 800-946-6228	March	Personal Growth & Job Opportunities	2,000	**	***	**	**	***	***	***	The networks network
National Bar Association 202-842-3900	August	National Legal Issues	2,500	*	***	***	*	***	***	***	The kingmakers meet
Nat. Black MBA Association 312-236-2622	September	Employment, Business	8,000	****	****	***	**	****	****	****	Gen X Buppies set a new agenda
Nat. Bro. of Skiers Inc. 773-955-4100	February	Recreational, Social	4,000	NA	NA	**	*	NA	***	**	Powder, pleasure, and power
Nat. Conf. of Black Mayors ... 404-765-6444	March	Political Strategy	1,500	*	***	****	**	***	***	***	Power politics

Event	Date	Agenda	Estimated Attendance	Booths & Displays	Workshops	VIPs & Receptions	Entertainment	Keynote Speakers	Networking Opportunities	Overall Rating	Comments
Nat. Forum for Black Pub. Adm. 202-408-9300	April	Public Policy	2,500	***	***	**	**	***	***	***	Leadership influences policy
National Medical Association 202-347-1895	August	Health Care	2,000	**	***	**	*	***	***	***	Health care powerhouse
Nat. Min. Supp. Dev. Council Inc. 212-944-2430	November	Business/Supplier Development	3,000	***	***	***	**	***	***	***	Power meetings and business-to-business
Nat. Newspaper Publishers Assc. 202-588-8764	January	Communications & Editorial	1,000	*	***	***	**	***	***	***	Power publishers
Nat. Prof. Network Cruise 301-565-0070	August	Business/Professional Development	500	*	***	***	**	***	***	***	Strictly business mixed with pleasure
Nat. Society of Black Engineers 703-549-2207	March	Scholarship, Jobs	2,000	***	***	**	**	***	***	***	Corporations line up at the door
National Urban League 212-558-5300	July	Training, Jobs	15,000	****	****	****	****	****	****	****	Power message
PowerNetwork Conf. ext 330 216-691-6886	June	Networking, Bus. to Bus. Prof. Develop.	3,500	***	***	****	****	***	****	****	PowerNetworking training at its best
Tom Joyner Fantastic Voy. Cruise 972-789-1058	May	Recreational, Social, Fundraising	3,000	NA	*	***	****	NA	***	***	Partying and networking meet
Urban Financial Ser. Coalition 202-289-8335	May	Financial Strategies & Upward Mobility	1,000	*	**	**	*	***	***	***	Bringing back the bacon to black America

Ratings: *Good **Great ***Excellent ****Don't miss it! Check with your local chapter for dates and locations of these events.

Appendix C

The Most Influential Black Speakers in America: "The Fabulous 50"

These are the professionals who inform, inspire, and communicate with power, commitment, and passion. Most of them speak on the average of thirty to forty times a year. Most of them charge five thousand dollars, or more, but they are worth it! Fees are negotiable. Most of them have agents; some represent themselves. Many of them are represented by two large speaker bureaus: Program Corporation of America, SPEAKERSPCA.COM; and the American Program Bureau, APBSPEAKERS.COM.

THE MOST INFLUENTIAL BLACK SPEAKERS IN AMERICA: "THE FABULOUS 50"

Speaker	Topics	Comments
Dr. Na'im Akbar	Personality and human transformation	Dynamic and powerful
Dr. Claud Anderson	Black economic development	Put on your seat belt
Dr. Maya Angelou	Poetry, social commentary	Eloquent and theatrical
Julian Bond	Civil rights, human rights	Articulate and smart; an icon
Les Brown	Inspiration and motivation	"The Motivator"

Tony Brown	Economics and self-help	The seasoned voice of experience
Rev. Dr. Juanita Bynum	Biblically based success principles	Mesmerizing
Dr. Johnnetta B. Cole	Education and black women	Dynamic, charismatic
George Curry	Social and political policy	Tells it like it is
Dr. Michael Eric Dyson	Social and political policy	Takes no prisoners, brilliant
Dr. Harry Edwards	Sports and the black athlete	Exciting and tough
Therman Evans MD	Health and wellness	The best on the topic
Minister Louis Farrakhan	Black power and self-determination	The king of the podium
Rev. Dr. Floyd Flake	Social policy and community development	A model for the new church
George C. Fraser	Networking and economic development	Black America's networking guru
Dr. Henry Lewis Gates	Literary critic, social commentary	A public intellectual with a powerful voice
Earl G. Graves	Business development and capitalism	African-American business icon
William Gray	Education and philanthropy	Great stature and leadership
Dick Gregory	Health, economics, and human rights	Great wit and street smarts
Dr. Asa Hilliard	Black history and Afrocentricity	Paints powerful new images
Rev. Jesse Jackson	Human rights, social policy	Brilliant and inspiring
Congressman Jesse Jackson, Jr.	Social and political policy	Apples don't fall far from the tree
Bishop T. D. Jakes	Family and relationships	The best on the planet
Bob Johnson	Capitalism and entrepreneurialism	Excellent ideas and strategy; an icon
Vernon Jordan, Jr.	Power, politics, and human rights	Charismatic and connected
Dr. Maulana Karenga	Kwanzaa and Afrocentricity	A visionary and icon
Dr. Dennis Kimbro	Success and entrepreneurialism	Great research, great stories

Rev. Bernice King	Human rights and empowerment	Following in dad MLKs footsteps
Dr. Jawanza Kunjufu	Education and black boys	Intelligent and charismatic
Dr. Joseph Lowery	Civil and human rights	A prophetic voice; an icon
Dr. Julianne Malveaux	Economics and social commentary	Compelling and strong
Patricia Russell-McCloud	Success principles, personal growth	Supercharged
Bishop Vashti McKenzie	Biblically based, success principles	A dynamic voice
Kwesi Mfume	Civil rights, human rights	Rational exuberance
Harriet Michel	Minority business development	Her actions match her words
Rev. Dr. Otis Moss	Human rights and community issues	The preacher's preacher
Dr. Myles Munroe	Passion and purpose	Consise, informative, charismatic
Alvin Poussaint, MD	Family and relationships	Brilliant and eloquent
Randall Robinson	Human rights, reparations	Dignified eloquence, a powerful voice
Rev. Al Sharpton	Politics and social policy	A courageous voice
Tavis Smiley	Social and political commentary	Important and keen observations
Rev. Gardner Taylor	Religion and philosophy	Stands alone; the master; an icon
Susan Taylor	Self-actualization and commentary	Magnificent messenger
Iyanla Vanzant	Family and women's issues	A bright star
Congresswomen Maxine Waters	Social policy	Inspiring leadership
Dennis Rahim Watson	Youth and self-help	Inspiring and energized
Dr. Frances Welsing	Racism and mental health	Eminent and dynamic
Oprah Winfrey	Anything she feels at the moment	Warm, passionate, funny
Dr. Cornel West	Race, religion, and politics	Dynamic intellectualism

Andrew Young	Human rights and politics	Stature, insight, wisdom; an icon

Five to Watch:

Cheryl Broussard	Money management and wealth	A model for money management
Jim Clingman	Black economic development	Thoughtful and pragmatic
Keith Harrell	Success principles	Smart, funny, entertaining
Willie Jolley	Success principles	Energy and enthusiasm personified
Jewell Diamond Taylor	Personal growth and development	Elegant and impactful

Appendix D

The Best Black Clubs and Organizations

A. Philip Randolph Institute and A. Philip Randolph Educational Fund
1444 "I" St., N.W., Ste. 300
Washington, DC 20005
www.apri.org

African-American Institute for Research and Empowerment
PO Box 2131
Radio City Station
New York, NY 10101–2131
www.tbwt.com

African-American Male Empowerment Summit
614 Central Ave., Ste. 6
E. Orange, NJ 07018
www.aames.org

African Methodist Epscopal Church
1134 11th St., N.W.
Washington, DC 20001
www.amecnet.org

Africare
440 "R" St., N.W.
Washington, DC 20001
www.africare.org

Afro-American Historical and Genealogical Society, Inc.
PO Box 73067
Washington, DC 20056
www.aahgs.org

Airport Minority Advisory Council
2800 Shirlington, Ste. 940
Arlington, VA 22206
www.amac-org.com

Alpha Kappa Alpha Sorority, Inc.
5656 S. Stony Island Ave.
Chicago, IL 60637
www.aka1908.com

Alpha Phi Alpha Fraternity, Inc.
2313 Saint Paul St.
Baltimore, MD 21218
www.alphaphialpha.net

American Association of Blacks in Energy
927 15th St., N.W., #200
Washington, DC 20005
www.aabe.org

American Health and Beauty Aids Institute
401 N. Michigan Ave., Ste. 2200
Chicago, IL 60611
www.proudlady.org

American League of Financial Institutions
900 19th St., N.W., Ste. 400
Washington, DC 20006
www.alfi.org

Associated Black Charities
105 E. 22nd St., Ste. 915
New York, NY 10010
www.assocblackcharities.org

Association for the Study of African American Life and History, Inc.
Howard University
C. B. Powell Building
525 Bryant St., Ste. C142
Washington, DC 20059
www.asalh.org

Association of African-American Women Business Owners
8604 2nd Ave., Ste. 125
Silver Spring, MD 20910
www.aaawbo.org

Association of Black Foundation Executives
23 Gramercy Park, S.
New York, NY 10003
bbelfer@egf-ny.org

Association of Black Psychologists
PO Box 55999
Washington, DC 20040–5999
www.abpsi.org

BDPA Information Technology Thought Leaders
9315 Largo Dr., W., Ste. 260
Largo, MD 20774
www.bdpa.org

Bethune-DuBois Institute
8401 Colesville Rd., Ste. 400
Silver Spring, MD 20910
www.bethune-dubois.org

Black Entertainment and Sports Lawyers Association
c/o RJ Productions
P. O. Box 441485
Port Washington, MD 20749-1481
www.besla.org

Black Flight Attendants of America, Inc.
1060 Crenshaw Blvd., Ste. 202
Los Angeles, CA 90019
www.blackflightattendants.org

Black Sports Agents Association
9255 Sunset Blvd., Ste. 1120
Los Angeles, CA 90069
www.blacksportsagents.com

Black Women's Network
PO Box 56106
Los Angeles, CA 90056
www.blackwomensnetwork.org

Blacks in Gaming
2021 Glistening Sands Dr.
Las Vegas, NV 89119
www.blacksingaming.com

Blacks in Government
3005 George Ave., N.W.
Washington, DC 20001
www.bignet.org

**Caribbean-American Chamber of
Commerce and Industry, Inc.**
Brooklyn Navy Yard
Bldg. #5, Mezzanine A
Brooklyn, NY 11205
www.caacci.org

Chi Eta Phi Sorority Inc.
3029 13th St., N.W.
Washington, DC 20009
www.chietaphi.com

Coalition of Black Trade Unionists
PO Box 66268
Washington, DC 20035–6268
www.cbtu.org

**Conference of Minority
Transportation Officials**
818 18th St., N.W., Ste. 850
Washington, DC 20006
www.comto.org

**Congress of National Black
Churches**
1225 "I" St., N.W., #750
Washington, DC 20005–0908
www.cnbc.org

**Congressional Black Caucus
Foundation**
1720 Massachusetts Ave., N.W.
Washington, DC 20036
www.cbcfonline.org

Constituency for Africa
2400 N St., Ste. 510
Washington, DC 20037
www.cfa-africa-series.org

**Consortium for Graduate Study in
Management**
5585 Pershing Ave., Ste. 240
St. Louis, MO 63112
www.cgsm.org

Council on Foundations
1828 "L" St., N.W., #300
Washington, DC 20036
www.cof.org

Delta Sigma Theta Sorority, Inc.
1707 New Hampshire Ave., N.W.
Washington, DC 20009
www.deltasigmatheta.org

Executive Leadership Council
1010 Wisconsin Ave., N.W., #520
Washington, DC 20007
www.elcinfo.com

Gamma Phi Delta Sorority, Inc.
2657 W. Grand Blvd.
Detroit, MI 48202
www.gammaphideltasorority.com

Harvest Institute
623 Florida Ave., N.W.
Washington, DC 20001
www.harvestinstitute.org

I.B.P.O Elks of the World
P.O Box 159
Winton, NC 27986
www.ibpoew.org

**International Association of
African-American Music**
PO Box 382
Gladwyne, PA 19035
www.iaaam.com

International Association of Black
Professional Firefighters
8700 Central Ave., #306
Landover, MD 20785
www.iabpff.org

International Black Buyers and
Manufacturers Expo and
Conference
312 Florida Ave., N.W.
Washington, DC 20001
www.ibbmec.com

International Black Women's
Congress
555 Fenchurch St., Ste. 102
Norfolk, VA 23510
www.ibwc1609@cs.com

International Organization of
Black Security Executives
Livermore, CA 94551
www.iobse.com

International Society on
Hypertension in Blacks
2045 Manchester St., N.E.
Atlanta, GA 30324
www.ishib.org

Jackie Robinson Foundation
3 W. 35th St., 11th Fl.
New York, NY 10001
www.jackierobinson.org

Joint Center for Political and
Economic Studies
1090 Vermont Ave., N.W., #1100
Washington, DC 20005
www.jointcenter.org

Kappa Alpha Psi
2322 N. Broad St.
Philadelphia, PA 19132
www.kappaalphapsi.com

Leadership Conference on Civil
Rights
1629 "K" St., N.W., #1010
Washington, DC 20006
www.civilrights.org

Marketing Opportunities in
Business Entertainment and
MOBE's Information Technology
Symposium Series
8 S. Michigan Ave., Ste. 1510
Chicago, IL 60603
www.mobe.com

National African-American
Speakers Association
PO Box 22
Park Forest, IL 60466
Phone: 708–747–2219
www.naasa.org

National Alliance for Positive
Action
614 E. Manchester Blvd.
Inglewood, CA 90301
www.natalliance.org

National Alliance of Black School
Educators
310 Pennsylvania Ave., S.E.
Washington, DC 20003
www.nabse.org

National Alliance of Market
Developers, Inc.
PO Box 44303
Philadelphia, PA 19104
www.namdntl.org

National Association for the
Advancement of Colored People
4805 Mt. Hope Dr.
Baltimore, MD 21215
www.naacp.org

NAACP Legal Defense and Education Fund, Inc.
99 Hudson St., #1600
New York, NY 10013
www.naacpldf.org

National Association of African Americans in Human Resources
PO Box 11467
Washington, DC 20008
www.NAAAHR.org

National Association of Black Accountants, Inc.
7249 "A" Hanover Pkwy.
Greenbelt, MD 20770
www.nabainc.org

National Association of Black Consulting Engineers
2705 Bladensburg Rd., N.E.
Washington, DC 20018
www.jnt.com

National Association of Black County Officials
440 First St., N.W., #410
Washington, DC 20001
www.nobco.org

National Association of Black Hotel Owners
3520 W. Broward Blvd., Ste. 218B
Fort Lauderdale, FL 33312
www.africanamericantravel.com/
nabhood

National Association of Black Journalists
8701 "A" Adelphi Rd.
Adelphi, MD 20783–1716
www.nabj.org

National Association of Black Owned Broadcasters, Inc.
1155 Connecticut Ave., N.W., 6th Fl.
Washington, DC 20036
www.nabob.org

National Association of Black Scuba Divers
1605 Crittenden St., N.E.
Washington, DC 20017
www.nabsdivers.org

National Association of Black Social Workers
8436 W. McNichols Ave.
Detroit, MI 48221
www.nabsw.org

National Association of Black Telecommunications Professionals, Inc.
1710 "H" St., N.W., 10th Fl.
Washington, DC 20006–4601
www.nabtp.org

National Association of Blacks in Criminal Justice
North Carolina Central University
PO Box 19788
Durham, NC 27707
www.nabcj.org

National Association of Health Services Executives
8630 Fenton St., Ste. 126
Silver Spring, MD 20910
www.nahse.org

National Association of Investment Companies
1300 Pennsylvania Ave., N.W., Ste. 700
Washington, DC 20004
www.naichq.org

National Association of Minority Contractors
666 11th St., N.W., #520
Washington, DC 20001
www.namconline.org

National Association of Minority Media Executives
1921 Gallows Rd., Ste. 600
Vienna, VA 22182
www.namme.org

National Association of Negro Business and Professional Women's Clubs, Inc.
1806 New Hampshire Ave., N.W.
Washington, DC 20009
www.nanbpwc.org

National Association of Real Estate Brokers, Inc.
9831 Greenbelt Rd., #309
Lanham, MD 20706
www.nareb.com

National Association of Securities Professionals
1212 New York Ave., N.W., #210
Washington, DC 20005–3987
www.nasphq.com

National Baptist Convention of America, Inc.
1320 Pierre Ave.
Shreveport, LA 71103
www.nbcamerica.com

National Baptist Convention U.S.A., Inc.
5240 Chestnut St.
White Rock Baptist Church
Philadelphia, PA 19139

National Bar Association, Inc.
1225 11th St., N.W.
Washington, DC 20001
www.nationalbar.org

National Beauty Culturists' League
25 Logan Cir., N.W.
Washington, DC 20005
www.nbcl.org

National Black Association for Speech, Language and Hearing
PO Box 959
Athens, OH 45701
www.nbaslh.org

National Black Caucus of State Legislators
444 N. Capital St., N.W., Ste. 622
Washington, DC 20001
www.nbcsl.com

National Black Child Development Institute
1101 15th St., N.W., Ste. 900
Washington, DC 20005
www.nbcdi.org

National Black Data Processing
9315 Largo Dr., W., Ste. 260
Largo, MD 20774
www.bdpa.org

National Black MBA Association
180 N. Michigan Ave., #1400
Chicago, IL 60601
www.nbmbaa.org

National Black Nurses Association
8630 Fenton St., Ste. 330
Silver Spring, MD 20910-3803
www.nbna.org

National Black Police Association
3251 Mt. Pleasant St., N.W., 2nd fl.
Washington, DC 20010-2103
www.blackpolice.org

National Black United Fund, Inc.
40 Clinton St., #4
Newark, NJ 07102
www.nbuf.org

National Brotherhood of Skiers, Inc.
1525 E. 53rd St., Ste. 418
Chicago, IL 60615
www.nbs.org

National Center for Black Philanthropy, Inc.
1110 Vermont Ave., N.W., Ste. 405
Washington, DC 20005
www.ncfbp.org

National Coalition of Black Meeting Planners
8630 Fenton St., #126
Silver Spring, MD 20910
www.ncbmp.com

National Coalition of 100 Black Women
38 W. 32nd St., Ste. 1610
New York, NY 10001
www.ncbw.org

National Conference of Black Mayors, Inc.
1151 Cleveland Ave., Bldg. D
East Point, GA 30344
www.blackmayors.org

National Council of Negro Women, Inc.
633 Pennsylvania Ave., N.W.
Washington, DC 20004
www.ncnw.org

National Dental Association
3517 16th St., N.W.
Washington, DC 20010
www.ndaonline.org

National Forum for Black Public Administrators
777 N. Capital St., N.E., Ste. 807
Washington, DC 20002–4239
www.nfbpa.org

National Funeral Directors and Morticians Association, Inc.
3951 Snapfinger Pkwy, #570
Omega World Center
Decatur, GA 30035
www.nfdma.com

National Medical Association
1012 10th St., N.W.
Washington, DC 20001
www.nma.net.org

National Minority Business Council, Inc.
25 W. 45th St., Ste. 301
New York, NY 10036
www.nmbc.org

National Minority Supplier Development Council
1040 Avenue of the Americas, 2nd Fl.
New York, NY 10018
www.nmsDCus.org

National Newspaper Publishers Association
3200 13th St., N.W.
Washington, DC 20010
www.blackpressusa.com

National Optometric Association
3723 Main St.
PO Box F
East Chicago, IN 46312
www.natoptassoc.org

National Organization of Black Law Enforcement Executives
4609 Pinecrest Officer Park Dr., 2nd Fl., Ste. F
Alexandria, VA 22312-1442
www.noblenatl.org

National Organization of Minority Architects
c/o School of Architecture and Design
College of Engineering, Architecture, and Computer Sciences
Howard University
2366 6th St., N.W., #100
Washington, DC 20059
www.noma.net

National Sales Network
2117 "L" St., N.W., Ste. 317
Washington, DC 200037
www.salesnetwork.org

National Society of Black Engineers
1454 Duke St.
Alexandria, VA 22314
www.nsbe.org

National Society of Real Estate Appraisers
3596 Lytle Rd.
Cleveland, OH 44122-4908
www.nsrea.org

National Urban League, Inc.
120 Wall St.
New York, NY 10005
www.nul.org

Omega Psi Phi Fraternity
3951 Snapfinger Pkwy.
Decatur, GA 30035
www.omegapsiphi.com

100 Black Men of America
141 Auburn Ave.
Atlanta, GA 30303
www.100blackmen.org

Organization of Black Designers
300 "M" St., S.W., Ste. N110
Washington, DC 20024
www.odb.org

Phi Beta Sigma Fraternity, Inc.
145 Kennedy St., N.W.
Washington, DC 20011
www.pbs1914.org

Race for Success Foundation, Inc.
2940 Noble Rd., Ste. 1
Cleveland Hts., OH 44121
www.frasernet.com

Rainbow/PUSH Coalition
930 E. 50th St.
Chicago, IL 60615-2702
www.rainbowpush.org

Schomburg Center for Research in Black Culture
515 Malcolm X Blvd.
New York, NY 10037–1801
www.nypl.org/research/sc

Sickle Cell Disease Association of America, Inc.
200 Corporate Pointe, Ste. 495
Culver City, CA 90230-8727
www.sicklecelldisease.org

Sigma Gamma Rho Sorority, Inc.
8800 S. Stony Island Ave.
Chicago, IL 60617
www.sgrho1922.org

**Southern Christian Leadership
Conference**
334 Auburn Ave., N.E.
Atlanta, GA 30312
www.sclcnational.com

**Student National Medical
Association**
5113 Georgia, N.W.
Washington, DC 20011
www.snma.org

**Thurgood Marshall Scholarship
Fund**
60 E. 42nd St., Ste. 833
New York, NY 10165
www.thurgoodmarshallfund.org

United Negro College Fund
8260 Willow Oaks Corp. Dr.
PO Box 10444
Fairfax, VA 22031-8044
www.uncf.org

Urban Financial Services Coalition
1300 "L" St., N.W., Ste. 825
Washington, DC 20005
www.ufscnet.org

Zeta Phi Beta Sorority, Inc.
1734 New Hampshire Ave., N.W.
Washington, DC 20009
www.zphib1920.org

Glossary

Afrocentric Networking Movement: Movement whose members develop contacts and relationships for the purpose of sharing information and/or resources for the good of the greater community and not just the individual.

Afrocentricity: Principles derived from early African tribal cultures that promote the oneness of all things. Cooperation, collectiveness, and sharing are the essential elements. Value is inherent in every human being and reflects the interconnectedness and interdependence of all things. All life is in harmony with nature. Community is above the individual.

Black-on-black set-aside programs: An objective in which a black person or business sets aside at least 10 percent of their annual expenditures for black businesses and professional services that offer competitive value for their products or services.

Black vs. African American: It is my opinion that for the purposes of making this book user-friendly to a global black audience, using the term *black* instead of *African American* is more inclusive. Additionally the growing U.S. population of those from Africa, the Caribbean, and South and Central America does not want to be referred to as *African American*. African Americans generally do not mind being referred to as black.

Therefore I've chosen to use the term *black* as the dominant reference in this book.

Eurocentricity: Principles that promote survival of the fittest. Competition is the common denominator that permeates man's interaction with both nature and all other men. Life is played out on various battlefields. Human value or worth is measured by utility; therefore, materiality is paramount.

Excellence: Reinvesting one's personal achievement back into the community to improve the human condition.

Fraser Guidelines for Effective Networking: A list of ten principles that synthesize the author's thirty-five years of experience, ideas, and theories in the field of networking for the collective good of black people. (See page 257.)

FraserNet: The twenty thousand black professionals and business owners from all professional, technical, and entrepreneurial disciplines who belong to a network brought together and managed by the author. To join and to be listed in *SuccessGuide Worldwide,* send a business card to FraserNet, Inc, 2940 Noble Road, Cleveland Hts., Ohio 44121. You will also receive a free catalogue of products and services.

Intellectual capital: The estimated dollar value of the seven hundred and ten billion hours of formal education and professional training incurred between 1968 and 2000 by blacks in vocational, professional, technical, administrative, and business-ownership positions. The value has been estimated conservatively at ten dollars an hour or over seven trillion dollars.

Kwanzaa (kwahn-zah): A nonreligious seven-day cultural celebration established in 1966 by Dr. M. Ron Karenga. Designed for black people as a celebration of the fruits of their labor during the past year, it is a time of rejoicing, reflection, and commitment used to develop a greater sense of unity, identity, and purpose. There are Seven Principles (see **Nguzo Saba**) upon which Kwanzaa is based.

Mentoring: Acting as a trusted adviser, friend, and teacher. A mentor willingly shares his or her wisdom, experiences, and resources, usually in a one-on-one relationship that extends over the long term.

Networking: The identification and building of relationships for the purpose of sharing information, opportunities, and resources.

Networking agenda: The "street map" for determining how you will get to your goals.

Networking goals: Defining *what you want* in life for both the short and long term. All goals change as you change, and all are attained through networking with and through others.

New Underground Railroad: A metaphorical reference to the use of modern networking methods to link needy blacks with those who have achieved success, with the goal of helping to free them from poverty and lack of opportunity, just as the Underground Railroad network of free blacks and sympathetic whites helped thousands of slaves reach freedom.

Nguzo Saba (n-goo-zoo sah'-bah): African name for the Seven Principles of Kwanzaa. The principles cover spiritual, cultural, family, educational, economic, community, and youth activities.

PowerNetworking: An annual conference that trains black professionals how to successfully create connections that take their life, business, organizations, and/or community to a higher level.

Race-lynching: Spreading unsubstantiated, vicious, and put-down gossip, rumors, or innuendos about a fellow black person, contributing to self-defeating mistrust, division, and conflict within the black community.

Rites of Passage: A ritual that teaches us to recognize our own beauty, goodness, and power. Based on African culture and traditions, the ritual builds character, self-esteem, and unity among black people of all ages and cultures.

Role modeling: Serving as a positive example to others either personally or professionally. A role model may be emulated for his or her style, accomplishments, work habits, etc. Unlike a mentor, a role model need have no formal contact with his or her emulators, and there need not be any commitment by either to acknowledge the other.

Selective buying: Purchasing products and services only from those businesses and service providers that demonstrate outreach, appreciation, support, and employment practices that are beneficial to the black community.

Social entrepreneurialism: Making fundamental changes and solving complex problems with fresh, market-oriented solutions that are profitable and create jobs and wealth. Also known as "doing well by doing good."

Soul-O-Dex: An extensive file of business contacts from black professionals and entrepreneurs. Used to access information and resources before utilizing nonblack contacts.

SuccessGuide Worldwide: The Networking Guide to Black Resources: Published annually and supported by national corporate advertisers. Lists thousands of top black professionals, business owners, and community leaders. Used as a network to help people find jobs, customers, and contacts. Networking protocols must be adhered to by all those using the guide. Protocols are listed on each guide page.

Tribalism: The belief in being faithful to one's own kind, defined by ethnicity, language, culture, and religion. According to futurist John Naisbitt, this belief is flourishing. According to *Tribes* author Joel Kotkin, "Tribes utilize their historically conditioned values and beliefs to cope successfully with change. Those identifiable values include strong ethnic identity, a belief in self-help, hard work, thrift, education, and the family. Modern-day tribalism must be leavened with a willingness to learn from and accept others. Or it will prove ultimately destructive."

Urban Village: Literal and figurative term applied to efforts by the established black middle and upper classes to reach back and assist those blacks still struggling to achieve prosperity. Many of those still struggling live in once-flourishing black urban neighborhoods that have become isolated because of the exodus of successful black people. There is a growing movement for successful blacks to give back and/or move back and help rebuild those neighborhoods into the "new Urban Villages."

Vertical networking: Applying your unique gifts, personal achievements, and resources in a way that reaches down and lifts up those who are still struggling to achieve new levels or are stuck in the cycle of poverty.

Suggested Reading

Anderson, Claud, Ed.D. *Black Labor, White Wealth: The Search for Power and Economic Justice*. Bethesda, Md.: PowerNomics Corp. of America, Inc., 1994.

Asanti, Molefi. *Kemet, Afrocentricity and Knowledge*. Trenton, N.J.: Africa World Press, 1990.

Billingsley, Andrew. *Climbing Jacob's Ladder: The Enduring Legacy of African-American Families*. New York: Simon & Schuster, 1992.

Brown, Les. *It's Not Over Till You Win*. New York: Simon & Schuster, 1997.

Chideya, Farai. *Don't Believe the Hype: Fighting Cultural Misinformation About African Americans*. New York: Plume Books, 1995.

Cobbs, Price M., and Judith L. Turnock. *Cracking the Corporate Code: From Survival to Mastery, Real Stories of African-American Success*. New York: Executive Leadership Council, 2000.

Covey, Stephen R. *Seven Habits of Highly Effective People*. New York: Simon & Schuster, 1989.

Edwards, Audrey, and Dr. Craig K. Polite. *Children of the Dream*. New York: Doubleday, 1992.

Fraser, George C. *Race for Success: The Ten Best Business Opportuni-

ties for Blacks in America. New York: William Morrow and Company, Inc., 1998.

Graves, Earl. *How to Succeed in Business Without Being White.* New York: HarperCollins, 1997.

Hooks, Bell. *Black Looks: Race and Representation.* Boston: South End Press, 1992.

Johnson, John H. *Succeeding Against the Odds.* New York: Warner, 1989.

Kimbro, Dennis, and Napoleon Hill. *Think and Grow Rich: A Black Choice.* New York: Warner, 1989.

Kiyosaki, Robert T., and Sharon L. Lecter. *Rich Dad, Poor Dad.* New York: Warner, 2000.

Kotkin, Joel. *Tribes: How Race, Religion and Identity Determine Success in the New Global Economy.* New York: Random House, 1993.

Lesau, Charlotte, and Worl Lesau. *African Proverbs.* White Plains, N.Y.: Peter Pauper, 1962.

Misner, Ph.D., and Don Morgan. *Masters of Networking: Building Relationships for Your Pocketbook.* Atlanta, Ga.: Bard Press, 2000.

Munroe, Dr. Myles. *The Burden of Freedom.* Lake Mary, Fla. Strang Communications, 2000.

Stanley, Thomas J., and William D. Danko. *The Millionaire Next Door: The Surprising Secrets of America's Wealthy.* New York: Simon & Schuster, 1998.

Thomas, David A., and John J. Gabarro. *Breaking Through: The Making of Minority Executives in Corporate America.* Boston: Harvard Business School Press, 1999.

Walker, Blair, and Reginald Lewis. *Why Should the White Guys Have All the Fun?* New York: John Wiley & Sons, 1995.

West, Cornel. *Race Matters.* Boston: Beacon Press, 1993.

Williams, Chancellor. *The Destruction of Black Civilization.* Chicago: Third World Press, 1987.

Your Comments, Please

We would like your feedback on this book so as to make our next one even better. Please complete the questionnaire, copy this page, and mail it to George C. Fraser, FraserNet, Inc., 2940 Noble Rd., Ste. 1, Cleveland Hts., OH 44121 or e-mail it to gfraser@frasernet.com

1. In future books I would like to see a new chapter or chapters on the following topics related to those you explored in *Success Runs in Our Race*:

_____

_____

_____

2. Here is how I intend to use *Success Runs in Our Race* or the *SuccessGuide* publication:

_____

_____

_____

3. ☐ I am a black professional and/or entrepreneur. I would like to be listed in *SuccessGuide Worldwide*. I agree to assist those who contact me through *SuccessGuide*.

☐ Attached is my business card (include e-mail please)

☐ I am in either a leadership, executive, managerial, supervisory, professional specialty (i.e., engineer, dietitian, accountant, etc.), sales, or business ownership position.

☐ I would like to be included in your network, and I agree to assist those who contact me through your network.

☐ Additional information (please)

Name _____

Title _____

Business Name _____

Address _____

City_____State_____Zip_____

Phone_____Fax _____

e-mail_____

Under what category would your business be listed in the Yellow Pages? (no more than 3 words) _____

4. I need to make a networking contact in the following area of expertise in the following cities:

Expertise: City:

_____   _____

_____   _____

_____   _____

_____   _____

_____   _____

_____   _____

_____   _____

_____   _____

Please fax (216–691–6685) or mail a copy of this form to: FraserNet, Inc., 2940 Noble Rd., Ste. 1, Cleveland Hts., Ohio 44121

Visit www.FraserNet.com for information to purchase membership, *SuccessGuide Worldwide*, books and tapes, or to attend the annual PowerNetworking Conference.

The FraserNet product and program resources include:

FraserNet.com
FraserNet Memberships:
Networking Tips, Facts, and Ideas
Books and Tapes
African American Business Hall of Fame & Museum (a 501(c)(3))

Special Events
PowerNetworking Conference (annual: June)

Publications
SuccessGuide Worldwide: The Networking Guide to Black Resources
Race for Success: The Ten Best Business Opportunities
for Blacks in America
Success Runs in Our Race: The Complete Guide to Effective
Networking in the Black Community
Success Runs in Our Race Teachers Manual and Student Workbook

Tapes
PowerNetworking Conference audio- and videotapes
(Complete set of all media: 37 audiotapes, 15 CDs, 4 videotapes)
Speaking Out: George C. Fraser's Greatest Speeches
(two 60-minute audiotapes)
For Your Success: Ten Guiding Principles of Power Networking
(six 60-minute audiotapes)
Race for Success: The Ten Best Business Opportunities for Blacks
in America (two audio cassettes)
Success Runs in Our Race: The Complete Guide to Effective
Networking in the Black Community (two audio cassettes)

Speaking Engagements
Special Appearances
Successories (T-shirts and Caps)

FraserNet, Inc.
2940 Noble Rd., Ste. 1
Cleveland Heights, Ohio 44121
B: (216) 691–6686
F: (216) 691–6685
Email: gfraser@frasernet.com

About the Author

George Fraser is the author of two books, including the critically acclaimed best-seller, *Race for Success: The Ten Best Business Opportunities for Blacks in America*. He is also the creator and publisher of the award-winning *SuccessGuide Worldwide: The Networking Guide to Black Resources*. A new edition is published annually. He is the creator of the annual *PowerNetworking Conference*, one of black America's largest conferences.

George Fraser is a frequent contributor to scholarly journals on a wide range of topics that include business ethics and economic development. He has been featured in the *New York Times* best-seller *Masters of Networking*, along with Colin Powell. His latest book, *Race for Success: The Ten Best Business Opportunities for Blacks in America*, was published by the William Morrow Company, and selected as one of *the ten best business books of the year* by *Booklist* magazine.

Mr. Fraser has served on numerous boards and has received many awards and citations for his community service, including the United Negro College Fund National Volunteer of the Year

Award. Allstate Insurance recently presented to him on national TV its Architect of the Village Award. He has been appointed to state and city commissions by both the governor and the mayor of his home state and city of Cleveland, Ohio.

Mr. Fraser spent seventeen years in management with Procter & Gamble, United Way, and Ford Motor Company. Today, as a popular speaker and author, Mr. Fraser has appeared on more than 250 television and radio talk shows. His views are solicited by media as diverse as CNN and *The Wall Street Journal.* He speaks nearly 120 times per year all around the world. His inspiring talks on success principles, effective networking, wealth creation, ethics, and valuing diversity are as popular among corporate professionals as they are among college students.

His words and ideas have been taped and televised. Over the last decade the prestigious publication *Vital Speeches of the Day* has selected five of Mr. Fraser's speeches to be reprinted and distributed worldwide, a first for any professional speaker in America.

Upscale magazine name him one of the top 50 power brokers in Black America. *Black Enterprise* magazine called him black America's #1 networker and featured him on its cover. Personal growth "guru" Stephen Covey called Mr. Fraser a "masterful teacher." TV host and journalist Tony Brown called him a "visionary with the rare combination of leadership and management skills." Many have called him a new voice for people of African descent. He is considered by many to be one of the foremost authorities on networking and building effective relationships.

Mr. Fraser received his executive training at the Amos Tuck School of Business at Dartmouth College. He was awarded an Honorary Doctorate Degree of Humane Letters from Jarvis Christian College. He has been married to Nora Jean for thirty-one years; they have two sons, Kyle and Scott.

Index

ABC Radio Networks, 16
abundance mentality, 132–33
ACN, 247
acquaintances, 157, 215
Active Transportation, 274
advertising, 73–74, 80, 281
Advertising Council, 83
Aerial Capital Management, Inc., 17
African American Business Hall of Fame
    and Museum, 52–54, 187
African American Chamber of
    Commerce of Northeast Ohio, 305
African American/Diversity Newswire,
    17
African American Faculty and Staff of
    Case Western Reserve University,
    305
African culture, 4–5, 10, 58, 60–64,
    214–15. See also Afrocentricity;
    Kwanzaa
  cooperative effort and, 9
  Kwanzaa and, 89–91
  tribal success and, 87
African Proverbs (Leslau and Leslau),
    99
Afrocentricity, 4–11, 214
  business cards and, 171
  community and, 87
  essential elements of, 4
  Eurocentricity vs., 62–65
  principles of, xxxvii, 284–85, 307

  Rites of Passage and, 65
Afrocentric networking, 50, 134–37
  black organizations and, 5–6, 293
  success for all and, 6–11, 285–308
  Web sites and, 117
agenda, 157, 195–97
  black, 92–95
  conventions and, 238–39
  conversation and, 208
  networking exercise, 324
  preparing, 263, 323
Allen, Carolyn Watts, 128–29, 131
Allen, Robert, 128
Allen AME church (Queens, New
    York), 297
Alpha Kappa Alpha, 5
Alpha Phi Alpha, 5, 159, 293
alumni groups, 5
American Association of Blacks in
    Energy, 6
American Dream, 64–65
American Express Company, 17
American Journal of Sociology, 157
American Program Bureau, 336
America Works, Inc., 298–300
Amos, Wally "Famous," 31, 166
Amway, 247
Angelou, Maya, 117, 189, 306
Anheuser-Busch, 122
appearance, 187, 193–94, 236
appointments, 278

Aquarian Conspiracy, The (Ferguson), 132
Arabs, 108, 270
Ariel Capital Management, 70, 116
Armstrong, Howard, 219
Arrington, Freddy, 24, 25
Ashe, Arthur, 54, 75, 121
Asians, 13, 108, 110, 111, 272, 290
assertiveness, 191, 192
Association of Black Insurance Professionals, 83
Athletes Building Better Communities LLC (AABC), 7
Atkins, Connie, 305
Atlanta, Georgia, 112
Atlanta Business League, 126
Atlanta Tribune, 302
Atlas, James, 33
AT&T, 290, 303
    Diversity Board, 304
Avant, Clarence, 52
Avon, 247
awards ceremonies, 176–80

Baba (Yoruba priest), 60, 61, 65–66
Baber, Anne, 189
Bad Boy Worldwide Entertainment Group, 52
Bakewell, Danny J., 101
Baldwin, James, 35, 184, 189
"Balloonfest 1986," 28
Bank of America, 17
banks, 100, 116, 278
    loans and, 300–303
    as sponsors, 174
"Barbadian network," 9
Barkeley, Charles, 163
Barrow, Joe Jouis, 267
Basket Case, 302, 303
Beal, Bernard, 76–77
BE Company of the Year, 12
BE Industrial/Service 100s, 14–15
"Being Seen at Negro Conventions" (Nivri), 236–37
Bell, Ed, 246
Bellamy, Werten, Jr., 15
Belton, Marc, 16
Bennett, William J., 99
Bethel AME Church (Birmingham), 297
Big Brothers and Big Sisters, 82
Billingsley, Andrew, 49–50, 52, 87
Bing, Dave, 53

Black, Wilbur, 194
black Americans. *See also* black community; black-owned businesses; *and specific age groups, professions, and social classes*
    advertising and loan rate of, 76
    buying power of, 12–13, 18, 89, 26, 116–17, 272–75   dividing, 44–45
    economics and, 287
    images and stereotypes of, 72–84
    lobbying for, 82–83
    magazines targeting, 74
    police and, 79
    self-perception problems of, 49, 73
    start–up business barriers and, 111–14
    success among, 9–10
    successful, reaching back, 300–304
    tips for whites networking with, 280–82
    value of networking and, 133
    wealth controlled by, 108
    white-dominated law firms and, 75
black business networks, 134–35
black chamber of commerce, 124, 126
black community. *See also* Afrocentricity; Urban Village; Underground Railroad
    Afrocentric networking and, 135–37
    agenda for, 92–95
    black professional organizations to aid, 6, 10
    cultural knowledge, passing on, 57
    divisions in, 44–45
    economic development and, 52–54
    economic success in neighborhoods of, 45–46
    empowering, 57
    encouraging positive media coverage of, 80
    entrepreneurship strengthens, 109–10
    families and, 49–50
    focusing on success to advance, 11–15, 18–19
    goals and action steps, 93, 94
    intellectual capital and, 86–87
    interdependence of, 89
    Kwanzaa and, 90–91
    neighborhood businesses and, 117
    networking and purchasing first in, 270–75
    reuniting, 10

spiritual connection and, 65–67
success of, networking for, xxxvii
success of, individual vs., 86–87
black conferencing, 236–37
Black Data Processing Associates, 305
Black Educational Development Inc., 25
Black Enterprise, 7, 12, 13, 14, 16, 74, 75, 80, 133, 185, 274, 285
Networking Forum of 1987, 29–30
Black Expo, 154
black history, 84, 93
Black Leadership Council, 19
black middle and upper classes, 52
economic and educational agenda for, 89
exodus of, from cities, 38–39, 300
helping underclass, 88
media image of blacks and, 78–79
Rites of Passage and, 67–68
stratification of black community and, 44–45
targeted as market, 281
black-on-black buying, 273–75
exercise, 329, 330
black organizations, 5–6. *See also* specific types
finding, 83
positive images and, 82–83
whites on boards of, 280
black-owned businesses. *See also* entrepreneurship; minority businesses
areas of opportunity for, 116–19
buying from, 124–26, 272–74
employment by, 14–15
number of, 11–12, 14
professionals and, 88
revenues of, 85–86, 110–11
supporting, 82, 94
Black Pages, 259
Black Power movement, 52, 214
black "power networking," 7–8
Black Professionals Association, 305
black resources, business cards and, 172
Blacks in Government, 305
Blacks in Management, 305
Blackwell, Gene, 25–26
Blige, Mary J., 81
blue-collar jobs, 13
board appointments, 243–46
minority position and, 244–45

body language, 202, 249–50
Bol, Manute, 57
Bond, Julian, 163
Book of Virtues, The (Bennett), 99
Boston Federal Reserve Bank, 76
Bowes, Lee, 298–300
Boy Scouts, 82
BP America, 174
Brewster, Bob, 247
Bridges, Ken, 12
Brimmer, Dr. Andrew, 244
British, as tribe, 214
Brotherhood Crusade Black United Fund (Los Angeles), 100, 101
Broussard, Cheryl, 283
Brown, Carl, 50
Brown, Carolyn M., 7
Brown, Les, 26, 31, 81, 152, 189, 224, 235
Brown, Ron, 31, 267
Brown, Tony, 31, 182, 270
Brzezinski memorandum, 43–45
Budweiser, 174
Burger King, 295–96
Burnett, Leo, 73
Burrell, Tom, 53
Bush, Barbara, 71
Bush, George W., 185
business cards, 166–71, 263, 277
Afrocentric thinking and, 171
blank, 169–70
design of, 167
names and, 204
notes on, 169
number to carry, 168
organizing, 168–69, 171–73
recent college graduates and, 228
Business Consortium Fund (BCF), 302–4
business. *See also* black-owned businesses; entrepreneurship
planning, 124
start-up barriers, 111–14
buying, 122–23
from black community first, 271–75, 329
selective, 274–75, 330
Byrd, Carolyn Baldwin, 15

Cain, Herman, 53
CALPERS, 8
Campbell, Joseph, 107

capital, 113–14, 120–21, 123
 fiinding, for minority business,
  300–303
Caribbean–American Chamber of
  Commerce and Industry, 48
Carr, Frank, 290–91
Carruthers, George R., 16
Carter, Jimmy, 44
Census report of 2001, 14
Center for Community Change, 76
Center for the Advancement of African
  American Entrepreneurship, 53
Central County Burglary Investigators
  Group, 212
Chance, Jim, 255
charity, 82
Charles, Ray, 24
charter schools, 116
Chenault, Ken, 52–53
chewing gum, 279
children. *See also* young people
 family goals and, 93
 goals and jobs for, 158
 role models for, 97–99
Children's Book of Home and Family, The
  (Bennett), 99
Chinese, 214, 270
Chisholm, Samuel J., 53
churches
 networking by, 6, 296–98
 networking through, 134
 mentoring and role modeling and, 97
civil rights laws, 85, 112
civil rights movement, 6
 next phase of, 11–19
Clemmons, Mack, 270
Cleveland, 101, 304–5
 becomes majority-poor, 38–39
 black leadership in, 304–6
 Renaissance Project in, 128–31
Cleveland African American Library
  Association, 305
Cleveland Foundation, 246
Cleveland State University Black
  Alumni Organization, 305
Cleveland Women's Council of the
  National Association of Real Estate
  Brokers, 305
clients
 looking for potential, 124
 networking for, 229–32
Climbing Jacob's Ladder (Billingsley), 52

Clinkscales, Keith, 8, 36
Clinton, Bill, 185
clubs, 174
 best black, 340–48
 mentoring and role modeling and, 97
Coca–Cola Company, 17, 122, 174
Cole, Dr. Johnnetta, 244
Coleman, Don, 8
Coleman, Trevor, 18–19
collective work and responsibility
  (*Ujima*) principle, 4, 91, 135
college
 helping young blacks go to, 289–90
 network and, 225–26
college graduate, job hunt and, 224–28
colleges, black, image of, 83–84
Combs, Sean "P. Diddy," 52
Coming of Age (Hill), 62
"communicate with network" principle,
  145
communications industry, 80
communication skills, 189–90. *See also*
  conversation; listening skills;
  people skills
community, Afrocentric principle of,
  xxxvii, 4, 9. *See also* black
  community
Community Development Corporations
  (CDCs), 56, 297
community groups, 82
community influence, networking for,
  244
community reinvestment, personal goals
  exercise, 329
Community Reinvestment Act (1977),
  100, 101
Compliments
 accepting, 278
 whites and faint praise of blacks,
  280–81
computer, 172
confident mind-set, 242. *See also* self-
  assurance; self-esteem
Congressional Black Caucus, 44
Congressional Black Caucus
  Foundation, 10
connectors, 163–64, 315
Consortium of African American
  Organizations, 304–6
consumer base, expanding, 125
contact(s)
 following up with, 240

information seeking and, 242
job seeking and, 218–20
multiplying, 156–57
number of, 156
secondary, 157
staying in touch with, 228
unexpected, 270
Continental Airlines, 174
conventions and conferences, 236–40
conversation, 199–210
closing, 208–10
common ground in, 207–8
finding topics for, 263
introductions and, 202–5
key to relaxing in, 207–8
moving along, 207–8
opening lines in, 199–202, 322
rules and tools of, 205–10
Coolidge, Calvin, 115
Cooperation
Afrocentric principle of, xxxvii, 4
power through, 15
cooperative economics (*Ujamaa*)
principle, 91
investment clubs and, 286, 287
Koreans as model for, 47–48
networking and, 135
reason for lack of, 49
successful blacks and, 300–304
Copeland, Margot James, 16
Corporations
appointment to boards of, 245, 246
finding mentors in, 234
law firms and, 236
living dual existence in, 37
networking for career success and,
232–36
outreach to black community and,
330
preparing minority youth for, 291
responsibility of, 125
Cosby, Bill, 73, 289
Cose, Ellis, 281–82
Cove, Peter, 298
cover charge, 175–77
cover letter, 220–22
Covey, Stephen R., 158, 197
coworkers, 24
creativity (*Kuumba*) principle, 91, 136
credit unions, 295–96
Crest toothpaste, 74
crime reporting, 78, 84

Crump, Randy, 292–94
customers, 205, 229–32

DaimlerChrysler, 123, 126
Dash, Damon, 252
Davis, Miles, 75
Day, Thomas, 111
Def Jam Recordings, 51
Delta Sigma Theta, 5
Denny's, 47
Denson, Reginald R., 16
Dickson, Reginald, 291, 292
Disney Corporation, 125
distrust, 138–39
doctors, 115
Dominic, Virgil, 141
Donovan, Kyle, 15
Dorsey, Julius C., Jr., 97–98
Dortch, Tommy, 162–63
Douglass, Frederick, 37, 212
Dress for Success (Molloy), 193
DuBois, W. E. B., 37–38
Dudley Products, 12
Duggins, Linda, 81
Dyson, Dr. Michael Eric, 189

East Brooklyn Congregations (EBC), 56
East End Neighborhoood House, 58,
60–61, 66
Eaton Corporation, 293
Ebony, 12, 74, 80, 90
economic boycotts, 47
economic empowerment, 35, 50, 95,
285–97
investment clubs and, 288–89
goals and action steps for, 94
inroads for, creating, 290–94
mentoring and, 100–102
redemption and, 295–97
economic success, five global tribes and,
214
Edelin, Dr. Ramona Hoage, 10
Edison Plaza Shopping Center, 56
Edley, Chris, Jr., 74
education, 93–99. *See also* college;
schools
black passion for, 214
as business opportunity area, 116
church programs and, 296
entrepreneurship and, 112–13
goals and action steps for, 93–94
intellectual capital and, 85

(continued)
jobs and, 40–41
mentors and role models and, 96–99
programs to aid blacks to get,
289–90
Eleanor and Julius Dorsey, Sr.,
Education Fund, 98
ElecTech, 294
Ellison, Ralph, 71
Emerge, 18–19, 236
Emerson, Robert, 304
employment (jobs). *See also* job hunting;
unemployment
black-owned businesses and, 15, 111,
114
black losses, 13
of blacks, in places you shop, 271–72,
274–75
creating, 108–10, 114
education and, 40–41
Encyclopaedia Britannica, 25
entertainment, 115, 118
entrance, making great, 198
entrepreneurship, 107–26
areas of opportunity for, 116–19
blacks vs. other minorities and,
110–11
factors for success and, 119–22
impact of, on community, 109–10
history of blacks and, 111–14
negative perceptions and, 76
resources and information for, 113
resurgence of blacks and, 139–40
role models and, 112–13
self-made millionaires and, 115
social, 298–300
ten steps to, 123–24
entry-level job, 224–28
environment, in group dynamics, 233
Environmental Data Consultants, 255
Envy of the World, The (Cose), 281–82
Erving, Julius "Dr. J," 8
Essence, 72–73, 74, 80
Essence Communications, 187
E-Style catalogue, 12–13
ethnic identity, 214
Eurocentricity, 62–65
Evans, Benny (half brother), 22
Evans, Myra (half sister), 23
event. *See also* conventions
going alone, 280
preparing for, 263–64, 278

excellence
embracing, 95
personal achievement vs., 87–89
executives, 115
exercises, 310–31
conversation openers, 322
huggers and shakers, 315
identify your network, 310
information sources, 320–21
mentoring activities review, 316
networking agenda, 324
networking dos and don'ts, 331
networking opportunities, 313
networking plan, 318
networking skills evaluation, 311
networking skills improvement, 312
network to achieve organizational
goals, 328
personal and professional goals, 314
personal goals for community
reinvestment, 329
question preparation, 323
role-model attributes review, 317
selective buying review, 330
self-assurance checkup, 325–26
self-introduction script, 319
skills inventory, 327
expertise, sharing, 238
extended network, 157
job hunting and, 215, 218–19
Exxon Mobil, 290
eye contact, 188, 199
"Eye on America" (TV show), 164

"Fabulous 50," 175, 336–39
Fairchild, Denise, 56
faith (*Imani*) principle, 91, 136
family, 95
goals and action steps for, 93
Farr, Mel, 274
Fatburger, 8
Fauntroy, Rev. Walter E., 44
favorites, 145
Feagin, Dr. Joseph, 75
fears and doubts, 197–203
Feaster, Lynn, 154–55, 157
Federal Communications Commission,
258–59
Ferguson, Ken, 262
Ferguson, Marilyn, 132
"fess up" rule, 144
filing, 171–72

finance, 116
first class, flying, 279
first impressions, 192
Fisk, Jason, 7
Fitzhugh, Howard Naylor, 52
"Five–P's" philosophy, 263
flirting, 248–52, 279
follow-through, 170
follow-up, after convention, 240
Fondon, Janine and Tom, 17
food, 175–76
Ford, Harold E., Jr., 17
Ford, Henry (athlete), 7
Ford, Henry (auto manufacturer), 122–23
Ford Foundation, 56
Ford Marketing Institute, 29
Ford Motor company, 31, 122–23, 125, 126, 147–49, 174
   Dealership Development program, 29, 30
Forest City Dental Society, 305
for-profit ventures, 173
Fort, Howard, 246
Forten, James , Sr., 111
Fortune, 7, 48, 86, 123, 290, 302
Francis, James, 77
Franklin, Rebecca, 164
Fraser, Edward (brother), 21, 163
Fraser, Emma (sister), 20, 22, 32
Fraser, George, background and personal story of, 19–32
Fraser, Ida Mae Baldwin (mother), 20
Fraser, Joseph (brother), 20, 22, 32
Fraser, Kyle (son), 27
Fraser, Scotland (brother), 21
Fraser, Scott (son), 27, 268–69
Fraser, Walter (brother), 21, 163
Fraser, Walter Frederick (father), 20, 22, 163
Fraser Guidelines, 256, 257–73
FraserNet, Inc., 9, 33, 52
   core values of, 34–35
   goals for, 160–81
   guiding principles of, 34
   mission statement, 34
   overall goal of, 35
   vision statement, 34
FraserNet Workbook, 309–31
fraternities, black, 5, 84, 97, 159
"Free Frank: A Black Pioneer on the Antebellum Frontier" (Walker),4
FUBU, 12, 50–51

Gallman, Vanessa, 67–69
Gallup Organization, 112
Garnett-Thomas, Gwendolyn, 17
Garvey, Marcus, 48
Gary, Willie, 164
Gaston, A. G., 193
Gault, Stan, 246
Gelb, Vic, 28
General Electric, 188, 307
General Mills, 16
General Motors, 123, 126
Gilchrist, Richard, 26–27, 163
Girl Scouts, 82
"give first, expect nothing in return" guideline, 156, 265–66
GlobalAutomotiveAlliance, 16–17
global commerce, 119
Global Hue, 8
global network, 214–15, 256
GlobalTech Financial, LLC, 15
Glover, Danny, 31
Glover, John, 150, 265
goals conversation and, 208
   defining, 157–59
   exercises, 314, 328, 329
   long–term, 157, 159, 160
   narrowing, 195–96
   setting, 159–62
   short–term, 157, 159, 160
   spiritual, 92–93
Goldston, Nathaniel, III, 53
Good Morning America (TV program), 70
"good provider" principle, 145
goodwill gestures, 141
Goodyear, 246
Gordon, Bruce, 53, 308
Gordy, Berry, 52
"Gospel of Equity," 100
gossiping, 280
government, 114–15, 242–43
Graham, Stedman, 31
Granovetter, Mark, 157
gratitude, 146, 157, 242, 276–77, 278
Graves, Earl, Jr., 72
Graves, Earl G., 29–30, 52, 53, 75, 133, 163, 244
Gray, Willie, 211
Great Connections (Baber), 189
Greater Christ Baptist Church (Detroit), 295
grooming, 187, 193–94, 236, 278, 280

group dynamic, 233
  how to enter, 202–3
  leadership, 234
Grugg & Ellis Real Estate Company,
  7

Hafed, Ali, 55–56
Hairston, Teresa, 127
Halle Brothers Department Store, 24
Hamilton Securities Group, 118
handshake, 199, 278
Hansberry, Lorraine, 154
hard sell, 230
Harlem book fair, 81
Harris, E. Lynn, 117
Harris, Stayce D., 16
Hartsfield, Rev. William, 297
Harvard Business Review, 291
Hawkins Food Group, 15
Hayes, Eleanor, 141
health care, 118–19
Heart & Soul, 74, 80, 117
Heider, John, 15
"help line" guideline, 276
high school students
  entrepreneurship and, 112–13
  overcoming negative perceptions,
    76
  programs to aid, 289
Hill, Paul, Jr., 58, 62–63, 64
hip-hop music, 12
Hispanic Chamber of Commerce, 140
Hispanic-owned businesses, 110, 111
Hispanics, 13, 108
Hobson, Mellody, 17, 70
Holder, Geoffrey, 31
Hooks, Benjamin, 18
Hoover, Carole, 162
Hoover Milstein, 162
"host, not guest" rule, 143
hotels, 174
housing, low-income, 297
Hubbard, Marilyn French, 183
Hudson, Joseph R., 124, 125, 126,
  302–3
Hudson Strategic Group, 124, 302
huggers, 161–62, 315
Huggins, Hosiah, Jr., 198
Hughes, Cathy, 52
human resources infrastructure, 156
humor, 206
Hurston, Zora Neale, 198

IBM, 122, 290
ideas, being source of, 229–30
image, of blacks, 79–84. *See also*
  perceptions; self-image; stereotypes
  as obstacle, 79–80, 138–39
  promoting positive, in media, 80–84
  self-esteem and, 84
  success despite negative, 85
immigrant groups, 108
incorporation stage, 65, 67
Indians, 214
individual, community success vs.,
  86–87
influence, networking for, 147–49
informal meetings, 234
information
  loop, formal and informal, 236
  networking for, 140, 146–47, 240–43
  sources exercise, 320–21
inner-city schools
  promoting positive images and role
    models, 82
  role modeling and supporting, 97–98
inquisitiveness, 190–91
Inroads program, 290–94
insecurity, 197. *See also* self-assurance;
  self-esteem
insurance industry, 158–59
integration generation, 95
"integration shock," 77
intellectual capital, 84–87
interdependence, as goal, 89
*International Library of Negro Life and
  History*, xxvi, 25–26
internships, 225–26
  preparing minority youth for, 290
interruptions, 205–7, 280
introductions
  of others, etiquette of, 204–5
  script exercise, 319
  self-, 199–200, 263, 278
inventions, 115
inventory
  job hunting, 217–18
  of skills exercise, 327
investment clubs, 285–88
invisibility, 76–77
Irish, 270
IVDS, 258

Jackson, Rev. Jesse, 47, 303
Jakes, Bishop T. D., 81

Jamaicans, 48, 270
Japanese, 87, 133, 214, 270
Jews, 108, 133, 214, 270, 272
job hunting, 215–24. *See also*
   employment
   contact list for, 218–19
   hidden job market and, 215–16
   networking and, 134, 147
   new college graduate and, 224–28
   positioning self and, 223–24
   résumé and letter for, 219–22
   taking inventory for, 217–18
   welfare recipients and, 298–300
job training, 299–300
Johns, Daymond, 50
Johnson, Bob, 244
Johnson, Charlie, 274
Johnson, John H., 11, 31, 52, 82, 133,
   193
Johnson, Magic, 7–8, 52, 88
Johnson, Robert L., 52, 118
Johnson, Roy, 8
Johnson Development Corporation, 7–8
Johnson Publishing, 11–12, 82
joint ventures, 124
jokes, 206, 279, 281
Jolley, Willie, 153
Jones, Cynthia, 264–65
Jones, James Earl, 31, 55, 189
Jones, Mike D., 7
Jones, Quincy, 53, 244
Jordan, Vernon, 83, 244
Journal of Negro History, 25

Kani, Karl, 12, 51
Kappa Alpha Psi Fraternity Inc, 305
Karenga, Maulana "Ron," 89–91
Kauffman, Mel, 168
Keating, W. Dennis, 39
keiretsu (Japanese business alliance),
   47–48
Kennedy, John (attorney), 164
KeyCorp, 16
keynote address, 180
Khayat, Saad, 155
Kim, Jin Agyuk, 46
Kimbro, Dennis, 31, 193
King, Rev. Martin Luther, Jr., 5, 206,
   290
Kmart, 300, 301, 303
"knots, not net" rule, 142
know–how, 121–22

knowledge, shared, 33
Koppel, Ted, 78
Koreans, 46–48, 133, 270
Kotkin, Joel, 48–49, 213–14
Kwanzaa, 19, 62, 89–91
   Holiday Expos, 90
   Seven Principles of, 89, 91–92,
      135–36, 285, 307

Landers, Ann, 263
Lanier, Bob, 259
lawyers, 115, 164, 278, 297
leadership, sharing, 7
Lee, Marshall O., 72–73
Legacy of John Brown, The (DuBois),
   37–38
Leo's Casino, 24
Lerdesdorff, William, 111–12
Leslau, Charlotte and Wolf, 99
letters to the editor, 80
leveraging purchasing power, 122–23,
   274–75
Lewellen, Michael, 265–66
Lewis, Byron, 53
Lewis, Ed, 52
Lewis, Mr. (Port Authority supervisor),
   23
Lewis, Reginald, 52, 116
Lewis & Murray, 15
Liberty City Entrepreneurial Education
   Center, 56
libraries, 242–43
life crises, 65
Lincoln, Abraham, 206
listening skills, 186, 187–88, 277–78
   body language tips, 188
   guidelines, 268–69
Live Your Dreams (Brown), 224
Llewellyn, J. Bruce, 8
loan(s)
   guarantees for minority-owned
      businesses, 302–3
   negative perceptions and, 76
   unfair lending practices and, 113
Local Initiatives Support Corporation,
   56
Lombard, kenneth, 7–8
London, Mel and Sheryl, 180–82
long-windedness, 206, 279
Lorayne, Harry, 203
Love, Helen, 148
Lowenstein, Barbara, 181, 182

Lynch, Willie, 41–42, 45
lynching, 41

McCants, Yvonne, 255
Macdonald, Hugh, 86
McDonald's, 123
McMillan, Terry, 117
McNeal, Glenda G., 17
McVeigh, Timothy, 203
McWorter, Free Frank, 3–4, 5, 50, 284
McWorter, Lucy, 4
mailing lists, 175
Make College Affordable Act, 17
Malcolm X, 5, 25
Manners, Miss, 204
Mantra, 31
marketing, 73–74, 80
    advice, 101–2
    to blacks, by whites, 281
    yourself, as recent college graduate,
        227 (*see also* job hunting)
Marlboro cigarettes, 73–74
Marshall, Sam, 29
Martin, J. Alexander, 50
Mashow, John, 111
MATAH network, 12, 247
match test, 199
Mathis, Pat, 304
Maxwell, 81
Maynard, Robert, 9
MBE (Minority Business Entrepreneur),
    77
meals, at events, 179–80
media
    promoting positive coverage in,
        79–84
    negative images of blacks in, 78–79
Megatrends (Naisbitt), 140, 240
Mel Farr Ford, 274
Mensah, Anthony J., 38, 66–67
mentoring, 5, 94, 98–102
    activities review exercise, 316
    of blacks by whites, 281
    in corporation, 235
    economic, 100–102
    keys to successful, 98–100
    weekend, 101–2
mentors, 27
    attracting, 234–35
    identifying, 315
    as network shakers, 162–63
Merrill Lynch, 290

Metropolitan Missionary Baptist
    Church (Kansas City), 297
Miami-Dade Community College, 56
Michel, Harriet, 274
Microsoft, 290
Millionaires
    first black, 112
    self-made, 115
Million Man March of 1994, 12
Milstein, Howard, 162
minority businesses, 123, 294. *See also*
        black-owned businesses
    books on, 124
    loan guarantees for, 302–3
    number and revenue of, 110–11,
        124–25
    reasons for doing business with,
        124–26
Minority Business Report (TV program),
    70
Minority Link Inc., 305
minority position, on board, 244–45
Minter, Steve, 246
mission, 158
Mitchell, Bert N., 16
Mitchell & Titus, LLP, 16
Molloy, John, 75, 193
Monroe, Sylvester, 100, 101
Moore, Jim, 188
Morel, Madeleine, 181, 182
Morris, Frank, 3
Morrison, Toni, 117
Morse, Ariah (foster father), 20–21,
    163
Morse, Frances (foster mother), 20
mortgages, 76
Mosley, Walter, 117
"Mother Teresa" factor, 244
M R Beal and Associates, 76
multilevel marketing (MLM), 247
mutual funds, 116

Naisbitt, John, 140, 240
Names
    introductions and, 205, 279
    remembering, 203–4
    spelling, 221, 280
name tags, 166, 170–71, 204
National 100 Black Men of America,
    100, 163
National African-American Insurance
    Association, 159

National Alliance of Market Developers, 305
National Association of Black Accountants, 305
National Association of Black Developers, 180
National Association of Black Journalists, 6
National Association of Black Social Workers, 5
National Association of Black Women Entrepreneurs, 183
National Association of Investment Corporation (NAIC), 286, 288
National Bar Association, 84
National Black Leadership Roundtable, 44
National Black MBA Association, 19, 84, 140, 255, 305
National Center for Neighborhood Enterprise, 302
National Conference on Black Entrepreneurialism, 248
National Minority Supplier Development Council (NMSDC), 124, 125, 126, 274, 300, 302
National Networking Month, 150–52
National Opinion Research Center, 71
National Society of Black Engineers, 5, 305
National Technical Association, 305
National Urban League, 113, 237, 263
Nationwide Insurance Agency, 158
Naval Research Laboratory, 16
NBA franchises, 118
Nehemiah Homes Project, 56
Networking Forum, 29–31
network marketing, 247–48
network(s) and networking
  in action, 180–82
  Afrocentrism and, 5–6, 134–35
  agenda exercise, 324
  "always be prepared" guideline, 262–65
  avoiding abuse of connections and, 141–42
  awards ceremonies and, 176–80
  basic principle of, 24
  being known and, 137–38
  board appointments and, 243–46
  card for job hunting and, 228
  career success and, 232–36
    categories of, 146
    cleaning up, 165
    commitment guideline, 257–58
    community infrastructure and, 41
    conventions and, 236–40
    conversations and, 184–210
    customers and, 229–32
    doing good and, xxxvii, 149–50, 298–306
    dos and don'ts for, 277–80
    economic empowerment and, 285–97
    economic power of, 7–8, 15
    entrepreneurship and, 113
    establishing base for, 156–57
    fears and, 197–202
    forms of, 132
    goals and, 157–61
    how-tos, 133–34, 136–37
    huggers and shakers and, 161–64
    identifying, exercise, 310
    influence and, 147–49
    information gathering and, 140, 146–47, 240–43
    intellectual capital and, 86–87
    job hunt and, 215–24
    job hunt for working poor and, 299–300
    keeping sex out of, 248–52
    keys to nurturing, 144–46
    media images and, 79–80
    mind-set and, xxxvi
    mongrels and, 165
    nemeses of, 164–65
    "no abuse" principle and, 144–45
    office politics and, 233–36
    opportunity identification exercise, 313
    organizational goals exercise, 328
    pact, *SuccessGuide* and, 15
    personal growth and, 15, 88–89
    personal story of success through, 19–32
    plan creation exercise, 318
    for public good, 298–306
    purpose and, 135, 195–96, 212–51
    pushing, 145–46
    quick check of, 137–39
    resources and, 149
    selective buying review exercise, 331
    self-esteem and, 138–40
    skills evaluation exercise, 311
    skills improvement exercise, 312

(continued)
social, 24–25
social reform and, 6–7, 9–10
starting event for, 173–76
staying in touch with, 228
success for all and, 134–35, 306–8
thirty best places for, 332–35
tools for, 165–73
21st century tribe and, 132
as way of life, 255–83
wealth sharing and, 128–33
by whites with blacks, 280–82
work and, 284–308
working for you, 154–83
New American Strategies Group, 8
New Dress for Success, The (Molloy), 75
newspapers, 80, 174
black reporters and, 81
job ads, 216
reading, 263
Newsweek, 7
New Vision Magazine, 74
New York National Bank (NYNB),
304
New York Times, 23, 72, 75
Nightline (TV show), 78
Nivri, Tang, 236–237
Nixon, Richard M., 184–85
nonprofit groups, 173, 245
No One Need Apply (Bowes), 299
notebook filing system, 172
Nunn, Sam, 163
NV Magazine, 15–16

Ochman, B. L., 208
office politics, 233–36
Ogilvy, David, 221, 223
Ohio Association of Insurance
Professionals, 158–59
100 Black Men/Women, 19, 100, 163,
289, 290
opening lines, 199–202, 322
opportunity, 24
entrepreneurial success and, 120
Oprah, 164
organization, need for, in group
dynamics, 233
Organization for a New Equality
(ONE), 100, 101
organizations. *See also* corporations
best black, 340–48
culture of, 235–37

goals of, exercise, 328
mentoring and role modeling in, 97

parenting, 95–97, 144, 163
Parson, Richard, 52
passion, 123
PDA (personal digital assistant), 165–66,
172
People Organized to Work for
Economic Recovery (POWER),
296
people skills, 186–95
Pepsi-Cola, 122, 174
perceptions, of blacks
effect of negative, 71–78
excellence and, 87–89
fixing, 79–84
lack of networking and, 138–39
Perkins, Rev. James, 295, 296, 297
Perrin, Keith, 50
personal achievement, excellence vs.,
87–89
personal vision, 158
Peters, Howard A., 96
Peters, Johnnie Mae, 96
Petersen, Donald, 147–49
Pickard, William, 16
Pinckney, Jerry, 23
Pinder, Jessie, 286, 287–88
Pitts, Otis, 56
Poitier, Sidney, 289
police, 79
political board appointments, 245
political savvy, 244
Polote, Benjamin, 303–4
poor and poverty. *See also* underclass
Afrocentric networking and, 10–12
images and, 84
job hunting and, 299–300
lack of "success network" for, 38–40
networking to empower, 41
overcoming, 74
sharing resources and, 92
wealth-building to create jobs for,
108
position, job hunt and specifying, 221
positioning, 223–24
positive feedback, 99
positive profile, board appointments
and, 244
positive reinforcement, 157
positive self-talk, 198, 202

Poussaint, Dr. Alvin, 5, 31, 138, 139, 244
PowerNetworking Conference 2002, 52
PowerNetworking Conference, 237–38
prejudging, 156
Pre–Paid Legal, 247
Preparation
  entrepreneurship and, 124
  guideline, 262–65
  job hunting and, 216–17
President's Council, 305
"presumption of incompetence," 74–76
Price, Chuck, 29
Price, Hugh, 244
PRINK, 208
priorities, 197
private enterprise. *See also* black-owned
    business; entrepreneurship
  jobs and, 108–9
  public good and, 298–306
private schools, 116
Procope, Ernesta, 52
Procter & Gamble, 26–27, 37, 74, 147, 163
professional organizations, 5–6
professional resource guides, 140
professionals, black, 11, 18
  emergence of, 139–40
  helping businesses, 88
  helping professionals, 88
  image of, 83, 84
  networking forums for, 30–31
  "presumed incompetence" and, 75
  resentment of, 68
  Seven Principles and, 91–92
  young urban, 13
Program Corporation of America, 336
promises, 143–44, 278
promotion, of event, 175
Pryor, Fred, 186
public good, 298–306
public relations, 80
public-sector jobs, 108–109
public service, board appointments and, 244
publishing, 117
purpose, 135, 195–96, 212–51
  principle (*Nia*), 91

qualifications
  assessing, 217
  job hunt and, 221, 223–24

questions
  answering, 279
  conversations and, 207
  opening, 200–202
  prepare good, exercise, 323
  seeking information and, 242
  techniques, 190–91

Race for Success Inc., 53
*Race for Success: The Ten Best Business
    Opportunities for Blacks in America*, 115–16
racial attitudes, 71–73. *See also* images;
    perceptions; stereotypes
racism, 49, 73–74, 78–79, 84, 138
Radio One, 80
radio stations, 174
Raphaelson, Joel, 220–21
rapport, building, 266–67
Rawls, Lou, 27
real estate development, 117–18
recession, 13
reciprocity, 122–23, 274–75
referrals and references
  finding clients and, 231–32
  giving, to newcomers, 165
  volunteer work and, 226–29
reintroducing self, 204
Reitman, Bob, 28
relationships
  board appointments and, 246
  building and maintaining, 141–44
  business card and, 168
  finding clients and, 229
  networks built on, 156
religion, 95. *See also* churches
Renaissance Project, 129–31
resources
  matching, with needs, 156
  networking for, 149
restaurants, 117
résumé
  riting, 220–21, 228
Ries, Al, 73
risk-averse culture, 114
Rites of Passage, 57–62, 65–67, 94
Robinson, Eddie, Jr., 7
Robinson, Randall, 215
Rodriguez, Max, 81
Rogers, John, 116
role model(s), 23
  attributes review exercise, 317

(continued)
entrepreneurial, 112
identifying, 315
need for, 39, 81, 82, 95
programs for, 5
serving as, 94–98
as shakers, 163
Roman, Kenneth, 220–21
RSVP, 279
Rubbermaid, 246
Ruckeyser, Louis, 31
Rush Communications of NYC, 12, 51
Russell-McCloud, Patricia, 16

SAD (Self-Absorption Disorder), 268
sales
jobs, 115, 247–48
network marketing ventures, 247–48
soft vs. hard, 230
SAT score, 89
Saunders-Jones, Ingrid, 17
saving, 123
Savoy, 8, 74, 80, 117
SBC Ameritech, 246
schools, 82. *See also* education
black entrepreneurs and, 116
role models for, 97–98
script event, 178–79
self-introduction, 319
self-assurance, 187, 191–93
overcoming fears and, 198–202
checkup exercise, 325–26
self-determination (*Kujichagulia*)
principle, 91, 135
self-employed, 111, 115
self-esteem
lack of cooperative economics, 49
networking and, 138–40
passing on, 57
personal achievement and, 88
Rites of Passage to build, 58–62
self-help, 95
self-image. *See also* self-assurance; self-esteem; "victim mentality"
overcoming negative, 197–202
networking for information and, 242
separation stage, 65, 67
September 11, 108
service, 15
service clubs, 5
Seven Habits of Highly Effective People, The (Covey), 158

sex, 248–52
shakers, 162–64
SHARE (Successful Hair Designers Annual Resource Expo), 194
sharing, 4, 33, 131–32, 194–95
Shatz, Adam, 75
Shaw University, 164
Shorebank Corporation, 57
shyness, 197, 198
Simmons, Russell, 12, 51
Simpson, Carole, 31
skills gaining recognition for, 233–34
inventory exercise, 327
slave mentality, 41–45
slave owners, 42–43
slavery, 3–4, 49–50, 112, 138
Sloan, Maceo K., 17
Sloan Financial Group, 17
Small, Eric, 116
small business development, 116–17
small talk, 184–85, 263
Smikle, Ken, 275
Smith, Clarence, 52, 187
Smith, Hilton O., 17
Smith, Oscar, 185–86
Smith, Winston, 303–4
smoking, 279
social clubs, 134
soft sell, 230
Sony/Loews Cineplex Entertainment, 8
sororities, black, 5, 84, 97
Soul-O-Dex (Rolodex), 5, 31–32, 140, 241
Source, The (magazine), 12
sources, key, in organizations, 236
speakers
events and, 174–75, 179–80
Fabulous 50, 336–39
length of speech, 179
speaking, tone and speed of, 189–90
spelling, 221, 280
Spencer, Nora Jean (wife), 26
Spiegel catalogues, 13
spiritual goals, 92–93
sponsor, 174, 176
sports, 115, 118
Starbucks, 8
State Farm Insurance, 225–26
"stay loose" principle, 145
Steele, Shelby, 77
stereotypes. *See also* image; perceptions
avoiding racial, 280–81
changing, 80, 108

Stith, Rev. Charles R., 100–101
stock market, 115
strength
from within, 33
job hunting from position of, 223
"Strength of Weak Ties, The"
(Granovetter), 157, 215
structure, in group dynamics, 233
success. *See also* wealth
community, vs. individual, 86–87
entrepreneurial, key factors in,
119–22
seeking clients and, 230–31
"successful cultural offensive," 10
SuccessGuides, xxvii, 15, 32, 33, 164, 180,
264–65
SuccessGuides Worldwide, 9, 15–18,
33–34, 52, 140
SuccessNet Forum, xxvii, 31, 147–48,
173
SuccessSource, Inc., 31, 32, 33
Sullivan, Rev. Leon, 215
Survey of Minority-Owned business
Enterprices, 110

table manners, 279
Tacolcy Economic Development
Corporation (TEDC), 56
talent, 119–20
Tao of Leadership (Heider), 15
Target Market News, 13, 275
Taylor, Susan, 31, 81, 189
technology, 11, 117, 214
telephone calls, 269, 277
television, 80
Tell, William, 129
Tennessee Titans, 7
Terry, Roy, 51
Terry, Rudolph, 51
Texaco, 47
T.G.I. Friday's, 8
thank-you notes. *See* gratitude
Think and Grow Rich (Kimbro), 193
Thomas, Fred, 78
Thomas, Isiah, 118
three-by-five-inch card system, 173
Tillman, Jerald T., 158–59
Time, 100, 101
timing, of events, 177–79
tokenism, 281
Toyota, 126
TransAfrica, 215

transition stage, 65, 67
"treat everyone with dignity" guideline,
269–70
Tribes (Kotkin), 213–14
Tribune (Oakland, California), 9
Trout, Jack, 73, 223
trust, 143–44, 218
global tribes and, 214–15
Truth, Sojourner, 5
Tubman, Harriet, 5
Turner Construction Company, 17
"two–ness" (duality), 37–38

underclass, 75. *See also* poor
black middle class and, 38, 300
image of blacks and, 73
need to uplift, 10, 11, 88
Underground Railroad, 4, 6–7
new, 4–10, 18, 35, 50, 87, 92, 102,
307
unemployment, 11, 13, 84
United Airlines, 16
United Negro College Fund (UNCF),
27, 83, 94, 150, 226, 265
United States Air Force, 16
U.S. Chamber of Commerce, 124
U.S. Congress, 17
U.S. Department of Commerce, 110
U.S. Health Advisors, 247
United Way, 27–29, 82, 150, 226
unity, 19, 135
(*Umoja*) principle, 91
Unity First Online, 17
Universal Negro Improvement
Association, 48
UniWorld Group, 126
unwritten rules, 234
"up front" rule, 142–43
Urban Financial Services Coalition, 305
Urban Village
black agenda as manifesto for, 95–102
renewing, 54–57, 69, 92, 307
utilities, 174

Valdry, Warren, 289, 290
Vanguarde Media (VMI), 8, 36
Verizon, 53
Vibes, 117
"victim mentality"
economics and, 287
freeing self from, 50
freeing youth of, 292

violence, media and, 78–79
Visions Investment Club, 288
Voices and Silences (Jones), 189
volunteer work, 27, 94
  board appointments and, 245–46
  job networking in, 226–27
  networking for good and, 149–50
  networking for resources, 149

Waitley, Denis, 31
Walker, Carl, 125
Walker, Don, 23
Walker, Juliet E. K., 3–4, 4
Walker, Madame C. J., 52, 53
Wall Street Journal, 13, 23, 289–90
Wall Street Project Conference, 303
Washington, Ben, 300
Washington, Booker T., 53, 109, 284
Washington Researchers, 140
Watkins, Paul G., 284, 285–89
Watson, Fannie, 300–303
wealth
  board appointments and, 244
  freedom created by, 107–8
  gap, closing, 107
Welch, John, Jr., 307
welfare, job programs and, 298–300
Wellington, Al, 12
West Indians, 48–49
Wharton, Dr. Clifton, Jr., 53
Wharton School, 12
What's My Line? (TV show), 202
Whitaker, David, Jr. (lawyer), 53, 64
Whitaker, Dr. David, 57–58, 271
White, Michael R., 128, 130, 149
white guilt, 281–82
whites, 13
  acceptance by, 45, 49
  college degrees and, 290
  corporate world of, and "duality," 37
  median incomes vs., 48–49
  misperceptions of blacks and, 71–73
  networking with, Afrocentricism and, 135
  reporters, promoting positive stories by, 81

seeking to network with blacks, tips for, 280–82
Williams, Corky, 190
Williams, Gregory, 31, 59
Williams, John, 41
Williams, Terrie, 169
Willis, George, 212–13
Wills, Cheryle, 28
Wilson, William Julius, 38
Winfrey, Oprah, 52, 103
Winn-Dixie chain, 56
Winston, Peggy, 257–61
Winston, Sherry, 180
win-win situation, creating, 156
WJW-TV 8, 141
Women
  improper flirting by, 250
  improper male behavior and, 251–52
  introducing, 205
  as listeners, 187–188
  media stereotypes of black, 80
Woodson, Carter G., 84
Woodson, Robert, 302
working the room, 240
World African Network, 90
World Wide Technology Inc., 11
writing
  job hunt and, 220–22
  self-introduction, 319
Writing That Works (Roman and Raphaelson), 220–21

Young, Andrew, 163, 244
Young, Whitney, 263
Young Black Scholars program, 289
young people (youth), 289–94
  goal and action steps for, 94–95
  jobs to aid "at risk," 40
  mentors and role models for, 38–40, 54–57, 99
  preparing, for college, 289–290
  preparing, to be leaders, 290–92
  Rites of Passage and, 57–62
Young & Rubicam, 83

Zebraa Communications, 198